ENZO FERRARI

Richard Williams is the *Guardian*'s chief sports writer
and the author of two highly acclaimed books –
The Death of Ayrton Senna and *Racers*, which was shortlisted
for the 1998 William Hill Sports Book of the Year

ENZO FERRARI

A Life

RICHARD WILLIAMS

Yellow Jersey Press
LONDON

Published by Yellow Jersey Press 2002

2 4 6 8 10 9 7 5 3

First published in Great Britain in 2001 by
Yellow Jersey Press

Yellow Jersey Press
Random House, 20 Vauxhall Bridge Road,
London SW1V 2SA

Random House Australia (Pty) Limited
20 Alfred Street, Milsons Point, Sydney,
New South Wales 2061, Australia

Random House New Zealand Limited
18 Poland Road, Glenfield,
Auckland 10, New Zealand

Random House (Pty) Limited
Endulini, 5a Jubilee Road, Parktown 2193, South Africa

Random House UK Limited Reg. No. 954009

www.randomhouse.co.uk

A CIP catalogue record for this book
is available from the British Library

ISBN 0-224-05986-6

Typeset in Bembo by MATS, Southend-on-Sea, Essex
Printed and bound in Great Britain by
Bookmarque Ltd, Croydon, Surrey

For Jane

Contents

List of Illustrations   ix

An Agitator of Men   1

Chapter One   9
Chapter Two   41
Chapter Three   73
Chapter Four   109
Chapter Five   123
Chapter Six   161
Chapter Seven   185
Chapter Eight   209
Chapter Nine   241
Chapter Ten   263
Chapter Eleven   285

The Last Enemy   299

Notes on Sources   304
Acknowledgements   313
Index   315

Illustrations

1 Enzo Ferrari, Modena, 1931
  (Ferruccio Testi/Spitzley-Zagari
  Collection)   xii
2 Enzo Ferrari in his first race, 1919
  (Odoardo Gandolfi/Spitzley-Zagari
  Collection)   8
3 The Scuderia Ferrari at Livorno, 1930
  (Ferruccio Testi/Spitzley-Zagari
  Collection)   40
4 Enzo Ferrari with Achille Varzi,
  Monte Piantonia, 1934 (Ferruccio
  Testi/Spitzley-Zagari Collection)   72
5 Enzo and Dino Ferrari, c.1943
  (Ferrari family archive)   108
6 Bruno Sterzi, Maranello, 1948
  (Giuseppe Panini archive)   122
7 Enzo Ferrari with Alberto Ascari,
  early 1950s (Hulton Archive)   160
8 Enzo Ferrari, Martino Severi,
  Federico Giberti and Peter Collins,
  Maranello, 1957 (Louis Klemantaski/
  The Klemantaski Collection)   184
9 Laura and Enzo Ferrari with other
  constructors, Monza, 1961 (Ferrari
  family archive)   208
10 Lorenzo Bandini, Modena, 1965
  (Peter Coltrin/The Klemantaski
  Collection)   240

11 Enzo Ferrari with Mauro Forghieri,
   1975 (R. Gremigniani/Scuderia
   Ferrari archive)   262
12 Enzo Ferrari with Gilles Villeneuve,
   Imola, 1979 (Giampietro Sanna/
   Foto Olimpia Imola)   284
13 Enzo Ferrari, Monza, 1976 (Franco
   Varisco)   298

The race track justifies tendencies and behaviour which would be condemned as antisocial in other circumstances.

Anna Kavan, *World of Heroes*

– What is it?
– It's a Ferrari.
– Does it run?
– Does it run! She won the Grand Prix last year. I bought it from Simonelli's widow. Paid her a hundred quid for it.
– What are you going to do with it?
– Race it, of course . . .

Exchange between Moira (Ava Gardner) and
Julian (Fred Astaire), from *On The Beach*
(dir. Stanley Kramer, 1958)

Enzo Ferrari, Modena, 1931.

An Agitator of Men

In the end, in his last days, what frightened him most was the idea of losing his memory. He talked about it constantly. He tried medicines that promised to arrest the slow decay. Medicines that would help him hold on to the ghosts and the stories of nine decades. Memories of shooting arrows at a target with his brother Alfredo outside their father's workshops. Of lying in a hospital for incurables at the end of the Great War. Of the roar of the first engine to carry his name, summoned to life on a chilly spring morning in Emilia. Of his dead son, bending over a drawing board. Of taking a racing driver to lunch in the private room of the restaurant across the road and watching his face and his hands as they discussed money. Of the dogs who had accompanied him on his excursions, a poodle called Sambo and a German shepherd called Box, travelling in the boot of his car. Of evenings in the hotel across the square, with cards and drink and girls. Of Sunday afternoons in his farmhouse at the test track, watching the races on the television and waiting for the phone to ring. Of the men who were close to him, not the famous ones, the ones who drove his cars and sometimes died in them, but men like Bazzi, his right arm for fifty years, and Peppino, who had known more than anyone about all the lives he had led.

His routine seldom varied. On a weekday he rose at eight in his bedroom on the first floor of the big dark four-storey house that stood opposite the Fountain of the Graces in the Largo Garibaldi. Half an hour later, after a five-minute walk past the opera house and through the gate in the old city walls, he would be at the barber's shop, seated in his regular chair, the first on the left. Antonio D'Elia had cut the *Ingegnere*'s hair in his salon in the

Corso Canalgrande since the 1950s. Antonio was the brother-in-law of Gozzi, the most enduring of his *consiglieri*. Now Massimo, his son, had taken over. If it was a Monday, they would talk about how the local football club had got on and Ferrari would tease Massimo about Internazionale's latest defeat. Then the barber would remove the towel from around his neck and Dino, Peppino's successor, would arrive to drive him to the outskirts of the town, to the cemetery of San Cataldo, to the marble tomb he had built for the family in 1956, where the cast-iron latticework gates would be unlocked and he would spend a few minutes with his parents and his wife, Laura, and their son. When Peppino was alive, Ferrari had always taken the wheel himself. Now he was old and he let Dino do the driving as they went back to the Modena office, to the building at 11 viale Trento e Trieste, where it had all begun. There, in the rooms above the old workshops, where he and his wife and their son had lived for forty years, he would spend an hour or so, dealing with his mail and perhaps seeing a supplicant or two. And he read the newspapers. Always the newspapers. He read *Il Resto del Carlino*, *Il Tempo*, *La Nazione*, *La Repubblica*, *Il Giornale*, *La Stampa*, *Il Corriere della Sera* and *La Gazzetta di Modena*. He read *La Gazzetta dello Sport* and *Il Corriere dello Sport* and *Tuttosport*. He read *L'Equipe* and its Belgian counterpart, *Les Sports*. Sometimes Gozzi would present him with items clipped from other papers; perhaps *L'Osservatore Romana*, the Vatican's mouthpiece, had been inveighing against the sinfulness of motor racing again. In the early days, his mother had kept books in which she pasted the stories announcing her son's triumphs.

And at about eleven o'clock he would summon Dino to drive him to Maranello. The car would seldom be a Ferrari. Usually it would be something relatively humble – it had been a little Lancia Ardea in the early days, or a Fiat 1100, for a while even a Mini-Cooper. There had once been a Renault that amused him because it gave the driver messages: please close the door, please fasten your belt, your oil is running out. He wanted to buy it, but Renault, naturally, wanted to give it to him as a present, for the prestige – Mr Ferrari drives a Renault! He said, no, I want to buy it. I don't want it as a present. But if you give me 50 per cent off, I'll buy it. That was the sort of deal he would have offered to someone himself, as he did to John Surtees, who turned up at Maranello at the wheel of his much-loved BMW and was told, '*Beh, macchina tedesco* – no, you must drive a Ferrari,' and ended up being given 15 per cent discount on a 330GT with the balance of the cost being taken off his salary at source.

At the Maranello factory he would say good morning to his workers, local men from Sassuolo, from Fiorano, from Vignola, from Castelnuovo, from Formigine, from all the nearby small towns and hamlets in the foothills of the Apennines, the men who worked in his foundry, his engine department, his paint shop and his holy of holies, the *gestione sportiva*, the racing department. In his office, just inside the gate, under the archway and through the first door on the left in the low ochre block, he would greet his secretaries and deal with more paperwork, signing letters and writing notes in his violet ink until one o'clock or a quarter past one, and then he would walk out through the factory gates and across the via Giardini. In the old days lunch would be in the private room at the Ristorante Cavallino, which he had set up in the farm building that came with the land. But from the early Seventies, when the *pista Fiorano* had been opened, he would instead walk over to the test track, to another old farmhouse where he had his own apartment, including a kitchen and a cook, and there he would have lunch – perhaps with Gozzi, or his son Piero, or with one of the drivers, during a break from their testing duties; or perhaps a favoured long-term client, someone like Prince Bernhard of the Netherlands, a good friend since the Fifties, who always came in person to pick up his latest car and sometimes stayed for *salsicce cotto* and *tortellini alla panna*. Afterwards there would be a rest until four o'clock, and then he would return to the office at Maranello, where he had an armchair and a television. He would stay there until about eight o'clock, and then go back home.

There he would find Lina, his mistress, who had brought up

Piero in a parallel life that had been an open secret to most of Ferrari's friends, if not to his mother or his wife. Piero, Ferrari's only surviving child after the death of his first son in 1956, had grown up using his mother's surname to disguise his patrimony. When Laura died in 1978 it was decided that he could now use the precious name – ironically, the most common in the region. Piero Lardi at last became Piero Ferrari, although the change of name did not bring about an alteration to the gentle, modest character that the boy had inherited from his mother. What he did not have was his father's stubbornness, the quality that made people say: 'That's the Old Man – if you tell him to go left, he'll go right.'

At the weekends, when nobody else was working, his routine altered hardly at all. Saturday and Sunday, the same thing – to the barber's, to the cemetery, to Maranello, to the *pista*. Dino would drive him then, too. Everybody remembered how Peppino, his predecessor, had left Ferrari's side only once a year, on Easter Day, when his wife and children demanded his presence. But that was a day when Ferrari traditionally held a morning conference of his closest aides. One year during the meeting he needed some medication for his asthma, and asked for Peppino. No, he was told, remember Peppino doesn't work on Easter Day. 'When you need him', Ferrari exclaimed, 'he's never here.'

On Saturday, he would have his closest friends to lunch. Sergio Scaglietti, for example, a bricklayer's son whose Modenese craftsmen had provided the aluminium bodies for generations of Ferrari road and racing cars. Carlo Benzi, his accountant, who had been with him since just after the war, who knew the secrets of his personal Swiss bank accounts, and who had learnt how to cope with his obsessively precise ways and his extraordinarily exact memory. His bodyguard, Valdemaro Valentini, a former policeman. And Gozzi, and Dino. These were his *amici del sabato*, his Saturday friends. But while he would use the familiar *tu* when addressing them, they retained the formal, respectful *lei* with him. For many years these Saturday lunches would take place in trattorias or taverns in neighbouring towns and villages. Later Ferrari took to entertaining them at

Fiorano, where Pina, his cook, created constant variations on the theme of risotto. They would stay with him until four or five, and then he would most probably go home. Once, when his wife was still alive, he would have detoured to see Lina, at the farmhouse not far away where she was bringing up Piero. Then, instead of going back to the house, he might have gone across the road to the Hotel Real, to meet other pals and find girls. That had been easier when he still lived around the corner, before Laura could look out of the window and watch the Real's entrance to see who was coming and going. But now a bank stood where the hotel had been. There was a bank, too, in the building that had housed the Hotel Palace, another refuge and the scene of late-night adventures. Anyway, that was long ago. So he would probably stay at home and read a book. Not Machiavelli or Dante, as some had come to imagine, although he didn't mind borrowing their epigrams. (Over the years he was often called Machiavellian, but he had never read *The Prince*. With him, it was instinct.) He liked Steinbeck and Stendhal, and Giovanni Guareschi's comic parables of small-town life in the Po Valley, and biographies of great military leaders: Napoleon, Horatio Nelson, Alexander the Great. On Sunday he might spend some time with his granddaughter, Antonella, Piero's daughter. If there was a grand prix that weekend he would settle down in front of the television in his farmhouse by the test track, having made sure to load a cassette into the video recorder so that when the drivers came in the following week he would be able to show them exactly where and how they had committed the errors that had cost his cars another race.

As Gozzi said, he was a liar, yes, but only when it was important. He could open the door of a prototype grand touring car for a woman and tell her, 'If you like this car, we'll make it. If you don't, we won't.' Ten years after Ferrari's death, sitting in an anonymous office above the multistorey car park that had been built on the site of the original Scuderia Ferrari garage, Gozzi spoke of his skill at the art of being many things to many people. Movie stars, great conductors, Japanese businessmen, racing

[5]

drivers, racing drivers' widows – he may not have been genuinely interested in any of them, except perhaps a widow or two, but each one went away believing they had the key to his personality.

As a young man, Enzo Ferrari had looked in the mirror and asked himself: 'Who am I in this world?' Yet even when the answer was all around him, he was not satisfied. He needed to maintain control. He had to feel that the lives of those with whom he dealt were his to command. So he left people waiting at his door. He set spies on others. His collaborators lived in daily fear of making a mistake, since he was unsparing of the slightest error. He operated within a climate of creative tension that often turned destructive yet was too deeply ingrained to be changed, even at times when the need seemed obvious to everyone else. *Divide et imperare*, that was his motto. He was harsh and capricious, cynical about human nature and devoted to a single set of imperatives, and he was always liable to start shouting in the middle of a restaurant if he felt threatened or betrayed. On the telephone he was a monster. But he could be generous and warm and amusing, loving a joke and capable of laughing at his own imperfections, sometimes – usually when least expected – ready to bestow small tokens that let his people know their work was appreciated. In this world he was the *padrone*, the one who provided livelihoods and thereby gave a community its sense of pride. As Gozzi said, Ferrari was a universe. And when outsiders entered his universe, whether it be the President of the Republic or the Pope, it was on his terms.

Quite early on, he stopped venturing outside its frontiers. The most famous name in motor racing did not go to the races. Nor would he travel to business meetings. This served only to increase his charisma and his power. One went to him, as the *clienti* always had, and then waited to be admitted to the dark office, illuminated only by the light above the portrait of the dead son, before facing the old man with the hawk's nose and the white hair who hid his thoughts and his memories behind a pair of dark glasses. He sent his team around the world in search of glory, but he stayed firmly within the world he knew. People said that he had seen too many drivers die in his cars, or that he could not bear to see his precious machines damaged, or that his love of racing had somehow died along with Dino in 1956. The truth was that he had given up attending races more than twenty years earlier. He was afraid of flying, elevators gave him claustrophobia, and he was no longer curious about the outside world. He discovered that if he stayed at home, and waited for others to bring him the news, then it made him happier. And then he was no longer responsible for the day-to-day problems. Others could take the blame. And he could indulge in his love of conspiracy, playing off one man against another until a winner emerged, a winner for him.

He was a man of pride in his appearance and in his achievements, but he was not vain. Italians are fond of titles, yet they meant little to him, or at least only in one specific sense. Between the wars he was made first a *Cavaliere* and then a *Commendatore*, the rough equivalents of a knighthood or a *Légion d'honneur*. He had no use for them. Anyway, he always said that *Commendatore* was a Fascist title. He preferred to be addressed as *Ingegnere*, a gesture of relative modesty by which he seemed to put himself on a level with many of those he employed, as well as linking himself to the seriousness and integrity of their work. Not until the University of Bologna awarded him an honorary degree, when he was already over sixty, did he actually qualify for it. He was also widely referred to as *Il Drake,* the Dragon, indicating respect and fear, albeit of a slightly pantomimic sort. Later, to the English-speakers, he was just the Old Man, a term often uttered with a mixture of affection and exasperation. But to his workers, as he entered the factory every day and walked among them, speaking to them in the Modenese dialect as he asked about the health and progress of their wives and children, it was a simpler matter. *C'e capo*. Here's the boss.

'Who am I in this world?' Eventually he found an answer. To people who imagined that Ferraris were designed by the man called Ferrari, he said: I am not the designer. Other people do that. *Sono un agitatore di uomini*. I am an agitator of men.

Enzo Ferrari at the wheel of a CMN in his first race, the Parma–Poggio di Berceto hillclimb in 1919, with Nino Berretta in the mechanic's seat.

One

Men do not make history; they endure it, as they endure geography. And history, anyhow, is all a matter of geography.

Giovanni Guareschi, *The Little World of Don Camillo*

Even when he was at the height of his fame and fortune, his name heard around the world, granting or denying audiences to Hollywood stars and names from the *Alamanach de Gotha*, his mother could sometimes be heard to say, 'Ah, but the better of my sons is dead.'

Who knows what effect such words might have had on the survivor, a boy with strange hooded eyes, and what seeds of a tendency towards the sardonic and the dismissive they may have implanted? At any rate she was, so his friends and acquaintances said, the only person, man or woman, of whom Enzo Anselmo Ferrari was ever frightened. 'Enzo, Enzo!' she would shout. The reply from the grown man was instant. 'Yes, Mother?'

Adalgisa Bisbini came to Modena from her family home in Forlì, sixty kilometres along the via Emilia towards Rimini, to marry Alfredo Ferrari. Born in 1859, the elder of the couple by thirteen years, Alfredo was a grocer's son from Carpi, a few kilometres north. Both were from modestly prosperous petit-bourgeois families. Alfredo, who had been a supervisor at the Rizzi metalworks, started his own business in Modena, fabricating metal parts. His workshops, and the family house, were sited at 264 via Camurri, next to the railway line running through the northern end of the town; the national railway system became his biggest client. The buildings stand there today, now renamed and renumbered but looking almost exactly as they did then, except for the television aerials sprouting from the roof of the two-storey house. From the road, the house appears deserted, the long, low workshops disused. But round the side, where the railway track passes along the front, up there on the brickwork of the upper floor of the house, the name FERRARI can just be seen, carefully lettered in white paint that may be only a decade or two from fading completely.

Alfredo and Adalgisa Ferrari had two sons. The first, also called Alfredo, was born in 1896, followed two years later by Enzo. The younger son's birth certificate indicates that he was born on 20 February 1898; in fact his appearance in the world had come two days earlier, coinciding with the arrival of a snowstorm so heavy that it prevented his father from travelling to the registry office to report the birth until two days later.

In those days, Modena had a population of about sixty thousand. Originally the base of a wandering tribe of Celts called the Boii, it was captured in 218 BC by the Romans, who named it Mutina. It became a station on the via Emilia, the road from Ariminum (Rimini) to Mediolanum (Milan) laid down in 187 BC by Marcus Aemilius Lapidus, and the centre of a region in which retired legionaries settled on land given them after twenty-five years' service to the state. It was also where Spartacus and his rebel army of escaped gladiators and slaves faced two legions under Gaius Cassius in 72 BC. Although wearied by a long march from Meta Ponte on the sole of the Italian mainland, Spartacus's band slaughtered their opponents almost to a man before heading away on a journey into the Alps, which was to end in their own destruction. Thirty years later, Mutina was where Mark Antony finally caught and captured one of the nobles who had conspired in the assassination of Julius Caesar. After passing through the hands of various invading barbarians, Modena settled down again and developed into a thriving regional centre. The Cathedral of San Geminiano, begun in 1099 by the architect Lanfranco and decorated with friezes and gargoyles by the sculptor Wiligelmo, is one of the glories of Renaissance Italy. In the seventeenth century the town joined the Lombard League and benefited from the commercial activities of the Este family, whose influence radiated throughout the regions of Emilia and Romagna. When they were ejected from their base in a magnificent palace in Ferrara, Modena became their new headquarters. Their Palazzo Ducale, built in 1634, later became a military academy whose students, in their striking fuschia-coloured uniforms, were the country's military leaders in the making. In 1673 Maria Beatrice D'Este, known as Maria of Modena, left Italy to marry James, Duke of York, the future James II of England. Modena's sons included the great eighteenth-century historian Lodovico Antonio Muratori, author of the vast *Annali d'Italia*, the composers Marco Uccellini and Alessandro Stradella, the poet Fulvio Testi and the pioneering gynaecologist Gabriele Falloppia. There was also the hat manufacturer and ardent nationalist Ciro Menotti, who one night in 1831 was supposed to rise from his seat in the Teatro Ducale and interrupt an opera festival by offering the crown of a united Italy to the Duke of Modena. Instead he was arrested at his home in the Corso Canalgrande and later executed.

It is the sort of city the English writer Jonathan Keates describes as 'perfect north Italy, the small, accessible metropolis, with enough air to breathe and a sufficient veneer of worldliness, in which you might live without annoyance'. Not always enough air to breathe, however. Its climate veers between suffocating heat and winter fogs; the Romans had to drain swamps in order to make it habitable. By the time Enzo Ferrari came into the world it was also noted for a sparkling red wine called Lambrusco, for many varieties of *aceto balsamico*, or balsamic vinegar, for a dish of pigs' trotters known as *zampone*, for the pervasiveness of *tortellini in brodo*, and for countless small workshops in which men hammered and cut and twisted and produced almost anything that could be made in metal. The origins of this particular regional speciality are obscure, but the men of Modena and the surrounding small towns earned a reputation for craft skills and ingenuity in the manufacture of the sort of thing – axles, cart springs, bodywork – that made the transfer from the age of the horse and cart to the era of the automobile. And these were the men, around thirty of them employed by his father, among whom Enzo Ferrari grew up.

He later wrote that he and his brother shared a bedroom over the workshop; thanks to an absence of heating and curtains, it never got warm in the winter. 'We were awakened in the morning by the ringing of hammers. My father . . . acted as the manager, the designer, the salesman and the typist of his firm all at the same time.' But he was successful enough to buy three-speed bicycles for his sons, and there was enough room for the boys to keep homing-pigeons in a loft in one of the workshops. The modest but handsome four-room house, after all, had a pink marble staircase – 'the only luxury'. Enzo remembered his father as a man dedicated to his business but with time for culture, and for music in particular. Alfredo senior had played the cello, and there was a piano in the house. He was also a fastidious man, drafting his correspondence on the backs of envelopes before typing a final version on a Royal typewriter, keeping copies made in violet ink on a small duplicating machine. Those copies left a lasting impression on his younger son, who used violet ink in his fountain pen for the rest of his life.

Alfredo junior, known as Dino, was a good scholar, quiet and studious. Enzo, however, disliked school. He would rather be out riding his bike, rollerskating, running foot-races on a hundred-metre course marked out in front of the workshops, shooting rats, or entering his pigeons in competitions. His boyhood ambitions, he wrote, were to be 'an opera singer, a sports writer, and lastly a racing driver', vocations not dependent on academic qualifications.

The desire to be a racing driver had its roots in his father's acquisition, in 1903, of a motor car, one of only twenty-seven in Modena. It was a single-cylinder De Dion Bouton, of French manufacture, and the family acquired a combined chauffeur and handyman to keep it in good fettle. Other cars followed the De Dion, and one of them carried the two Ferrari boys, dressed in identical sailor suits, to their first communion, at which Enzo was presented with a silver watch by his godfather, Anselmo Chiarli, in whose honour he had been given his middle name.

On 6 September 1908, Alfredo Ferrari took his sons to see their first motor race. The Circuito di Bologna was a star-studded event featuring two of the greatest drivers of the day, the tall, blue-eyed Felice Nazzaro of Turin, twenty-seven years old, and Vincenzo Lancia, a Piedmontese, a year younger, racing their giant Fiats over a fifty-kilometre course formed from public roads on the city's outskirts, incorporating part of the via Emilia. Lancia made the fastest lap but Nazzaro won the race, at an average of 74 mph over the fast, straight roads.

Naturally, the young Enzo was entranced by the spectacle of motor racing in its infancy. The two Fiats were painted red; a year earlier, for the French Grand Prix at Dieppe, new regulations required entrants to paint their cars in their national colours – blue for France, white for Germany, green for Britain, red for Italy. The identities of those members of the governing body who determined the match of countries and colours are lost to historians, as are the reasons behind their decisions. But it may reasonably be assumed that the French, being the principal organisers of early motor racing, gave themselves the first choice, and took the blue with which their country is identified. It seems likely that the association of red with Italy came about through the popularity of Garibaldi, the nineteenth-century leader of the nationalist movement, whose soldiers were famous for their red shirts. The dramatic appearance of the cars of Nazzaro and Lancia must have made an impression on the small boy. But in his later recollections Enzo Ferrari remarked that he was also struck by a novel safety

[13]

feature: at the most dangerous bend, where the crowd was thickest, the spectators were separated from the track by a strip of land forty yards wide which had been flooded with water.

A year later he was back for more, a spectator at the time trial over a measured mile on the straight stretch of the road at Navicello, between Modena and Ferrara, organised by the fledgling Modena Automobile Association. He walked two miles from his home, crossing three fields and a railway line, to watch the event, in which some of the better-known Italian drivers of the time took part. Attendants with water barrels damped down the unmade surface before each competitor set off. The event was won by a driver called Da Zara, who recorded an average of 87 mph. 'I found these events immensely exciting,' Ferrari reported.

More exciting, certainly, than his studies. Enzo recalled an August night in his fifteenth year when he was walking along with his friend, a boy named Peppino, and was using a car magazine to swat away the mosquitoes. Suddenly Peppino asked him what he was going to do when he grew up. Under the flickering light of the gas street lamps, Enzo pointed to a picture of Ralph De Palma, the winner of the Indianapolis 500. 'I will be a racing driver,' he said. 'Good,' Peppino answered. 'If you succeed, that will be a good profession.'

Enzo and Alfredo practised writing their signatures in the ice that formed on their bedroom window, looking ahead to the day when they would be famous men, pursued for their autographs. Alfredo did not allow the fantasy to distract him. When Enzo came home with a bad school report, however, his father beat him. 'I can still remember the weight of his hand,' he wrote more than half a century later. 'He said, "You must become an engineer!"' There is no record of his father's reaction when, in 1914, the sixteen-year-old Enzo became a published writer, contributing the first of several football reports to *La Gazzetta dello Sport*, Italy's celebrated national sports daily newspaper. One of them described the 7–1 defeat of his home-town team at the hands of Internazionale, the team of stars who had only recently broken away from their parent club AC Milan.

In 1915 Italy entered the Great War, and Dino joined the rush to sign up with the Red Cross volunteers, taking with him one of the family's cars, a red four-cylinder Diatto Torpedo, which he pressed into service as an ambulance, ferrying wounded soldiers from the battleground in the mountains to the hospitals in the Po Valley. But after a few weeks he enlisted in the Air Force, joining the ground crew of Squadriglia 912. This outfit's most celebrated member was the fighter ace Francesco Baracca, who shot down thirty-four enemy aircraft in his French-built Spad biplane before plunging out of the sky to his own death in 1918, an event which was to make its mark on the Ferrari family's history.

Enzo was still living at home when Alfredo senior suffered an attack of bronchitis early in 1916. It quickly turned into pneumonia, and within days he was dead. Later in the year the elder son, too, died in a sanatorium at Sortenna di Sondrio from an unspecified malady contracted at the front. 'That', Ferrari wrote, 'left me desperately alone with a mother who would have loved to keep me by her as life began pitilessly to draw me away from her side.'

Not only was the head of the family business gone, but so was his presumed heir. All that was left was an eighteen-year-old boy who wanted to be an opera singer but did not have the voice, who wanted to be a sports journalist but did not have the training, and who wanted to be a racing driver but no longer had access to the sort of family income that might have provided him with the means to make a start. Without his father, the Ferrari metal-fabrication business was finished. Young Enzo, waiting to be drafted, got a job with the local fire brigade as an instructor in their lathe-workers school, using the knowledge he had picked up from his father. In 1917 his call-up papers arrived, ordering him to join the 3rd Mountain Artillery in the Val Seriana, north of Bergamo, where a Piedmontese second lieutenant, noting his background, gave him the job of shoeing

[15]

the mules that were dragging field guns through the Dolomites.

Perhaps the Modenese climate of a hundred years ago was not the healthiest in which to grow up. Within months of joining his mountain regiment Enzo too fell ill, seemingly with pleurisy, and was transported to a hospital in Brescia, where two operations prevented him joining his father and brother in the next world. His complete recovery came only after a prolonged and dismal period of convalescence at the Barracano centre in Bologna, a group of old huts reputedly intended for incurables where he could hear, as he lay in his bunk, the coffinmakers' hammers echoing the early-morning sound his father's workmen had made what now seemed like a lifetime ago.

He returned to the war at the wheel of a Fiat, as a driver for a man called Pacchiani who was in charge of supplies. On the morning of 11 November 1918 he awoke from a night spent sleeping on a bag of onions in a warehouse to discover that an armistice had been announced. 'I saw a group of workers around a street light changing the bluish bulb used for the curfew for a bright white one,' he wrote. 'That was how I knew the war was over.' Of the 5,000,000 Italians who fought in the war, 700,000 had died and 250,000 had ended it as invalids.

He was quickly demobbed. There was a home for him back in Modena, where his mother was waiting with pleas for him to return, but he had no idea of what to do next. 'I was back where I had started,' he wrote. 'No money, no experience, limited education. All I had was a passion to get somewhere.' A passion and, in his pocket, a standard letter from his commanding officer, recommending him for employment. Straight away he took it to Turin, where he made an appointment at Fiat. Founded in 1899, the Fabbrica Italiana Automobili Torino had been taken over in 1907 by one of its three founders, Giovanni Agnelli, and his family, and was already involved in many levels of industry as well as motor cars. Wartime production had enabled it to quadruple its employment roll to 18,000, and it was about to launch the 501 model, which would become Italy's first mass-production economy car. But it was Fiat's commitment to a racing programme, enshrined in his memories of Nazzaro and Lancia hurling their machines around the roads near Bologna, that fired Ferrari's dreams of joining the company.

On a cold winter's day he found his way to the company's offices on the Corso Dante, where he was ushered into the presence of the engineer Diego Seria, 'a stalwart man with close-cropped reddish hair turning grey', who sat behind a mahogany desk in a room furnished with green velvet drapes. Having explained his desire to work with automobiles, the interviewee received a polite but conclusive response. Fiat, Seria said, wasn't big enough to provide jobs for all the unemployed ex-servicemen in Italy.

Ferrari left the plush warmth of Seria's office and returned to the Corso Dante. Walking down the broad boulevard, the wind biting through his clothes, he reached Valentino Park. He found a bench overlooking the banks of the River Po. He brushed the snow from the seat.

'I was alone,' he wrote. 'My father and my brother were no more. Overcome by loneliness and despair, I wept.'

He wept, but he did not give up. He stayed in Turin, living off the remains of a 'tiny inheritance' from his father, and found his way to the Bar Nord, not far from the main railway station, the Porto Nuova. The Nord was frequented by aviators and automobilists, and it was there that he befriended Romolo Bonacini, a mechanic who pointed him towards lodgings at the nearby Hotel Bologna, where he took a small room in the middle of the hotel, near the laundry room. Soon he also had a boost to his morale in the form of a job, thanks to a man named Giovannoni, a Bolognese with a garage on via Ormea. Post-war Italy was developing a ravenous appetite for motor cars, and demand was outstripping supply. In order to help satisfy it, Giovannoni took Lancia Zeta light trucks, stripped off the bodies, reconditioned the parts, and prepared the chassis for delivery to coachbuilders who would provide them with new passenger-car bodies. Ferrari tested the unclothed chassis and engines, then drove them to one of the three workshops of Carrozeria Italo-Argentina of Milan, where fashionable 'torpedo' bodies were installed for the benefit of the customers who visited the firm's showroom.

In Milan he would stop by the Café Vittorio Emanuele, where sporting types and would-be wheeler-dealers gathered. There he met Marco Garelli, soon to be famous for building motorcycles, and Ugo Sivocci, a former bicycle racer who had competed in the 1913 Targa Florio, the eighth running of a race around the Madonie mountains of Sicily. Sivocci had just taken a job as the chief test driver with a new company called CMN, Costruzioni Meccaniche Nazionali, which until the armistice had been making four-wheel-drive tractors for towing guns, replacing the mules Ferrari had shod. Now CMN was assembling passenger cars from surplus parts discarded by the Isotta Fraschini company. Sivocci was happy to recommend his new friend's qualities to one of CMN's directors, and by Easter 1919 the company had taken him on as an extra driver to test and deliver their cars. He rented a room from a widow at 1 corso Vittorio Emanuele and plunged into another new world. When Garelli entered one of his new motorcycles in a race from Milan to Naples, Ferrari and Sivocci followed the rider, Girardi, in a CMN car which they had turned into a refuelling wagon. When Girardi broke a wheel in Capua, they helped him mend it.

It was during adventures such as this that Ferrari began to sense a reawakening of his childhood ambition to become a racing driver. On Sunday, 5 October 1919 he took part in his first competition, the Parma–Poggio di Berceto hillclimb, a time trial up a fifty-kilometre course on the slopes of Monte Piantonia in the foothills of the Apennines. Driving a 2.3-litre CMN Tipo 15/20 tourer, which he had just bought at a considerable discount, he was competing against rivals driving Fiats, Opels, Bianchis, Bugattis, Aquilas, Italas and Alfas. The regulations issued by the Pro Parma club required him to be accompanied by a riding mechanic, as all racers were in those days, to help with wheel changes and mechanical mishaps. Ferrari chose Nino Berretta – 'a young man who had been around a lot, brilliant, enterprising, and very much liked by a lot of women'.

He was familiar with the road, originally built by Marie Louise, the Duchess of Parma and the second wife of Napoleon, to link her estates in Emilia with others she owned in Lunigiana. But on a cold and damp day, with wisps of fog lingering in the valleys, it presented an intimidating test. He waited for the start, with the number 29 painted on the sides of his bonnet, watching the aces preparing themselves, chief among them Antonio Ascari in his thoroughbred 1914 Fiat Grand Prix, with a 4.5-litre engine which he tuned himself in his garage in Milan.

The first car, the Aquila of Count Carlo Alberto Conelli, left at 7.30 a.m. Ferrari was not due to see the starter's flag until 10.55. By that time Ascari had already made his ascent, breaking the record and setting a time of 38 minutes and 11.2 seconds, an average speed of 52 mph. When Ferrari set off, along roads lined with spectators, he felt that he was being thrown scraps of applause which were all that was left after Ascari's triumphant passage. But by the time he reached the famous Piantonia steps, a steep climb with many hairpin bends, the spectators had thinned out and his attention was occupied by the demands of the unmade road with its unstable verges, unpredictable gutters, rock walls and unprotected drops. Hauling on a vast steering wheel almost two feet in diameter, trying to coax every last ounce of power from the CMN's engine, he climbed from 200 ft to 2,700 ft above sea level in a time of 50 minutes and 13.2 seconds, good enough for twelfth place overall and fifth in the 3-litre class.

In those days all motor races, even local hillclimbs, presented an enormous challenge. Few events ever presented a more fearsome one than the Targa Florio, the invention of Count Vincenzo Florio of Sicily, a renowned motoring pioneer.

Florio's plate was the reward for the winner of a time trial around the Madonie mountains in the north of the island, passing through the narrow streets of villages such as Cerda, Collesano and Campofelice. But in 1919 merely reaching the event was an accomplishment, particularly if you had to start from Milan. Ferrari and Sivocci both entered the Targa Florio, taking Berretta and another mechanic, Ripamonti, with them. They left Milan in their CMNs, planning to drive down to Naples where they would load the cars on to a steamer, the *Città di Siracusa*. But as they passed through the Abruzzi mountains they faced an unexpected ordeal. 'We found ourselves in a blizzard', Ferrari wrote, 'and we were chased by wolves. They were put to flight, however, by shots from the revolver I always kept under the seat cushion, and by the arrival of a group of road gangers armed with torches and guns.'

They arrived in Naples just as the *Città di Siracusa* was about to cast off its mooring ropes, but the stevedores were persuaded to reopen the loading doors – thanks to 'the unspoken understanding between the unprivileged and poor', Ferrari claimed, adding that he had started out with only 450 lire in his pocket. That night he and his companions suffered terribly from the combined effects of a rough crossing and predatory insects.

The 1919 Targa Florio, the tenth edition of a race that was to survive more or less unchanged for another fifty years, had attracted a powerful field. The Italian entries, headed by Ascari's Fiat and the Alfa of Giuseppe Campari, a would-be opera singer, were opposed by two French teams, the Peugeots of André Boillot and Rémy Reville and the eight-cylinder Ballot of René Thomas, a former motorcycle racer. Ferrari and Berretta, swathed in overcoats and caps, set off the day before the event to try to learn as much of the 108-kilometre Medio Circuito della Madonie as they could manage in a single day, preparing for a race in which the competitors would be required to complete four laps. Ferrari and Berretta were in the middle of their reconnaissance lap when a violent storm forced them to abandon their efforts. Even when, years later, the course was cut in half again, it was still terrifying. In its longer forms its challenge was nothing short of elemental. Such a course could be closed to normal traffic only in the loosest of senses. At any moment a peasant on a bicycle, wobbling along with a load of hay on his back, might wander into the road. And the lap was too long for the sort of communications that would provide the competitors with an idea of where they stood in the race at any given moment. All they could do was give it everything, or as much as they dared on the stark and inhospitable mountain roads of Sicily.

The day of the race produced rain on the low-lying sections, snow in the mountains, and mud everywhere. Goggles quickly became caked. Some drivers used gauze masks to keep the stuff out of their mouths and noses. Within a lap, a car's racing number would be illegible. Ferrari started at 8.02 a.m., just behind Boillot's Peugeot, but his effort was hampered within the first few miles by a loose petrol tank. He and Berretta spent more than forty minutes stationary while they repaired the fastening that secured the tank to the chassis, relegating them to last place. Then, on the final lap, as their car entered Campofelice, they met three policemen standing in the road, arms raised. The *carabinieri* told the puzzled racers that they would have to wait: the new President of Italy, Vittorio Emanuele Orlando, a Sicilian elected only a week earlier, was making a speech in the village square. Ferrari and his companion waited with mounting frustration while Orlando, not a man of few words, continued his oration. And even when he had finished, the CMN was forced to let the President leave first in his big black De Dion Bouton limousine and to follow behind at a processional pace until, after several miles, the official party turned off.

Ferrari pushed the CMN as hard as he could, but by the time he reached the finish line the officials and spectators had disappeared, relieved to escape the weather. Only a single policeman was left, charged with the duty of recording the last stragglers, all of them outside the official limit of ten hours. The policeman had an alarm clock with which to take their times, and he was rounding them out to the nearest minute. The following day a furious Ferrari stormed into the Palermo office of Vincenzo Florio, demanding justice. Having listened to his case, Florio agreed to list him as the last official finisher, in ninth position, two places behind Sivocci. The race was won, at an average speed of about 40 mph, by Boillot, who had not been able to avoid running into a wandering spectator near the finish line, with fatal results. Ascari and his mechanic ended up in hospital after overturning their car in the mountains. Newspaper reports of the race presented a variety of versions of the events surrounding Ferrari's unusual result; decades later the finding that Vittorio Emanuele Orlando had apparently visited Termini Imerese rather than Campofelice that day seemed to throw doubt on the specific accuracy of Ferrari's own account – not the last time his version of an event would be questioned.

That was his last race for CMN. The company was having little commercial success and for his first race of 1920, a return to the Parma–Poggio di Berceto hillclimb, he acquired a more powerful vehicle, a 1913 Isotta Fraschini with a 7-litre engine, four-wheel brakes and a rakishly streamlined radiator. A new mechanic, Guglielmo Carraroli, seated alongside him, Ferrari raced to his first significant result: second in his class and third overall. Giuseppe Campari, the opera singer, won the race in his Alfa. Ascari had missed the deadline for entries by half an hour, and had been refused the chance to defend his trophy. From a brief meeting with Campari there developed a lasting bond. 'We became close friends,' Ferrari said. 'There was something very special about Campari. So open, so sincere and straightforward that he remained unassuming, even at the height of his fame. He was not just an exceptionally skilful driver but also an indefatigable fighter, a man for whom risk was part of the act of winning.'

There were two more insignificant and unsuccessful races in the Isotta, but for his return to the Targa Florio in October he established a relationship that was to exert a decisive effect on the shape of his life. His involvement with Alfa Romeo of Milan was to turn him into a star in the motor-racing firmament, and then to cast him out in such a way as to turn his implacable need for revenge into a powerful weapon.

It began with a bit of a joke. Alfa Romeo had its origins in a company – Anonima Lombarda Fabbrica Automobili – founded by Cavaliere Ugo Stella, a Milanese notable, in partnership with the French firm Darracq. The joint concern took over the derelict Darracq factory in Portello, a suburb of Milan, but the partnership lapsed during the war, when the Italian side of the company switched to making shells and trucks for the army. Afterwards Nicola Romeo, a mathematics professor, had taken a leading role and given his name to the rejuvenated company, which soon began to participate in racing once more and was developing fast, lean, responsive machines that would get results and attract customers. Ferrari joined their number when he ordered a G1 model, a powerful 6-litre car based on the design of an American car, the Pierce-Arrow. He had placed his order with Giorgio Rimini, Alfa's sales and racing manager. Described by Ferrari as 'swarthy of complexion, with staring eyes and a cigarette permanently hanging from his lips ... keen, intelligent and full of drive', it was Rimini who responded to Ferrari's complaints about the non-appearance of the car by producing the signed contract. Somewhere near the bottom of the small print was a clause proclaiming that the car would be delivered 'as soon as possible, or even earlier'. That experience, Ferrari recalled, taught him to read every contract down to the very last word before signing on the dotted line.

The incident certainly did nothing to damage his growing friendship with Rimini, who gave him a place as a junior member of the Alfa Romeo team, where he would line up alongside some of Italy's finest drivers and work with engineers and technicians who would be at the leading edge of the development of racing cars in the years between the wars. It was a time of turmoil for Italy, communists and anarchists making common cause against the black-shirted Fascists, and coinciding with Ferrari's appointment in August was the occupation of the Portello works by Alfa Romeo's workers, who flew the red flag from the factory pole and shut down production as part of a general wave of action throughout Milan.

By October, normal working hours had been restored. There were three Alfa Romeo cars ready at the start of the 1920 Targa Florio, led by Campari. Michele Conti was in the mechanic's seat of Ferrari's car, a modified pre-war touring machine. Again the conditions were dreadful, constant rain during the week of the race washing away much of the loose road surface, often leaving sharp stones projecting out of the earth. In an effort to mitigate the effects of the weather, the Alfas were equipped with gauze screens and mudflaps added by the firm's chief designer, Giuseppe Merosi, a qualified surveyor whose assistant, Antonio Santoni, was a pharmacist. This time there were neither wolves nor presidential parades to obstruct Ferrari's progress, just a rival driver, Guido Meregalli, in a car manufactured under Nazzaro's name. Meregalli saw Campari, the pre-race favourite, retire on the second lap with water fouling the low-mounted spark plugs of his engine, and held off Ferrari, whose determined attack in the closing stages earned him second place overall and victory in his class. Meregalli, distressed and exhausted by the ferocity of the race, tried to get out of his car at the finish line but found himself unable to stand up. The first truly outstanding result of Ferrari's career, at the wheel of an unremarkable car in a very demanding race, it confirmed his place in a team whose number soon expanded to include Antonio Ascari.

Ferrari developed a particular regard for the more experienced driver, the son of a grain merchant from Mantua. 'Antonio was a man of real character, exceptionally energetic and truly brave,' he wrote. 'He was utterly fearless, with a talent for improvisation – the sort of driver we used to call a *garibaldino*, meaning the reckless, intuitive kind who didn't scrupulously walk the course in advance but felt their way into every bend, getting closer and closer to the very limits of tyre grip as lap followed lap.' To Ferrari, it may have been equally significant that Ascari had also established a business relationship with Alfa Romeo, becoming the firm's dealer for the Lombardy region, using his own successes to boost sales.

Not until 1923 and a race called the Circuito di Savio was Ferrari able to achieve his ambition of passing the chequered flag as a winner. Held on 17 June on roads outside Ravenna, starting and finishing in front of the basilica of Sant'Apollinare in Classe, the race plunged through pine forests and down long full-throttle straights. With a young Alfa mechanic named Giulio Ramponi alongside him, Ferrari held off a fifteen-strong field over the distance of 225 miles and was borne aloft in triumph by the crowd, who had broken the police lines. That afternoon, before he and Ramponi drove back home to Modena in the dust-covered Alfa, he was introduced to Count Enrico Baracca, the father of the late fighter ace in whose squadron his brother Dino had served. 'From this meeting', Ferrari wrote, 'another followed with the mother, Countess Paolina. It was she who told me one day, "Ferrari, put the prancing horse of my son on your racing car. It will bring you luck." I still keep the photograph of Baracca with the dedication by the parents in which they entrusted me with the emblem. The horse was, and has remained, black, but I myself added the yellow background, this being the colour of Modena.'

Scepticism has often accompanied Ferrari's account of how he acquired the device of the *cavallino rampante*, which has become such a potent symbol of the company, its cars, its victories, and its all-pervasive myth. Some believe that the horse was not Baracca's emblem at all, but that of the whole Squadriglia 912, and therefore not within the gift of his parents. Others claim that, since the rearing black horse is in fact the symbol of the city of Stuttgart, Baracca must have cut it from the fabric fuselage of the aeroplane of one of the German pilots he shot down, as aces on both sides were wont to do whenever there was the opportunity to follow a victim down. Indeed, Baracca is said to have shot down an Albatross carrying such a shield, piloted by an unnamed German from Stuttgart, over Tolmezzo, near Udine, in November 1916.

The fact that Ferrari did not use the emblem until 1932 has been presented as another reason to cast doubt on the integrity of his tale and to accuse him of embroidering the story of his meeting with Baracca's mother in order to add colour to his own myth. Ferrari was certainly shrewd enough to be thinking already about the appeal of such a connection. But until 1930 he did not have a team of his own, so before then he could hardly have had any practical use for a symbol of his own. When he considered the time was right to express the autonomy of his own organisation, the prancing horse was ready to be unveiled.

Francesco Baracca's horse would be joining a crowded field. Motor racing was exploding in popularity as the 1920s progressed. By the end of the decade, the four-leafed clover of Alfa Romeo, the trident of Bologna to be found on the cars of the Maserati brothers, the horseshoe-shaped radiator grille of the Bugattis, and the three-pointed star of Mercedes-Benz would be jostling for position and capturing the imagination of a growing public, pushing out the established names of Sunbeam, Peugeot, Renault and Fiat. Ordinary roads were still being closed for full-scale races, but new permanent circuits were also being erected throughout Europe, including the autodrome in the royal park at Monza, outside Milan, and the combined speed bowls and road tracks at Brooklands and Montlhéry, in the countryside near London and Paris respectively.

It was a good time to be moving up in the sports-car business, and though Ferrari was still pursuing his career as a driver it was soon evident that he had no illusions about his own abilities. It was on his recommendation that Giorgio Rimini persuaded Ugo Sivocci to leave the ailing CMN concern and join the Alfa team's complement of drivers, first as head of the test department and later as a member of the grand prix squad, even though it effectively pushed Ferrari himself down the pecking order. He was also instrumental in bringing Luigi Bazzi, a talented thirty-year-old Fiat engine specialist, from Turin to Milan. Bazzi had fallen out with Fiat's chief engineer, Guido Fornaca, at the French Grand Prix, when Fornaca had peremptorily ordered him to put more petrol into Pietro Bordino's stationary car, ignoring Bazzi's protestations that the problem was a broken supercharger. Now Bazzi joined Alfa Romeo to work alongside Giuseppe Merosi, whose limitations – and those of his pharmacist assistant – were becoming apparent. What this activity provided was evidence that Ferrari was keen to pin his future to a wider involvement in the burgeoning managerial and entrepreneurial sides of motor racing. At Alfa Romeo he was making himself useful in a variety of roles, travelling on the firm's behalf to important motor shows in France and Switzerland, and to Brooklands where, on his only visit to England, he encountered Mario Lombardini, the British representative of the Pirelli tyre company. Lombardini was to become a 'second father' to Ferrari, some-body whose views on the importance of the links between racing and the motor industry helped form his philosophy, and who was to be of considerable help as he developed his business.

Ferrari was also still a racing driver, at least intermittently, and now he was turning up at the tracks with a regular companion. On a business trip to Turin in 1921 he had met Laura Domenica Garello, a striking and extrovert girl two years his junior who came from a modest background in Racconigi, a village outside the city. *Una donna buffa*, someone was to describe her in later years – a bit of a card. According to Ferrari, they met under the arches near the Porto Nuevo railway station. 'Laura was pretty, blonde, graceful, *simpatica*,' he remembered. Before long they were living and travelling together. Over the next fifty years Laura was to play a vital role in Ferrari's destiny, but for a while the nature of their liaison had to be concealed from his mother back in Modena.

The following year, however, he delighted Adalgisa by

deciding to move his base of operations back to his home town. She seems to have been somewhat less enthralled when, on 28 April 1923, he and Laura were married in Turin, in a church near the Fiat works, in a ceremony attended only by twenty of the bride's relatives, who also had to be coaxed into accepting the advisability of the match. The relationship between Laura and her mother-in-law seems to have been a stormy and acrimonious one: two strong women were beginning a long struggle for the right to the attention of a man who, before too long, was to prove himself intent on spending a good proportion of his time out of the way of either of them.

His real attention was on his work. Deepening his involvement with Alfa Romeo, Ferrari established a business largely devoted to selling the firm's cars in the region around Modena. The first company, Carrozzeria Emilia, reflected in its title the location of its headquarters, in a garage just outside the old town walls. It was here, too, that he began his career as an employer, giving work to local people and thereby setting himself on the path to establishing his status as a local *padrone*, with power over the livelihoods and wellbeing of men and their families. By using the reputation he had gained as a racing driver to sell fast cars to the more affluent and sporting members of the community, he had begun to discover his true métier.

How good a driver was he? Contemporary newspaper reports often contain high praise based on individual performances, but inevitably lack perspective. The reporter who described him as 'audacious and ready, confident and perfect' as early as 1919 was probably trying too hard to make an impression of his own. 'He should be considered among the best of Italian drivers,' another wrote after the 1920 Targa Florio. Yet Rimini clearly did not consider him to be on the same level as Ascari or Campari, since he restricted Ferrari to races of the second rank, and only four or five a season of those, consistently overlooking him when selecting the team for the major grand prix events. 'I can't honestly swear that if I'd kept it up I would ever have become a great driver,' Ferrari said.

[28]

'Even then I had my doubts. If you want spectacular results, you have to know how to treat your car badly. Ill treatment means excessive gear shifts, pushing the car further than the engine will bear, reckless braking, all the things that got in the way of my feeling for the machinery. The fact is that I don't drive simply to get from A to B. I enjoy feeling the car's reactions, becoming part of it, forming a single unit. I couldn't inflict suffering on it.' There have been suggestions that he lacked the commitment, and perhaps the ultimate courage, necessary to join the very top rank. 'Ferrari had too great a respect for the cars that were entrusted to him, and perhaps he was not foolhardy enough,' his friend and chronicler Gino Rancati wrote. This may be true, although no driver capable of finishing second in the Targa Florio could ever have been considered a coward.

After his triumph in the Circuito di Savio, the year 1923 ended in tragedy. The photographs of the Alfa Romeo team before the Italian Grand Prix at Monza show the trio of star drivers – Ascari, Campari and Sivocci – and their mechanics in the cockpits of three of Merosi's low-slung P1 machines, with Ferrari, Bazzi and Rimini standing in attendance. Contemplating an imminent confrontation with powerful opposition from Fiat, Sunbeam and Bugatti, the team smile for the camera without undue ebullience, although there is an amusing snap of them posed outside the Monza garage, sharing the spoof ritual of swearing allegiance to a brand of motor oil. Ferrari himself planned to take part in the practice sessions, apparently without intending to compete. Two laps into the race, however, Sivocci's P1 left the track at high speed on the left-hand bend at the back of the circuit. Ferrari sped to the scene. 'I was one of the first to reach Sivocci's car,' he wrote. 'I gathered him into my arms and tried to give him first aid, but sadly there was nothing anybody could do for him.' An English spectator volunteered the use of his car to take Sivocci to hospital in the town. A photographer was there to record the scene as, perched on the tail of the car with Sivocci dying in the back seat, a soldier hanging on to the passenger door, and the Englishman at

[29]

the wheel in his overcoat, gloves and trilby hat, Ferrari said goodbye to the man who had convinced him that motor racing might provide the basis of a career. As a mark of the team's distress, Rimini withdrew the remaining two cars from the race. Sivocci's car had been carrying the number 17, which in later years Ferrari would associate with misfortune.

It was already clear that Merosi's new P1 was not up to the job of competing with the best of its rivals. When Rimini asked for suggestions, Ferrari turned to Bazzi, who mentioned with enthusiasm that a young and gifted Fiat engineer named Vittorio Jano might be able to provide some of the answers. Rimini ordered Ferrari to travel to Turin and find him. Thanks to Guglielmo Carraroli, who had ridden as Ferrari's mechanic in the early days and still lived in Turin, he was able to discover Jano's home address. Ferrari's own description of the fateful meeting makes it sound straightforward. 'I climbed up to an apartment on the third floor of an unpretentious house in the via San Massimo. Jano's wife, Rosina, answered my ring at the door. Suspiciously, she wanted to know the reason for my call and, without beating about the bush, I told her I had come to persuade her husband to give up his job at the Fiat works and come over to Alfa. Just as she was replying that her husband was too much of a Piedmontese to think of leaving Turin, Jano himself arrived. We had a talk, I told him the advantages of joining Alfa, and the following day he signed up.' Jano's version, confided to the American historian Griffith Borgeson in 1964, a year before his death, is slightly different. He knew all about Ferrari, he said, and was aware that he had Nicola Romeo's trust, but considered him an insufficiently senior figure with whom to conclude such an important arrangement. To begin with, then, he turned down the offer. Only when an approach was made from a more exalted level did he accept the deal, which raised his earnings from the 1,800 lire he was making each month at Fiat to 3,500 lire; within eighteen months of his arrival in Milan, he was earning three times his Turin salary.

No one disputed that he was worth the money. 'Bazzi had

described him as strong-willed,' Ferrari wrote. 'But that, as I was to find, was putting it mildly. Once in Milan, Jano took command of the situation, establishing a military discipline.' He completely reworked Merosi's P1, enabling the team to start the 1924 season with its successor, the P2. Bristling with a host of innovations from its supercharged eight-cylinder engine, with two valves per cylinder, to its hydraulic brakes, the P2 immediately cut a swathe through its adversaries, even before Jano's men had time to apply a coat of Alfa's deep red paint. 'Ascari's first lap made an enormous impression,' the journalist Giovanni Canestrini wrote after witnessing the car's first practice session for its debut race, the Circuito di Cremona. 'While waiting along the edge of the road with eyes pointed at the course, it seemed to us that a bullet had just passed us by. The silver car proceeded firmly on that imperfect surface, and the singing of the engine gave the impression of uncommon power.' Ascari took it to victory in Cremona, Campari won the Grand Prix of Europe, and the team's four cars made a clean sweep of the Italian Grand Prix at Monza, a priceless victory in terms of prestige.

Ferrari's absence from the triumphant quartet betrayed evidence of his strange year in the cockpit. In 1924 he raced a total of five times and scored three wins in a row in the Circuits of Savio, Polesine and Pescara, partnered in all of them by Eugenio Siena, a cousin of Campari. Repeating his success in the Savio race, he finished two laps ahead of the little Chiribiri in second place, driven by one Tazio Nuvolari, a former motorcycle champion from Mantua who was making the transition to four wheels at the advanced age of thirty-one. But it was at Pescara that Ferrari achieved his best result to date, winning the Coppa Acerbo, a major event, despite using an old six-cylinder Tipo RL/Targa Florio sports car, a piece of equipment much inferior to the P2 with which his team mate Campari started the race.

The circuit at Pescara, 15.8 miles long, began on the long, flat road leading through the resort on the Adriatic coast before turning sharply up into the hills, where it twisted through a pair of mountain villages, between churches and farmyards, before swooping back down to the coast road. One of the most majestic settings ever devised for a massed-start motor race, it made equal demands on the drivers' skill and courage, on the properties of their cars' chassis and on the ability of their engines to sustain long periods of running at peak revs. Those finding themselves in the vicinity today can still drive the roads that once formed the track, which are little altered in almost eighty years, although the staff in the office of the local automobile club, situated not far from the old start line, are a little hazy about the precise configuration of the circuit that brought fame and honour to their otherwise unremarkable resort town. Up in the villages of Spoltore, Cappelle and Montesilvano, so little has changed that it is easy to imagine generations of heroes thundering through, from the Bugattis and Alfas of the golden age up to Stirling Moss in his Vanwall, trouncing Luigi Musso's lone Ferrari on a baking-hot afternoon in 1957, in the last big race ever held in Pescara.

Back in 1924 Enzo Ferrari took the lead from the start, looking over his shoulder at the two Mercedes of Count Masetti and Count Bonmartini, and waiting for Campari's P2 to come by. But Campari, whose gearbox broke in the early stages, had devised the ruse of pushing his broken car up an alley and out of sight, in order to leave the Mercedes drivers in ignorance of his retirement as long as possible. Ferrari, too, wondered where his team mate had got to. 'Lap after lap I looked in my mirrors,' he wrote. 'But there was no sign of the P2. Worried by its absence – it was a much faster car than mine – and by the way the Mercedes were sitting on my tail, I glanced at Siena and slowed slightly. Siena, however, let out a roar in which there was not the slightest shadow of concern over the absence of his cousin. "Keep going," he shouted. "We're going to win!"' Sufficiently confused, Masetti and Bonmartini failed to press their attack and Ferrari took the chequered flag, pulling up to be congratulated by a welcoming committee including Air

Marshal Italo Balbo, the Duke of Abruzzi, and Professor Giacomo Acerbo, a member of Mussolini's cabinet and brother of the dead Great War hero in whose honour the race had been given its name. The winner's rewards were a large silver cup, made by a Florentine craftsman, and a cheque for 5,000 lire. 'I had really made my name as a driver,' Ferrari reflected.

An even greater reward seemed to have arrived with the announcement that he would be drafted into the squad for the French Grand Prix in Lyons three weeks later. Completing the four-car team, he would line up alongside Ascari, Campari and the veteran French driver Louis Wagner, all with Jano's brand-new P2 machines. The role of Ferrari's riding mechanic would be taken by his friend Bazzi. But what should have been his best chance to establish himself as a top-line driver turned into one of the stranger episodes in grand prix history. 'After the practice laps, which went very well, I felt completely shattered,' Ferrari wrote. 'It made me so ill that I had to withdraw from the race.' He had been rundown all year, he added. 'My indisposition, in fact, was grave enough to compel me to cut down and practically give up driving.' This opaque explanation has satisfied few historians, particularly since Ferrari arrived in Lyons on the back of three consecutive wins over a ten-week period. Any ambitious driver would have been grateful for the opportunity to show his paces in the P2 and to measure himself against the best. But Ferrari, it seemed, simply packed his bag and took the train home to Modena. Never again would he be invited to race such a car. His chance of grand prix immortality seemed to have gone for good.

In later years, he spoke of the strange retreat from Lyons in terms of a deeper malady. 'The truth', he said, 'is that I was sick, suffering from the first symptoms of an illness which, in 1969, affected me so badly that it made me sell 50 per cent of my company to Fiat.' Behind this enigmatic utterance lie several possibilities. The first is that he was influenced by his family, specifically by his wife and his mother, who wanted to see him reduce his commitments. The second is that he was indeed suffering from some sort of intermittent clinical depression. A third interpretation is that his words, written many years later, were putting up a smokescreen to help him avoid giving a proper explanation of the negotiations for the sale of his company, which would have involved an admission of a different kind of weakness. None of these interpretations seems any more or less credible than the others. But whatever the reason behind his sudden and unexpected return home in August 1924, his decision at least had the virtue of enabling him to clear his mind and get on with the business of establishing himself in the motor industry.

Neither did it damage his links with Alfa Romeo. Six weeks later he was at Monza, in his racing overalls but with a silk scarf around his neck in place of a pair of goggles, smiling for the photographer as part of a happy group including Wagner, Rimini and Nicola Romeo, on the eve of what would be a triumphant team performance in the Italian Grand Prix. After all, it was his contribution to the defection of Bazzi and Jano from Fiat that had made Alfa's success possible. Is it simply the mischievous imagination that wonders why he is on the edge of the group, and slightly to the rear, and giving a smile which might almost be described as shy? He is also in the background as Ascari poses for a photograph with his son, six-year-old Alberto, who is standing on the driver's seat of the Alfa with the number 1 painted on its radiator, which his father will drive to victory the next day.

It would be three years before Enzo Ferrari raced again. In this time he concentrated on expanding his business and on reinforcing his network of contacts. Now appointed as Alfa Romeo's dealer for Emilia-Romagna and the Marches, he invested in a new building on the via Emilia and set up an office in Bologna. At a time when Italy was experiencing the Fascist dictatorship of Benito Mussolini, a regime strong on road-building programmes, railway timetables, and threats to invade weak North African nations, Ferrari seemed happy to be left alone to consolidate his own affairs. He had met Mussolini once, during a state tour of the region in 1924, when he was asked to drive his own car ahead of the dictator's new Alfa Romeo in order to act as a guide to the house of the local senator, where lunch had been laid on. Mussolini insisted on taking the wheel of his own car, and while Ferrari was having his lunch in a side room, the official chauffeur approached him with an urgent request to go slowly as he led the way back to Modena, since the roads were wet and *Il Duce*'s violent skids had been making him turn green.

Alfa's racing team faced 1925 in a confident frame of mind, but the heart was torn out of them in July, when Antonio Ascari crashed and died while leading the French Grand Prix on the banked track at Linas–Montlhéry, in search of his third win in a row. In light rain, his winged hubcap clipped a post and sent the P2 into a series of somersaults, from which it landed upside down in a ditch. He died almost before the ambulance had left the circuit, and once again the team withdrew from the race as a mark of respect. Ferrari, too, was devasted. Ascari's ability to combine sport and business had been a beacon to him, as had the older man's attitude to getting things done. 'If he came upon a technical problem that he couldn't solve,' Ferrari said, 'he was not afraid to ask for suggestions from someone who knew more than he did.' Ferrari knew a bit about cars, but he also understood the limits of his knowledge, and he would never be too proud to call for assistance, even though he might some-times take a while to accept that it was his own prejudices which had created the problem. 'He was a model father and husband, as well as a great companion,' Ferrari continued. 'He was generous with his money and generous in every sense and, when necessary, he was humble. Ascari did not get a good education but he was a man of great knowledge.' The whole team attended Ascari's funeral and the burial in Milan's Cimiterio Monumental. Flowers were dropped from a low-flying aeroplane. It was Campari, the big, jolly, life-affirming part-time opera singer, who lifted up the dead man's son, Alberto, just turned seven, and told him: 'Some day you will arrive at the heights, as he did. Perhaps you will be even more famous.'

Ferrari told Rimini to try to secure the services of Tazio Nuvolari, the little Mantuan motorbike racer who had finished second to him at the Circuito di Savio, as a replacement for Ascari. But Nuvolari made a mess of his test drive, leaving the track at Monza and rolling down a slope in his P2 before getting painfully caught in a barbed-wire fence, from which a group of soldiers had to free him. Surveying the damaged car, and much more bothered about the bent metal than about Nuvolari's painful gashes, Jano was not pleased.

In September at the same circuit Alfa Romeo again won the Italian Grand Prix. This time Gastone Brilli-Perri, a thirty-two-year-old Florentine nobleman and a newcomer to the team, took the victory and with it the world championship. But that day Alfa Romeo also announced their retirement from grand prix racing. Rimini left the company after a disagreement, Merosi also resigned, and Jano, who had been named director of design, moved on to create a new series of fast, light road cars, the six-cylinder 1600 and 1750 series which, with their lovely coachbuilt bodies by Zagato and Touring, would establish a reputation for beautifully designed, well-packaged, rapid and responsive cars with a sporting heritage. To dealers such as Ferrari they offered the sort of product that did not need a hard sell.

The urge to race, however, had not deserted him. In the spring of 1927 he put a toe back in the water by using an old Alfa RLSS to win the grand touring class in the Circuito di Alessandria. Three weeks later, driving a new 6C–1500SS, a highly tuned version of the new road sports car with a handsome Zagato body, he had the satisfaction of winning a race in his own backyard. No one had given him much of a chance in the 250-mile Circuito di Modena, and bigger cars, led by the Isotta Fraschini of Count Aymo Maggi, took the initiative at the start. Halfway through the race, however, a torrential rainstorm brought chaos. By the time the skies cleared, Ferrari had slipped into the lead. As he stepped out of the car, having won by eleven seconds, he was greeted with a passionate kiss by Signora Laura, smartly dressed in a dark overcoat and hat, two-tone leather handbag and high-heeled shoes, the very picture of a successful racing driver's consort. Probably every bit as significant as this display of wifely affection, however, was the first appearance of a young man named Peppino Verdelli, his mechanic at this race, who was to stay with him for more than forty years, becoming his chauffeur (or rather his passenger, since Ferrari always insisted on taking the wheel) and most trusted confidant. Peppino had a wife and children but his true home, it was soon being said, was the *casa* Ferrari.

Ferrari's participation in these small races indicated his renewed appetite for driving, and perhaps his recovery from the traumatic withdrawal from the race at Lyons. His interest in competition was also aroused by the creation of the Mille Miglia, a thousand-mile race around Italy for sports and touring cars, starting and finishing in Brescia. Races from city to city were how motor racing had begun, but they had almost died out by the time four men, two aristocrats and two journalists, devised an event that would bring publicity to their home town as well as satisfying their love of motor sport. Aymo Maggi and Franco Mazzotti, friends from boyhood and keen amateur racing drivers, joined up with Renzo Castagneto and Giovanni Canestrini to plan a race that would go from Brescia to Rome and back, circumnavigating half of Italy. When Castagneto jotted some figures down on the back of an envelope and remarked that the cars would cover a distance of 1,600 kilometres, Count Mazzotti responded: 'That's a thousand miles. Why don't we call it the Coppa della Mille Miglia?'

It was a wonderful idea and Enzo Ferrari, with Rimini out of the picture, took on the management of a three-car Alfa Romeo team in the inaugural event. 'The Mille Miglia was a race that not only made a sizeable contribution to the technical evolution of the automobile but also identified real champions,' he wrote later. 'No driver could consider his credits complete without a victory in Brescia. In the very first edition of the race there was a test of the maturity of our cars and our industry. The course was very different from what it became: the roads had deep grooves cut by the steel wheels of carts, there were curves within curves, and there were stones, rocks, gravel and mud. The railway crossing could appear suddenly in the middle of a blind curve. For the driver and the car, it was the ultimate test of reflexes.' Like the Le Mans 24-hour race, started four years earlier, the Mille Miglia was intended to attract teams from manufacturers keen to display the speed and reliability of their cars.

The Alfa team consisted of three of Merosi's durable six-cylinder RL SS models, with special 'torpedo' bodies. The first of them, driven by Brilli-Perri, set the pace. Ferrari himself made the journey through the hill country to the Raticosa Pass, in the Apennines between Bologna and Florence, to watch the cars go by, and at that stage he could take confidence from their showing. But as they travelled from Florence to Siena and on through Rome to Perugia and back up the Adriatic coast via Ancona and Pesaro, one by one the Alfas began to fall away, leaving victory to another great Italian driver, Nando Minoia, who had averaged 47 mph for twenty-one hours in an OM, built in Brescia. Maggi, Mazzotti, Castagneto and Canestrini could give themselves a pat on the back and celebrate with an extra glass of grappa. They had created an event which, over the next thirty years, would pass into legend, epitomising as nothing else could all the romance and danger of motor racing in the era before drivers became cocooned in carbon fibre and restrained by safety straps, or spectators protected by crash barriers and run-off zones. The Mille Miglia was motor racing in the raw, the way it had been invented by the pioneers at the turn of the century, and it said something about Italy that it was the last European country to sanction such an activity on the open roads. While the British outlawed the use of public highways for racing, millions of ordinary Italians believed it an honour to have the Mille Miglia pass through their towns and villages, with its parade of heroes and hardware. And from its origins right up to its final moments thirty years later, Enzo Ferrari would play a central role in its destiny.

The Scuderia Ferrari leaving a Livorno hotel for the start of the Coppa Ciano
on 3 August 1930: Enzo and Laura are in the front seats of their stripped-
down Alfa Romeo, with Baconin Borzacchini and Luigi Arcangeli behind,
Augusto Caniato at the rear and Tazio Nuvolari on the right.

Two

Of all the drivers with whom he was associated in the early days, Enzo Ferrari had a particular fondness for Giuseppe Campari. With Alfa Romeo out of grand prix racing, Campari's answer was to buy a P2 of his own from the factory. He was still dreaming of a singing career – he had just married a *diva* named Lina Cavalleri – but he had also opened a garage business near his home in San Siro, a Milan suburb. Ferrari's recollections of a dinner party at the *casa* Campari charmingly evoke a sense of time and place. 'I pushed my way into the kitchen to observe the scenery,' he wrote. 'Dressed in grey pyjamas with blue stripes, with the look of a prison uniform, the great racing driver was bending over the pots among clouds of steam and bursts of flame. The sauce received, among other exquisite ingredients, droplets of sweat. At the table, I excused myself by explaining that I was suffering from a special allergy to pasta. My friend found the *riccioline*, a sort of cut-up spaghetti which was a typical Milanese dish, excellent, if a bit salty. The night ended with a duet by the host and hostess: the first act of *La Traviata*.'

When Campari took his P2 to Pescara to win the Coppa Acerbo, Luigi Bazzi went along to look after the car. Notwithstanding the pause in activity that followed Ascari's death, the members of the old team were still in contact. In 1928 Ferrari also accompanied Campari on a practice run over the Mille Miglia course, and came back with a story which he used to illustrate his friend's furious will to win. Campari, he said, was a man who stopped at nothing, and for nothing. Going over the Raticosa pass, Ferrari suddenly noticed water splashing on the floor. Over the roar of the engine, he yelled at Campari: 'I think a radiator hose may have broken! Let's stop to check!' No answer from Campari. Glancing down, Ferrari noticed that from the bottom of the driver's cotton long johns, which protruded from the hems of his overalls and were fastened to his socks with tape, liquid was streaming out. 'Well,' Campari shouted as he wrestled the car around another hairpin, 'what did you want me to do? We can't stop when we're racing! You just have to piss in your pants, that's all!' Campari won that year's race, and the one after it, thus establishing Alfa Romeo's special relationship with the event; Giulio Ramponi was the mechanic who risked a drenching in pursuit of glory.

Ferrari himself returned to the wheel that year, repeating his victory in the Circuito di Alessandria although, like all his fellow competitors, he was mourning the unexpected absence of Pietro Bordino, a great Italian champion. Bordino had been killed during a practice run when a dog ran under the front of his Bugatti, jamming the steering, locking the wheels and sending the car hurtling into a ditch. Ferrari also won again in Modena and finished third in the Circuito di Mugello, on both occasions with Peppino Verdelli in the mechanic's seat. Although those three races comprised his entire programme for the season, he was nevertheless listed tenth in the order of Italy's highest-earning drivers that year, with 45,000 lire in winnings to his credit. Third was Campari, with 152,000 lire. But it was the top two, Emilio Materassi (185,000 lire) and Tazio Nuvolari (178,000 lire), whose activities most interested Ferrari.

In addition to their own individual achievements, both men had also started their own teams, or *scuderie*, that season, offering cars for hire to wealthy amateurs. Materassi, a thirty-nine-year-old mechanic from Florence, took over the cars and equipment of the Talbot team after the French company decided to close its racing operation. As well as three Talbot grand prix cars, he also acquired two Bugattis, two Italas, an Amilcar and a Chrysler. His first driver was Luigi Arcangeli, known as the Lion of Romagna, a twenty-six-year-old motorcycle champion. Nuvolari's team, based in Mantua, comprised five

[42]

Bugattis. His partners were a local landowner and Achille Varzi, a textile merchant's son of exaggeratedly elegant appearance and sombre demeanour. The twenty-four-year-old Varzi had been Nuvolari's chief opponent on motorcycles; soon they would create a legendary rivalry on four wheels.

Ferrari was attracted by the idea of creating a proper team of his own, free from the influence of a manufacturer but with guaranteed financial backing. While he began to lay plans, his own racing career was dwindling away. In 1929 he again raced only three times, crashing out of the Circuito di Alessandria, finishing fifth in the Circuito del Pozzo after losing his rear brakes, and placing eighth in the Circuito di Mugello, where he became ill during a race run in extreme heat. Much more significant to Ferrari's future was a race in which he did not drive. On 1 September the entrants for the Circuito delle Tre Provincie, starting and finishing at Bagni di Porretta, included three young men with brand-new Alfa Romeos: Peppino Adami of Modena, Alfredo Caniato from Ferrara, and Mario Tadini from Bologna. All three were making their debuts, and all three had bought their cars from Enzo Ferrari.

A month later, at a formal dinner held in Bologna's Casa del Fascio to celebrate the achievement of Baconin Borzacchini in establishing a new world speed record in his sixteen-cylinder Maserati, Ferrari took the next step. Seated at his table were two of his customers, Caniato and Tadini. Caniato and his brother Augusto were textile manufacturers; Tadini was from an affluent family with origins in Bergamo. As they talked, Ferrari put his proposal for the creation of a racing stable. They would come up with the basic finance and he would provide the experience, the contacts, and the expertise. The two young men were clearly impressed. On 1 December they visited the office of Enzo Levi, a Modenese lawyer, where they signed the documents that brought into existence the Società Anonima Scuderia Ferrari, a joint-stock company. Tadini and the Caniato brothers would provide 130,000 lire, more than half the funding. Ferrari himself would stake 50,000 lire, with a further

5,000 lire coming from his friend *Dottore* Ferruccio Testi, a local veterinary surgeon who also had a business distributing beer, soft drinks and mineral water.

To put flesh on the financial bones provided by Caniato and Tadini, Ferrari began doing the rounds of his contacts. First he went to Portello, where he was warmly received by the Alfa Romeo executives, who could see that his plan would relieve them of at least some of the problems associated with running a racing programme. Unsure of whether to run their own team or not, they were in no doubt of the benefits accruing from the publicity associated with a good showing in competition, and Ferrari's background gave them confidence in his ability to deliver the necessary results. The Scuderia's partners were offered shares in exchange for guarantees of technical co-operation and the supply of certain basic tools, and an agreement was quickly made. Alfa Romeo contributed a token amount of 10,000 lire. Pirelli, the Milanese tyre manufacturer, came up with half that sum.

Whatever claims to originality or innovation Ferrari was to make, it was in this arrangement, rather than in the technical specifications of any of the cars whose manufacture he was to supervise, that such qualities could truly be found. Ferrari's achievement was twofold. First, his prescience enabled him to envision the benefits which a relationship with a small, responsive, specialist concern could bring to a larger manufacturer when it came to adapting to the needs of a competition strategy. 'Alfa Romeo never saw the Scuderia Ferrari as a competitor,' he wrote later, 'nor certainly did they imagine it as the embryo of a future motor-car factory. There was no hint of future rivalry. In Alfa's view, the Scuderia offered it a chance to enter a lot of races and maintain a racing image despite no longer wanting to be directly involved. Alfa also derived another benefit from the Scuderia Ferrari, which was not spectacular but very practical. I always used to keep Alfa informed about my own experiments with the cars and about what our competitors were doing. In this way the Scuderia became a small detachment of ultra-loyal Alfa clients who shared a common passion for racing as well as engineering and financial interests.' Second, he saw how a racing team could be pieced together using contributions, financial and technical, from outside parties. So after his success with Alfa Romeo and Pirelli he visited Bosch, makers of spark plugs, and Shell, suppliers of carburants and lubricants, and from each he secured an agreement which formed another piece of the mosaic. Ferrari did not invent trade sponsorship, but he may have been responsible for turning it into a system. And from such pioneering agreements sprang a wider form of patronage, spreading its reach far beyond the manufacturers of automobile components to embrace multinational companies whose businesses had nothing to do with cars but who realised the dividend to be achieved from an association with the winners in a glamorous sport with a worldwide audience.

The Scuderia made its headquarters in the old Gatti machine-tool workshops on the via Emilia. Here they prepared their five cars, three Alfa 1750s and two 1500s, plus others belonging to their clients. Ferrari appointed as his first *direttore sportivo*, or team manager, another, unrelated, bearer of Modena's most common surname, Saracco Ferrari. The small complement of mechanics included Peppino Verdelli, and a Citroën van was acquired as the team's back-up vehicle. A third driver, Luigi Scarfiotti, a local Fascist politician and a member of the lower chamber of the Italian parliament, was added to the strength. And plans were laid for the Scuderia to make its first appearance at the Mille Miglia, which would have its fourth running on the weekend of 12 and 13 April 1930.

The field was a formidable one. OM, the first winners, were present with three cars. Mercedes-Benz entered Rudolf Caracciola in a massive 7-litre SSK. The Maserati brothers from Bologna, in their second year as manufacturers, had Luigi Arcangeli in their fast Tipo 26M. Lancia were there. And the Alfa factory, boosted by Campari's efforts in 1928 and 1929, had entered no fewer than six of their 1750 SS models, their drivers including Nuvolari and Varzi as well as Campari. (Brilli-Perri, who would have been among them, had been killed in Tripoli a few weeks earlier, driving one of Materassi's Talbots.) The Scuderia Ferrari's entries were for Tadini and Siena, Caniato and Sozzi, and Scarfiotti and Carraroli. It was hardly a glorious debut. Ferrari, stationed at a refuelling point near Bologna, saw all his cars go through, but none of them got much further. The real story of the race was to be found elsewhere, in a famous battle between Nuvolari and Varzi, two men who would one day leave their imprints on the Scuderia.

In the Mille Miglia, the cars left the start on the viale Rebuffone in Brescia at one-minute intervals, the smallest departing first, beginning in the middle of the night. The fastest competitors were flagged away before dawn, which was when Nuvolari began his chase of Varzi, who had left one minute earlier. At first, as they headed down to Florence via Piacenza and Bologna, Arcangeli's Maserati held the lead. As Nuvolari flew through the cold night over the Raticosa and Futa passes, slithering around the hairpin bends with their unmade surfaces, his mechanic, Gianbattista Guidotti, pulled himself down into his seat, clutching the grab handles. Sweet tea was available to both men from a flask attached to the bottom of the dashboard. From time to time, when the road straightened between hills and towns, Guidotti would peel Nuvolari an orange or hand him a piece of barley sugar. By the time they reached Florence, in a pale spring dawn, they had taken the lead. Varzi attacked between Florence and Poggibonsi, as the sun was rising. As they came into Rome, the halfway point, averaging more than 60 mph, the lead was his. Nuvolari went through the Rome control point and had his card stamped by the race official without actually bringing his car to a halt, earning him the cheers of the large crowd. But by the time they had crossed the plateaux of the Abruzzi and reached the Adriatic, Varzi had a lead of two minutes.

As they set off on the flat-out run up the coast, Nuvolari could do nothing against a rival in a car with an equally powerful engine. At the Venice control, Varzi's lead was unchanged. But as they returned to twisty dust-covered country roads, Nuvolari's virtuosity and courage began to tell. By the time they reached Lake Garda, he had cut the lead to half a minute. Guidotti was advising him to ease up, believing that the car could not stand such violent treatment. Nuvolari ignored him, and between Verona and Peschiera he had reduced the gap to a handful of seconds. By now it was dusk, and as they roared along a straight road leading into Peschiera, Nuvolari spotted the tail lights of Varzi's car. That gave him an idea. As they entered the illuminated streets of the town, Nuvolari switched off his own lights. Varzi failed to spot his rival creeping up behind him, and when they left the town and plunged back into the rural darkness, Nuvolari was close enough to be able to drive by following his rival's beams. A banner across the road announced that the finish in Brescia was only three kilometres away. Nuvolari waited. Varzi still had not seen him. Nuvolari waited some more. Then, with his foot hard down and the engine at peak revs, he pulled out to the left and blasted by Varzi's car, switching on his lights as he did so. As he had calculated, an astonished Varzi had no time to mount a counter-attack. Nuvolari, who had set a new record average speed of 62 mph, was lifted from his car and carried on the shoulders of his fans. Varzi kept calm but swore revenge. The members of the Scuderia Ferrari were already on their way back to Modena, planning their next move.

Ferrari entered himself in a 1750 in their next race, the Circuito di Alessandria, a week later. In the morning all the drivers attended a ceremony to dedicate a memorial at the spot where Pietro Bordino had been killed the previous year. Varzi won the race in a modified P2, but Ferrari finished third, earning the team's first podium position. The Scuderia entered no cars in the Targa Florio, but Ferrari's continuing role as a special adviser to Alfa Romeo's board was visible in his presence at a celebration in Milan to welcome back the victor. Varzi had exacted early revenge on Nuvolari by insisting that the factory allow him to race in the P2, a pure grand prix car with a 2-litre engine and almost twice the power of the 1750 sports model with which his team mates, including Nuvolari, were equipped.

The Scuderia's standing rose when Campari joined them for races at Caserta, where he finished third, and on the Tre Fontane circuit in Rome, where he was fifth and Tadini seventh in a much stronger field. These respectable results, added to Ferrari's ceaseless efforts to strengthen the relationship with the factory, prefaced Alfa Romeo's decision to help the team increase its competitiveness by sending it a P2, which had been returned from an owner in South America and had received the latest modifications in line with the cars raced by the works drivers. As a quid pro quo, Campari returned to the factory squad. But to drive the sleek grand prix car, in its first appearances for the Scuderia, Ferrari secured the services of none other than Tazio Nuvolari.

Towards the end of his life, when he was asked which driver, out of all those he had known, Enzo Ferrari considered to be the greatest, he replied with a single word: 'Nuvolari.'

Their first meeting took place in 1924: 'It was in front of the basilica of Sant'Apollinare in Classe, on the Ravenna road, where they had set up our pits for the second Circuit of Savio. At the start, I remember, I didn't pay much attention to this skinny little fellow called Nuvolari, but as the race went on it became obvious that he was the only competitor capable of threatening my progress. I was in a 3-litre Alfa Romeo, he was in a Chiribiri, and it was in that order that we finished. A week later, at the Circuito di Polesine, the same thing happened. And we became friends.'

By all accounts, their friendship took some time to ripen. The Scuderia Nuvolari, after all, had made its appearance before the Scuderia Ferrari, but the Mantuan had proved himself less suited to team management than his rival in Modena. Nor was Nuvolari as gifted at the politician's arts. And he had upset Jano,

[48]

when Ferrari suggested him as Ascari's replacement, by wrecking one of the precious P2s on his trial run at Monza. 'You're an idiot,' Jano had told him. 'You'll never make a racing driver.'

Although sometimes Nuvolari drove like an urchin, his background was comfortable and he was a man of some style. His father, Arturo, was a landowner in Castel d'Ario, a village in the Veneto twenty kilometres from Mantua, the city of Virgil and the Gonzaga. The Nuvolari family could trace its position in the region back to the eighteenth century. The large house occupied by Arturo and his wife Emma, where their son was born in 1892, stood in the main square. Tazio was a puny child, and at first his father did not expect him to live. But although he remained small, he grew stronger once the family had moved, along with his uncle Giuseppe, to a farm in Ronchesana, a few kilometres away. There Tazio had plenty of scope to exercise his growing love of speed, either on a bicycle or on his favourite black horse, which he rode without saddle or bridle, and rode so fast that one evening he was thrown off and landed in a ditch, breaking his leg.

A love of competition ran in the family. Both Tazio's father and his uncle were keen on bicycle racing, and Giuseppe turned out to have a talent for it. After dominating local and regional races, he graduated to higher levels. Eventually he became national champion three times, and travelled to events in Berlin, London and Paris, from which he would send postcards home to his nephew. Giuseppe thought Tazio had the build and the instincts to become a jockey. Arturo, however, knew that a stable-lad's training routine would bore such a restless character. And when Giuseppe settled back in Ronchesana and started to set himself up as a motor-car dealer, Arturo saw the possibility for his son to learn a trade, one that would certainly appeal to him, given the boy's enthusiastic reaction to the rare sight of early automobiles passing through the village. So it was that Tazio Nuvolari began to devote his life to automobiles, spending all his time at his uncle's business, either in the workshop, helping the mechanic and learning the principles of the motor car, or on trips with Giuseppe to Milan or Brescia. On these he was eventually allowed to take the wheel, immediately displaying a keen enjoyment of the sensation of taking bends as fast as possible as well as an urgent desire to get past any vehicle – haywagon, oxcart or motor car – that appeared in front of him. In a shed next to the farm he set up his own workshop, in which he messed about with an old engine. He made a painfully unsuccessful attempt to fly, leaping from the shed roof using a kind of parachute made with canvas cut from discarded car hoods. Undeterred, he and a friend, Rossene Poletto, purchased a dismantled Blériot monoplane for a couple of thousand lire. They brought it home and rebuilt it over a period of three weeks, but its maiden flight, in the farmyard, came to a fiery end in a haystack, from which Tazio emerged in a rage, complaining that the plane had refused to perform according to his careful calculations.

No longer quite so keen on flying, he returned to a world in which motorcycles offered a young man the cheapest and most spectacular route to speed. At thirteen he had been given his first motorbike, handed down from his uncle. Although he never grew taller than five feet five inches, Nuvolari cut a dashing figure as he roared around the country lanes, drawing admiring glances from the local girls. He spent his Great War service as a driver, some of it in Sicily, where he earned a remarkable rebuke from one officer, who disliked the brio with which he negotiated mountain roads: 'You should be a stretcher-bearer – driving is not the job for you.' On his return he married a local beauty, Carolina Perrina, had a first son, Giorgio, and went to work selling cars in Mantua.

By 1920 he was racing. Initially he made more impact on motorcycles than in cars, eventually graduating to the Bianchi works team, on one of whose famous *Freccia Celeste* – blue arrow – machines he scored his most notable victory at the Gran Premio delle Nazioni at Monza in 1925. He was in a four-wheeled Bianchi for the first Mille Miglia, in 1927, finishing fifth in the 3-litre class after taking a shade over twenty-three hours to complete the course. The first enthusiastic notices for his ability in a car came after he won the 1927 Gran Premio Reale in Rome, beating better-known and more handsomely mounted drivers in an unsupercharged Bugatti Type 35, one of two he had purchased with the proceeds from the sale of a small farm. The Bugattis were the start of Scuderia Nuvolari, in which he was assisted by a young mechanic, Decimo Compagnoni. In 1928 he won the Circuito del Garda, the Tripoli Grand Prix and the Circuito del Pozzo, all against second-rank opposition. His third place in the European Grand Prix at Monza was more impressive, but the race was darkened by the death of Emilio Materassi and twenty-one spectators in the main grandstand when Materassi lost control of his Talbot as he came off the banked section on to the pits straight.

Before the 1929 season Nuvolari launched an ambitious attempt to make progress when he hired a young engineer, Alberto Massimino, to create a new design based on his old Bugatti. But the result was thoroughly disappointing, and he returned to a standard Bugatti to take second place, behind Borzacchini's Maserati, in the Tripoli Grand Prix. He had done enough to persuade Jano to give him the second chance of a test for Alfa Romeo, and there were outings in a 1750 at Mugello and in the Coppa Ciano, in which he earned praise for finishing second, behind Varzi's P2. All of this set the scene for the dramatic duel in the Mille Miglia of 1930, in which he created the legend of a man who drove with a ragged fury and would never give up as long as he had four wheels under him and a teaspoon of fuel in the tank.

Few men, Ferrari believed, knew Nuvolari well. Ferrari noted his extreme self-confidence and his caustic sense of humour, and remembered an exchange on the day he had sent his drivers off to the Targa Florio in 1932, handing them return tickets for the long journey to Sicily. 'They told me you were a good manager,' Nuvolari said, examining the ticket. 'But now I know that isn't true. You ought to have got only a single ticket, because when anyone goes off to a race it means there's always the possibility that he'll be coming back in a wooden box.' For that race Ferrari gave him Paride Mambelli, a young and inexperienced member of the Scuderia, and a protégé of Arcangeli, to be his riding mechanic. Nuvolari looked the lad up and down and asked him if he was sure that he wouldn't be too frightened to race next to him. He warned him that if he, Nuvolari, thought he was taking a curve too fast to stay on the road, he would shout loudly, at which point the boy should dive under the dashboard for protection. When they returned to Palermo at the end of the race, Ferrari asked Mambelli how it had gone. 'Nuvolari started shouting when we got to the first curve', he replied, 'and he didn't stop until we got to the finish. So I spent the whole race under the dashboard and didn't see a thing.'

Nuvolari's debut with the Scuderia in 1930 could hardly have been more propitious. He and the P2 were entered in three hillclimbs in June and July – the Trieste–Opicina, the Cuneo–Colle della Maddalena, and the Vittorio Veneto–Cansiglio. At the first of them, on 15 June, he registered Scuderia Ferrari's inaugural victory and smashed the course record. The whole outfit, four cars with their drivers and mechanics, plus engineers and a few passers-by, posed proudly for a team photograph, with Ferrari himself standing between the P2 of Nuvolari and the 1750 of Eugenio Siena, who had finished fourth. The team's second victory came on the climb to the Colle della Maddalena, where Nuvolari outstripped Caracciola's Mercedes. The hat-trick was completed against little opposition, and the Scuderia headed for their next circuit race, the Coppa Ciano at Livorno, in particularly good spirits. Nuvolari's P2 was to be joined by the 1750s of two other top-flight drivers, Arcangeli and Borzacchini, while Campari and Varzi would be in the factory's P2s.

On a blazingly hot day, Varzi and Nuvolari raced each other with such ferocity that neither of their Alfas could stand the pace. Before he retired, Nuvolari astonished spectators on the

tricky downhill stretch at Montenero by twice missing a fast
bend, opting instead to carry straight on at full speed through
the forecourt of a small filling station, passing between the
pumps and the kiosk – a gap later measured by his own
mechanics, who had heard about the incident, and found to be
no more than a few centimetres wider than the P2. The best-
placed of the Scuderia's finishers was Borzacchini in fourth
position.

Now the greatest threat to the Alfa Romeos was coming
from Maserati, whose team was joined by Arcangeli and Varzi
in time for the Coppa Acerbo in Pescara. Nuvolari took the
battle to them, but experienced plug trouble and fell back to
fourth, leaving Varzi to win the race. Two more hillclimbs, at
Senigallia and Pontedecimo, fell to Arcangeli and Borzacchini
in the Scuderia's cars, but although Alfa Romeo provided the
team with a second P2 for the Italian Grand Prix, Varzi and
Arcangeli finished in the top two places in Maseratis. Another
failure in Brno, in Czechoslovakia, where Nuvolari's car
suffered from a broken water pump and was overtaken by two
Bugattis just short of the finish line, marked the end of the road
for the P2s, which had been subjected to all sorts of
modifications during their seven years of competitive life.

At the end-of-season dinner in the San Carlo Hotel in
Modena, in front of about sixty drivers, sponsors, mechanics
and other associates, including Luigi Bazzi and Giulio
Ramponi, who were still employed at Portello, Enzo Ferrari
could look back on a successful first year. Fifty entries had been
made in twenty-two events; eight outright victories and many
good placings represented a satisfying haul. He had laid the
foundations. And now, on a site at number 11 viale Trento e
Trieste, a hundred metres or so from the crossroads with the via
Emilia on the eastern side of Modena, he was creating a new
headquarters for the team, itself a statement of high confidence
and powerful intent.

To buy the premises, in which draught-horses had formerly
been stabled, Ferrari and his lawyer, Enzo Levi, had gone to see

Giuseppe Casoli, the manager of Banco di San Geminiano e San Prospero in Modena, to ask for a million-lire loan (the equivalent of about £90,000 today). Casoli listened in silence, staring at the floor and twiddling his thumbs as Ferrari spoke for an hour about his plans. When the speech was over, the banker looked at the lawyer and said, 'This young man has told me a fascinating story. So what should we do? Should we give him his million?' The money was provided to acquire the solid nineteenth-century two-storey building with its triple frontage and a low extension at the back, thus also securing Enzo Ferrari's lifelong loyalty to the Banco di San Geminiano e San Prospero, named after Modena's two patron saints. On the upper floor of the new property were the offices, and a small apartment for Enzo and Laura. Downstairs would be the workshops, and in the extension a variety of industrial drills, milling machines and belt-driven lathes was installed. Posters for the team's sponsors – Bosch, Pirelli, Shell – were pinned to the walls. A Shell petrol pump was put up next to one of the front doors. At the rear would be parked two new transporters, a Lancia and a Ceirano, with special bodies built by Carrozzeria Emilia to hold two racing cars each, the trademarks of the team's suppliers prominently emblazoned on their sides.

The Scuderia began the new season with a strong roster of drivers and an even closer relationship with Alfa Romeo. The professionals were promised their retainers plus a share of their prize money and of any appearance money accumulated by the team. The percentages varied, with Nuvolari at the top, to be given 30 per cent of his winnings plus a 100 per cent of any starting money paid to him by race organisers. All his travelling expenses were guaranteed, and an insurance policy worth 50,000 lire was taken out by the team on his behalf. The gentlemen amateurs, on the other hand, would be paying the team to prepare and enter the cars on their behalf.

For Alfa, Jano was completing work on the sports and single-seater versions of his new eight-cylinder 2.3 model. The factory team still existed, but a pair of the two-seaters was sent to

Modena in April in preparation for the Mille Miglia, probably because Alfa Romeo wanted to give the car a low-key debut in which failure would not be a public-relations disaster. Nuvolari took one of these handsome cars and Arcangeli the other; although the new model showed great promise, the drivers' efforts to keep up with Varzi's 5-litre Bugatti and Caracciola's Mercedes were undermined by problems with their Pirelli tyres. Nuvolari could finish no higher than ninth, although Campari managed second, behind Caracciola, in his 1750, and Alfredo Caniato also won his class in a 1500.

After Nuvolari had won the Targa Florio in a factory-entered car, the official Alfa team gave the grand prix version of the 2300 its debut in the Italian Grand Prix in May, along with another new model, the Tipo A, in which two 1750 engines were placed side by side to form a V12. There were no entries from the Scuderia, but Ferrari was present when the noisy, gregarious Arcangeli died during the practice sessions after his Tipo A spun off into the trees at the fast Lesmo curves; earlier he had posed for the cameras with a hare which his car had killed. Campari and Nuvolari teamed up to win the ten-hour race, averaging almost 100 mph in their 8C–2300, a model which would henceforward be universally known as the 'Monza'.

The death of Arcangeli, one of several drivers whose season was to have alternated between drives for Ferrari and Alfa Romeo, dealt a blow to the Scuderia's plans. Nor was the team's first experience of the 8C Monza encouraging. Nuvolari finished a poor fourth in the German Grand Prix thanks to the the inefficiency of the Continental tyres the team were using around the tortuous fourteen-mile Nürburgring circuit, the result of a one-off deal to use the German company's products. Nevertheless the Scuderia was growing in scale all the time, now perfectly capable of sending teams to two or sometimes even more meetings on the same weekend. In the small events it was registering consistently impressive results for its cast of gentlemen amateurs, while Nuvolari piloted the Scuderia's 8C

Monza to victory over a very strong field in the Coppa Ciano in Livorno, after taking the grid as one of the team's eight entries.

One week after the Coppa Ciano, on 9 August 1931, Enzo Ferrari made his last appearance as a racing driver in the Circuito delle Tre Provincie, a time trial that led into the hills south of Bologna. He was thirty-three years old, and a month earlier Laura had announced that she was pregnant. Once again the team was present in numbers, but the *padrone* showed his intention to go out in style by entering himself along with Borzacchini in a pair of 8C Monzas, while the great Nuvolari, who did not make up his mind to participate until the day before the race, was relegated to a six-cylinder 1750. Nuvolari arrived in Bagni della Poretta only four hours before the start, which was scheduled for half past four in the afternoon. He was not familiar with the eighty-mile circuit, which wound over the Abetone pass, so he and Ferrari set off on a last-minute reconnaissance lap in the 1750, with Nuvolari at the wheel. For Ferrari, it was an opportunity to find out, at last, how Nuvolari did it. 'At the first corner,' he reported, 'I was certain that Tazio had taken it badly and that we were going to end up in a ditch. I braced myself for the shock. Instead we found ourselves at the beginning of the straight with the car pointing down it. I looked at Nuvolari. His rugged face betrayed not the slightest emotion, not the slightest relief at having avoided a 180-degree skid. At the second bend, and again at the third, the same thing happened. At the fourth and the fifth I began to understand how he managed it, for from the corner of my eye I noticed that he never took his foot off the accelerator, but kept it pressed flat to the floorboards. Bend by bend, I discovered his secret. Nuvolari went into the bend rather sooner than would have been suggested to me by my own driving instinct. But he went into it in an unusual way: that is to say, suddenly pointing the nose of the car at the inner verge just where the bend started. With the throttle wide open – and having, of course, changed down into the right gear before that terrifying charge – he put the car into a controlled four-wheel skid, utilising the centrifugal force and keeping the machine on the road by the driving force of its rear wheels. Right round the whole of the bend, the car's nose shaved the inner verge and, when the bend came to an end, the machine was pointing down the straight without any need to correct its trajectory.' Thanks to Nuvolari, Ferrari had discovered the existence of the four-wheel drift, albeit too late for the technique to have any effect on his own career. The car's old-fashioned suspension and the high-pressure tyres of the day helped Nuvolari to control the car at such extreme angles, but the driver's own unwillingness to ease off the throttle was the key element. Ferrari concluded that 'there was probably no one who combined so high a degree of driving sensitivity with an almost superhuman courage'. A few hours later Ferrari got the chance to put what he had seen into practice. What he experienced, however, was defeat at the hands of an unearthly genius.

In the two big 8C Monzas, Ferrari and Borzacchini started confidently. Nuvolari, on the other hand, teased the crowd at the start by creeping away from the line in his smaller 1750. Once round the first corner, however, he put his foot down. But the car was hardly out of Poretta when it plunged into a short tunnel. What Nuvolari did not remember was that the tunnel ended with a level crossing, with a deep trough hidden between the railway lines. When the car hit the trough at full speed, Decimo Compagnoni was thrown out of the mechanic's seat so violently that both grab handles came away in his hands. He landed on the back of the car, and while Nuvolari struggled to regain control with one hand he had to use the other to hang on to his companion's leg and keep him aboard. Once Nuvolari had brought the car to a halt, the pair got out to inspect the damage. Seeing that the throttle control was broken, Compagnoni removed his leather belt and tied it to the broken connection, passing the belt under the bonnet and into his side of the cockpit. For the remainder of the race he would operate the accelerator by tugging on the belt while Nuvolari worked the steering and the brakes.

And after all that, they won. Borzacchini helped by retiring after only three miles, but Ferrari was still ahead. 'You won't make it, Signor Nuvolari,' the respectful Compagnoni suggested over the noise of the wind and the exhaust. 'Their 2300 is faster than our 1750.' 'You'll find', Nuvolari shouted, 'that we go faster downhill.' And down they plunged. 'Those who saw Nuvolari descend the Abetone,' the reporter for *Il Littoriale* commented, 'those who saw him come down like a hawk from Sestola and Lizzano, say the scene was unforgettable.' At Sestola, a group of Nuvolari's fans had informed him of the gap to Ferrari – he was still forty seconds behind, with twenty-two miles to go. 'Pull in the belt, Decimo,' Nuvolari ordered, 'and don't ease it once.' Down they flew, arriving at the finish, where Ferrari had prematurely been acclaimed the winner. They had made up not just the deficit of forty seconds, but another thirty-two besides. 'I've never worked so hard in my life,' Nuvolari told his employer. 'Yes,' Decimo Compagnoni muttered, rubbing his sore hands, 'and I've never been half so scared.'

Nuvolari had established the standard against which Enzo Ferrari would judge his drivers. 'Unlike just about all drivers, of whatever era, Nuvolari was never discouraged if he was given a car of inferior performance,' he wrote. 'He never left the starting line already beaten, and whatever position he was in, even if he was seventh or tenth, he always fought like a lion.' This was the quality that Ferrari would come to demand of his own drivers, that they show fire even when he could not provide them with the best equipment. 'That passion of his, that indomitable pride,' he concluded, 'was perceived by the fans and made him their hero.'

But Ferrari was always on the lookout for new talent, and towards the end of 1931 he issued an invitation to a racing motorcyclist named Piero Taruffi. Already twenty-five years old, the son of a successful Roman surgeon, Taruffi had been bitten by the speed bug as a child when his father took him to watch a motorcycle race on the Tiber circuit. At seventeen he won a reliability run from Rome to Viterbo, driving the parental Fiat tourer. The following year he travelled to Lyons to watch his first grand prix, coincidentally the very race from which Enzo Ferrari so mysteriously withdrew. Taruffi's career as a motorcycle racer reached the first of its peaks in 1928, when he won the Royal Grand Prix in Rome, beating the Bianchis of Nuvolari and Varzi on his old Norton 500. Thanks to his knowledge of the Tre Fontane course, on which he had practised endlessly as a youth, and to the flexibility and good handling of the English bike, he was able to register a significant success over the finest Italian riders of his day. The Bianchi pair made a particular impression on him – 'a beautiful contrast, as always, Varzi in beautiful check plus-fours and brown suede jacket, Nuvolari in a pale blue jersey hanging out from a sleeveless jerkin, with a spare chain hanging round his neck like a halter and a leather tool bag at his waist with chain-changing implements, plug spanner, and the like'.

When he switched to four wheels, a good showing in a 2-litre Itala sports in the Coppa Ciano, which Nuvolari won for the Scuderia, must have caught Ferrari's eye. He may also have been impressed when Taruffi, back in the saddle of his Norton, set the fastest lap in the 1931 Monza Motorcycle Grand Prix at 112 mph, having modified the bike according to aerodynamic principles by fitting a narrow fuel tank and setting the footrests further back to give him a lower riding position. Taruffi, who was studying to be an engineer, tried to go even further in this direction by adding shrouds to the spoked wheels, but the effect was to make the bike weave unpredictably. Ferrari appreciated the skills of motorcycle racers, and believed that the discipline provided a good grounding for a successful transition to high-powered cars, enabling racers to develop their sensitivity to the contact between tyre and road surface while also accustoming them to racing in close company.

Taruffi received the summons by telephone, and was soon on the road to Modena. His memory of the encounter provides a portrait perhaps surprising in its warmth, given Ferrari's subsequent reputation. 'Although the Scuderia was in its early days,' he wrote, 'Ferrari himself was well known, being the man who controlled the racing destiny of Alfa Romeo. I arrived feeling rather nervous, but he immediately put me at my ease. He was brief and explicit: "There's an event down your way in a week's time. Two events, actually, a regularity run and a speed trial. You're an engineer, so you should be able to cope with the regularity run. As for the hillclimb, just do your best. Now go and choose a car – you can have either a 1750 Alfa or a 2.3, both supercharged. Take them out and see which one you want." I came back an hour later, having chosen the 2.3. "Very well," he said, "but don't overdo it. I don't want you to hurt yourself. Or to wreck the machinery. Cars are expensive." They gave me the usual indemnity forms and a contract to sign. I was to get my expenses and 25 per cent of any prize money. I was a real professional, complete with contract. I signed, without raising a single query.' Ferrari sent Peppino Verdelli along to look after the young driver. A careful study of the regulations gave Taruffi the victory in the reliability run, held over two laps of Lake Bolsena. Several practice runs over the eight-mile hillclimb for the Coppa Frigo, between the villages of Bolsena and Montefiascone, gave him the confidence to go all out. He won that, too, by more than seventeen seconds from the 2-litre Bugatti of Clemente Biondetti, a first-class driver. 'I now felt officially launched,' he wrote, and the Scuderia had another driver who was to play a part in years to come.

To celebrate the close of the 1931 season Ferrari organised another lavish banquet, this time at the Ristorante Boninsegna in Modena. The drivers each received a gold neck-chain on which his name had been engraved, while the Alfa Romeo mechanics received a pair of gold cuff-links. For the Scuderia's own mechanics there were silver cuff-links and bonus cheques. Now that Ferrari was no longer making any pretence of being a racing driver, even though he had taken the precaution of renewing his competition licence for another year, his standing as their patron was even more clearly defined. And to emphasise the achievements of the team bearing his name, he commissioned his friend Ferruccio Testi to produce a brochure detailing and celebrating the team's record since it came into existence. In addition to his work as a vet and his business interests, Testi was also a first-class amateur photographer. It was to him that Enzo Ferrari owed the tradition that began with the publication called '*Due Anni di Corse*' ('Two Years of Races'), the first of the official booklets recording the team's successes that were sent to contacts and customers and people whom Ferrari hoped to influence. In time Testi's publications grew to contain advertisements for the Scuderia's sponsors and letters of endorsement and encouragement from its friends. Their pages provide a portrait of racing in the 1930s; and after the war, when the nature of the Scuderia changed, the tradition continued, becoming an even more important statement of Ferrari's identity.

His success in 1931 was endorsed by the cover of the magazine *Motori Aero Cicli e Sports*, which carried a picture of the team competing at the Masarykring in Czechoslovakia and the caption '*Per il prestigio dello sport e dell'industria automobilistica nazionale*' – For the prestige of the nation's sport and motor industry.

Dino Ferrari was born on 19 January 1932, and christened Alfredo, after his grandfather and his dead uncle. 'I decided I would never race again,' Enzo Ferrari declared, although his driving career had been running down for some time, and had really come to an end after his nervous withdrawal from Lyons in 1924. On the day he came second to Nuvolari in the Circuito delle Tre Provinci, he said, he had concluded that if Laura produced a son he would give up driving to concentrate on the management and business side of the Scuderia. A son, that is. No mention of a daughter.

Ten years after their meeting, the marriage of Enzo and Laura had evolved into an arrangement based on the accommodation of each to the other's interests. Three years before Dino's birth, Enzo had begun a relationship with Lina Lardi, a tall, elegant dark-haired girl whom he had met in the office of his friend Renzo Orlandi, a coachbuilder. Lina was from Castelvetro, a medieval hill village a few miles south of Modena, across the Abetone road from the hamlet of Maranello. Her quiet demeanour no doubt provided a respite from the frequent eruptions of the spirited Laura, and from Laura's constant quarrelling with Ferrari's mother. Their relationship, conducted on a daily basis, would last the rest of his life, as well as, in the end, delivering the dynastic succession he craved.

There were changes in the structure of the Scuderia at the start of 1932. Alfredo Caniato, who had bought Tadini's shares, decided that it was all getting a bit too ambitious for him and sold the combined holding to Count Carlo Felice Trossi, already known to Ferrari as a talented amateur driver. Trossi paid for the shares with money from Banco Sella, his family's bank, and became the president of the operation. 'Didi' Trossi belied his languid appearance and established his credentials by registering the team's first win of the year at the wheel of an 8C in the Coppa Gallenga. 'He was a unique character,' Ferrari said. 'In his whimsical, casual manner he did things, in his private life and on the track, that others would have thought impossible. Tall, fair-haired, loose-limbed, he brought a unique tone of carefree aristocracy into the team. And he was a great driver. He never became a motor-racing legend because he couldn't be bothered to make the effort to achieve the domination for which he had the talent. In fact he was a dilettante all his life, flitting from flower to flower, sipping at his pleasures: speedboats, planes, cars, collections of rare birds, rebuilding his castle in Gaglianico, a marina at Paraggi, a wool factory. So you might say not the most positive of men but no one who knew him ever forgot this extraordinary character.'

One day Trossi announced that Count Giacomo Acerbo, a government minister, and the brother of Captain Tito Acerbo, the war hero whose name had been given to the Coppa Acerbo, would be paying a visit to the Modena workshops. A picture of the occasion shows the company's managers done up in their best suits to greet the visiting dignitary, with a group of soldiers and *carabinieri*, and off to the side, hardly part of the main group at all, a line of half a dozen mechanics in their overalls, grinning with their enjoyment of the unexpected moment.

The growing scale of the team's operations could be seen in its entry for the Mille Miglia, where it supported the four official Alfa entries with five 2300s, three 1750s and a 1500. Among the 1750s was one to be driven by Baroness Maria Antonietta Avanzo, the most famous Italian woman racing driver of the inter-war period, who had made her start in motor sport with a twelve-cylinder Packard which she took to a sand race meeting on the beaches of the island of Fano, in Denmark. When the huge torpedo-bodied car caught fire while travelling at full speed, she drove it into the sea to quench the flames. As she emerged, Antonio Ascari overheard her remark that she'd be happy to swap it for a Fiat. On her return home she found a bright red Fiat awaiting her, and Ascari got the Packard, which was repaired and put back into use. Whenever Ferrari saw this dramatic car, it reminded him of the distinctive sound of the Packard 'twin-sixes' that American army officers had driven during the Great War, a sound that, or so he claimed, was to hang around inside his head and to emerge as a source of inspiration when the time came for him to commission the design of an engine bearing his own name.

On 7 April the team lined up outside Modena, all the cars with their Mille Miglia starting numbers already painted on their flanks, a stirring sight as they prepared to set off for Brescia, with a big Alfa saloon at their head. Borzacchini won the Mille Miglia for the factory, but Trossi and Scarfiotti finished second and third for the Scuderia, while other Alfas filled eight of the next nine places. The Baroness had run as high as tenth before her car gave up at Perugia. Taruffi, sharing an 8C with Eugenio Siena, managed to persuade his co-driver to wear a crash helmet, a practice he had brought over from his experience with motorcycles.

This was to be a season in which the official factory racing team concentrated on quality, particularly after Jano had unveiled his masterpiece, the single-seater Tipo B (or P3, as it became known) at the Italian Grand Prix in June. The Scuderia mostly had to make do with quantity. The Mille Miglia entry had been an indication that, for the moment, there was more profitable business to be done with wealthy amateurs, or at least amateurs with wealthy patrons, such as a man named Soffietti, a ski instructor from Sestriere who had found the favour of the Principessa di Piemonte, then second in line to the throne of Italy, or one Enrico Ziegler, the protégé of the president of the Royal Italian Automobile Club. The Scuderia also diversified into motorcycles, running a team of Rudge and Norton machines in national events for a group of riders including Giordano Aldrighetti, Mario Ghersi and sometimes Taruffi. The workshops were always busy as the growing staff of mechanics, including Nuvolari's man Decimo Compagnoni, worked long hours on their fleet of Alfa Romeos to extract greater performance. Eugenio Siena, now the team's test driver, verified the results with a blast down the via Emilia. And an important new association had been formed with the Bolognese carburettor-manufacturing firm of Edoardo Weber. The advantages of industrial co-operation were exploited when Ferrari encouraged Weber to collaborate with Shell, another of his commercial partners, in research that would advance the understanding of combustion. Virtually unknown at the time, Weber's name was to become the most famous in its field, a brand synonymous with high-performance engineering, not least because the characteristic noise produced as its twin-choke carburettors sucked air into the engine made a significant contribution to the feral sound of an Alfa or, later, a Ferrari or a Maserati. And the sight of two or three twin-choke Webers attached to such an engine, with their elegant mini-trumpets, became as much a piece of Italian automotive sculpture as a

Zagato body or a set of Borrani wire-spoked wheels.

By July, too, the yellow shield carrying Francesco Baracca's black prancing horse was seen on the bonnets of the team's cars for the first time, on the 8C–2300s which came first and second in the twenty-four-hour race at Spa in Belgium, the winner driven by Antonio Brivio and Eugenio Siena, ahead of Piero Taruffi and Guido D'Ippolito. It is said, without evidence, that Ferrari paid a visit to Baracca's parents in 1931 or 1932 to ask their permission to take such a step. After the cars had been driven in convoy to Belgium over the San Gottardo pass, that day in Belgium witnessed the unveiling of what was to become one of the world's best-known symbols, boldly emblazoned inside a yellow shield on the long red engine covers.

Not until August did the factory lend the Scuderia a P3, Nuvolari exploiting the power of its twin-supercharged straight-eight engine as he drove it to a comfortable victory in the Coppa Acerbo. When Borzacchini took over the car for the Masarykring race in Brno, the brake problems that cost him the race produced the P3's only failure to win that season. It was a car that went as well as it looked. Its lean, functional *monoposto* body, with louvres covering its bonnet, big-bore exhaust pipes running the length of both flanks, and a beautifully tapering tail, made it the very picture of a thoroughbred 1930s racing car, the product of an era in which something designed for speed was almost bound to look beautiful, too.

The men who made it, however, were having their hands tied. At Alfa Romeo, the priority had become the fulfilment of government contracts to supply military vehicles. Mussolini's empire-building was taking precedence over the specialist demands of an in-house racing team and, in any case, the company's financial position had been weakened by the effect of the Depression on the demand for sports cars. Competition, particularly the sort of constant research and experimentation demanded by grand prix racing, had further drained the company's coffers. At the beginning of 1933, Alfa Romeo announced a complete suspension of all competition activity.

[65]

Effectively, the company had been taken over by the government, absorbed into a scheme called the Istituto di Ricostruzione Industriale, or IRI, a form of state protection under which it was to remain. In the light of all this, Enzo Ferrari had been working furiously behind the scenes to convince Alfa to allow the Scuderia to take over its activities. The team's achievements, he pointed out, fully justified the plan. Scuderia Ferrari had represented Alfa Romeo's interests inside and outside Italy for three years, with considerable success. It had built up expertise in engine-tuning and chassis development. It had many friends and powerful partners. In the previous season it had entered fifty events and gained twenty-six victories. And it knew how to exploit those victories for publicity purposes. But the answer was no. To Ferrari's intense frustration, Alfa's management – led by a new man, Ugo Gobbato – locked their six P3s away. Europe's fastest competition cars lay silent under shrouds in the Portello works.

There they were to stay for the remainder of the season, while the Scuderia Ferrari soldiered on with its eleven 8Cs, six of them Monzas and five sports models, plus a couple of 1750s and various cars belonging to clients. To compensate for the lack of new machines from Alfa Romeo, steps were taken to order a Duesenberg-based single-seater, built for the Indianapolis 500, from America, while thoughts turned to the possibility of acquiring machines from other sources, possibly from Maserati or MG. Among Ferrari's problems was the fact that he now had something close to a monopoly of Italian driving talent; there simply were not enough cars with which to satisfy all their demands, which put extra pressure on his diplomatic skills. What helped him make a decision, of course, was when a driver showed an interest in buying one of the cars, and then pledging to race it in the team colours. 'Certainly money talked,' Piero Taruffi remembered.

It turned out to be a season of constant activity, many good results, much turmoil, some controversy, and ultimately tragedy. In March, Nuvolari won a chilly Tunis Grand Prix and followed it by winning a comparatively uneventful Mille Miglia (his exhaust pipe fell off in the Apennines, making the car sound like a low-flying aircraft). And then, in Monaco on 23 April, he and Achille Varzi went head-to-head in the race that defined their rivalry. Nuvolari led the Scuderia's entry of four 8C Monzas, their engines enlarged to 2.6 litres in the Modena workshop. Varzi was in a factory-entered 2.3-litre Bugatti Type 51, the product of a designer who came from a Milanese family but had chosen to establish his little empire in Alsace-Lorraine. The Monaco Grand Prix had been run since 1923, and an improbable circuit was already producing improbably thrilling races. In the half-bowl of the principality, noise and colour entwined to create a special magic. Everything that was motor racing could be found in the Monte Carlo circuit, compressed in such a way as to heighten the excitement. The cars needed power to lift them up the road climbing from the harbour to the square in front of the casino. They needed agility and resilience to negotiate the bumps and hairpins on the descent to the sea front. They needed to be able to dance through the chicane at the end of the pitch-black tunnel, to cling to the limit of adhesion through the left-hand curve called Tabac, and to transfer all their power to the tarmac while sliding around what used to be called the Gasometer Hairpin under the eyes of a crowd spilling out of balconies and clinging to the hillside beneath the royal palace.

Taruffi, who was not given a drive, watched the race and marvelled at the intensity of the struggle, which raged without respite for ninety-nine laps and three hours, the bitterness of the rivalry undiminished by the cordiality that always existed between the two men. Certainly it was exacerbated, as such rivalries always are, by the contrast between them. Varzi, the younger by ten years, had a stern face and eyes that seemed to be looking inwards, towards the dark secrets of the soul. He raced in beautifully tailored white overalls and a white leather helmet. His hair was immaculately parted and brushed flat on his skull. Nuvolari, by contrast, seemed full of colour and humour and expression, in his blue helmet, yellow shirt, blue trousers and yellow shoelaces – yellow was his lucky colour. He never raced without carrying in his hip pocket a wallet containing photographs of his wife and two sons, and another of his father and uncle out hunting. Varzi, however, seemed far beyond such superstitions. 'He had created his own inimitable driving style,' the journalist and amateur driver Count Johnny Lurani wrote. 'His style was methodical, cold-blooded and precise, comparable to the best Swiss watch, while Nuvolari could be likened to a cuckoo clock, liable to strike at the most unexpected moment and always full of surprises.' Taruffi, too, was fascinated by the contrast between the two men, whose abilities he had first seen expressed in their duels on two wheels. On four wheels, he wrote, 'they were still just as different in temperament, and still just as equally matched, Nuvolari acrobatic and daring, Varzi deadly accurate and self-possessed. Nuvolari, the maestro of over-the-limit motoring, delighted the crowds with his wizardry, while Varzi, cornering like a white line, used to leave many spectators almost indifferent. Even the experts timing the two men through a corner found it hard to say which was the better.'

For ninety-nine of the hundred laps the red Alfa and the pale blue Bugatti chased each other through the streets, blisters forming on the palms of the drivers' hands from the thousands of gearchanges around the tight switchback circuit. Five laps from the end, after almost three and a half hours of racing, Nuvolari felt his engine falter slightly. Varzi took the lead at the Gasometer Hairpin as they entered into the penultimate lap, but Nuvolari managed to squeeze past going up the hill into Casino Square and was still ahead when the hundredth lap began. Now Varzi was waiting to pounce. When he made his move, Nuvolari responded – only to see flames shoot out from the engine cover. He stopped the car, leapt out, and tried to push it to the finish. A mechanic came to his aid, against the regulations, and their efforts were halted by officials brandishing fire extinguishers. Varzi, who had not won a race for more than a year, now had his revenge for the Mille Miglia. When, back in Modena, the Scuderia's mechanics stripped down Nuvolari's engine, they found virtually nothing worth saving.

Nuvolari was unimpressed by the equipment with which the Scuderia expected him to win races. The cars were showing their age. When pushed by the new Maseratis, the much-modified Alfas were proving themselves to be badly overstressed. On a night in June, after one of the team's cars had again let him down during the Marne Grand Prix, Nuvolari signed a contract with the Maserati brothers to race their 3-litre car at Spa the following week. When he told Ferrari, there was an explosion. Out of it came a temporary compromise: the Maserati would be entered by Scuderia Ferrari, although the prancing-horse shield would not appear on it. And Ferrari could take little comfort from Nuvolari's crushing win, or for the one that followed in the Coppa Ciano, since they prefaced an announcement that the Mantuan intended to leave the team for good, and would be taking not only his mechanic, Compagnoni, but also his friend Borzacchini to Maserati along with him. Taruffi went, too, having tired of the limited opportunities; he had taken to racing his own Norton against the Scuderia's motorcycle team, and relationships had not been helped when he defeated them. 'Ferrari hated seeing his own riders beaten,' he noted. Nor, perhaps, did he enjoy watching one of his own riders depriving the team of prize money.

The desertions had a profound and immediate effect. Ferrari knew that Alfa Romeo would be disconcerted by Nuvolari's defection to one of their rivals. He called his friend Mario Lombardini at Pirelli, who promised support. At a lunch in the Ristorante Pipori in Milan, Ferrari and Trossi sat down with Lombardini and other Pirelli executives to work out a sponsorship arrangement that would allow the Scuderia to acquire the P3s from the factory. Finally Ugo Gobbato agreed to the deal on Alfa's behalf, although it did not come cheap. Every year since 1930, Ferrari's payments to Alfa Romeo had virtually doubled – from 271,000 lire to 473,000 lire to 844,000 lire. Now they were to double again, to 1,676,000 lire. Before long, trucks were rolling from Milan to Modena carrying the six racing cars and their spare parts. With them, too, came extra personnel, including Attilio Marinoni, a test driver, and Luigi Bazzi, who was able to resume his close partnership with the man who had taken him from Fiat to Alfa Romeo in the first place, and was rewarded with the title of technical director.

To put some experience back into the driving line-up, and to ensure that the squad would have drivers capable of doing justice to the potential of the P3s, Ferrari invited his old friend Campari back into the team. He also signed Luigi Fagioli, known as the Abruzzi Bandit, thirty-five years old, talented and uncompromising on the track, and Louis Chiron, a Monegasque two years younger. Results came immediately. Fagioli won the Coppa Acerbo, beating the Maseratis of Nuvolari, Borzacchini and Taruffi. He won again in the Comminges Grand Prix, and finished second at Miramas behind Chiron, who, delighted by the lightness of the Alfa's handling, returned to the pits with his arms aloft, shouting: 'It's like a bicycle!'

Two races were scheduled for Monza on 10 September 1933. The first, and more important, was the Italian Grand Prix, held over the combined road course and banked high-speed track, won by Fagioli with an exhilarating final sprint after Nuvolari had made a late pit stop. Even though the early start and poor weather had kept the crowds away, this was already the Scuderia's proudest day. In the afternoon, however, the banked track alone was used for a second event, the Monza Grand Prix, held over three heats and a final. Seven cars lined up for the second heat, but only three of them emerged on to the pits straight to complete the opening lap. In a four-car crash at the South Curve, both Campari and Borzacchini were killed. The other two drivers involved, Count Carlo Castelbarco and Nando Barbieri, were unharmed. The members of the Scuderia, stunned by their first fatality, packed up and went home. The final went ahead without them, only for Count

[70]

Czaikowski to die at the same spot when his Bugatti left the track and caught fire. Like the cars of Campari and Borzacchini, his machine had shot over the lip of the banking and crashed to earth on the other side. According to some accounts – including that of Taruffi, who took part in the morning's race but not in the afternoon's – the disasters had been caused by oil dropped on the South Curve that morning from a blown engine. The course marshals, the safety-conscious Taruffi noted, had tried to cover it with sand. He himself was left to thank his stars that Nuvolari had produced an unfriendly reponse to a request to borrow a spare Maserati axle to replace one broken in the morning's race. 'Typically, in his half-brusque, half-sarcastic way, he refused point-blank. I did not argue and left it at that. It probably saved my life.'

Ferrari mourned the death of a friend, one who had given him the material for countless anecdotes, such as the time Campari managed to persuade a theatre manager in Bergamo to let him sing. The audience booed, and one spectator shouted that he would be better off racing his cars. Campari stopped, peered into the darkness, and said with mock sorrow: 'When I race, they tell me to go and sing. When I sing, they tell me to go and race. What am I to do?' To Ferrari his death, at the age of forty, marked the end of an era, the passing of the first generation of great Italian racing drivers.

Enzo Ferrari confers with Achille Varzi during a test session with the
Alfa Romeo P3 on Monte Piantonia in 1934.

Three

Early in Dino's life, it became obvious that he was not a strong child. One boy in five thousand is born with the genetic defect known as Duchenne's muscular dystrophy, and Enzo Ferrari's first son was the one. The disease, which attacks the muscle cells and creates the phenomenon called wasting, is normally diagnosed between the ages of two and seven; most commonly, its victims die at around the age of twenty.

It attacks boys because it is present in the X chromosome, from which it sends messages to the cells inhibiting growth and provoking decay. Boys have one X chromosome. Girls have two, and the effect of the second X chromosome is to counter-act the aberrant behaviour of the first, preventing it from causing damage. Girls do not die prematurely from Duchenne's muscular dystrophy, although it can attack them later in life. When the parents of the young Dino Ferrari were told the cause of his mysterious weakness, his mother inevitably saw herself as the carrier of the disease. And so, perhaps, as he looked at her through a furious grief that he allowed to grow to almost mystical proportions, did his father. In an age before the invention of counselling and psychotherapy, before the exist-ence of magnetic resonance imaging scans and complex drugs, the reactions of those closest to the victim may have been conditioned by instincts that would seem, in a new century, bizarrely primitive.

Enzo and Laura Ferrari were united, as he was to say many years later, by a love of automobiles and the world in which they existed. There were rooms in the house of Ferrari from which Laura was excluded simply by virtue of her gender; as could be seen in Ferruccio Testi's photographs of celebratory dinners and visits from important local and national figures, where no females were to be seen. Nevertheless she had played an important part in the formation and evolution of the team, encouraging and criticising and keeping an eye on the purse, sometimes with a forthrightness that her husband's associates could find irritating or even obstructive. And as Enzo Ferrari spent more and more time in Modena, choosing not to travel with the team on its adventures, Laura often took his place, joining the convoys of cars and vans as they measured the length and breadth of Italy in their mission to expand the Scuderia's reputation. Dino's illness, and the sombre prognosis accompanying the news, opened the first real rift in their relationship. Before, their friends could hardly see daylight between them. Now, and for ever, there was a shaft of darkness.

Campari was dead. Nuvolari and Taruffi had gone. Fagioli announced that Mercedes-Benz had offered him a lot of money, and that he intended to accept it. Eugenio Siena, the talented test driver, departed to start his own team. Ferrari's summary at the end of the 1933 season, published in the latest of Testi's annual brochures, was downbeat. 'The last four years of our lives' work have not been without difficulties of various kinds – novel tasks, unexpected problems, sad endings,' he wrote. In terms of results, however, they had improved their average, entering fifty-one events and coming away with thirty-four wins. And as he surveyed the annual dinner at the Ristorante Boninsegna, turning his thoughts to 1934, there were reasons for optimism. To replace Nuvolari as his standard-bearer, he had hired Achille Varzi. Ferrari never cared much for Varzi, but he was in no doubt of his value. 'Varzi the driver', he wrote, 'was no different from Varzi the man: intelligent, calculating, grim when necessary, ferocious in exploiting the first weakness, mistake or mishap of his adversaries. He could well be described as pitiless.'

Alfa Romeo made it clear that they had no plans for a return to racing, and that Scuderia Ferrari would be given a free hand to run the cars. Bazzi supervised the conversion of the P3s to the new formula presented to grand prix teams, which imposed a maximum weight limit of 750 kg. In return, Alfa Romeo stipulated that Ferrari was to give driving contracts to two Algerians who had been promised P3s that now would never be built. The pair were Marcel Lehoux and a young man whose name is barely remembered now but who, given a kinder treatment by fate, might well have ranked with the very greatest.

Born in Algeria in 1910, the son of Catalan parents, Guy Moll was twenty-two and had just completed his national service when his friend Lehoux offered to sell him a Bugatti. He went to his father, who owned a transport company and a vineyard. When his father turned him down, Moll didn't hesitate. Buy me that Bugatti, he said, or you'll never see me again. A few weeks later he was guiding the car to third place, behind Raymond Sommer and Tazio Nuvolari, in the Grand Prix de Marseille at Miramas. A season with an 8C Monza in 1933 yielded a further crop of respectable results, but there was no reason to envision that his entry into the ranks of the Scuderia Ferrari would herald the arrival of a phenomenon. Nor, to judge by Moll's contract, did Ferrari predict such a thing: the young man was awarded a salary of 1,500 lire a month for a nine-month season, plus 30 per cent of his prize money and starting money, racing whenever and wherever the team ordered, and he was required to pay his own insurance premium.

Ferrari sent five cars, with engines increased to 2.9 litres, to Monaco. He got a hint of Varzi's strange attitudes when the driver said that his seat was the wrong height. He spent a long time messing about with different cushions, piling them up on the seat. Eventually he explained the problem to Bazzi. Two cushions made it not quite high enough, he said, but the third made it too high. Bazzi told him to go away and have a cup of

[75]

coffee. When he came back, the engineer promised, everything would be all right. As soon as Varzi was gone, Bazzi snatched Ferrari's newspaper, folded it in four, and put it under the seat. Varzi returned, proclaimed the height perfect, and thanked Bazzi warmly. 'The newspaper had six pages and made no appreciable difference to the height,' Ferrari remarked scornfully. 'But Varzi was capable of the greatest conviction, even when an absurdity was involved. Anything he believed in, he would defend to the bitter end.' But in the race the great Varzi, in his first appearance for the Scuderia Ferrari, found himself beaten by the newcomer on the circuit where he had humbled Nuvolari a year earlier. Chiron, in another of the P3s, had taken what looked like a winning lead. Moll hounded him and on the last lap, when Chiron appeared to be carried away by the thought of winning his home grand prix and spun off the track, the Algerian took his chance. 'That day', Ferrari wrote, 'Moll revealed the style of a great champion, asserted his personality as a driver and vindicated my faith in him.'

Ferrari loved to tell the story of Moll at Montenero that season, when the Algerian had overtaken Varzi but was delayed by a flat tyre. After changing the wheel, Moll set off in a mad pursuit and quickly caught his adversary. Ferrari, thinking about the team, was in the process of signalling him to back off when Moll suddenly went into a half-spin and slid backwards down the road. But even as he was recovering, wrestling the car back into the right direction, Moll managed to send Ferrari a hand signal that acknowleged the instruction. 'I was amazed,' Ferrari said. 'Never have I seen such coolness and self-assurance in the face of danger. Moll had what it took to be one of the all-time greats.'

The 1934 season began wonderfully for the Scuderia. The Mille Miglia was no longer such a priority for a team that now concentrated on grand prix racing, but it was to enable Varzi to take further revenge on Nuvolari. Both men were driving Alfas, Nuvolari's entered by Siena, who was also his co-driver. The race started in rain, and Varzi was leading as they reached Terni. When the skies cleared, Nuvolari attacked and at Bologna he had a lead of almost three minutes. Then the rain started again, falling intermittently, which allowed Ferrari himself to take a hand. He was waiting at the Imola refuelling stop, on the return leg of the race, when Varzi pulled in. Ferrari had been told on the telephone that the rain was likely to start again and persist all the way back to Brescia, so he ordered the mechanics to prepare a set of wheels mounted with tyres whose grooves had been hand-cut with a special tool to give them better grip in the wet. 'What are those for?' Varzi asked him, in an irritated sort of way. An argument began, which was soon wasting so much time that Ferrari threw up his arms. 'Have it your own way,' he said. Varzi thought for a moment, and made up his mind. 'Oh, go ahead,' he said. The mechanics fitted the wheels. And just before he engaged the clutch to start on the last leg, the first drops of rain fell. 'You were right after all,' he shouted to Ferrari. 'Thanks!' While Nuvolari slithered about on the wet roads, Varzi was able to make up time and win the race.

Varzi led Moll and Chiron home in a clean sweep of the Tripoli Grand Prix, having been forced to deal roughly with the young Algerian, who caught his team mates after recovering from a pit stop to change a tyre. Instead of keeping station, Moll raced the great Italian neck-and-neck to the finish line, to the excitement of the crowd and the consternation of the team management. None of the three drivers was happy. Varzi had been pushed unnecessarily hard by a team mate, Moll had failed to win a race that could have been his, and Chiron had been beaten by the newcomer.

Chiron won the Moroccan Grand Prix, and Varzi the Targa Florio. But the first stirrings of the threat that was to undermine the team's long-term prospects were felt in May, when the streamlined rear-engined Auto Union, designed by Ferdinand Porsche, made its debut at the Avus circuit in Berlin, a high-speed track consisting of two lengths of autobahn linked by a steeply banked brick-faced turn at one end and a flat hairpin bend at the other. Ferrari responded swiftly by ordering a special streamlined body to be commissioned from the Breda aircraft and armaments company. *Ingegnere* Cesare Pallavicino's dramatic design, featuring enclosed front suspension, a head-rest extended into a tail fin, and fairings around the wheels, underwent its only test on the Milan–Laghi autostrada and was in action in Berlin three days later. Varzi tried it but complained of vibration from the bodywork and opted for his usual mount. Moll, who at twenty-five still had the smooth, round face of a schoolboy, displayed no such qualms. Retirements among the leading runners worked to his advantage and he came home the winner, to Ferrari's delight.

But the Auto Unions had shown glimpses of their potential, and when Mercedes-Benz reappeared at the Nürburgring, the shadows began to close on Ferrari. The German teams, benefiting from the support of Hitler's government, had made lavish preparations. They were introducing technology beyond the dreams of the Italians, whose attitudes had evolved steadily and organically from a heritage of backyard improvisation – the sort of thing that produced the inspired guesswork of Pallavicino's streamlined body. The German engineers were making a quantum leap, both in the philosophy and the science of racing-car design. Manfred von Brauchitsch's new Mercedes W25 won on its debut, with Hans Stuck's Auto Union second. Both had independent suspension and hydraulic brakes all round. The stubby silver bodies of the Auto Unions made them look like spaceships or submarines. Chiron's upright Alfa managed third, and suddenly resembled something in an old photograph.

Ferrari hired a new man to act as *direttore sportivo*, Nello Ugolini taking over from Marco Lolli in a role that was becoming increasingly significant. Ugolini came from Vignola, a small town near Modena. His background was in managing football teams, at which he was (and would be) extremely successful. His career had begun in the late 1920s, when his diligence as assistant secretary of the Modena football club brought him to the attention of the man who had once written football reports for the *Gazzetta dello Sport*. 'This is a smart fellow, with a head on his shoulders,' Ferrari remarked. Those who mistook Ugolini's charming and emollient manner for weakness were making a mistake, and his abilities earned him the informally bestowed but universally employed sobriquet of 'Maestro'. He had no difficulty in transferring the principles of management from one sport to another, and he quickly reached an effective modus vivendi with Ferrari himself, learning the paramount value of being first on the telephone to the boss after a practice session or a race.

At Montlhéry the German teams turned out in force but, after outclassing the Alfas in practice, ran into mechanical trouble and left the podium to Chiron, Varzi, and Trossi, whose car was shared by Moll. The Algerian's late inclusion came on the orders of Ferrari, who had initially left the young man on the sidelines but then told Ugolini to let him have a go, sensing that Moll's desire to impress would make him set times fast enough to inspire the older drivers to snap out of their torpor and speed up. The Italian press foolishly took the result as evidence of the Scuderia's ability to master the German threat, an impression blown apart at the Nürburgring, where Stuck won for Auto Union with Fagioli second in a Mercedes. Again, Chiron salvaged a third place. Now the team's only successes were coming when the German teams were absent, either because the events were beneath their consideration or the organisers refused to meet their financial requirements. Only the performance of the new Alfa 6C–2300 cars, which had replaced the 1750s, was giving Ferrari cause for satisfaction, with wins in events like the Targa Abruzzo 24-hour race at Pescara.

The Targa Abruzzo shared a meeting with the Coppa Acerbo, for grand prix cars, in which the Alfas again confronted the German teams. Chiron's P3 was eliminated by a fire in the pits, caused when an inattentive mechanic splashed fuel on the car's exhaust pipe. Varzi took over Pietro Ghersi's car after his own gearbox failed, but was too far behind to make a challenge. But the Germans, too, were suffering. Caracciola's Mercedes crashed out of the lead, and Stuck's Auto Union retired. That left Moll, driving so brilliantly on the fast and tricky course that as the race neared its conclusion he was outpacing Nuvolari's third-placed Maserati and closing on the leader, Fagioli. Lap by lap he bit into Fagioli's lead, although at one point he spun, stalled, and had to get out in order to restart the car. But still he was making inroads, until as he left the village of Capelle and started the straight drop back to the sea he came up to lap the Auto Union of the former motorcycle racer Ernst Henne. Moll was believed to be travelling at his maximum speed of around 165 mph when he eased his Alfa past the silver car. But then suddenly he swerved, running over the verge and into a ditch. For fifty yards the car continued in a straight line, with Moll trying to wrestle it back on to the road. Then it hit a low stone pillar, part of the parapet of a small bridge, and was launched into the air, somersaulting and tossing out the driver before cutting through telegraph wires, smashing back into the ground, and rebounding until finally it crashed into the side of a house. Moll himself had hit a concrete post and died instantly. Barely four months after his debut, a sensation had come and gone. In Ferrari's view, he was the only driver fit to compare with the man he admired above all other drivers: 'In fact he resembled Nuvolari in certain singular mental traits, in his aggressive spirit, in the calm assurance with which he drove and in the equanimity with which he was prepared to face death.' His funeral procession, at the Maison Carrée cemetery in Algiers, might have been that of a Hollywood star.

At Monza, the organisers added chicanes in order to slow the German cars and give the supposedly more agile Italian machines a chance. But it was a useless ploy, thanks to the better brakes and suspension of the Mercedes and Auto Unions. Varzi was reduced to scrapping with Nuvolari for third place; even that was denied them when two Auto Unions, driven by Prince von Leiningen and Christian Momberger, neither of them remotely in the class of the Italian drivers, slipped easily past, reducing the pair to also-rans. Varzi eventually retired with transmission trouble, leaving Nuvolari to finish fifth in a car whose brakes had long since disappeared. For the Scuderia, the final insult came when Nuvolari arrived in Modena with a Maserati and trounced the Scuderia's five Alfas on their home ground.

A season that had promised much was ending in dismay and uncertainty. Varzi had many fans, particularly in the area of the Piedmont around his home town of Galliate, but few inside the Scuderia Ferrari. His temperament made him a difficult man to deal with, particularly for the mechanics, who resented his constant expressions of dissatisfaction with the equipment he was offered. Few inside the team expressed disappointment when Varzi announced that he would be driving for Auto Union the following season. After trying Hans Stuck's car at a Monza test session just before the Italian Grand Prix, he accepted the German company's offer – and just pipped Nuvolari, who had made his interest in joining the team known too late.

The Scuderia's staff might have bidden Varzi a more regretful farewell had they known that during his first season with Auto Union he would fall disastrously in love with the wife of one of his new team mates. Ilse Hubach had been married to Paul Pietsch less than a year. She was a sort of blonde version of the silent-movie actress Louise Brooks: a woman whose beauty and style were particularly apparent whenever she turned up in the pits in a white sun-dress with matching accessories. Pietsch, twenty-two years old, a member of the Porsche family and a very junior figure of the team, was her second husband. When she met Varzi, their *amour fou* led them both to leave their partners, with tragic results. Ilse had become addicted to morphine during a stay in hospital, and when Varzi went into a temporary depression she offered to introduce him to its properties. Reluctant at first, he eventually gave in. The subsequent dependency came close to destroying his career and both their lives.

Just as Varzi had replaced Nuvolari, so Nuvolari cheered the hearts of the Scuderia's employees by announcing his intention to return for the 1935 season. He had sworn, on his departure barely a year earlier, never to work with Enzo Ferrari again, but Vittorio Jano made the peace, after a great deal of toing and froing in which letters and telephone calls paved the way for a meeting between the two protagonists on neutral ground, the Croce Bianca hotel in Piacenza. Nuvolari had spent the winter by the lakes, where he visited the great poet Gabriele D'Annunzio, a half-blind and dying man who gave the driver the small brown shell of a tortoise with a plaque bearing the inscription: 'To Tazio Nuvolari of good Mantuan blood, who, true to his race, has joined courage with poetry, the most desperate risk to the most obedient mechanical power, and lastly life unto death in the path of victory.' Nuvolari adopted the tortoise as his emblem, while the shell was arranged in a place of honour in the glass memento case in his fine new villa in Mantua. Nuvolari was now forty-three. He was in no hurry to slow down, but he no longer wanted to be at the team manager's beck and call, and the deal brokered by Jano was for grand prix events only. Nuvolari would receive a large salary plus expenses and 50 per cent of his winnings and appearance money, far more than Ferrari had previously allowed any driver.

His new team mate would be René Dreyfus, the former Bugatti driver, who paid tribute to the effectiveness of the peacemaker's work. 'Jano was good at that sort of thing,' he said. 'He was a quiet, serious engineer given to pragmatic solutions to difficult personal dilemmas. He was seldom known to smile, but to me he was a delight. He was warm and gracious.' Jano returned to Portello to work on the replacement for the P3, the car that would enable the Scuderia and its drivers to get back on terms with the Germans. For Alfa Romeo, however, such work was not high on the agenda; investment in racing would be reduced and Jano was encouraged to involve himself in other areas. It would be almost a full season before the fruits of his work emerged, at a time when the two German teams were increasing the pace of development by the month, racing each other and leaving the Italians and French to cope with the dust and fumes in their wake.

Ferrari, however, saw an opportunity to take the initiative. While he could not summon the technical expertise or the material resources necessary to confront the Germans effectively in the 750 kg formula, he could still challenge them in the Formula Libre category, in which there were no restrictions in weight or engine capacity. So he commissioned Bazzi to create a new single-seater, using two P3 engines – one at the front and one in the tail – linked to a single three-speed gearbox. The *Bimotore*, as it became known, would obviously be massively overweight for the grand prix rules, but in theory it would have enough power to give the Mercedes and Auto Unions a scare in the free-formula races. Principally assisted by Arnaldo Roselli, another former Alfa engineer, Bazzi worked with his usual discipline, eating and sleeping little and devoting all his energies to the task. He also banned smoking in the workshops, which initially created consternation but was to become a permanent rule. In a sense, the *Bimotore* was nothing more than a parts-bin special, since most of its components came from the previous cars, but its conception was undeniably audacious. Not only did Bazzi and his men produce the first of two cars within four months, they also produced a car that worked – even if some of the team's drivers were terrified by the prospect of handling such a beast, and despite its prodigious appetite for consuming its Belgian-made Englebert tyres. But on its first run, on the road from Formigine to Maranello, it was said to have reached a speed of 178 mph in the brave hands of Attilio Marinoni, one more transplanted ex-Alfa employee who had worked closely with Bazzi on the project. Nuvolari, too, had a go, and pronounced himself enthusiastic to a watching group which included Ferrari, Jano, and a delegation of Alfa's senior personnel. 'Jano wasn't directly involved,' Ferrari said, 'but he always kept an eye on our digressions.' The car was called an Alfa Romeo, although it was designed and constructed by Scuderia Ferrari personnel in their own workshops. For the first time, too, the prancing horse of Baracca was seen not on a shield on the side of the car but on a small enamel badge above the radiator, replacing the viper and the cross of Alfa Romeo.

While Bazzi laboured to complete the new grand prix car, the Scuderia began the season with a one-two for Nuvolari and Dreyfus around the streets of Pau, driving P3s. This was followed by a victory in the Mille Miglia for Carlo Pintacuda, a new arrival, at the wheel of a P3 modified to take a second seat and with lights and mudguards attached. A Sicilian who lived in Florence, Pintacuda had joined the team by the straightforward expedient of buying his car. The result was made even sweeter for the Scuderia by the fate of Varzi, who had accepted a one-off drive in a Maserati but whose car shed its body parts all over Italy before succumbing to lubrication problems. This was the first of Pintacuda's two wins in the thousand-mile event. He was less convincing in grand prix machines on closed circuits, and Ferrari concluded that open-road racing was his forte. When he came into the pits during the Coppa Ciano, complaining that the brakes of his single-seater were not working properly, Nuvolari, whose rear axle had broken, jumped in and won the race. To journalists who asked how he had done it, Nuvolari replied: 'If you want to go fast, you don't need brakes.' This was a joke that, in Ferrari's words, Pintacuda 'took some time to digest'.

Antonio Brivio won the Targa Florio for the team, but in the grands prix of Monaco and Tunis the Alfas were thoroughly beaten by the latest Mercedes and Auto Unions in the hands of Fagioli and Varzi. Now was the time to unleash the *Bimotori*, and the very fast Mellaha circuit in Tunis provided the opportunity. Both cars were present, the 6.3-litre car for Nuvolari and the 5.8-litre for Chiron. But after only three laps Nuvolari, who had been running in second place, came into the pits with shredded tyres. The 1,100 kg weight of the *Bimotore* and the abrasive effect of the sand blowing across the track turned his race into a farce. Others suffered, too, even Caracciola's winning Mercedes, but the German teams had anticipated the problem. Their cars were fitted with built-in compressed air jacks which lifted them off the ground in a second, while their mechanics had been practising the art of changing wheels. A job which had previously taken two minutes now occupied half that time. In fact Alfred Neubauer, the Mercedes team manager, could be seen timing the crews as they went through the drill during practice. Nuvolari, enjoying no such advantages, had to change no fewer than thirteen tyres during the race, in somewhat less scientific circumstances, and did well to finish fourth, ahead of Chiron.

There were similar problems at the Avus track, where the German teams unveiled a new generation of streamlined cars, although Chiron managed to finish second by driving with his mind almost wholly focused on conserving his tyres. When the team took the larger *Bimotore* to the Firenze–Mare autostrada in order to earn some publicity points by breaking a speed record, the car was fitted with tyres from Dunlop. On a stretch of dual carriageway near Lucca, Nuvolari set off early in the morning and succeeded in shattering the existing records for the flying kilometre and flying mile with speeds of 199 mph and 200 mph respectively, the latter eclipsing the mark established by Stuck in an Auto Union on the same stretch of road a few weeks earlier. That achievement, however, was effectively the end of the line for the *Bimotore*, a magnificent if misguided project. The Nuvolari car was broken up, its components returned to the parts bin, while the smaller car was sold to an English enthusiast who planned to race it at Brooklands.

The 1935 grand prix season continued with what was beginning to look like an endless series of victories for the Silver Arrows of the German teams. There seemed no reason for any change to the new natural order of things when they arrived at the Nürburgring for the German Grand Prix. But on 28 July Tazio Nuvolari produced one of the greatest drives in the history of grand prix racing – so great, in fact, that it would not be equalled for more than twenty years.

The crowd had assembled to acclaim a German victory,

virtually every one of more than a quarter of a million spectators anticipating a walkover by the five Mercedes and four Auto Unions. But the Nürburgring, above all, was a driver's circuit, its 174 corners forming a sort of mini Mille Miglia that encouraged those with the highest skills and the greatest instinct for improvisation to take their chance against superior machinery. Nuvolari had begun the meeting by surprising the Germans when he posted a practice time as fast as that of Bernd Rosemeyer, Auto Union's new ace, another former motorcyclist who had been discovered by Dr Porsche. What followed was a race handed down from Olympus.

There was rain on the morning of the race, ending a spell of fine weather and dispersing the smoke lingering from a thousand barbecues. National Socialist flags fluttered from a line of poles above the grandstand. Swastikas had been painted on the head-rest fairings of the German cars. Bands played. The prototype of the Stuka, the dive bomber that was to be turned on the Spanish people in the destruction of Guernica and on the British army in the retreat from Dunkirk, swooped down to demonstrate its abilities to a thrilled crowd, the sirens in its wheel-spats screaming. *Korpsführer* Adolf Huhnlein, Hitler's sports minister, took his seat. In his pocket was a speech congratulating the German teams on their victory.

Nuvolari appeared wearing a red leather helmet instead of his usual blue linen bonnet, with a silk scarf round his neck in the red, white and green of the Italian *tricolore*. A replica of D'Annunzio's tortoise had been woven on to the breast of his yellow shirt. The drivers of the German teams marched on together, in identical white overalls. As the Scuderia Ferrari crew members made their final preparations, Decimo Compagnoni leaned over to Nuvolari. '*In bocca al lupo*,' he said. May you go into the mouth of the wolf (and, it was understood in this traditional Italian benediction, may you return safely). Nuvolari smiled. 'I think the weather's going to clear up,' he remarked.

Ten seconds before the start, and anxious to avoid getting boxed in by the silver machines, he began slipping the clutch.

When the flag fell Caracciola and Fagioli got away first, with Nuvolari tucked in behind them. Halfway through the opening lap he passed Fagioli, crossing the line in second place, albeit twelve seconds behind Caracciola. Soon Rosemeyer went by, then von Brauchitsch, then Fagioli. But Nuvolari was feeling good, happy with the handling of the car, confident that he could match his opponents. The race was not going so well for his team mates. First Brivio retired, then Chiron. It seemed only a matter of time before Nuvolari's ageing Alfa would succumb too to the stresses imposed by the demanding circuit and the hectic tempo of the race. But, having sat back as Caracciola and Rosemeyer got on with what looked very much like a battle for victory between Mercedes and Auto Union, in the middle of the race Nuvolari launched his attack.

Gradually he made ground, creeping up to the German cars. By the tenth lap, astonishingly, he was in the lead. Two laps later, however, there was a setback. The cars stopped for refuelling and a change of tyres. Caracciola was in and out in sixty-seven seconds. Von Brauchitsch's crew had the second car on its way in forty-seven seconds. In the Scuderia's pit, the mechanics were filling Nuvolari's petrol tank and fitting his car with a new set of wheels shod with special Englebert tyres, their treads 6 mm deep rather than the usual 4 mm to take account of the extra wear encountered at the Nürburgring. But Nello Ugolini watched in horror as the pressure pump refused to deliver its fuel to the car's tank, forcing the mechanics to complete the task using gravity and a funnel. Two minutes and fourteen seconds after coming to rest, Nuvolari was on his way.

Now he was in sixth place, and the chase began. In a single lap he overtook four cars. This was total concentration, total aggression, a blend of competitive savagery and the utmost sensitivity to the messages being delivered by the cracked and undulating concrete of the track, by the thousand stretched and straining components of the car, by the sound of the engine and the tyres, and by the visual information from kerbstones, trees, and hoardings, all of them fed through seat, hands, ears and eyes, and translated into the quick, darting movements that sent the car slaloming and dancing through the turns, clipping verges as it slid, bucking over the famous humps that sent all four wheels off the ground. By these means he was gradually pulling back the only man who still lay ahead.

In the Mercedes pit, Neubauer was peering anxiously at von Brauchitsch's tyres each time the leader went past. With two laps to go, the team manager spotted what he had been looking for. The breaker strip, a layer of white under the tread, was showing through. In the heat of the race, the tyres were wearing faster than he had anticipated. How much longer could they last? Tyre technicians and mechanics stood by, ready to make a quick change. But Neubauer said no. 'Brauchitsch will make it', he shouted, 'and so will the tyres. It's only a question of a few minutes.'

As the cars passed the pits to start the last of the twenty-two laps, the Mercedes still had a lead of thirty-five seconds over the Alfa. Von Brauchitsch, an aristocrat who resented the promotion to the driving squad of men who had started their careers as mere mechanics, was doing everything he could to keep Nuvolari at bay, aided by Neubauer's sophisticated system of pit signals. But over the fourteen miles of the Nürburgring, thirty-five seconds was not an insurmountable gap, at least not to a genius in full flight. With less than half the final lap to go, von Brauchitsch could see Nuvolari in his mirrors, a distant speck of dark red. He might nevertheless have held the Italian off, using the massive power of the Mercedes' supercharged straight-eight engine for a final blast on the finishing straight, had an abused tyre not finally burst as he left the banked turn called the *Karussell*, just six miles from the chequered flag. His race was over. Nuvolari tore past and crossed the line.

In the Scuderia Ferrari pit there was pandemonium. In the grandstands there was a moment of stunned silence before applause broke out in recognition of an astonishing feat. *Korpsführer* Huhnlein put his hand in his pocket, crumpled his prepared speech into a ball, and got ready to improvise something polite for the waiting microphones. It was several minutes before an Italian flag could be found to be run up the pole for the prizegiving ceremony. No one in the stewards' office had a recording of the Italian national anthem to play – until Decimo Compagnoni remembered the 78 rpm disc that Nuvolari always carried with him, for luck, carefully packed in his suitcase. The mechanic ran back to get it, and the *Marcia Reale* rang out across the Eifel mountains.

'As far as I'm concerned,' Ferrari would say several decades later, 'there has been only one truly great racing driver. There is a perfect balance between a car and its driver – fifty per cent car and fifty per cent driver. With Nuvolari, this relationship was overturned. He contributed at least seventy-five per cent of the total.'

Although Nuvolari won enough secondary races – Pau, Bergamo, Biella, Turin, Adenau, Livorno and Modena – to make him Italian champion in 1935, the truth was obvious. The triumph at the Nürburgring had been merely the exception to the rule of Germany's absolute mastery over grand prix racing. Not until September did Jano produce his new car. Instead, at the instruction of Ugo Gobbato, Alfa Romeo's new chairman, he had been spending his time trying to design an engine for fighter aircraft as part of the commitment to providing the equipment for Mussolini's military adventure in Abyssinia. And even then the delivery of the new 8C-35 had to be rushed forward in response to crushing defeats for the team in the Coppa Acerbo and the Swiss Grand Prix towards the end of the season. Between those two races there was so much unrest among the drivers that Enzo Ferrari was forced to respond to the growing volume of complaints by sending them all a letter in which he ordered them not to gossip to the press about the Scuderia's problems with its cars.

When the 8C-35 finally appeared, two things were evident. First, although it was undeniably handsome, and clearly a step forward from the P3, it still did not look like a modern grand prix car, as redefined by the designers of Mercedes-Benz in Stuttgart and Auto Union in Zwickau. Jano had adhered to the old paradigm, believing that a slim upright car would be as aerodynamically efficient as a low flat one. At that stage, the science of aerodynamics had more to do with guesswork and aesthetics than facts derived from practical research. Lacking a wind tunnel, Jano had to follow his instincts. In this case, they were wrong. Somehow the concept of the centre of gravity had escaped him. And if the car, from a visual point of view, looked like a schoolboy's copy of the Mercedes W25 of two years earlier, then its engine was even more disappointing. Jano had been working on a new twelve-cylinder engine with which to bridge the gap in power to the German engines, but there was no sign of it. Instead he had merely provided an improved version of the old eight-cylinder engine from the P3, a design basically ten years old. What the car did have, admittedly, was independent suspension all round and hydraulic brakes.

Although this was little more than an interim solution, the Italian press built up expectations of a machine that would finally get the better of the detested silver cars. When the new Alfas made their first appearance at Monza, Ugo Gobbato was present, and so was Ferrari, which had become unusual. Already, as Dreyfus observed, 'You really could only be sure of seeing him at the end-of-season banquet.' Nuvolari did his best to satisfy his bosses' hopes, setting the fastest race lap in his own car before a piston broke as he passed the pits. Dreyfus was now in second place, and as Nuvolari walked back in front of the grandstands the crowd began to chant: 'Nuvolari la macchina! Nuvolari la macchina!' When the Frenchman came in to refuel, Ferrari and Gobbato asked him if he would mind handing the car over. 'Of course I wouldn't,' Dreyfus said. 'Tazio was the team captain. He beamed, and said grazie. I was a big fan of Tazio's, and I was proud he was my friend.' Then Nuvolari was off, finishing a fighting second in Dreyfus's machine, which ended up with worn-out brakes and an engine firing on only seven cylinders. The following week he registered the 8C–35's first win, in the team's home race in Modena, with no Germans in the entry list. Seven days later he was firmly beaten by Rosemeyer in Brno.

The twelve-cylinder engine would not arrive until the following May, and in the meantime there had been further changes at the top of the Scuderia. The principal departure was that of Count Trossi, an amateur of the old school in an increasingly professional world, leaving Enzo Ferrari to take over the chairmanship of the new board. Nuvolari stayed, but Louis Chiron announced that in 1936 he would be racing for Mercedes-Benz, and Dreyfus went back to France to join Talbot. The principal new arrival would be Giuseppe Farina, aged twenty-nine, a doctor of political science and a member of the large coachbuilding family, who had raced for the Maserati brothers in 1935 and was something of a protégé of Nuvolari.

Global politics had already obstructed the development of the new car, and when the Scuderia attempted to open the season with the Pau Grand Prix in late February they found world affairs making an even more direct intervention. France had been a signatory to the League of Nations' motion condemning Italy's invasion of Abyssinia, and the Scuderia Ferrari's trucks, containing the cars of Nuvolari, Farina and Brivio, were turned back from the border crossing at Ponte San Luigi.

Jano had also supplied the team with new 8C–2900 sports cars, which Brivio and *Dottore* Farina used to come first and second in the Mille Miglia, the former victorious at a record speed despite losing his lights in the later stages. It was a good start to the season, but deceptive. At Monaco, where four 8C–35s faced the new and more powerful sixteen-cylinder Auto Unions, there was chaos from the start. Brivio's Alfa was seen to be leaking oil on the grid. He switched cars with Tadini, who spent the first lap laying a carpet of lubricant around the streets of the principality, already wet from rain. When Chiron arrived at the Tabac, at the head of the field in his Mercedes, he

[91]

lost control on the mixture of oil and water and started a six-car pile-up. Nuvolari was among the survivors, and took the lead from Caracciola on the tenth lap, but handling problems had forced him back into fourth place by the end.

At the Tripoli Grand Prix there was a surprise guest. Dr Joseph Bühler, Hitler's secretary of state, took the parade of cars and drivers alongside Air Marshal Balbo, a sign of the relationship between Italy and Germany following the signing of a royal decree in Rome which declared the establishment of a Fascist republic. Scuderia Ferrari celebrated by unveiling Jano's latest engine, sending a trio of the new 4-litre 12C–36 models on to the grid. Tadini had replaced Farina, who had been injured when a tyre burst during a test at Monza. When Nuvolari went out for his first practice lap on the wide, sweeping Mellaha circuit, shortly after Varzi had set a time with an average speed of 135 mph, the same thing happened. He was doing more than 120 mph when a rear tyre exploded, sending the car into a somersault. Nuvolari was thrown out, landing on a pile of weeds and grass which had been cut a few days earlier during the preparation of the course. It took them ten minutes to find him, and he was still unconscious when the ambulance took him to hospital. The comparatively soft landing restricted his injuries to a few broken ribs, which would have been enough to earn most drivers a sick note. But Nuvolari, fitted with a plaster corset, was back in his car the next morning, driving a little more conservatively but nevertheless finishing seventh. The Germans filled the first four places.

'The magic show is over,' Enzo Ferrari was reported to have said when he heard the result from Tripoli, but a month later on the Penya Rhin circuit, on the streets of a Barcelona suburb, Nuvolari gave the Scuderia's morale an important boost by using the 12C to beat two-car teams from Auto Union and Mercedes. Simultaneously, Pintacuda and Marinoni were involved in the Scuderia's first long-haul adventure, a combined sporting and sales trip to Brazil with two of the new 8C sports cars. After suffering transmission failure on the Gavéa circuit in

Rio de Janeiro, a track so spectacularly hilly that it was known as the Devil's Trampoline, they finished first and second in a race around the streets of São Paulo, following which the cars were sold to local enthusiasts anxious to get their hands on modern machinery from Europe. And as if to demonstrate the Scuderia's versatility, on the day of the second Brazilian race the team was also winning the Spa 24-hour race with the pairing of Siena and Raymond Sommer, the son of a Parisian textile manufacturer, having entered the race at the request of Englebert, their Belgian tyre suppliers. Sommer, something of a long-distance specialist, had won the Le Mans race – on which the Spa event was modelled – in factory-entered Alfa Romeos in 1932, sharing the wheel with a keen young Italian named Luigi Chinetti, and in 1933, partnering Nuvolari.

At the Nürburgring, Rosemeyer beat Nuvolari in the ten-lap Eifelrennen race with a drive through the fog which showed the young man taking on the master at his own game. Nuvolari's revenge came a week later in a Budapest park, followed by a win in Milan's Sempione Park. The 12Cs might not quite have had the pace for some tracks, but on street and parkland circuits they could be competitive, at least in Nuvolari's hands. Rosemeyer brooked no competition on their return to the Nürburgring for the German Grand Prix, but Nuvolari produced an unexpected answer at the Coppa Ciano at Livorno, when he responded to the cries of the public by taking over Pintacuda's 8C after his own twelve-cylinder had retired. Nuvolari dragged the machine, about which Pintacuda had been complaining, from the back of the field all the way to the front, nudging the tail of Rosemeyer's Auto Union as he tried to find a way by on the tight Montenero circuit and sweeping past Varzi to claim one of his greatest victories. Varzi, in fact, was so demoralised that he pulled off, convincing few observers with his claim to be suffering from a problem with his brakes.

There was further consolation for the Scuderia in the team's first trip to the United States, to compete in the Vanderbilt Cup. Promoted by a group of wealthy businessmen, the contest was intended to be a match race between the Old and New Worlds, reviving for the purpose the name of a series of races held before the Great War. In late September the Scuderia's trucks delivered three 12Cs and an 8C for loading on to the liner *Rex* in Genoa harbour. Nuvolari, Farina and Brivio were to be the drivers, with Marinoni in reserve and Bazzi and Ugolini in charge. Four mechanics – Meazza, Stefani, Mambelli and Bai – went along. Enzo Ferrari, as had become his habit, stayed at home, waiting for news.

In June, during a ceremony in which he was proclaimed champion of Italy by Mussolini in the historic setting of Siena's *campo*, Nuvolari had been told by the dictator: 'We must win in New York. Understood?' The Spanish Civil War had begun and Mussolini, who was sending Franco planes, tanks, guns and men to help in the fight against the republicans, was keen to exploit any opportunity to win American sympathy. 'We'll win, *Duce*,' Nuvolari replied. On 12 October forty-three cars lined up for the start of the Vanderbilt Cup on an artificial track laid out at Roosevelt Field, the aerodrome used by Lindbergh for his flight to Paris nine years earlier. A prize of six million lire was on offer for the winner. The European entries included Jean-Pierre Wimille's Bugatti and the ERAs of Earl Howe and Pat Fairfield, but the Americans were confidently expecting victory for one of their Indianapolis-type cars, most probably that of Mauri Rose. Nuvolari, however, set off like a hare and during the next four and a half hours lost the lead only once, while making a pit stop. Late stops pushed Brivio down from second place, which was inherited by Wimille, to third. Farina crashed. Raymond Sommer came fourth in another Alfa, and Fairfield's ERA finished fifth. The Americans were nowhere, the potential of their oval-track cars nullified by their own organisers' choice of a twisty circuit configuration which suited the Europeans. For the Scuderia Ferrari, the sale of the 8C to an American driver simply added to the financial dividends of the trip.

When Ugolini made the telephone call to Modena, it was with good tidings. There were late-night celebrations at El

Morocco, the famous Italian-owned Manhattan night spot. And the winner found himself besieged, in the American way, by people anxious to give him large sums of money simply for agreeing to endorse their brand of soap or soft drink. Nuvolari had pocketed the cheque for $32,000 without even opening the envelope to look at it, and he had no difficulty in turning their offers down, even the one that promised him $50,000 for a three-minute interview on a sponsored radio programme. Instead he accepted an invitation from a hard-up Italian immigrant to drive a few demonstration laps on a dirt track near New York. The immigrant had assured his friends that he could produce the champion. Success, he told Nuvolari, would set him up. The great Nuvolari responded.

Encouraged by Mussolini, who wanted to see Italian cars making a better showing against those of his Axis partner, the Alfa Romeo board decided to involve the company in the sporting programme once more. In March 1937 they approached Enzo Ferrari and settled on a new arrangement. They would buy 80 per cent of the share capital of the Società Anonima Scuderia Ferrari, on the understanding that Ferrari himself would continue to run the racing team and sell cars to private competitors from the Modena premises. On the face of it, this would mean little change in the daily operations of the team. But two months later, seemingly as part of the deal, Alfa Romeo transferred an engineer, Gioachino Colombo, to the Scuderia. Thirty-four years old, Colombo had worked with Jano at the Portello factory since 1924. He had assisted the designer on the P2, the 1750 series, and all the other significant models of the early Thirties. He had absorbed Jano's wisdom without acquiring his prejudices and blind spots. Now, long frustrated by the imposition of his mentor's seniority and fixed views, he wanted to express himself. In Modena he could breathe more easily as he conspired with Enzo Ferrari and his staff to outwit the German domination of top-level motor racing.

[95]

As with the genesis of *Bimotore*, Ferrari was thinking laterally. Since it seemed unlikely that the combined forces of Alfa Romeo and the Scuderia would ever be able to match those of the state-assisted German teams in the 750 kg formula, he needed to look elsewhere, for another form of racing that might catch the public's imagination. What he saw was the category called *voiturette* racing, a formula for smaller single-seater cars in which engine size was restricted to 1.5 litres, with or without superchargers. ERAs, Bugattis, Delages and Maseratis were already competing in this category; there were no Germans in sight.

'When I arrived in Modena', Colombo remembered, 'I already had a definite plan in mind: to build a small car with a rear engine, a kind of miniature Auto Union. For some time I had been thinking about this project, and I'd been studying some possible solutions in my spare time.' At the earliest opportunity, he explained them to Enzo Ferrari. The *padrone* listened closely and asked for explanations of this point and that. Gradually Colombo began to feel hopeful. And then, having heard all the evidence, Ferrari gave his verdict. 'No,' he said. 'It's always been the ox that pulls the cart.'

Nothing could have expressed more clearly Ferrari's inherent conservatism. Had he not, after all, just spent a season seeing his team, led by the world's finest driver, being regularly beaten by a team of cars in which the ox pushed the cart? But he had grown up in a world of real ox-drawn carts, he had shod the mules for gun carriages, and he was not going to betray his background. Not, at least, until he was faced with a situation in which there was absolutely no alternative. 'It was clear', Colombo continued, 'that this was his joking way of concluding the discussion on good terms. But I learned from then onwards that while Enzo Ferrari always gave his designers absolute freedom to put forward their ideas and paid the closest possible attention to what they said, he always reserved the final decision for himself.'

The new boy soon settled into the rhythms of life in the viale

Trento e Trieste, where the buildings had been extended across a neighbouring patch of land, forming a courtyard. There were long days in a small design office, working with Bazzi and a group of new and recent arrivals – Angelo Nasi, another engineer on loan from Alfa; Alberto Massimino, the ex-Fiat man formerly employed by Nuvolari to build a special based on his old Bugatti; and Federico Giberti, the nephew of the coachbuilder Renzo Orlandi, Ferrari's old friend. Fresh minds, fresh thinking. This time, they were working together to build a car from the ground up. There was a deadline, but there was no need to rush. 'We spent many Sundays working, first on the design and then on the car itself,' Giberti remembered. 'With Ferrari, whenever he fixed a date it was essential to keep it, or at least get very close to it. We were able to produce so much because there were people just right for the job, people who studied the plans and then knew how to work on their own.'

While they worked, the season's racing began with the Mille Miglia, in which Pintacuda secured his second victory, and the team's fifth in a row, after seeing off a challenge from Delahaye and Talbot. In international single-seater racing, the prospects were less rosy. The Germans were approaching the last year of the 750 kg formula by throwing money at their engineers, Mercedes unveiling the 5.6-litre W125 while Auto Union continued to develop their V16-engined car for Rosemeyer. Both teams were also bombarding Nuvolari with offers, and it seemed only a matter of time before he recognised the truth of the matter, that he was wasting his time with a losing cause. Hermann Lang, a former mechanic, won the first grand prix of the season for Mercedes, while the Scuderia's entry of half a dozen 12Cs failed to make an impression. Ferrari left the Germans to battle it out along the super-fast straights of the Avus, and the Alfas were then outclassed even at the Nürburgring, where the pace of the Germans' technical development allowed Rosemeyer to knock almost fifteen seconds off his own lap record from the previous year.

Nor was there joy to be had from a second trip to New York.

The managements of Mercedes and Auto Union had noted the publicity accruing to the Italian team from the 1936 victory, and both sent two-car teams, led by Caracciola and Rosemeyer. No doubt *Korpsführer* Huhnlein and his boss were also keen to make a point on the other side of the Atlantic by demonstrating to the Americans the invincibility of National Socialist technology and morale. Rosemeyer won easily, from the Mercedes of Dick Seaman, a young Englishman. Nuvolari and Farina managed fifth, sharing the latter's 8C after the 12C had broken.

Nuvolari had not wanted to be there at all. The elder of his sons, eighteen-year-old Giorgio, was seriously ill. At home in Tazio's Mantuan villa, the boy lay dying of pericarditis. Ferrari tried to persuade Nuvolari to go. 'Giorgio will be able to hold out until your return,' he said, according to the account given by Giovanni Lurani, Nuvolari's biographer, 'and there's always a chance that he'll recover. After all, he's made of the same stuff as his father.' It seems unlikely that Ferrari, whose own elder son, Dino, had already displayed the symptoms of a severe childhood illness, would put undue pressure on a worried father. And he had, according to Lurani, consulted Decimo Compagnoni about the prognosis. But it was apparently Giorgio's words that swayed Nuvolari's decision. 'What', he said to his father, 'would the team do without you?' On board the *Rex*, the members of the team tried to divert Nuvolari's thoughts. But one evening on the outward passage he was having dinner when a waiter came across with a tray carrying a piece of paper announcing that he was wanted on the ship's radio-telephone. On the line from Mantua, the distant voice of Compagnoni announced that Giorgio had gone.

Back in Europe, the humiliations continued. Nuvolari was paid an extra 100,000 lire by the factory to test a new low-chassis version of the 12C, and the Alfa management showed their intentions by entering it for its debut at Pescara under their name, rather than the Scuderia's. But its performance was so disappointing that it did not appear for the Swiss Grand Prix, to which Ferrari sent 12Cs for Farina and Sommer, only to discover that Nuvolari had turned up to drive for Auto Union. Nuvolari found it difficult to adapt to the handling of the mid-engined chassis and handed his car over to Rosemeyer before taking over Fagioli's machine to finish seventh. For the Scuderia, depression turned to farce when Sommer came into the pits and waved his broken gear-lever under the nose of *Ingegnere* Marinoni.

Within the Scuderia, morale had collapsed. Rumours of imminent changes were circulating freely. In Milan, all efforts at the Portello factory were being turned towards developing two new sixteen-cylinder engines, a supercharged 3-litre and an unblown 4.5, for the forthcoming season's new Grand Prix regulations. Workshops were being fitted out, a sign that fresh plans had been laid. Suddenly Jano was sacked, paying the price for fathering a generation of cars that had been consistently unable to keep pace with their German rivals. And Nuvolari, his patience exhausted, finally cracked and signed a contract to drive for Auto Union.

On 1 January 1938, eight years after it had been brought into existence during a conversation over dinner in Bologna, the Scuderia Ferrari ceased to exist. Ugo Gobbato, Alfa Romeo's chairman, announced that the company was regaining direct control of its own racing affairs. It had bought the Scuderia, whose complete effects would be moved to Milan. So away from Modena went the old cars, the spares, the machine tools and the entire Tipo 158 project. Rumours that Enzo Ferrari would be rejoining Vittorio Jano to start a completely new team proved unfounded. Jano went to Lancia while Ferrari, it was announced, would continue to run Alfa's racing team, to be known henceforward as Alfa Corse. His engineers would go with him. And, although it seemed an insignificant detail at the time, Ferrari's new contract with Alfa stipulated that should he leave the company, he would not be able to manufacture cars under his own name for a four-year period. Effectively, the old garage and workshops became an Alfa Romeo showroom and service centre. He had been well rewarded for the takeover, and his annual salary as the director of Alfa Corse was generous, but now he was just an employee.

In Milan, to which he commuted from the old headquarters, there were plenty of familiar faces. Bazzi, Ugolini and others had made the transfer with him. But he also found himself working with a new design team headed by a Spaniard, Wilfredo Ricart – or, as his passport put it, Wilfredo Pelaya Ricart y Medina. If Ferrari did not detest Ricart on sight, then he certainly gave that impression when he described the powerful loathing he felt for *lo spagnolo*. 'He appeared almost surreptitiously,' Ferrari wrote twenty years later, his bile undiluted by time, going on to suggest that Ricart's appointment to Alfa Romeo must have had a political dimension. 'This Spaniard, who spoke four or five languages fluently, captured – this is the only word for it – the trust of Gobbato. He impressed the latter, I believe, with the way in which he presented his plans, with the clear and elegant manner with which he expressed himself, with the ease with which he perused the publications of every country, and, finally, with the air of authority with which he knew how to submit explanatory diagrams prepared by a young graduate he had engaged as secretary for the Special Studies Office, namely *Ingegnere* Orazio Satta, today Alfa Romeo's design manager and the virtual father of the present-day Giulietta car.' In other words, Ferrari insinuated, Ricart was in the habit of taking the credit for the work of another, more talented designer. And Ferrari, of course, spoke only his native tongue and its Modenese dialect fluently, with a smattering of basic French. Even more scathing was his description of Ricart's 'sleek, oiled hair' and the smart clothes which he wore 'with a somewhat Levantine elegance', jackets with sleeves that came over his wrists and shoes with unusually thick rubber soles. When Ferrari asked him about the reason for the thickness of the rubber soles, Ricart replied that a great engineer's brain should not be jolted by unnecessarily severe contact with the ground. Finally, 'When he shook hands, it was like grasping the cold, lifeless hand of a corpse.'

When Ferrari approached Gobbato to suggest, with heavy sarcasm, that such enormous brainpower was surely wasted on the frivolous task of designing racing cars, the chairman, himself an engineer as well as an expert administrator, sent him away with a flea in his ear. 'Perhaps he thought I was jealous,' Ferrari wrote, obviously believing that his readers would see the absurdity of such an outlandish suggestion. More than half a century later the Ferrari-versus-Ricart argument still raged, the Catalan's supporters pointing to the potential of the prototypes and blueprints that fell victim to the start of World War II, including a startlingly beautiful mid-engined car for the *voiturette* formula ('just a mid-engined version of the Tipo 158 with a V12 motor', Ferrari sniffed) and a stunning teardrop-shaped two-seater Berlinetta with a supercharged 3-litre engine, also mounted behind the driver. Those making the case for Ferrari had the immediate and longer-term success of the Tipo 158 to support their contention that the Alfa Romeo board would have done better to give him a completely free hand with his own design staff.

Between Ferrari and Gobbato, however, there was a conceptual gulf that could not be bridged. 'He [Gobbato] was not a great believer in improvisation or in snap decisions,' Ferrari wrote. 'A great industrial organiser, he expected everything to be arranged in advance, with every last detail foreseen and worked out. He hated having to adapt himself to sudden changes, while for me the act of makeshift was almost a part of my religion. Gobbato believed that a racing car should be the product, the synthesis of products, of all the departments of a big works. I took the contrary view, that a racing car should be the compendium of the work of a small auxiliary workshop, well fitted out and with its own specialised staff, so that the ideas and designs of the engineers might rapidly be translated into reality.' It was, he added, 'an ideological contract, with repercussions on the practical level'.

A year after Gioachino Colombo had gone to Modena to start the project, the Alfa Romeo Tipo 158 ran for the first time in a test at Monza, in the hands of the Scuderia's test driver, Enrico Nardi. Its promise was obvious. This car broke away from the unspoken rules that seemed to have governed the design of its Jano-built predecessors. It sat low to the ground, its brakes were hydraulically operated, its wheels were independently suspended, its gearbox was mated with the differential to achieve a balanced weight distribution. Here was a modern single-seater racing car, and something more besides. It would surely be a match for the excellent machines being turned out by the Maserati brothers, who had suddenly turned into genuinely local rivals. Following the premature death in 1937 of Alfieri Maserati, the most inventive and dynamic member of the family, the remaining brothers sold a controlling interest in their company to the Orsi family of Modena. The Maseratis were in the process of moving the entire operation from Bologna to a new factory on the viale Ciro Menotti, on the other side of the via Emilia from the old Scuderia headquarters. The brothers had signed a ten-year deal, which would expire in 1947.

When Enzo Ferrari's Alfa Corse team arrived in Livorno in the first week of August for the *voiturette* race supporting the Coppa Ciano, the three cars were the centre of attention. The Scuderia Ferrari shields had gone, replaced by the old four-leafed clover, the *quadrifoglio*, of Alfa Romeo. Three new drivers had been engaged – Clemente Biondetti, Francesco Severi, and Emilio 'Mimi' Villoresi, a young Milanese whose brother Luigi, a Maserati works driver, had already won several *voiturette* races. Luigi – or 'Gigi' – had himself arrived in Livorno in a car specially modified to counter the threat from the Tipo 158.

The trio of Alfettas, as they would become known, started from the front row of the grid. Severi led from the start but was soon overtaken by Gigi Villoresi's Maserati. Mimi took up the challenge, and the two brothers raced each other so furiously that the Maserati's engine eventually broke under the strain, leaving the Tipo 158 to take a famous victory on its debut. The

Alfetta was to become one of the great racing cars, but not until another decade and more had elapsed. In its early races it fought neck-and-neck with the Maseratis, giving the Italian public something other than the demonstration runs that the German teams were continuing to produce in the grands prix. Alfa Corse continued to send bigger cars to these races, but still they trailed behind the Mercedes and Auto Unions. And, by the end of 1938, Tazio Nuvolari had finally mastered the art of putting the ox behind the cart. At forty-six, taking over the leadership of the Auto Union team following the death of Rosemeyer during a speed-record attempt, he won races at Monza and Donington Park with all his old mastery. So, late in the season, the Italian racing authorities came up with another scheme. From the beginning of 1939, they announced, all grand prix events in Italy would be run to the *voiturette* formula. This, they hoped, would enable their own teams to recapture their lost glory.

The first race held under the new formula would be the Tripoli Grand Prix on the sand-swept Mellaha circuit. The date of the race was 7 May. Thirty cars turned up. Twenty-eight of them were Italian, including a Maserati with a specially streamlined body, prepared for Gigi Villoresi. To the utter consternation of the Italian teams, the twenty-ninth and thirtieth cars, accompanied by crews in neat white uniforms, arrived from Stuttgart.

For months the Mercedes-Benz management had flatly denied rumours that they were building a car to the new regulations. When the English photographer George Monk-house wrote to his friend Dick Seaman, one of the team's star drivers, asking if the stories were true, he received a joky reply: '[Alfred] Neubauer says thanks for your letter about [the] 1.5-litre car, but knows nothing about it. Dr Kissel is, however, going to send you all the blueprints of the new 750 cc 24-cylinder 2-stroke Mercedes.' But the previous November, two months after the announcement of the new formula, Mercedes had begun, in conditions of great secrecy, to design and build the new car, the W165, which was virtually a miniaturised eight-cylinder version of their current V12 grand prix car. Six months later two of the new cars were not only finished but ready to race.

Even to their drivers, their existence was a surprise. Immediately after the Pau Grand Prix, Hermann Lang and Rudi Caracciola were told by telegram to report for testing at the Hockenheim circuit, normally a motorcycle track. 'Why to Hockenheim?' Lang wrote. 'Did Mercedes-Benz suddenly build motorcycles and wanted them tested?' They were driven at high speed to the rendezvous, where all was revealed. Only three days remained before they would need to embark for the Tripoli race and Neubauer had to decide whether to confirm their entry. This test was his last chance to assess the cars' chances of success. 'If the smallest thing went wrong', Lang continued, 'and even the slightest modification was necessary, all our hopes would have been in vain.' But the test was flawless, and the cars were prepared for shipment from Naples to North Africa.

The personnel of Alfa Corse, under the management of Meo Costatini, made the crossing on the same boat. The two teams played deck games against each other and at midnight the vastly proportioned Neubauer appeared in the guise of Neptune, covered from head to foot in seaweed, to deliver a message in Italian to the assembled company. When they arrived in Tripoli, the *ghibli* was blowing and the sky had turned a sulphurous yellow. Straight away, the Italians' worst fears were realised. In the hands of Lang and Caracciola, the two Mercedes were very fast indeed. Only Gigi Villoresi managed to outqualify them, much to the Germans' surprise. On the night before the race, Neubauer outlined his plan. Lang would act as the hare, going flat out in an attempt to stay with the leading bunch, but prepared to make a tyre change. Caracciola would drive more conservatively, in order to get through the race on one set of tyres.

Lang planned his start carefully. Air Marshal Italo Balbo, the governor of the colony, was to drop the flag, given his cue by a set of lights. Lang watched the lights rather than the flag and made the best start of his life, closely followed by his team mate. As Balbo watched aghast from the magnificent grandstand of the circuit that he had created, the two silver cars left Luigi Villoresi's Maserati, and the other twenty-seven Italian cars, standing. Within a lap, the streamliner's engine had blown up, wrecking the plan of the Villoresi brothers – racing for different teams, of course – to beat the Mercedes cars by running the race as a sort of relay, taking turns to lead in order to force their opponents to over-extend themselves. Farina, in the leading Alfa 158, made a superhuman effort to get on terms, but after he overtook Caracciola to take second place his engine also gave up the struggle. Lang's car behaved perfectly. In heat that reached 52 degrees Celsius on the track and 37 degrees in the shade, he and Caracciola finished first and second, with Mimi Villoresi a breathless and dispirited third in the only surviving Alfetta, several minutes behind. The Alfas had suffered from vapour lock in their fuel lines, as a result of the high temperatures. Years later Gigi Villoresi remembered that all the Italian drivers had finished the race with bloodshot eyes and swollen lips as a result of breathing the fumes from the German cars' exhaust pipes, a phenomenon suggesting that the Mercedes engineers had employed some potent new additive, probably with the capacity of lowering the temperature of the fuel. So affected was Ovodio Capelli, the driver of a privately entered Maserati, that when he stopped at the pits and was handed a slice of lemon to suck and a damp sponge to wash his face, he ate the sponge and wiped his face with the lemon. Less than a lap later he stopped the car, got out, and fainted.

The Mercedes team could hardly believe their own achievement. 'My reception at the pits was incredible,' Lang remembered. 'Neubauer was as pleased as a schoolboy. The mechanics pulled me out of the car to carry me on their shoulders, nearly breaking my legs in the process.' The award of the trophies showed the scale of the honours that had been prepared for the

Italian teams. Not just the main award but the Prince of Piedmont's cup for fastest lap, the Minister of Italian Africa's cup for leading at half-distance, the City of Milan cup for leading after ten laps, the Count Volpi cup for the runner-up, the King of Italy's cup for the winning entrant, and the Duke of Aosta's team cup all went to Mercedes-Benz and their drivers. On the return journey to Naples, Neubauer spent most of his time reading congratulatory telegrams while Meo Costantini prepared to give Enzo Ferrari the details of the unforeseen debacle.

For the Italians, the only good news was that the 1.5-litre Mercedes W165s were never to be seen again. War in Europe was on the horizon, but in any event the impression was given that the cars had been designed and constructed, using the company's vast resources over a period of six months, simply to make a point in Tripoli. At the end-of-season dinner in Stuttgart, Max Sailor, Mercedes' sporting director, made a speech clarifying their philosophy. 'Some people', he said, 'think that motor racing is no longer interesting, because Mercedes-Benz always win. We cannot help this, as we have been winning races for forty years and we do not propose to stop now, whether the formula is for 1.5-litre racing cars, or 4.5-litre sports cars, or whatever the powers that be like to make it. Mercedes, with their forty years of experience and tradition, and the best racing organisation in the world, will be on the starting line.'

Maserati went away to console themselves with the victory of their 8CTF car in the Indianapolis 500, driven by Wilbur Shaw, the first win in the event by a non-American car since 1919. The staff of Alfa Corse merely licked their wounds. A month later at Monza, the talented Mimi Villoresi was killed while testing the latest developments on a 158. Claiming the driver had been ill at the time of the test, Ferrari refused to sanction an insurance payment to the Villoresi family, which angered the dead man's brother considerably. 'Ferrari claimed the accident happened because Mimi had eaten too much,'

Villoresi said. 'It was proved afterwards that the steering had broken, but Ferrari refused to admit it. And that, as you might imagine, introduced a certain air of hostility into our encounters.'

It was only one of the problems afflicting the team. Within months of the Tripoli race, Gobbato told the director of Alfa Corse that his time with the company was over. Wearying of the feud between Ferrari and Ricart, the chairman had sided with the designer. 'I was sacked,' Ferrari said. 'It seemed to me to be the only logical solution to the problem.' As he cleared his desk in Milan and prepared to move back to an uncertain future in Modena, Ferrari was left contemplating the knowledge that a relationship with Alfa Romeo which had begun nineteen years earlier, with his second place in the Targa Florio, and in which hard work and ingenuity had been crowned with moments of exhilarating success, was over for good.

He made the best of it. He would show Gobbato and Alfa Romeo exactly what they had discarded. And he was happy to be home. 'My return to Modena,' he reflected, 'in order to transform myself from a racing driver and a team organiser into a small industrialist, marked not only the conclusion of what I might call an almost biological circle. It represented an attempt to prove to myself and to others that, during the twenty years I was with Alfa Romeo, not all my reputation was gained by the efforts and the skill of others. The time had come to see how far I could get by my own efforts.'

With blackout hoods over their bicycle lamps, Enzo and Dino Ferrari travel
the country roads from their home in Modena to the new factory in
Maranello during the last months of World War II.

Four

In Rome on 1 September 1939, while Hitler's stormtroopers were invading Poland, Mussolini proclaimed Italy's neutrality. Two days later the British and French governments declared war against Germany, and Italy had entered a curious period during which, although its sympathies were in no doubt, it stood aside while much of Europe prepared to tear itself apart.

When Ferrari read, in the newspaper *Il Popolo di Brescia*, that an edition of the Mille Miglia would be held in 1940, he wrote a letter, dated 1 November 1939, to Renzo Castagneto, one of the race's founders, welcoming the news. It was typed on notepaper bearing an old address – on the viale Trento e Trieste, Modena – but the name of a new company: Auto-Avio Costruzioni. Since, thanks to his agreement with Alfa Romeo, he was forbidden to start a car company which used the Ferrari name, he had come up with a new one. There was no sign of the prancing horse on the notepaper. 'Scuderia Ferrari was a joint-stock company,' he wrote, 'and as such it had been liquidated. With the proceeds from that liquidation and my own from Alfa, I founded Auto-Avio Costruzioni in Modena.' As the name suggests, the company's bread-and-butter business was to include the manufacture of aircraft parts. Within a short time, Ferrari had assembled a staff of more than forty employees, including Alberto Massimino, the Turin-born designer who had stayed behind in Modena after working on the Tipo 158. No doubt Ferrari believed that Massimino's spell in the aeronautical industry in the late 1920s would come in useful, given the new company's ambitions. He was joined in the enterprise by a Modenese engineer, Vittorio Bellentani, aged thirty-three, who had been working for a local motorcycle constructor.

In 1938, following a serious accident in the Mille Miglia, the government had announced a ban on open-road racing. A Lancia Aprilia driven by two amateurs from Genoa lost control after going over a level crossing near Bologna and ploughed into the crowd, killing ten people, seven of them children, and injuring a further twenty-three. As a result, in 1939 there had been no Mille Miglia. But a suggestion by Count Giovanni Lurani, one of the leading gentlemen amateurs, interested the organisers. 'Johnny' Lurani's idea was to run the race over a closed circuit measuring just over a hundred miles, around a triangle formed by the cities of Brescia, Cremona and Mantua, very reminiscent of the sort of race which had been held in the region during the early years of the century. Entries would be accepted from unsupercharged sports cars conforming to the Sport Nazionale regulations, which would be required to cover nine laps of the circuit – close enough to the thousand Roman miles of the title.

Soon after the plan had been made public, Ferrari was approached by one of his old customers. A member of an illustrious Modenese clan, the twenty-six-year-old Marchese Lotario Alfonso Rangoni Machiavelli held degrees in law and social and political sciences but worked on his family's estates. He had begun his racing career with a small Fiat before graduating to Alfas, among them one bought from and prepared by the Scuderia Ferrari. The Marchese's idea was that Ferrari might like to build him a car for this new-style Mille Miglia.

Almost simultaneously, Ferrari received another request along the same lines. This one touched his heart, since it came from the son of the late Antonio Ascari, who had been Ferrari's mentor before his death at Montlhéry in 1925. Alberto Ascari was only twenty-one when he visited his father's old friend, but he had already distinguished himself as a motorcycle racer, greatly to the displeasure of his mother, who had sent him to boarding school to try to divert his interest away from the sport that had killed her husband. On leaving school, however, Alberto went to work in his father's old business in Milan, selling Fiats, and increased his involvement in racing. It may well have been with money inherited on his twenty-first birthday – 13 July 1939 – burning a hole in his wallet that he approached Ferrari about the chance of being provided with a car for the Mille Miglia.

After consultations with Massimino and Bellentani, Ferrari offered his two potential customers a design which, to take best advantage of the limited time available, would make use of ready-made components. The new car would be based on the Fiat 508C, an excellent small saloon originally designed by the great Dante Giacosa, father of the Fiat Topolino and, after the war, of the *Cinquecento*. The 508C had an overhead-valve four-cylinder 1,100 cc engine, a four-speed gearbox, an X-braced chassis, and independent front suspension. In fact Giacosa himself had already produced a tuned-up version with a streamlined body, capable of 95 mph, which had taken part in the Mille Miglia races of 1937 and 1938. Ferrari, Massimino and Bellentani proposed taking two of the engines and arranging them end-to-end, creating an eight-cylinder engine with an overall capacity reduced to 1,500 cc, in order to avoid competition with the powerful Alfas in the bigger categories. It would also be eligible for a special cash prize offered by Fiat for the best finish by a car based on one of its designs.

The car, Ferrari decreed, would be called the 815, denoting its eight cylinders and 1.5-litre capacity. He told Ascari that the price for his car would be 20,000 lire. The Marchese's car would be completed to a higher standard of luxury, to be reflected in the invoice. With the agreement of the two customers, given over a celebratory Christmas Eve dinner, the workshop got down to business, ordering an aluminium cylinder block and sump from the Calzoni foundry in Bologna and an alloy body from Carrozeria Touring of Milan. The chassis, the suspension, the transmission, the brakes and the steering would come directly from the 508C, as would valve gear and connecting rods. The crankshaft and the camshaft would be machined by Ferrari's own workmen, who deliberated over the best way to mate the two engines. Massimino and Bellentani were helped by Enrico Nardi, the old Scuderia's last test driver.

At the Touring workshops in Milan, Felice Bianchi Anderloni and his coachbuilders prepared to apply their company's principle – 'Weight is the enemy, and wind resistance the obstacle' – to the two chassis sent by Ferrari, who told them that he wanted 'not just a racing car, but something with a touch of luxury'. It was clear that, by contrast with the earlier creations of the Modena premises, the *Bimotore* and the Tipo 158, he had an eye on a potential market for road cars. In the recollection of Bianchi Anderloni's son, he said, 'I want something that will make people say, "That's a Ferrari,"' which suggested, since the new car could not yet be called a Ferrari, that he had a longer-term scheme already in mind. Touring's designers created a one-tenth scale model and checked its efficiency in a primitive wind tunnel. Their bodies, it was always said, were 'drawn by the wind'. Later they would check the aerodynamic properties of the full-scale body by attaching tufts of wool and photographing their movement as the car travelled at various speeds. For the 815, these tests were carried out on a straight stretch of road near Lainate, between Milan and the lakes. Ascari, who lived in Milan, could not wait for the call from Ferrari to collect the completed car. He called in at the Touring works along with a friend, the motorcycle racer Silvio Vailati – 'We were just passing,' he said innocently – and had his picture taken while sitting in the car outside the offices. When the first car to be completed was taken out of the Modena works and on to the via Emilia for its initial test, the little team of engineers felt euphoric. 'Though I have to say', Ferrari remarked, 'that the joy masked a good deal of trepidation.'

By the time eighty-eight cars turned up in the last week of April to be scrutineered in Brescia's piazza della Vittoria, Italy was moving closer to war. On 18 March, Mussolini had met Hitler at the Brenner Pass in the South Tyrol. On 2 April *Il Duce* ordered all the young men of Italy over the age of fourteen to answer the call to bear arms. Only Italian and German entries contested the last pre-war Mille Miglia. In the class for the biggest cars, four representatives of Alfa Corse – who sent the 2500 model, also with beautiful Touring bodies, for a squad of drivers including Farina and Pintacuda – faced Delages, one driven by Taruffi. Five streamlined BMWs dominated the 2-litre class, one of them a Touring-bodied coupé which had won its class at Le Mans the previous summer. In the category for cars under 1,500 cc, which would be required to complete only eight laps, a gaggle of specials based on Fiats and Lancias were faced by the two brand-new 815 models from the Auto-Avio Costruzioni company of Modena, designed and developed in barely three months. Rangoni, as the Marchese was listed, took the wheel of one, with Nardi as his riding mechanic. In the other, Ascari was partnered by his cousin Giovanni Minozzi, a native of Castel d'Ario, Nuvolari's home village. Aged forty-two, Minozzi had raced with Alberto's father in the 1920s. His experience, it was thought, would temper the tendency towards over-exuberance of a boy half his age.

Sadly, there was little opportunity. The smallest cars set off at four o'clock in the morning of Sunday 28 April, led by a little red Fiat Topolino. Just over an hour later, wearing numbers 65 (Rangoni) and 66 (Ascari), the 815s left the starting line, not on the customary viale Rebuffone near the centre of Brescia, but on the outskirts, on a stretch of avenue where Castagneto had erected a grandstand and a giant leader-board. They set off auspiciously, leading their class at the end of the first lap; Ascari was ahead of Rangoni, a very respectable twelfth and thirteenth in the overall standings as they passed the point, just before Cremona, where Enzo Ferrari had set up a refuelling station. The day was dry, bright and still. Across the flat Padano plain, with its long straight roads, all the cars were setting a pace much higher than expected, and the strain told. On the second lap Ascari was forced to pull out with a broken rocker arm. The Marchese, taking over the lead in the class, lapped steadily for a further 600 miles, edging into the overall top ten before a rear-axle problem sent the second 815 into retirement. The gleaming white Touring-bodied BMW coupé of Huschke von Hanstein and Walter Baumer took the overall victory at an average of over 100 mph, to the dismay of the Alfa Romeo team and the Italian spectators. A Lancia Aprilia inherited the 1,500 cc class win.

In Ferrari's view, the failure of the new cars to live up to their promise was the fault of haste in manufacture, and the two 815s went back to Modena for repairs. The Marchese, an enthusiastic pilot, was soon to join the Italian air force and died during the war while testing a new plane. Eventually Ferrari sent his disassembled car back to the family estate, in boxes. When, after the end of the hostilities, Rangoni's younger brother Rolando came to try to put it back together, he discovered some parts were missing. Where, he asked Ferrari, were the missing bits? Sorry, Ferrari said, but all my car parts were given away during the war. Rolando did the best he could, but was then surprised to get a message from Ferrari, who wanted to buy the car. 'He made me such a ridiculous offer', the new Marchese said, 'that I told him quietly, "My dear Commendatore, when I came to you asking for spare parts, you cut me off with hardly a word. Now you would like me to practically give you the car. I'm sorry, but I have no intention of giving you anything."' According to Rolando, the car was later broken up.

Ascari collected his car, took it home, and sold it in 1943 to Enrico Beltracchini, a fellow Milanese who had taken part in the 1940 race, partnered by Arnaldo Roselli – a member of Ferrari's Tipo 158 design group – in the cockpit of a Fiat 1100 special. Beltracchini competed in the 815 for the first time at Piacenza on 11 May 1947, in the race in which the first car to bear Ferrari's name also made its debut. A handful of undistinguished performances later, Ascari's old 815 started a journey through several further pairs of hands before finding its way into the ownership of a well-known Emilian collector. In 1996, on the eve of the San Marino Grand Prix at the

Autodromo Enzo e Dino Ferrari in Imola, it took its place as the centrepiece of a small exhibition in the piazza Matteoti. The evening sun warmed its immaculate paintwork, the colour of ripening cherries.

Italy finally declared war against Britain and France on 10 June 1940. The announcement was made by Mussolini's Foreign Minister − none other than Galeazzo Ciano, the Count of Cortelazzo, who had donated the Coppa Ciano for the annual race at Livorno. Both Nuvolari and Varzi had received the cup from his hands, driving the Scuderia Ferrari's Alfa Romeos.

The husband of Mussolini's daughter, Edda, and a lover of Wallis Simpson before she took up with the Prince of Wales, Galeazzo Ciano had masterminded Italy's invasion of Albania; but he became opposed to Mussolini's alliance with Hitler, and the success of his arguments had been largely responsible for the declaration of neutrality in 1939. Now, however, Mussolini had his own way. 'With the courage of a jackal at the heels of a bolder beast of prey,' the New York Times thundered, 'Mussolini has now left his ambush. His motives in taking Italy into the war are as clear as day. He wants to share in the spoils which he believes will fall to Hitler, and he has chosen to enter the war when he thinks he can accomplish this at the least cost to himself.' As an exercise in geopolitical public relations, Scuderia Ferrari's Vanderbilt Cup adventure had clearly not exerted a lasting effect. By September, British soldiers in Egypt were fighting Italian armoured units pouring over the border from Abyssinia. In October, Mussolini's troops invaded Greece across the Albanian border, and Italian planes bombed Athens. By December the British were celebrating the capture of Sidi Barani from the Italians, only to discover, two months later, that it had provoked the arrival of Rommel's Afrika Korps in Tripoli.

At forty-two, Ferrari was too old for war service. He had joined the Fascist Party in 1934, and it seems he took out his membership, like many Italians in his position, without any great enthusiasm, more through convenience than conviction. In his part of Italy, after all, communism had made considerable inroads. When the time came for Italy to turn on the occupying German army, it was in the north-eastern provinces of Emilia and Romagna and Friuli and the Veneto that the partisans fought with the greatest vigour. In Ferrari's case, the association with Alfa Romeo must have made a show of Fascist sympathy something of a requirement. Ugo Gobbato, on whom he depended for money and material, was a definite enthusiast. Ferrari was polite to local and national government officials, because it was in his interests. The Scuderia Ferrari's annual magazine used the Fascist calendar, in which 1933, for example, became year XII, and carried photographs of *Il Duce* at the wheel of an Alfa Romeo. 'Our organisation is preparing itself for new international challenges,' Ferrari wrote in his introduction that year, 'confident above all of its own potential, which derives from an initiative that was born, was nurtured and has prospered in the industrial tranquillity created by the *Duce* – an initiative which many have tried to imitate, and which we will work with all our power to perfect and make increasingly worthy of our Fascist homeland.'

When war came, and the manufacture of sports and racing cars was no longer possible, it was natural that Ferrari's company would become a small cog in the war machine, and a profitable one. Under a contract with the Compagnia Nazionale Aeronautica of Rome, Auto-Avio Costruzioni had already begun manufacturing small four-cylinder aircraft engines for use in light trainer aircraft. The Calzoni foundry in Bologna, which had worked on the aluminium block of the 815 engine, produced the castings. The old workshops on the viale Trento e Trieste received rows of new lathes and other specialised machinery. Ferrari's own published version of his industrial metamorphosis describes the role played by Enrico Nardi, his former test driver, in introducing him to Corrado Gatti, the machine-tool manufacturer from Turin, in whose old Modena workshops on the via Emilia the Scuderia had made an early home. Gatti apparently suggested that Ferrari might care to go into the machine-tool business, setting himself up as the manufacturer of hydraulic grinding machines used in the manufacture of ball bearings, machines to which the Jung company of Germany held the patents. Ferrari described how he asked the Germans for a manufacturing licence, but was refused, being told that the machines were too complex and he would need help in installation and maintenance which could not be supplied. But his lawyer reminded him that since the machines were not being made in Italy, there was nothing in Italian copyright law – then and now notably elastic by the standards of other European countries – to prevent him going ahead and making them anyway. 'I therefore set to work in all humility to copy them,' he wrote, tongue firmly in cheek. His copies, he claimed, were so accurate that a leading Italian industrialist wrote to tell him that they worked as well as the originals. And to the side of each was screwed a rectangular metal badge bearing the prancing horse, with the letters SCUDERIA FERRARI and MODENA all but scoured into illegibility.

He was now working closely with Franco Cortese, a gentleman amateur from Livorno who had driven for Alfa Romeo before the war and had attached himself to Ferrari as a kind of roving super-salesman. Then in his late thirties, Cortese apparently introduced Ferrari to the firm of Ernesto Breda, manufacturers of guns, military vehicles and aircraft parts based in the Milan suburb of Sesto San Giovanni, a kind of Italian equivalent of Krupp in Germany or Vickers in Britain. There had been some previous contact between Ferrari and Breda, but not of a military nature: it had been a Breda engineer, Cesare Pallavicino, who designed the streamlined body for the P3 with which Guy Moll won a surprise victory against the Germans at Avus in 1934. Now Ferrari was invited to provide Breda with the grinding machines it needed for the manufacture of machine guns. Other commissions included orders for the manufacture of a reduction-gear unit for use with a Breda engine originally designed for the rail cars, enabling it to be adapted to power an army landing craft. Ferrari caused a fuss (and embarrassed Cortese) by refusing to travel to Milan to sign the contract, insisting that Breda's executives travel to Modena instead – which, after some argument, they did.

In 1942 it was suggested that Ferrari should think of moving his factory to a safer location, away from the urban centre of Modena, which the rail line and other factories made a potential target for Allied bombing. The idea coincided with his own longer-term thoughts. After failing to make a deal for land in the village of Formigine, just to the south of Modena, he settled – with the aid of a friend, Mino Amorotti, who scouted suitable locations – on a nearby hamlet. Its name was Maranello, and he already owned a small piece of land there. Eighteen kilometres south of Modena, it was situated on the via Giardini, a road built by an engineer of that name in the late seventeenth century at the request of Duke Francesco III of Modena as a way of linking his lands with the Duchy of Tuscany; later it became better known as the Abetone road, after the town in the Apennines through which it passed on its route south. Maranello had been occupied in the Bronze Age, the fifteenth century BC, and probably much earlier. In the second century BC its inhabitants, of Ligurian extraction, were overcome by Roman legions, the evidence of their conquerors' success – a kiln and other artefacts – left for archaeologists to discover. A fine sixteenth-century castle replaced a much older one destroyed, along with everything else, in a catastrophic earthquake in 1501. By the mid-nineteenth century the population stood at around a thousand, consisting almost entirely of argicultural workers and artisans. Its position in the foothills of the Apennines made it a favourite holiday destination of Modenese seeking respite from the summer heat and the mosquitoes that came with it. With his growing wealth, Ferrari had already bought himself a country house outside the village.

By the time, in 1942, that he decided to make his new base

there, the population numbered 6,500. Amorotti had found him a farm, the Fondo Cavani, which he decided to buy. At first its owners, Dante and Augusta Colombini, were uncertain. But at a second meeting they accepted Ferrari's offer, and the deal was settled with a handshake over a meal cooked by Signora Colombini. On 30 November Ferrari wrote to the Mayor of Maranello, on notepaper headed both Auto-Avio Costruzioni and, more prominently, Scuderia Ferrari, asking for a licence to build on the property. On 3 December the request was repeated, this time bearing the necessary six-lire stamp, and specifically requesting permission to build a prefabricated shed on the Cavani farm. On 4 December the mayor replied, giving authorisation. A handwritten contract covering the purchase of the Colombinis' property was drawn up by the notary, Ludovico Bassi, and signed on 16 December. The price for the land, which covered two hectares, and the farm building was 78,000 lire, plus 8,060.15 lire in tax and 78.50 lire for the notary's fee.

Since there is no record of Ferrari receiving private financial assistance, and since tales that his business was subsidised by money from his wife's family have long been discredited, it must be assumed that the capital costs came from his own savings, accumulated from the proceeds of his earlier enterprises, including his Alfa severance pay and his income from the sales of machine tools; his solid financial record and good relationships with Trossi's Banco Sella and Modena's Banco di San Geminiano e San Prospero would have helped. On 12 January a second application was made. Like the first, it mentioned the use of the property only for 'agricultural construction work'. It also listed all the properties Ferrari now owned, grouped together around the Abetone road: the Fontanile, Convoglio, Nuovo and San Martino farms, as well as the Fondo Cavani. Together these added up to a total of 306,228 square metres, and comprised almost the whole acreage of the site today covered by the Ferrari factory, the *gestione sportiva* – the racing department – and the Fiorano test track.

Even in 1942, with the war proceeding uncertainly and his destiny apparently tied in with machine tools, Ferrari had bigger aims in view.

It was around this time that Ferrari met Carlo Benzi, the teenage boyfriend of the daughter of the owners of a restaurant at Ubersetto, on the via Giardini between Maranello and Modena. One day in 1944, according to Benzi's account, a German officer wanted to ask Ferrari for some information. Ferrari spoke no German, so young Benzi offered his services as a translator. After the war, when he had taken his accountancy exams, his wife's sister asked Ferrari if he had a job for her young brother-in-law, and he was taken on as an assistant to Gardini, the company's financial manager. Later he became the company administrator, but in 1969, after the Fiat takeover, he left to concentrate his entire attention on Enzo Ferrari's private financial affairs.

Back in July 1943, as the factory took shape on the land across the road from the Cavani farm buildings, the Allies landed in Sicily. Two days later Mussolini was deposed and Italian soldiers began surrendering. In September the Fascist Party was abolished and the Italian government signed a document of unconditional surrender. But German troops marched into Rome, and the former dictator was rescued from an unspecified location. Under a new anti-Fascist prime minister, Marshal Badoglio, Italy had declared war on Germany. The Germans took reprisals, and there were ambushes and executions throughout Emilia. The war memorials in Bologna and Modena, consisting of enamelled postcard-size photographs of martyred partisans, and the plaques describing murders committed by the *nazifascisti* on many street corners in the towns of the region, attest to the scale of the desire to throw the Nazis out. In January 1944 the Allied landings at Anzio, south of Rome, presaged the long and bloody campaign that pushed the Germans up the spine of Italy.

On 4 November 1944 the new Ferrari factory was hit by the first of two Allied bombing raids. In April of the following year the workers were still clearing up the damage caused by the second attack when, in Milan's piazza Loretto, the *Duce* and his mistress, Clara Petacchi, were shot by partisans and hung by the ankles from the frame of a petrol station. A day later, the commanders of what remained of the German army in Italy offered their surrender, via the Archbishop of Milan. But before Italy could begin its reconstruction, a period of cleansing, a settling of scores, had to be endured. Ugo Gobbato, the apostle of Fascist efficiency, was shot dead by an anonymous assassin as he left the Alfa Romeo factory one evening. The carburettor manufacturer Edoardo Weber disappeared – paying with his life, in Ferrari's guarded view, 'for what were perhaps the mistakes of others'.

Test driver Bruno Sterzi swings a 166 Spider Corsa out of the factory yard
in 1948, the second year of production.

Five

On 22 May 1945, a month after the end of the war, Lina Lardi bore Enzo Ferrari his second son. They named him Piero. Even more than the adored Dino, who was now thirteen, Piero was to bear a strong physical resemblance to his father – the hooded, drooping eyes told the story.

The two households were to co-exist. One, the official family, represented his business, its history and, he continued to hope, its future, in the shape of Dino, the designated inheritor of the patrimony, despite his illness. The other offered a daily oasis of tranquillity, a chance to step temporarily out of the world he had made, with its demands and its urgencies and the conflicts that he generated and so relished. The 'agitator of men' could make a detour to Castelvetro during the journey from Maranello to Modena, turning up the narrow, winding road to the red-brick farmhouse where Lina grew cherries and plums and was bringing up Ferrari's second son. He could step from the incessant activity of one to the calm of the other – and then, in the evening, move on to a third plane of existence, the life he shared with his friends, at the Hotel Real or in various restaurants nearby, a man's life in which women occupied a very different role.

'Monogamy does not come naturally to man,' his compatriot Federico Fellini wrote. 'Physically, man is not a monogamous animal. No matter how hard he may try, to be so represents a tyranny over his natural instincts. He must naturally suppress the stirrings within him, which takes more energy than to give in to the drive. The myth is that when people marry, two people become one. It is not so. They are more likely to become two and a half, or three, or more.'

[123]

Twenty years younger than Ferrari, the director of *La Dolce Vita* and *Eight and a Half* was married from the age of twenty-three until his death fifty years later to Giulietta Massina, one of his leading ladies. 'Being a woman,' he observed, giving a view not uncommon among Italian men of the twentieth century, 'she naturally gravitates towards one man, who becomes her universe. Because the human male, on the other hand, is not monogamous by nature, marriage is an unnatural state of being for him. It is a tyranny he tolerates because he has been conditioned from birth to accept it, along with other mal-functioning ideologies we accept as natural law, but which are really only the mandates of men who ceased to exist aeons ago. I have tried for years to explain all this to Giulietta, but she has her own views on the subject, quite contrary to mine and equally implacable.'

Perhaps the nature of Ferrari's ability to function within two stable family relationships, while conducting at least one less formal affair and many transient ones, was clarified by his reaction when an old and close friend announced to him that he was leaving his wife and child for another woman. After the friend had presumptuously drawn a comparison between his situation and that of Ferrari, he found himself cut off for good. In Ferrari's mind, the two situations were not remotely comparable. He was behaving with some sort of honour, although he was too much of a cynic, where human nature was concerned, to use that term. But if he had not lived his life according to the teachings of the Church, then at least he had walked out on no one, and he had built a business that provided for them all.

When he told Franco Cortese, his highly effective travelling salesman, that he was planning to give up making machine tools and return to building sports cars, Cortese's reaction was immediate. '*Lei e matto a perdere un affare come questo,*' he said – 'Only a lunatic would dump a business as profitable as this.' But Ferrari, who had already lived through the painful aftermath of one war, was ready to move on. And since the Auto-Avio

Costruzioni and Scuderia Ferrari enterprise was no longer a limited company with shareholders but a privately owned business, he needed to depend on no one's approval when he decided the time was right to take his first step.

There was little time to waste. Less than a mile away from his apartment on the upper floor of the old Modena headquarters, on the other side of the via Emilia, the surviving Maserati brothers – Ernesto, Bindo and Ettore – had settled into their new premises and were making progress. Although they, too, had spent the war diversifying into peripheral areas, including machine tools, spark plugs, batteries, and electric vans and miniature trucks, they had also continued to work on designs for their next racing cars. Nuvolari had been willing to act as the conduit for secret negotiations with Dr Ferdinand Porsche over the possibility of a collaboration, although the idea had been abandoned. Instead they had raided Ferrari's staff to hire Alberto Massimino to work with Ernesto Maserati. The first fruit of their collaboration was to be seen outside the factory as early as April 1946 – a two-seater sports car with a shapely all-enveloping body and an unsupercharged six-cylinder 1,500 cc engine. By September it was racing.

Ferrari had begun to recruit his lieutenants within weeks of the official end of the war. Luigi Bazzi gladly came back from Milan, where he had spent the war with Alfa Romeo, who were now reduced to manufacturing cheap wood-burning stoves while trying to pick up the threads of the automobile projects planned before 1940 and set aside in favour of military projects. Vittorio Jano was unwilling to leave the safe haven he had found at Lancia after being tossed out of Alfa Romeo in 1938, but Gioachino Colombo, his former assistant, found himself temporarily suspended at the Portello works, while his membership of the Fascist Party was being investigated by a workers' body, the Internal Liberation Committee. Colombo was pleased to pick up the telephone and hear Ferrari's voice inviting him to a meeting in Modena. He later recalled the difficulty of travelling from Milan for the rendezvous, he and his friend Enrico Nardi traversing a war-scarred landscape and queuing for hours in the summer heat to drive their car on to a barge that would carry them across the Po, all the bridges having been destroyed by advancing or retreating armies. As they travelled, Colombo remembered the success of the Tipo 158 and the good times he had enjoyed with the small design team. But when he confronted Ferrari in the old office in the viale Trento e Trieste, the past disappeared. The future was the only item on the agenda.

'Colombo,' Ferrari said, 'I want to go back to making racing cars. I've had enough of utilities. What do you say – how would you design a 1500?'

This was a question for which Colombo had prepared himself. Maserati and Alfa, he pointed out, had eight-cylinder engines, ERA had a six.

'In my view,' he said, 'you should be making a twelve-cylinder.'

To his relief, Ferrari smiled.

'*Caro Colombo*,' he said, 'you've been reading my thoughts.'

Ferrari explained that he had long cherished the idea of building such an engine. He called it 'an ambitious dream', although there was nothing technically novel or adventurous about the decision to produce a V12 engine. The format had long seemed to promise a good blend of relatively compact dimensions and rapid piston speed. Auto Union had done it. Mercedes-Benz had done it. Even Alfa Romeo had done it, under the aegis of Jano – assisted by Colombo, of course – and the detested Ricart. But in the artisan-based culture of Modena, perhaps, it was a different breed of ox. And perhaps Ferrari's claims to have drawn inspiration from the sound of the Packards of US army officers and the Baroness Maria Antonietta Avanzo simply represented a later attempt to add colour to the legend.

But it was certainly significant that the engine came before the rest of the car. 'I have always paid more attention to the engine than the chassis,' Ferrari said, 'struggling to maximise power and engine efficiency in the belief that engine power

[126]

accounted for more than fifty per cent of success on the track.' As he admitted, the first vehicle to bear his name was a perfectly orthodox proposition. 'Our intention was simply to make a conventional engine, but one of exceptional quality,' he said. Later he felt that they had erred too greatly on the side of convention when designing the chassis. As long as they had more power than their rivals, his cars won races. 'However, once our rivals began to catch up with us, certain inadequacies in our chassis started to make their presence felt.' It was a fault which, he later reflected, would take years to work its way out of the company's system.

The first car was called the 125 S, and Colombo made his first drawings during a lunch party at his sister's house to celebrate *Ferragosto*, the religious festival of 15 August. While everyone else stayed at the table, he went out into the garden with a sheet of paper and sketched the layout of an engine with single camshafts and oversquare piston dimensions – in other words, the length of the piston travel was less than the diameter of the cylinder bore, theoretically permitting the engine to turn at higher revs. He was starting with the heart of the car before moving outwards to create the rest of the organism. Back in Milan he borrowed a drawing board from his cousin and sat in his small bedroom, creating the blueprint for the chassis frame and suspension. This was no adaptation of an existing production model, using off-the-shelf parts. This was a car designed from the ground up, with few compromises beyond the need to keep within reasonable budgetary limits. From the very start, therefore, it was a thoroughbred. To hurry the work along, Colombo called on help from Angelo Nasi, another former Tipo 158 man, who was working on diesel engines for Alfa Romeo and was delighted to be asked to draw up a five-speed racing gearbox. Word of the project was getting out, and Colombo received a visit at his apartment from Achille Castoldi, a motor-sports enthusiast who tried, without success, to buy the plans there and then. Instead the designer either took them back to the Maranello factory or sent them by trusted messenger. Colombo's final drawings were a combination of extremely detailed draughtsmanship and, touchingly, a boyish sense of fantasy – a helmeted driver sat at the wheel.

Ferrari's seriousness was immediately evident to Colombo. From the way he was approaching the project, it was obvious that he had it in mind to produce the car in numbers. But Colombo himself was soon in trouble with Alfa Romeo, where the directors had heard of his involvement. Although he was under suspension, objections were raised by activists and were upheld by the rest of the workforce, who – in Colombo's recollection – came close to staging a strike, claiming that he had no business working for an outside body while under investigation. Promised a return to his normal job, and fed the news that the company was thinking of rebuilding the 158s, which had spent the war hidden in a milk and cheese factory, and returning them to the race track, he told Ferrari that he would have to observe the terms of his contract and that his work on the 125 S was therefore at an end.

Among those now devoting their time to the project were Bazzi, Federico Giberti, in charge of purchasing, and Attileo Galetto, the machine-shop manager, plus a handful of influential newcomers, including Aurelio Lampredi, a thirty-year-old engineer, and Luciano Fochi, twenty-one, a draughts-man who had served his apprenticeship at Alfa. In charge of the construction of the prototype was Giuseppe Busso, yet another ex-Portello man, an expert in aero engines with no practical experience of automobiles, never mind racing cars. But Busso moved to Modena from Turin, his home town, with his family, and was made head of the technical office, responsible for injecting urgency into the project when the work went slowly and, as sometimes happened, fell behind schedule, occasionally for the soundest of reasons. When the Gilco company of Milan, who had been asked by Colombo to fabricate the oval steel frame tubes, produced a chassis weighing 56 kg, for example, they were told by Ferrari to take it away and not to come back until they had found a way of reducing it to less than 50 kg. The

[128]

version they eventually produced weighed in at 44 kg.

The work was almost done when, late in 1946, Ferrari received a visit from Luigi Chinetti. A Milan-born wheeler and dealer three years younger than Ferrari, Chinetti had been successful as a driver before the war; his true gift, however, was for making people want to buy things. He had run Alfa Romeo's distribution in Paris, and had switched the focus of his competition career to France in order to help publicise the cars. He set records at Montlhéry, and won at Le Mans in 1932 with Raymond Sommer and in 1934 with Philippe Etancelin. When war broke out he was in the United States, managing a team of Maseratis at Indianapolis, and when the liner *Rex* returned he stayed put, working for the local Rolls-Royce agency and marrying an American woman. In December 1946 they and their infant son flew to Paris on one of the first Lockheed Constellation flights and drove a pre-war Citroën *traction avant* down to Modena, arriving on Christmas Eve. At eleven o'clock that night, Chinetti walked into Ferrari's office.

Although each party later had his own version of what transpired, there can be no doubt that this was one of the more significant meetings of Ferrari's career. Before he had produced a single car, Chinetti wanted to talk to him about selling Ferraris in America. In the account he gave Brock Yates, Chinetti described Ferrari that night as haggard and dispirited, prematurely aged, surrounded in the semi-darkness by photographs and trophies that provided a somewhat ghoulish aura of past glories. The old Scuderia building, Yates wrote, reminded Chinetti of 'a musty tomb', and Ferrari's conversation was full of the 'broken dreams' of a man who appeared to 'dwell in the pathos of the past'. On the other hand, it might be remembered that Chinetti had spent the war in New York, where there were no blackouts or bombs, and where rationing – except of the *de facto* sort experienced by the poor – was unknown. He had also just driven down from Paris, where no bombs had fallen and even the Occupation had not really dimmed the bright lights. Modena's experience of the previous half-dozen years had been rather different. What seemed to Chinetti like terminal exhaustion might in reality have been the early signs of an awakening. And Ferrari might even have been lying doggo, waiting for Chinetti to try to sell him something. Or Chinetti may have been attempting to portray the transformation of Enzo Ferrari by the power of the American dollar as more dramatic than it really was.

But Chinetti had seen the prosperity of America, and he had witnessed the onward march of the consumer society. He had seen how Americans loved to spend money on items of display, and how so many of them loved to establish their superiority over their peers by parading their knowledge of, and access to, European style. He had watched them with their Rolls-Royces and Alfa Romeos and Delahayes and Hispano-Suizas. He had seen, too, how the American racing scene also featured many gentlemen amateurs, most of them keen to own cars with names ending in a vowel. And if it were true, as Chinetti had been told, that Ferrari was in the process of building a car that could be sold to the public, and if it turned out to be a car that embodied the racing heritage with which Ferrari had been associated in the days when he, Chinetti, had raced against the Scuderia, then there were good possibilities for them both.

According to Chinetti, Ferrari took some persuading. Fearful of committing himself wholly to his dreams, he seemed to be wedded to the idea of a partial return to the machine-tool business. Racing would be just a sideline. Chinetti told him that he had no future in an industry which would be dominated, in the post-war climate, by giant concerns. In racing, on the other hand, he could take a lead. And Chinetti would give him a start by promising to sell five cars to America. And if he could make twenty, he would sell those, too.

No doubt some version of this conversation took place, and no doubt Ferrari was encouraged by the thought of a wider market for his cars. He, too, had been a salesman, and he knew the lure of beautiful cars to rich people enjoying good times, or at least the semblance of them. In suggesting that this Christmas

Eve encounter laid the foundation stone of the Ferrari edifice, however, Chinetti may have been guilty of a little dramatic exaggeration.

The engine had already been bench-tested in September 1946, and was found to produce 60 horsepower at a modest 5,600 rpm. Bazzi, the wizard tuner, got to work. In November Ferrari told Cortese to stop trying to sell any more machine tools. The die, so to speak, was cast. In December he called a press conference, at which he announced his intention to manufacture three models – a 125 sport, a 125 competition, and a 125 Grand Prix car.

When the prototype 125 S was eventually ready for testing, Giuseppe Busso was there with his camera. It was 12 March 1947, twenty months after Colombo had arrived in Modena, and the week in which the worst European winter in living memory came to an end. In a photograph that survives from that day Busso captured Enzo Ferrari, in a dark double-breasted suit, a white shirt and a tie, his silvered hair neatly brushed back, sitting at the wheel of the car. It had yet to be provided with bodywork and, reduced to its naked components, it looks distinctly agricultural. The engine sits low in the frame. The air intake for the carburettors snakes over the cylinder heads. The tyres are narrow, the steel-disc wheels crude. Wires protrude from the backs of the dashboard instruments. Ferrari, three weeks past his forty-ninth birthday, is sitting for the first time at the wheel of a car bearing his own name, and is about to start the engine. He looks apprehensive. Behind him stand several young engineers, some in suits, others in overcoats and scarves, mostly smiling, flanked by mechanics in grease-stained overalls, their hands on their hips and their faces full of purpose.

Once he had fired up the little V12, Ferrari drove the car across the cobbles of the yard and out of the gates – a Ferrari swinging out on to the Abetone road for the first time – and pointed it in the direction of Modena, up a long, straight two-lane road. He got as far as Formigine, the nearest village, before turning round and heading back to the factory, a journey of less than ten miles. Back at the factory gates, Bazzi listened hard for the song of the returning engine. After Ferrari switched off the motor, his old comrade made a quick adjustment. Then it was Bazzi's turn to have a go, the second man in the world to drive a Ferrari. Swathed in his raincoat and scarf, he posed for Busso's camera before turning the car out of the gate.

There was still much to be done in the six weeks that remained before the first two cars were due to make their racing debuts. Lampredi, who had fallen out with Busso months earlier, finally made good an earlier threat to resign, and had gone off to work for Isotta Fraschini, leaving the team one experienced man short on the engineering side. But the mechanics, led by Adelmo Marchetti and Stefano Meazza, often worked through the night, while Ferdinando Righetti did the test driving. The competition debut would take place on 11 May at Piacenza, seventy miles from Maranello, and the two cars were completed on time, both with big, square radiator grilles with emphatic horizontal bars, like a giant cheese grater. Nino Farina was allocated a cycle-winged version with a 'cigar' body, while for Franco Cortese there was a more elegant variation with full-width coachwork. Cortese had been recompensed for his sterling wartime work as a machine-tools representative with a contract, signed on 7 April, for test and race driving, giving him a salary of 600,000 lire plus 50 per cent of the prize money. A solid but unspectacular competitor, he would be the ideal man to look after the new car, fast enough to explore its potential without running the risk of prematurely writing it off.

The Circuito di Piacenza was to be a conventional street race for sports cars. Maserati had promised to produce its new model in time for the race, as had Cisitalia, an ambitious new company which was in the process of exploiting Nuvolari's contacts with the Porsche family and was meanwhile producing small, cheap Fiat-based sports and racing cars. Both the Maserati and the Cisitalia, however, failed to appear. This was good news for Ferrari, whose own creation would not be immediately exposed to comparisons. Instead the competition came from a bunch of

Lancia Aprilia specials and a few older Maseratis and pre-war Alfa Romeos, plus Auto-Avio Costruzioni's 815, the ex-Ascari car, driven by Signor Beltracchini.

Enzo Ferrari was not present to see his car in its first race. As had become his firm habit during the 1930s, he stayed at home and waited for the phone to ring. On this occasion the voice on the other end of the line would be that of Federico Giberti, whom he had made his first post-war *direttore sportivo*. The physical distance presumably made it easier for Ferrari to exert his authority. The sentimental explanation, that he really could not bear to see his creations crash or lose, seems highly unlikely given that he was perfectly happy to send them to the scrapyard once their useful life was over, and that his favourite drivers were usually those who dealt the most grievous abuse to his cars in pursuit of glory.

At Piacenza, both Ferraris showed signs of being finished in a hurry. The panel-beating had been rushed, and neither car had a prancing-horse badge on show. After a small accident in practice, in which he spun and hit a kerbstone, Farina decided to pull out, displeasing Ferrari considerably. Cortese was left to fly the flag alone. He started well by setting the fastest practice time over the two-mile course, giving the first Ferrari pole position in its first race; but it was Nino Rovelli, a future petrochemicals magnate, who raced into the lead of the fifteen-strong field in a modified BMW 328. Rovelli pulled quickly away from Mario Angiolini's Maserati and ended the first lap of the scheduled thirty with a considerable lead. But as he took the first bend at the end of the via Farnese for the second time, Rovelli's ambition overruled his judgement and he slid into the straw bales, pieces of his car scattering across the track. Cortese, in the middle of the leading pack, had made a poor start and had a brief scare when his oil pressure dropped, but the problem solved itself and on lap twenty he took the lead from Angiolini, to the delight of Giberti, Bazzi, Meazza, and the rest of the Ferrari crew. But with only three laps left, and with a healthy lead over the Maserati, the engine began misfiring, signalling an imminent terminal malfunction of Cortese's petrol pump and a premature end to his race.

It was, Enzo Ferrari declared, 'a promising failure'. His car had been the fastest of an undistinguished field, although he could not have been particularly pleased that the race had been won by the car of a fellow Modenese whom he had known since boyhood. The laurels were taken by a Fiat-based special produced by Vittorio Stanguellini, whose grandfather invented pedal-tuned tympani for symphony orchestras and whose father had owned the first car in Modena, a 1910 Fiat bearing the registration 1 MO which was said to be one of the cars in which Ferrari himself had learned to drive. Vittorio was a skilled craftsman who had been building specials since before the war. But the difference between his dreams and Enzo Ferrari's could be measured in a word: ambition.

After the 'promising failure', Ferrari invited Colombo to come and take a look at his baby. The engineer was pleased with the way his plans had been executed. What Ferrari really had in mind was an attempt to lure him back into the fold, and he showed good timing: Colombo was about to fall out with Alfa Romeo again, having become embroiled in an ill-fated scheme to market a tiny two-seater sports car, the *Volpe* (Fox), which he had designed in his spare time. When the company failed to deliver cars to more than a thousand people who had believed the publicity campaign and put down deposits, the affair developed into a national scandal and Colombo, who was blameless, was once again relieved to be making the trip from Lombardy to Emilia.

While Ferrari awaited his arrival, two weeks after Piacenza the team travelled down to Rome for the second race of the 125 S's career. It was entered in the *Primavera Romana dei Motori*, as the local motor club called their series of three meetings, scheduled a fortnight apart. At the first of them, on 25 May, Cortese was present, again in the full-width 125 S, for a race to be run over the Terme di Caracalla circuit, laid out on tree-lined roads around the old Roman baths near the city centre. Facing the usual collection of specials and near-antiques, this time Cortese got away cleanly. Fernando Righetti's Fiat-Stanguellini took the lead, but several laps later the driver's mistake at the end of the viale Baccelli allowed Cortese past. He pulled away convincingly, and won with considerable ease from Righetti, whose car also began to suffer from magneto trouble. It was the first win for a car entered under the Ferrari name, and if Cortese was very far from being the most talented driver ever to race for the team, then at least he was someone who possessed an intimate knowledge and understanding of what Enzo Ferrari, back at home waiting for the news, had gone through to reach that moment of success.

Cortese embarked on a busy programme of racing. Within the next few weeks he won at Vercelli, Vigevano and Varese. A return to the baths of Caracalla was not as successful, but it did feature the cigar-bodied 125 S running for the first time without mudguards or lights, as an open-wheeled racing car. And by July, the successes had achieved one interesting effect: they brought Tazio Nuvolari back into the fold.

As soon as the war was over, Nuvolari had jumped into the first racing car he could find. He had been involved with the Cisitalia company, whose founder, Piero Dusio, had taken over the Porsche grand prix project that might have gone to Maserati. Now, at fifty-four years of age, with emphysema ravaging his lungs – the result of inhaling petrochemical fumes over so many years – Nuvolari went to see Ferrari and told him that he was ready to race for the Scuderia again, as long as the money was right. They came to an agreement: he would receive 145,000 lire for two races. At Forli he climbed into the 125 S, with its mudguards and lights refitted, and won a race dedicated to the memory of Luigi Arcangeli, once a Scuderia Ferrari driver. 'Once again', the British magazine *Motor* reported, 'Nuvolari confirmed his inexhaustible qualities as a champion.' That was on 6 July. A week later he was present for the Circuito di Parma, having spent the night before the race judging the Miss Parma contest. The next day, starting from pole position, his engine died on the grid. This inspired one of his most entertaining displays as he overtook fourteen cars in eighteen laps and eventually led Cortese home in the first ever Ferrari one–two. When the crowd engulfed him, he escaped by beckoning Miss Parma into the passenger's seat and leaving on an impromptu lap of honour. 'At the end of that lap', a journalist reported, 'the Ferrari mechanics – using energetic and persuasive methods – extracted him from the car and succeeded in accompanying him to another car and then back to the hotel.'

At the very least, Nuvolari had given wonderful value for his 145,000 lire. Under the terms of his Cisitalia contract he could not return to Ferrari until late August, when he and Cortese were entered for the race on the Montenero circuit at Livorno. Bazzi, out testing Nuvolari's car, was involved in an accident near the factory, breaking a leg and three ribs. Nuvolari took over Cortese's car, but was forced to retire with an attack of the carburation problems that had been regularly afflicting the 125 S. He would not be back in a Ferrari until the spring.

In the meantime Busso, Bazzi and their engineers were working on a supercharged version of the 1.5-litre engine. This would be fitted into a grand prix car with which Ferrari planned to challenge the Alfettas, now reassembled and about to make their return with a formidable trio of former Scuderia Ferrari drivers in Farina, Trossi and Varzi – who had recovered from his addiction to morphine and married the woman he had been with before falling for Ilse Pietsch – plus Jean-Pierre Wimille, a gifted Frenchman who had won the last post-war Le Mans race for Bugatti. But things were not going well for the Ferrari men. Colombo's adaptation of his own engine could not be made to produce a decent amount of power. Giulio Ramponi, an old friend from the pre-war days who had been working in England, came visiting and brought a set of 'thinwall' crankshaft bearings, manufactured in London under an American patent by the industrialist Tony Vandervell. They allowed the engine to rev more freely, but its output was still unimpressive.

Knowing that the Maserati brothers were about to launch a new 2-litre sports car, Busso enlarged the 125 engine to 1.9 litres, and a pair of cars took part in a race in Modena, at which both teams would be fighting for a home victory. Colombo was invited down from Milan, and was horrified when he saw Busso's modifications to the car's suspension. 'It's all wrong,' he exclaimed. 'I'll fix it myself.' He did, and Busso went into a sulk which ended later in the year with his departure back to Alfa Romeo. But the modifications availed the team nothing in front of their home-town crowd; the new Maseratis of the great friends Alberto Ascari and Luigi Villoresi pulled away to an easy victory over the new Ferrari 159s. Cortese briefly got between the Maseratis, but was forced to retire. The race was stopped prematurely after Giovanni Bracco's Delage hit Cortese's stationary car, sending the two cars into the crowd, killing two spectators and injuring others – the first fatal accident involving a Ferrari, albeit an immobile one. Fernando Righetti, hardly an ideal replacement for Nuvolari, could finish no higher than fifth, and the Scuderia Ferrari had been humbled by an important rival.

Revenge, of a sort, came quickly. For the first post-war Turin Grand Prix, two weeks later, Raymond Sommer returned to the Scuderia to drive a 159 which had been the recipient of further attention from Colombo. Sommer, now forty-one, had won the Spa 24 Hours for the team in 1936 and raced single-seaters for it the following year. According to Colombo, he took his payment in the form of cars which he took home and raced in France. On the grid at the Valentino Park circuit, a mechanic was still working on Sommer's car a few seconds before the start. When the flag fell, Ascari and Villoresi took off from the front row in their low-slung Maseratis and threatened to repeat the treatment handed out to Ferrari at Modena. Both Maseratis, however, retired early with transmission trouble, leaving Sommer to take the victory. The team had now won races with two different models.

[137]

In Ferrari's account of the race's aftermath, he tells us that he went to find the bench on which he had sat on a winter's day shortly after the end of the Great War, with the words of Diego Soria, that there was no job for him at Fiat, ringing in his ears.

'Now', he said, 'I went and sat on that same bench. The tears I shed that day, though, were of a very different kind.'

Tempting as it may be to see this as an example of Ferrari's talent for morbid self-mythologising, there must have been a certain emotional truth in his story. Coming to the end of his first season of racing with cars bearing his own name, he had recorded a decent number of victories and only one serious defeat. This achievement was of a very different order from those of the pre-war years, when he had been able to rely on Alfa Romeo's technology and the financial support of trade sponsors. Now, like many others, he was scuffling to find a foothold in a world still reshaping itself after a long and traumatic convulsion. He had advantages, including his own capital and his excellent contacts, not to mention the weakness of the vast majority of the opposition; but he was nevertheless managing to win races with cars that were not yet remarkable in design or performance, and he was pushing hard for improvement.

Lured by the perfume of glamour and victory, customers began arriving at Ferrari's door. Milanese counts and a White Russian prince were the first to scent the possibility that these little cars from Maranello, produced by a workforce now numbering 250, would become objects of widespread desire. The brothers Gabriele and Soave Besana, Lombardy aristocrats, are credited with the distinction of being the first customers for a Ferrari car, ordering a 166 Spider Corsa – the company's new model – at the end of 1947. That same year the Russian (or, to be more precise, Lithuanian) Prince Igor Troubetzkoy had married Barbara Hutton, the granddaughter of F. W. Woolworth and the inheritor, in 1933, of fifty million of the great shopkeeper's dollars. The fourth of the seven husbands who helped her to spend her way through the fortune, Prince Igor was stateless and penniless, and unlucky enough to encounter Barbara during her first period of addiction to pills and hashish. He was one of the few who did not abuse her in some way, but he was not the only one for whom she bought a Ferrari – merely the first. He, too, placed his order for a 2-litre 166.

Now Ferrari and Bazzi no longer needed to give each new car a try. Bruno Sterzi was the test driver, easing the cars out on to the via Giardini through a narrow gateway built into one corner of the factory buildings, where a rectangular shield with the prancing horse and the name 'Ferrari' was mounted next to the arch. Through this gate came the customers whom Ferrari, in later years, would unsentimentally divide into three categories: the sportsmen, the fifty-year-olds, and the exhibitionists. Troubetzkoy seems to have been in the first category. 'Some of these customers actually do take part in competitions with their cars', Ferrari wrote, 'and may continue to take an interest in motor sport for quite a number of years if they do not give it up after the first event or two'. Troubetzkoy, however, could claim the distinction of having taken part in Ferrari's first victory in a major international race when he and Clemente Biondetti won the first post-war Targa Florio on 3 and 4 May 1948, in a 166 Spider fitted with neat full-width bodywork by the coach-builder Allemano.

It is a matter of conjecture how much actual driving Prince Igor did as the pair dashed around Sicily's 600 miles of perimeter road, an old Giro di Sicilia route used because, of all the island's highways, these had been the least damaged during the Allied campaign to take the island, and had therefore been the most quickly repaired. Biondetti, a wealthy Tuscan, was a road-racing specialist, and surely took the lion's share of time at the wheel on the anticlockwise route, which started and finished in Palermo. But in the twelve hours and twelve minutes which they took to complete the course, at an average speed of 55 mph, the prince is likely to have had at least a brief spell of glory, possibly on the flat-out stretches of the return leg near Cefalù. They finished a mere sixteen minutes ahead of Taruffi in a Cisitalia 202 alloy-bodied coupé, a car that was to become a classic of Italian aesthetic principles, powered by an engine of only 1,100 cc, giving barely half the power of the Ferrari.

And a month after the Targa Florio, the team won its second international success in a race that was to go down as the most dramatic single event in Tazio Nuvolari's long career. The Flying Mantuan had been expected to race a Cisitalia in the 1948 Mille Miglia, but the car destined for him was damaged in a testing accident and he was told that there was no replacement. A call to Enzo Ferrari and a visit to Maranello produced a choice of two cars: a Spider Corsa with cycle mudguards and a distinctive horseshoe-shaped radiator grille destined for Prince Igor, or a Berlinetta coupé bodied by Allemano. With Troubetzkoy's blessing, Nuvolari chose the open car, while Clemente Biondetti was left with the Berlinetta. Nuvolari had spent the winter in a convent on Lake Garda, hoping to improve the condition of his lungs, and no one was prepared to tell him that, at fifty-five years of age, he should be relaxing at home in Mantua. His second son, Alberto, had died of kidney disease in 1946, aged eighteen. Nuvolari was tired of everything in his life, but ending his racing career did not seem to be the answer. He didn't know how to stop. Decimo Compagnoni, his old mechanic, had opted for retirement after the war, and warmly recommended his friend to do the same. But still Nuvolari drove, and sometimes drove on with flecks of blood on his lips, the evidence of his ruined lungs. More than ever, racing seemed to be both holding his life together and bringing it to a close.

As had happened the previous year, the Mille Miglia was run in a clockwise direction, featuring a shortened route along the Adriatic coast and an extension of the return leg to take in a visit to Turin. With Sergio Scapinelli, a Ferrari mechanic, by his side, Nuvolari was in contention from the start. Ascari led in his Maserati, but retired at Padua. Cortese led in the third Ferrari, but stopped with a broken gearbox. Consalvo Sanesi and Franco Rol, in the fast experimental Alfa Romeo coupés, both crashed. Taruffi's Cisitalia was finished. When Nuvolari reached Ravenna, he was in the lead.

By the time he got to Rome, however, having slithered up and down the Passo della Somma on his way through the Abruzzi mountains, the car was beginning to fall apart. As he pulled into the Rome checkpoint, where fuel and fresh tyres were waiting, it could be seen that the left front mudguard was missing, lost when he swiped a wall or an earth bank. Its engine cover had also disappeared; first it had come loose, then it blew away down a mountainside. The crowd pressed round the Ferrari as he pulled up. Eager faces bent to greet him. An Italian radio reporter pushed a microphone into the cockpit. Nuvolari's eyes, however, were staring down some invisible tunnel.

He drove on with a kind of fury, as though trying to exorcise all the tragedies of his life. On the Raticosa and Futa passes, his seat began to come adrift. He threw it away, and sat on a bag of oranges and lemons. At Bologna, three-quarters of the way round the route, he had an astonishing lead of twenty-nine minutes over Biondetti – who, ironically enough, was practically choking to death from the fumes penetrating the Berlinetta's closed cockpit. The entire population of Italy, listening to the radio commentary, now believed that the great man was going to win. Only the straight, flat roads of Lombardy and Piedmont remained. Nothing could stop him, not even a car that was progressively disintegrating.

Some claimed that when he reached Modena a priest was told to stand in the road to make him give up. No use. By Reggio nell'Emilia his rear brakes had packed up. And then, approaching the Villa Ospizio refuelling stop, with less than 200 miles of relatively easy running to go and all his rivals eliminated, a leaf-spring bolt, weakened when the car smashed over a pothole, suddenly sheared. Nuvolari kept the car on the road and brought it slewing to a halt at the point where Enzo

Ferrari was waiting. The driver wanted to carry on, but they both knew his race was over.

'Don't be downhearted, Tazio,' Ferrari said, 'we'll do it again next year.'

'At our age, Ferrari,' the driver replied, 'days like this don't come along too often.'

Nuvolari walked to the parish church and asked the priest for a bed. It was four o'clock in the afternoon. After two hours' sleep, he was ready to go home. His last ride for Ferrari would come the following month, at Mantua, his home town, where he started from the front row in the Coppa Alberto e Giorgio Nuvolari, a race dedicated to his dead sons. He led from the start, perhaps by general agreement; but after seven of the fifty laps, after he had been overtaken by Felice Bonetto, his incessant coughing forced him to give up.

The 1948 Mille Miglia would always be remembered for Nuvolari's heroic ordeal, but when Clemente Biondetti brought the Berlinetta to victory at an average speed of 75 mph it meant that the Ferrari team, almost exactly a year after its debut, had now won two of the world's three most famous sports-car endurance classics.

Back at the factory, the mechanics started making a list of all the bits that were missing from Troubetzkoy's Spider Corsa. Two weeks later Prince Igor was in the car and on the starting grid for the first post-war Monaco Grand Prix. In a race featuring the Maseratis of Farina, Ascari and Villoresi, he had to be content with a role among the supporting cast. Nevertheless he ran steadily until he crashed at the chicane on the fifty-eighth lap, by which time he had made his mark on history as the driver of the first Ferrari to enter a grand prix – even if it was not actually a grand prix car.

Troubetzkoy's car also earned another distinction when, a fortnight later, in the hands of Clemente Biondetti, it won the Stockholm Grand Prix, the first victory by a Ferrari outside Italy. This was, to say the least, a hotly disputed affair, since the driver listed as B. Bira – otherwise Prince Birabongse of Siam –

had clearly won the race with an exuberantly aggressive drive in a Gordini, only to be disqualified for leaving the circuit before the prizes had been awarded.

Although the success of the sports cars was generating plenty of interest among potential customers, for Ferrari the priority was to make his mark on the grand prix world. Having resisted Busso's attentions, Colombo's original V12 design was barely responding to the ministrations of its originator. Nor did the chassis design of the grand prix car, known as the 125GPC, seem promising. Alfa Romeo, on the other hand, were back in strength, entering the season with a developed version of the Tipo 158 and a team of drivers led by Varzi, with Trossi and Wimille joined by Consalvo Sanesi, who had replaced Farina. Maserati, too, had a promising new model, the 4CLT/48, a slender little car developed by Alberto Massimino and driven by the talented and harmonious team of Ascari and Villoresi.

Alfa Romeo's supremacy seemed obvious. Then, on the eve of the season's opening grand prix, Varzi was killed during a practice session on the Bremgarten circuit in Berne. While following Wimille, his Alfetta had spun on the rain-slicked surface during a zig-zag descent, hit an earth bank, and overturned. It was 1 June. His widow, Norma, persuaded the team not to withdraw but to stay and race. The funeral took place six days later in the little church of San Giuseppe in Galliate. Varzi was buried with his helmet, his goggles and his steering wheel. 'He's gone,' Tazio Nuvolari said. 'Now it's time for me to go, too.'

Didi Trossi, the Scuderia's old chairman, won the Swiss Grand Prix, but not long afterwards was diagnosed as suffering from lung cancer, and within the year he, too, was dead. 'He was a man on whom drama made no more impact than water on a duck's back,' Ferrari remembered, 'and he was a great driver.'

After Wimille had won at Rheims in an Alfa, the third race of the season was scheduled to be held on 5 September at Valentino Park in Turin, a place of some significance to Enzo Ferrari, although it must have been a coincidence that this was where his cars made their full grand prix debut. Colombo and his staff completed three 125GPCs, to be driven by Farina, Sommer and B. Bira, the Siamese prince, one of three Eton-educated brothers and a name well known to habitués of Brooklands and Donington Park, where he had raced ERA *voiturettes* and a Maserati grand prix car before the war. The reason for Bira's sudden and brief appearance in the Ferrari team, at the age of thirty-four, is unknown. Perhaps he paid for the drive; more likely, he had turned up in Modena on a shopping trip and shown an interest in ordering a car. His talent, though, was not in doubt.

Farina had tested the car on the circuit before dawn in the week before the meeting, but compared with the Alfas and Maseratis it looked heavy and clumsy. The race was run in pouring rain and Farina, driving in front of his home-town crowd, was soon out with a damaged radiator after going off the road. Bira's transmission broke, but Sommer, having qualified third, kept up with the leading group and finished behind Wimille's Alfa and Villoresi's Maserati. To earn a podium position in the team's first grand prix, against proven and highly developed designs from their two major competitors, was hardly a negligible start.

Seven weeks later over the circuit along the banks of Lake Garda, in a minor meeting against less exalted opposition, Farina took the 125GPC to its first victory. At Monza, Sommer and Farina started from the second row but an asthma attack halted the former and the latter's gearbox broke. On their home track, the Alfa Romeos finished in the first four places. Bira was back in the team at the Penya Rhin Grand Prix on Barcelona's Pedralbes circuit, but his transmission failed while he was in the lead, as did Farina's. Julio Pola, a local man, blew up the engine of the third car.

Abbreviated as it may have been, Ferrari's first grand prix season contained important lessons. The team needed a settled line-up of drivers, and a much better car. And during the winter came Alfa Romeo's announcement that, preoccupied with launching new road cars, and concerned about the expense of maintaining Alfa Corse, it would not be participating in grand prix racing the following season.

In Argentina, the new President Perón saw motor racing as a way of giving his supporters entertainment. In the winter of 1948–49 his government offered financial inducements to the Italian teams to ship their cars and drivers across the Atlantic for a series of races called the *Temporada*. Alfa, on the brink of withdrawal, declined. Enzo Ferrari, however, sensed not just a quick payday but a commercial opportunity. So did Count Omer Orsi, now in full control of Maserati following the end of the brothers' contract. Both sent teams. What they encountered was a man who would shape their future.

Juan Manuel Fangio was already thirty-six years old, and a veteran of several seasons in the local version of long-distance road racing, known as *turismo carretera*, in which stripped-down and heavily modified American coupés competed over vast distances in events that lasted for days on end. The Gran Premio del Norte, for example, covered 5,920 miles from Buenos Aires to Lima and back, through the Bolivian Andes. Fangio, the son of an accordion-playing house painter who had emigrated from the Abruzzi as a child in the late nineteenth century, had won that marathon in 1940 in his Chevrolet, and several other major races besides. He had also starred in the *mecanica nacional* formula for single-seaters, in a Chevrolet special, built to resemble an Italian grand prix car as closely as possible. When the European grand prix teams first arrived, in the winter of 1947–48, he had made a good showing in a real Maserati against the likes of Farina, Villoresi and Varzi. That summer the state paid for him to try his luck on the old continent. In San Remo, Varzi had recognised him and taken the trouble to invite him to lunch at his family's house in Galliate. He had been at Berne when Varzi died, and attended the enormous funeral. A few weeks later, at a reception in Paris, Jean-Pierre Wimille put an arm around his shoulder and told the correspondent of *L'Equipe*: 'This is the man you'll be writing about one day.'

When the 1949 *Temporada* opened in late January, with the Gran Premio Juan Domingo Perón, Fangio was equipped with a new Maserati. Ascari and Villoresi represented the works team. Farina was in the sole 125GPS Ferrari, now fitted by Lampredi with a supercharged 166 engine ('It was the sort of technical immorality Enzo Ferrari prided himself on,' Colombo sniffed). He was accompanied by a single mechanic, Stefano Meazza. In the absence of Alfa Romeo, Wimille was entered in a little Simca-Gordini. The race was to be held over a circuit in and around Palermo Park, which separates the centre of Buenos Aires from the banks of the River Plate estuary. At half past seven in the morning on the first day of practice, Wimille went out in his Simca-Gordini. On his third lap, as he approached the fast Golf Club curve on the Avenida de los Ombues, something happened. Perhaps a dog ran into the road. Perhaps a pedestrian had not understood the closure signs. Perhaps Wimille was momentarily blinded by the low morning sun. He lost control at high speed, crashed, and died minutes later on the way to hospital. Villoresi, Farina, Ascari and Fangio were among his pallbearers at a funeral service in the Recoleta cemetery.

Three hundred thousand fans turned up for the race, in which Ascari and Villoresi came first and second, with Fangio fourth. Farina, whose car had been fitted with a 1.2-litre engine (presumably from a non-Ferrari source) after a last-minute emergency, retired with a broken supercharger. A week later, in the Gran Premio Eva Duarte Perón, he hit a kerb and damaged a hub. But the following week in Rosario, after Meazza added lead ballast to the tail of his car in accordance with instructions received in a telegram from Maranello, Farina won a convincing victory. His car broke again, however, in the fourth and final race of the series, in Mar del Plata, where Fangio won, beating Ascari and Villoresi fair and square under the eyes of a crowd including 30,000 jubilant supporters who had made the thirty-five-mile journey from Balcarce, his home town.

[146]

From Argentina, Enzo Ferrari sent Farina and the little team north to Brazil, where the car retired from a race at Interlagos, outside São Paulo, but won on the tricky circuit at Gavéa, in Rio. The cars were sold, as were two more of the old 125GPSs, this time to England, where they were bought by Peter Whitehead, an amateur driver, and by Tony Vandervell, whose bearings had improved the performance of Ferrari's engines. Vandervell had become involved in the publicly funded British Racing Motors project, an attempt to create a genuinely competitive British grand prix car. It would be useful and instructive, he felt, if the BRM's designers could have a close look at what Italians were up to. Unfortunately they chose to go in the opposite direction, building a highly complex V16 whose repeated failures eventually turned the car into a national embarrassment. Vandervell said goodbye to BRM, painted his Ferrari green, and campaigned it as the 'Thinwall Special', promoting his brand of bearings while using it as a test-bed for developments which would emerge within a few years as his own team of Vanwall grand prix cars.

Once the Italian teams were back in Europe, Ferrari lost no time in making strenuous efforts to hire Ascari and Villoresi, the best pair of drivers available. He called Villoresi, the older of the two friends, and invited him to Modena for a meeting in his apartment above the old workshops. When Villoresi arrived, Ferrari was lying down and pretending to be asleep, his hands folded across his chest. Villoresi said nothing. Ferrari did not move. This went on for several minutes. 'Enough of this nonsense,' Villoresi said. 'I'm off.' And then, as if by magic, Ferrari woke up. The two men settled their old differences over the insurance claim following Mimi Villoresi's fatal crash. Deals were made for both Ascari and Villoresi, each of whom would receive a monthly salary of 100,000 lire plus 50 per cent of all starting and prize money. Towards Ascari, whose father he had admired, and who had come to him for a Mille Miglia car in 1940, Ferrari nurtured a genuine affection. When it came to Villoresi, however, his opinion was altogether brisker. 'Gigi

Villoresi was a true champion in style and passion and was Milan's favourite son for many years,' he wrote. 'Resourceful, with a malicious intelligence, he knew how to take advantage both of his car's strengths and his colleagues' failings, a skill he exploited with ruthless efficiency.'

Ascari and Villoresi made their joint Ferrari grand prix debuts at Spa, too many refuelling stops costing them victory as they came in second and third behind the old and slow but fuel-efficient 4.5-litre Talbot of Louis Rosier. Colombo was trying hard to provide the new driving team with more effective cars, revising the suspension and developing a modified engine with twin camshafts, but the future was drifting out of his control. Aurelio Lampredi had returned to the company, and had set to work on another kind of engine altogether: an unsupercharged V12 of 4.5 litres which he believed might be the way forward. Ferrari, noting the Talbot's reliability and frugality at Spa, and wondering what might have happened if it had actually been fast as well, gave his guarded approval. The two designers were clearly working on divergent paths, and only one could prevail. The company, now employing 250 people, was apparently big enough to accommodate such duplication of effort, as long as it produced results.

Ferraris were also starting to make headway with the group of hedonistic celebrities and partygoers which had come to be known as the jet set. The neo-realist film director Roberto Rossellini was among the early converts, and in 1949 became the first of his kind to make the pilgrimage to Maranello. Enzo Ferrari was happy to see him, and even happier that he had brought along Ingrid Bergman, for whom Rossellini had just left another actress, Anna Magnani. Bergman had abandoned her Swedish husband and three daughters to take up with the director, causing an international scandal. They would be married in 1950, as soon as the divorce papers cleared the courts, but Ferrari's delight at being close to such a dramatic affair is clearly visible in the photographs taken around the restaurant table.

Now, too, young Dino Ferrari was starting to be seen more regularly around the company's yard. At seventeen, with his father's encouragement, he was showing a keen interest in the technical side of the business. As a student at the Corni Institute of Technology in Modena, he was being taught by Sergio Scapinelli, a local man who had joined Scuderia Ferrari in 1937 aged seventeen, and had worked on the 1940 Mille Miglia cars. In 1948 Scapinelli had been chosen by Enzo Ferrari to partner Nuvolari in the Mille Miglia. Now he was passing on his knowledge to a new generation. In the workshops at Maranello Dino would watch the engineers and sometimes ask them questions which were met with patient and careful explanations of what they were up to. When the cars were tested he was often there in the background, a handsome, dark-haired boy, as tall as his father, standing in the shadows of the Monza pits or smiling with sudden pleasure as a single-seater was rolled out through the gates and fired up for a blast down the Abetone road, scattering chickens and cyclists with the scream from its engine. But the symptoms of his mysterious illness had begun to worsen. A boy who had loved cars and speed from birth, who had cycled happily from Modena to Maranello alongside his father on bright spring days, suffered from symptoms including kidney infections that were turning into nephritis, a chronic condition. Enzo Ferrari remembered one of his mother's proverbs, the wisdom of a widow whose husband and elder son had gone to miserably premature deaths. 'He who has good health', she used to say, 'is rich without even knowing it.'

Ascari started to win races in the old 125GPC, taking the Swiss Grand Prix, his first proper grand prix victory, followed by the *Daily Express* Trophy at Silverstone. After Lampredi had lengthened the wheelbase and added a two-stage supercharger to Colombo's engine, significantly improving the power, Ascari took full advantage at Monza and led the Italian Grand Prix from flag to flag, winning so convincingly that Farina, thoroughly outpaced in his Maserati, simply gave up in disgust. The cars now had radiator grilles in which the longitudinal bars of the old cheese grater were joined by vertical strips, creating the effect of an aluminium egg crate. This was to become the characteristic 'face' of the early Ferraris, helping to create an image so powerful that, more than half a century later, road-car designers were still using it as a styling resource when they needed to make a family saloon look more rakish and sporty.

Since entries for the grand prix races were so scanty and of such variable quality, thanks to the absence of Alfa Romeo and the failure of BRM and Cisitalia-Porsche to make their promised appearances, the idea of a second category reasserted itself. The new Formula Two would be run for unsupercharged 2-litre cars, producing bigger fields by allowing firms such as Ferrari and Maserati to create machines based around their existing sports cars. Eight such cars were ready in time for a race at Monza, where Fangio, making his first appearance in a Ferrari, won from Bonetto, Ascari, Cortese and a Brazilian, Chico Landi, all in cars built in Maranello. Fangio's car was one of two ordered by Perón's government on behalf of the Automobile Club of Argentina, for the standard price of $11,000 (then about £3,000) each. When the driver and his companions from the ACA got to Maranello, however, they were surprised to discover that the 166 F2 had not been painted in the Argentine racing colours of blue and yellow, as had been requested. Well, they were told, that must be because no one has paid for it yet. After much discussion, the matter was referred to Ferrari, who agreed to accept an IOU from the club officials, albeit at some cost to their nerves, since they would now be personally responsible for accident damage. The car was painted in the required livery and Fangio won the race. Eventually the money was paid and both cars were shipped off to Buenos Aires, where Fangio campaigned them in the next *Temporada*.

Installed in the sports cars, the 2-litre engine was beginning to provide the company's bread and butter. Following negotiations with Felice Bianchi Anderloni at Touring, Enzo Ferrari published a brochure advertising the availability of two variations on the 166 theme, an open *barchetta* (little boat) called the MM Spider and a coupé to be known as the Inter, both with bodywork built according to Touring's *superleggera* method, using light aluminium panels shaped and beaten and then laid over a network of thin-gauge tubing, providing both rigidity and lightness. With the open car, in particular, Anderloni had found an elegant resolution to the problem of clothing a rather stubby basic form without descending to effete decoration. The car was both chic and purposeful, as befitted a machine intended for road and track. When the designer died, as the prototypes were being prepared, his son took over, with a negligible difference to the output of the company – an example of the sort of family continuity that Enzo Ferrari would have looked forward to emulating with his own son, had illness not been casting a shadow over Dino's future.

Late in 1948 the two Touring-bodied 166 models were shown at the Turin auto show, where they created a sensation. While their racing heritage was explicit, they were both finished in such a way as to suggest an unexpected degree of luxury. With their leather upholstery and their heaters and wind-up windows, they were eminently suitable for a Saturday-afternoon cruise along the via Veneto or the rue de Rivoli. Nevertheless their suitability for racing was not in question, and in May 1949 Clemente Biondetti drove a 166 MM to victory in the Mille Miglia, his fourth consecutive victory in the race and Ferrari's second. Behind him was Felice Bonetto. Taruffi, in the third factory car, was leading at Ravenna, two hours from the finish, when his transmission broke. A second Mille Miglia was nothing in publicity terms, however, compared to what happened on the weekend of 25–26 June, when a Ferrari made its first appearance at Le Mans.

Luigi Chinetti had stayed in close touch with Enzo Ferrari after their Christmas Eve meeting, constantly emphasising his ability to sell cars in the United States, where the Sports Car Club of America was starting to run a programme of races for amateurs almost universally equipped with European machinery. With Lord Selsdon, a British amateur, he had won the 12 Heures de Paris at Montlhéry in a 166SC which he then sold for $9,000 to Briggs Cunningham, the Procter and Gamble heir who ran a racing team of his own. That made Cunningham the first American to take delivery of a Ferrari. Chinetti also bought the *barchetta* exhibited at the Turin show, which went to Tommy Lee, a Los Angeles car dealer who thus became the proud owner of the first Ferrari in California.

But Chinetti had an even more important role to play when he took his place among the forty-nine starters in the first Le Mans 24-hour race since the war. The rules had been amended to accept prototypes, and there were two Ferraris present: his own, again shared with Lord Selsdon; and another 166 in the hands of two Frenchmen, Jean Lucas and 'Ferret' (a pseudonym hiding the identity of one Pierre-Louis Dreyfus). Two big Delahayes took the lead, to the delight of the majority of a crowd estimated at 200,000, but Chinetti kept the Ferrari in contention throughout the evening and into the night, long after the French Ferrari had crashed and retired. Before dawn on Sunday morning, with the Delahayes out of the picture, Lord Selsdon took over; but after a break of barely an hour the voracious Chinetti, just a month short of his forty-eighth birthday, was back at the wheel. He had, after all, won the race twice before the war; no one had a better idea of what it took to succeed in this extraordinary event. Pressed by a pair of Delages and a Frazer-Nash, he was forced to compensate for a slipping clutch in the final hours of the race, but when he crossed the line – 'at touring speed', according to a witness – he was still a lap ahead of his nearest pursuer, having driven for almost twenty-three hours. The winners received the Coupe du Président de la République from the hands of the President himself, Vincent Auriol.

Considering the ostensible value of his contribution to setting up an American market for Ferrari, Chinetti was to receive remarkably short shrift in Enzo Ferrari's memoirs. A couple of terse sentences, in connection with the visit of the US presidential candidate Adlai Stevenson to Maranello, do little more than record Chinetti's existence. The uncharitable con-clusion would be that Ferrari hated the idea of the commercial success of his road cars overshadowing their performance on the track, and that he was not keen to share the credit for his company's success, particularly with a man who may have spotted an opportunity before it had occurred to him. At any rate, there could be no doubt that Chinetti's drive at Le Mans, besides giving Ferrari a clean sweep of the major European long-distance races, had increased the reputation of the com-pany's cars not just for speed but for reliability. Ferrari's sports cars, it seemed, were thoroughbreds with staying power, a com-bination that was beginning to be irresistible to those with money to spend in a post-war world emerging from austerity and getting ready for a boom.

But something urgently needed to be done about the grand prix cars, and Aurelio Lampredi, beginning tests of his new 4.5-litre engine, was already doing it. 'Ferrari is a man who instils enthusiasm into those around him,' Lampredi said, 'but he is no technician.' At a staff meeting, Ferrari announced that Lampredi would take sole responsibility for the next season's campaign. Colombo was furious, and harsh words were followed by threats of resignation, at which point Ferrari threatened to send the police to the designer's lodgings in Modena to make sure that when he left the company he would not be in possession of its precious blueprints. When Colombo continued to protest, Ferrari picked up the phone and placed a call to Modena's chief of police, whom he asked to institute such action unless Ferrari personally issued an instruction to the contrary within the next few minutes. Colombo gave what was described as a 'contemptuous' reply, but the call was made and the search did not take place. The entire staff, including the designer, went out to dinner to toast the new arrangement. The following day the two men met in private and Ferrari told Colombo that, from 1950, he would be responsible only for sports and grand touring cars. Clearly this was a blow to Colombo's pride, although in his writings he softened the impact, and even praised his employer for his far-sightedness in recognising that unsupercharged engines were the way to proceed, so that Ferrari was 'dressed and ready to go' when the moment came. As for Colombo's new job, 'By this well-balanced decision Ferrari ensured my continuing collaboration, and the experience of a well-proven designer, while avoiding situations that might prove to be embarrassing.'

The next playboy to get his hands on a Ferrari was in a class of his own. When Porfirio Rubirosa took Doris Duke as his third wife, she celebrated the wedding by giving him an eighteenth-century château on the rue de Bellechasse near Notre-Dame, a private aircraft, half a million dollars in cash, and five Ferraris. Rubirosa, the son of a Dominican general, was forty years old and extremely notorious. In his twenties he had seduced Flor de Oro Trujillo, the seventeen-year-old daughter of his country's dictator. The day they married was declared a national holiday. But he accepted diplomatic postings to Berlin and Paris, and a divorce was inevitable. Saint Moritz, Monte Carlo, Biarritz and Deauville were his playgrounds. His womanising became legendary.

'Don't you ever work?' a gossip columnist asked him.

'I don't have time to work,' he replied.

A Puerto Rican woman sold her jewellery to subsidise him, but in 1942 he married the young film star Danielle Darrieux. It lasted five years, a record for him. Next came an affair with an Argentine millionairess, followed by Doris Duke and the five Ferraris.

That's the story in the cuttings file. Since Rubi and Doris were married on 1 September 1947 and divorced thirteen months later, it seems highly unlikely. The château, the plane and the cash were hard facts. The only question mark surrounds the five Ferraris, since Enzo Ferrari's total production had barely reached that figure by the time the lawyers shook hands to terminate the Rubirosas' marriage.

By 1950, shortly before he was simultaneously cited in the divorce cases of both the Texas oil heiress Joanne Connolly and the wife of the heir to the R. J. Reynolds tobacco company, Rubirosa certainly had his hands on at least one Ferrari, a 166 MM entered by Luigi Chinetti at Le Mans. Rubirosa and his French co-driver, Pierre Leygonie, ran in the top ten for the first hour but then retired, like all the five Ferraris attempting to repeat Chinetti's success of the previous year.

Ferrari had entered fourteen races in 1947, twenty-eight in 1948 and forty-eight in 1949. Three cars had been built in the first year, five in the second, and twenty-one in the third. The figures for 1950 would be seventy-three races entered and twenty-six cars produced. Such growth meant that the company had begun to occupy a significant role in the life of Maranello, beyond the impact made by the sound of racing cars being tested up and down the Abetone road. Ferrari himself continued to live in Modena, where he also kept an office. The old workshops were gradually being turned into the *assistenza clienti* – the place where customers would bring their cars for servicing or repairs. And at Modena, too, there was a useful new facility, the *aeroautodromo*, a wartime military airport now adapted for dual use. Its first race meeting was held in May 1950, and thereafter it was open for use to any of the local companies that needed a test track. Ferrari, Maserati and Stanguellini were the most frequent users, giving the local people wonderful free entertainment as well as a sense of being part of a small but thriving industry. Often Enzo Ferrari would watch his engineers at work on their latest creation, accompanied by one or two of his cronies and often also by Don Sergio Mantovani, the local parish priest, who loved racing cars and their drivers. At the beginning of each year, an altar would be set up at the end of the long straight bisecting the circuit and the workers at the local automobile factories would receive a blessing from Archbishop Boccoleri. The track's owners liked to call it 'the little Indianapolis in Europe', thanks to its basically rectangular shape. It was not a particularly interesting or demanding circuit, although Martino Severi, Ferrari's chief test driver, became such a specialist there that even the very greatest of the factory's drivers, to their intense frustration, often found it hard to match the times set by a man who always wore black trousers, a black sweater and a black helmet, and who was unable to make an impact anywhere else. But the heart of the Ferrari company was now in Maranello, and it was there that Lampredi prepared the cars for the first year of the Formula One world championship, to be run for cars conforming to the existing grand prix specification.

The year began with a blessing. When the team returned from the *Temporada* series in Argentina, where they had won all three races using Formula Two cars with the name of Fernet Branca, the aperitif manufacturer, in letters a foot high on their bonnets, they were received at the Vatican by Pope Pius XII. Various wives and mothers went along, as did Enzo Ferrari, who could occasionally be persuaded to observe such public rituals even if he had no real interest in the Catholic Church. While the rest of the group stood around the pontiff for the formal photograph, the wife of Nino Farina went down on her knees, her handbag decorously placed on the carpet while she clasped her hands together.

Lampredi's unsupercharged 4.5-litre car would not be ready to race until late in the year. The Scuderia Ferrari would be going into the season with improved versions of the old 125, once again facing the full might of Alfa Romeo, whose management had decided that the publicity offered by success in the new championship made the expenditure worthwhile. And during their sabbatical, the Alfa personnel had seen nothing to suggest that their cars would be facing stiffer competition. Just in case, however, they had developed the Tipo 158 still further, and had assembled a formidable driving team featuring the three Fs: Farina, Fagioli and Fangio, all three familiar to the Scuderia.

The story of the season's six championship rounds was simple. Farina won at Silverstone, Bremgarten and Monza, Fangio at Monte Carlo, Spa and Rheims. Since Farina picked up more points for additional placings and fastest laps, he won the title ahead of a severely disappointed Fangio, with Fagioli third in the final standings. The three Alfa drivers scored an aggregate of eighty-five points for the season. The remainder of the field – eighteen points-scoring drivers – managed eighty-two between them. Farina finished the season with thirty points, while Ferrari's four works drivers could muster only sixteen. Villoresi had missed the latter part of the season after skidding and crashing into the crowd during the Grand Prix des Nations in Geneva, killing three spectators and suffering broken bones and head injuries. There was a glimmer of competitive promise at Monza, where Lampredi is said to have fainted with nervous anticipation when his two new cars, the 375 model, were pushed out on to the circuit in front of the packed grandstand. Ascari gave the designer even greater cause for excitement by holding the lead for two laps in the middle of the race, until his rear axle broke. Only at the end of the season, in the Penya Rhin Grand Prix at Pedralbes, did the first success for the unsupercharged cars arrive, Ascari leading home Dorino Serafini, Villoresi's replacement, and Taruffi, albeit in the absence of the Alfettas.

Colombo, who was languishing in the road-car department, accepted an invitation to return to Alfa Romeo in 1951. His bitterness was later intensified by Ferrari's apparent refusal to acknowledge his contribution, or to reply to his occasional letters. But one of Colombo's Ferrari engines won the Mille Miglia again in 1950, this time mounted in a 166 driven by Giannino Marzotto, who drove the whole course wearing a double-breasted lounge suit and a tie. The race was characterised by constant rain and mist, with occasional outbreaks of hail. Ferrari's first-line entries, including 3.3-litre *barchettas* for Ascari and Villoresi and an open 2.3-litre car for Vittorio Marzotto, the winner's brother, all hit trouble. Into second place came Serafini, a former motorcycle racer, in a second 2.3-litre car. Their chief rival had been Fangio in an experimental Alfa, and Serafini remembered being issued one urgent instruction shortly before the start: 'You're starting two minutes after Fangio,' Ferrari told him. 'Get past him, and then don't let him by.' The race was also notable for a proliferation of accidents, three of which produced fatalities.

Giannino Marzotto, one of seven sons of Count Gaetano Marzotto, a textile magnate and automobile enthusiast, was then just twenty-two years old and in the process of becoming a cornerstone of Ferrari's clientele. In 1948 he had ordered what he believed to be the fourth Ferrari sold to a customer, a 166 Inter. 'The details required a great deal of time,' he remembered, 'because in those days it was like a tailor-made suit, and the customer could add his own personal touch.' During the fittings he was able to spend some time with Enzo Ferrari. '[He was] a man with a strong personality and fascinating dialectical skills for a young man as curious as I was, with numerous very clear ideas about a great number of topics.' Ferrari, to whom the four racing Marzotto brothers represented important customers, was particularly taken with Giannino: 'He was a real speed merchant, a young Varzi in his cold, calculating earnestness. The successes in the Mille Miglia were a sure sign of his dedication and enough to show that he would have made an excellent professional driver, perhaps even a champion.'

Ferrari won the Mille Miglia again in 1951, this time with a professional driver, the fully recovered Villoresi, at the wheel of a Vignale-bodied coupé powered by one of Lampredi's engines, an unsupercharged 4.1-litre V12. Again the weather was poor, and there were many accidents. Ascari left the road after being dazzled by a light shone by a spectator who was trying to decipher the numbers of the competing cars; an onlooker was killed in the accident, and a manslaughter charge hung over Ascari for the next four years. Serafini crashed and was badly injured. Villoresi finished the race after an accident on the flyover near Ferrara left his car with a crumpled nose. Also at the wheel of a Ferrari was the twenty-one-year-old Eugenio Castellotti, another customer. A wild, handsome and ambitious young country gentleman from Lodi, outside Milan, Castellotti had an attitude that made an immediate appeal to Ferrari's tastes: 'It cannot be said that he was a driver of outstanding class or impeccable style, but none can deny that he was a big-hearted and generous man.' Comparing him to Antonio Ascari, Ferrari called him a *garibaldino*, the sort of man who, like Garibaldi's red-coated soldiers, put a love of risk above a calculation of the percentages.

At the dinner held in a Modena restaurant to celebrate Villoresi's victory, however, the family tragedy that had been looming for years finally exploded. The preface can be seen in the image preserved by the photographer, who called the assembled drivers, engineers, mechanics and other employees and friends of the Scuderia – even Ferrari's barber, Antonio D'Elia – to gather at one end of the long table for a commemorative picture. Most of the faces are turned to the camera, smiling with the pleasure of an evening's conviviality. But young Dino, who is standing on the edge of the group, is not smiling. He is looking down and across at his father. And Enzo, proudly seated in the centre with the trophy on the white tablecloth in front of him, has turned his eyes to meet Dino's, with a smile freezing on his lips. Dino's illness had suddenly erupted, the dinner was about to be prematurely terminated, and the father who had made his son the repository of his hopes was on the brink of being told that the boy's decline had become irreversible. For the next five years he would be torn between a refusal to accept the inevitability of Dino's impending death and a knowledge that mourning would not be long deferred.

Enzo Ferrari and Alberto Ascari, his first world champion and the son of one of his mentors, at Monza in the early 1950s.

Six

Victories at Le Mans and in the Mille Miglia and the Targa Florio certainly helped to sell Ferraris to the young and fashionable of Lombardy, Emilia and the Piedmont, beginning the process of establishing a solid commercial platform for the company. But winning races with sports cars was all very well. As the 1951 season began, only one kind of success really interested Enzo Ferrari. And standing in his way was his old employer, the company that had nurtured him and provided him with equipment and had even stood by him during his breakdown, before eventually rejecting him in the most conclusive manner, for reasons he was never able to accept.

While they prepared for the new year's racing programme to begin, Alfa Romeo's executives, engineers and drivers saw absolutely no reason why they should not maintain their dominance of the previous year. Farina had stayed on to defend his championship, with Fangio and Fagioli again at his side, while Colombo had worked on a new development of the Alfetta. With more power, a new rear suspension and better brakes, it was now called the Tipo 159, although it was still recognisably the machine that had been born in the workshops of the Scuderia Ferrari in Modena. Enzo Ferrari, however, was confident that Lampredi's big, bruising 4.5-litre 375 would finally expose the Alfa's age, which had been disguised as much by the lack of genuine competition as by the car's intrinsic excellence.

Alfa, as usual, ignored the springtime non-championship races, but the Scuderia profited from the absence of its chief rival to secure morale-boosting wins for Villoresi at Syracuse and Pau and for Ascari at San Remo. And at Silverstone in May, in the *Daily*

Express Trophy, there was the hint of a chink in the Alfa Romeo armour when Reg Parnell, an English driver in the cockpit of a 1950 Ferrari 375 which Tony Vandervell had bought, painted green, and rechristened the second Thinwall Special, was given the chequered flag after only six laps of a race run in near-monson conditions. He had used the greater flexibility of the unsupercharged Ferrari engine and his own local knowledge to establish a lead over the Tipo 159s, really only taking part in a reconnaissance mission for the grand prix, which lay two months ahead. After the race the teams gathered for a glass of champagne in the warm and dry environment of a large caravan brought along by Vandervell – who was thus responsible, in the view of photographer Louis Klemantaski, for the creation of motor racing's first hospitality unit. In Berne, however, the usual order reasserted itself. Fangio won the Swiss Grand Prix, with Taruffi's Ferrari second. It was Farina's turn at Spa, and Fangio won again at Rheims, albeit after a furious battle with Ascari. But the latter race had seen the arrival in the Scuderia's ranks of a new driver, one who seemed every bit as brutish as the cars.

José Froilàn González had served his apprenticeship at home in Argentina in the *turismo carretera* series. Since his elder brother had died racing, he disguised his own identity from his parents by competing under the aliases 'Canuto' and 'Montemaro'. The previous winter he had won two Perón Cup races in Buenos Aires, driving a 166 Formula Libre car and beating Juan Manuel Fangio in a much more powerful pre-war W163 Mercedes, which brought González a congratulatory message from Enzo Ferrari. With the usual push from the government and the Argentine Automobile Club, he followed the first of the great Argentines to Europe. Eleven years younger than Fangio, González was a very different type. By contrast with his jockey-sized friend, the new man was so corpulent that he seemed to flow over the sides of a single-seater cockpit, belying his abilities as a footballer, swimmer and cyclist. His style, too, was more obviously aggressive and somewhat erratic. As Ferrari said, 'Whereas Fangio could be counted on to keep going as regularly as clockwork, González alternated bursts of furious speed with spells in which he seemed to be taking his time. When he was in the lead, he would inexplicably slacken speed and let himself be overtaken; while when he was in pursuit, he ate up his adversaries.' He was certainly a colourful figure. In Argentina he had become known as *El Cabezón*, the Wild One. In Europe he was christened the Pampas Bull. His friends called him Pepe, or Pepito.

González finished second in the French Grand Prix, held in the blazing heat of the Champagne country, but it was on the chilly wastes of the Northamptonshire plateau that he was to write himself into Ferrari history. Given an older and less highly developed machine than those allotted to Ascari and Villoresi, he nevertheless amazed the paddock by recording the fastest practice lap, the first time an Alfa Romeo had not been on pole position since the inauguration of the world championship. On race day, 14 July, he went into the lead from the start, his elbows flailing outside the cockpit as he held off the Alfas. Fangio briefly took the lead, but González regained it before half-distance. While Ascari and Villoresi, in their newer and more powerful cars, disappeared with gearbox and clutch problems, their new team mate steamed on and, helped by the need of the thirsty Alfas to take on sixty-five gallons of fuel during their pit stops, he was never headed again. He stalled the engine during his final pit stop, and appeared to be making as if to get out of the car, perhaps imagining that he was supposed to hand over to Ascari. But he was urged back into the cockpit, not least by Ascari himself, and went back to win the race by more than a minute from Fangio, with Villoresi third. As the big red Ferrari with the number 12 on its nose cruised into the pit lane after its lap of honour, the driver was mobbed by a crew of overjoyed mechanics and embraced by his wife, Amalia.

And that was it. For the jubilant team, and for followers of the post-war world championship in general, the news was that the Alfa Romeo stranglehold had finally been broken. But when Federico Giberti made the telephone call to Modena, the man at

[163]

the other end of the line was experiencing a much richer and more complex set of emotions. Enzo Ferrari's mind went back to the bitterness of his sacking from Alfa Romeo in 1939, the end of a relationship lasting almost twenty years. 'I cried for joy,' he remembered. 'But my tears of enthusiasm were mixed with those of sorrow because I thought, today I have killed my mother.'

If he had killed her at Silverstone, he buried her at the Nürburgring, where Ascari took pole position and led González home to take his first world-championship victory, followed by a second at Monza, in front of his home fans, with González again on the next step of the podium. The teams arrived in Barcelona, the final race of the season, with Fangio leading Ascari by two points and a great deal of psychological warfare going on. Alfa's engineers quietly let it be known that they had fitted extra fuel tanks inside the flanks of their cars, ensuring that they would be able to run through the race without refuelling. In fact this was a bluff, but Fangio was not let in on the secret, for fear that he would tell his friend González, until the cars were on the starting grid and Colombo walked up to give him the news. Ferrari, however, had already made a disastrous error over their choice of small-diameter tyres. Unexpected wear caused by the rough surface of the Pedralbes track was forcing Ascari into the pits for fresh rubber every nine laps. That made it comparatively easy for Fangio, taking care not to slide his car unnecessarily on the abrasive surface, to win his third grand prix of the season and claim his first world championship. The two rivals had agreed that whoever won the title would pay for a banquet, to be held back in Milan in the Ristorante Savini. It cost Fangio the equivalent of 30,000 pesos, including the fee for a Spanish band. From there he went back home to Argentina, where a welcoming crowd blocked the six-lane avenue that runs through the centre of Buenos Aires and the Peróns greeted him at the Casa Rosada. Ascari went back to Modena to talk to Enzo Ferrari about their chances of doing better next time.

One driver who would not be part of their plans was the new star of British motor racing. Always on the lookout for fresh talent, Ferrari could not help but notice the performances of young Stirling Moss. In 1949, aged nineteen, Moss had chased Ferraris in the hands of experienced drivers around the lakeside circuits of Garda and Lausanne in a tiny Cooper fitted with a 1,000 cc motorcycle engine. In Monaco the following year he had won the Formula Three race, a fine showcase for young talent, and in a Formula Two event at Terme di Caracalla in Rome his British HWM had finished third to the works Ferraris of Ascari and Villoresi. With the same car in 1951 he had finished eighth in the Swiss Grand Prix, against Alfettas and Ferraris with twice the power. As he completed the race with a shattered windscreen, other team managers noted that he had been timed second fastest over one difficult section, only a fifth of a second behind Fangio. Enzo Ferrari let it be known that he would like to offer the young Englishman a ride. The news encouraged Moss, driving home from a race in Switzerland, to make a long detour in his Morris Minor to pay a visit to Modena.

They conversed in French. 'We seemed to get on well enough,' Moss remembered. Ferrari asked him to drive a new four-cylinder car at Bari on 9 September, if it had been completed in time, or failing that at the Italian Grand Prix on 16 September. 'He then made me the enormously tempting offer to accompany Ascari and Villoresi to the Argentine Temporada series in the new year, and asked me to join his team exclusively for 1952.' This was a considerable honour, since Dick Seaman, who drove for Mercedes-Benz before his death in 1939, was the only British driver ever to be invited into the squad of one of the top Continental teams. Moss, however, responded cautiously, since he had already received an approach from BRM, and was aware of his patriotic duty at a time when British teams were struggling to make an impact. But he agreed, at least, to drive the car in Bari.

After contacting the organisers to confirm the promise of starting money, Moss and his father set off on the long journey to southern Italy, by air to Rome and sleeper train to their destination. When they got to the track, Moss went to the

Ferrari garage to check that the new four-cylinder Ferrari was present and ready to race. The following morning he returned, only to be asked by a mechanic what he thought he was doing. That car, he was told, was due to be driven by Piero Taruffi. Infuriated by the discourtesy, Moss stormed off, vowing that he would rather spend the rest of his life driving a London bus than accept another offer to drive for Enzo Ferrari – who was, of course, nowhere to be found. In the race Taruffi finished third, behind Fangio and Villoresi in the larger, faster grand prix cars, leaving Moss wondering whether that proved Ferrari's judgement correct, or whether he might have done just as well as the veteran Italian driver – or even better. 'I did not forget', he concluded, 'and I would not forgive.'

This incident has always been paraded as an example of Enzo Ferrari's arrogance, and an indication of how it might sometimes have obstructed his judgement. After all, he botched the chance to sign up a driver who might have brought him three or four world championships, and he made an enemy into the bargain. For many years afterwards, Moss was to take a particular delight in getting the better of the cars from Maranello. On the other hand, Ferrari had acknowledged the talent in embryo. And he had, by Moss's account, made an offer not just for a single race but for a winter series and the full European championship season beyond that. Moss's cautious response must have made Ferrari raise an eyebrow, particularly if the Englishman mentioned the name BRM. After all, even in 1951 talented young drivers were already beating Ferrari's door down in their efforts to be awarded a drive. Why should he show much latitude to a young man who treated his offer with what may have seemed to be a measure of disdain?

They were both wrong. Moss would have been wiser to show more enthusiasm; the BRM project was a non-starter. And Ferrari was ill-advised to play fast and loose with the hopes of a young man – of any young man, never mind one who in later years he came to bracket alongside Tazio Nuvolari and Guy Moll as the very best he had seen.

In November Ferrari sent two 2.6-litre coupés to Mexico, where they were to take part in the second running of the Carrera Panamericana, a five-day race covering almost 2,000 miles of wild, mostly unmade roads from Tuxtla Gutiérrez to Ciudad Juarez by way of Oaxaca, Mexico City, Durango and Chihuahua. Stripped-down American saloons had dominated the inaugural race, won by Hershel McGriff, an Oregonian, in an Oldsmobile. The arrival of the Europeans put an end to all that. Piero Taruffi and Luigi Chinetti shared the winning car, with Ascari and Villoresi close behind. And Ferrari had opened up yet another market.

On the set of Jean Renoir's *La Carrozza d'oro* early in 1952, Anna Magnani posed with her foot on the bumper of a two-tone Ferrari 212 Inter, the skirt of her dress – the costume of an eighteenth-century *commedia dell'arte* player – not quite obscuring the car's egg-crate grille. A copy of the print was sent to Maranello, a dedication to Enzo Ferrari – 'with enthusiasm and good wishes' – scrawled on it by the actress. *The Golden Coach* wasn't Renoir's greatest film, although it had its admirers, but the 212 Inter wasn't Ferrari's greatest car, either. And Ferrari had a soft spot for Magnani, a 'tremendously human and quite disconcerting' person who had intrigued him by confiding, during a drive from Maranello to Modena, that the vibrations of an engine turning at full speed did something curious to her insides.

The products of Maranello may have been on their way to becoming the people's car of the *Cinecittà* crowd, thanks in part to the increasingly voluptuous bodywork with which many of them were now clothed by the designer Giovanbattista 'Pinin' Farina and his son Sergio, but the serious business was motor racing. No fewer than twenty-six Ferraris were among the 501 entries for the 1952 Mille Miglia, and Giovanni Bracco, another beneficiary of a family textile fortune, made it the fifth victory in a row for the company, smoking cigarettes and taking the occasional nip from a flask of Chianti as he drove through the rain in his 250 MM Berlinetta, outpacing the sleek new Mercedes-Benz 300 coupés of Karl Kling and the ageing Rudi Caracciola. To watch the cars pass through Modena, the beer and soft-drinks wholesaler Ferruccio Testi, one of the Scuderia's original supporters, created a miniature grandstand for himself and his friends by drawing up a pair of his firm's three-wheeled Aer-Macchi delivery trucks and setting café tables on their flatbeds, complete with parasols.

A few weeks later, the Mercedes cars were to take the top two places at Le Mans, their first success in Europe since the war. Yet their return sounded no note of warning in the grand prix world. Following the announcement of yet another withdrawal by Alfa Romeo (a sabbatical, this time, to last almost thirty years), the sport's governing body, the Fédération Internationale de l'Automobile, decided that the old Formula One was no longer viable. There was not going to be a Cisitalia-Porsche, there was no sign of the BRM, the Talbots were antiques, Maserati had no new car capable of challenging the Ferrari, and at that point Mercedes seemed interested only in sports cars. For 1952 and 1953, therefore, the grands prix would be run to Formula Two rules, since there were plenty of competitive unsupercharged 2-litre single-seaters capable of providing a good spectacle. And for 1954 a new set of regulations would be drawn up around cars of 2.5 litres' capacity, unsupercharged.

Deprived of his chance to capitalise on the advantage he had so painfully gained at the end of 1951, Enzo Ferrari was nevertheless well placed. Had he wanted to, he could have built a new design around Colombo's proven V12. Instead, making the first of many breaks from the engine format with which his cars have always been popularly associated, he plumped for a new four-cylinder layout presented by Lampredi. This reversal of the trend towards high-revving multi-cylinder complexity was typical of the engineer, who cherished simplicity and was apparently inspired by the four-cylinder Offenhauser engines which had dominated the Indianapolis 500. The new Lampredi four was placed in an equally unfussy chassis, a modified version of the previous year's 375, with a smoothly tapered body featuring a recessed radiator that gave it a hungry look. The Ferrari 500 would be rugged and reliable as well as fast, and Ascari, Villoresi and Taruffi would be available to exploit its potential, along with Farina, who had been rehired following the exit of Alfa Romeo. Fangio, after winning four out of the five *Temporada* events in a modified Formula Libre 166, went off to join Maserati.

Nello Ugolini returned to the team, replacing Giberti as *direttore sportivo*, and with him came the decision to put the prancing-horse shield on the cockpit sides of the cars for the first time since Ferrari had disbanded the original Scuderia and left Modena to run Alfa Corse in 1938. The pattern for the season was set when Ascari opened with a hat-trick of wins in the non-championship races at Syracuse, Pau and Marseilles. But when the field assembled for the first time in 1952 with championship points at stake, at Bremgarten for the Swiss Grand Prix, the main contender was otherwise engaged. Alberto Ascari was to be found that weekend en route to Indianapolis, where a team from Maranello was heading at the behest of Luigi Chinetti.

Remembering Wilbur Shaw's back-to-back successes at the Brickyard track with a Maserati ten years earlier, Chinetti was convinced that a Ferrari challenge could succeed. If he was right, it would give an enormous boost to sales of the road cars in the United States. Ferrari saw it as an opportunity to make use of the obsolete Formula One cars, and annoyed Chinetti by selling three cars to private entrants without telling him. The factory-entered car, which would be supervised by Ugolini, Lampredi and the mechanic Stefano Meazza, had been modified with the demands of the fast two-and-a-half-mile oval track in mind. The 'Ferrari Special', as it said in large letters on the bonnet, qualified only twenty-fifth fastest in a field of thirty-three, at a speed of 134 mph, but Ascari had hauled it up to eighth in the race when a rear hub failed and he spun into the infield. The other Ferraris, including one rechristened the Grant Piston Ring Special, failed to qualify, merely emphasising that cars developed to meet the parameters of European road racing were not necessarily the right equipment for high-speed ovals. But this was nevertheless a pioneering effort, and its lessons would not have been lost on John Cooper and Colin Chapman, who within a decade had begun the European conquest of America's most famous race.

Back home, the lucky pale blue helmet and pale blue long-sleeved woollen polo shirt of the highly superstitious Alberto Ascari became the dominant sight in grand prix racing. In his absence Taruffi had won the first round, but the major threat to Ascari's title was removed early in June when Fangio was injured in a non-championship race at Monza while giving the new Maserati its debut. He had raced a BRM at Dundrod the previous day, took a fog-delayed flight that evening to Paris, and then drove through the night in a borrowed Renault, down through France and northern Italy, arriving at the track two hours before the start. Not having practised, he lined up on the back row of the grid. On the second lap, in a highly uncharacteristic misjudgement clearly caused by fatigue, he took a curve too fast, overturned, and was thrown out, injuring the vertebrae of his neck as he landed on a patch of grass and soft earth. It was not yet midsummer, and the reigning world champion's season was over.

Ascari scooped up the remaining six races, from Spa to Monza via Rouen, Silverstone, the Nürburgring and Zandvoort, with hardly a backward glance. Only in a non-title race at Rheims, where he was surprisingly outpaced by the little Gordini of Jean Behra, a tough Niçois, was there a hint of vulnerability. Otherwise Ascari was unquestionably the class of the field, a man at the peak of his powers, thirty-four years old and making up for the seasons that he had lost to the war. He was a stylist who prepared carefully for every race and, like Jim Clark in later years, excelled at winning races from the front. 'When leading', Ferrari observed, 'he could not easily be overtaken – indeed I will go so far as to say that it was virtually impossible to overtake him. When he lay second, however, or even farther back, he had not the combative spirit I should have liked to have seen on certain occasions. This was not because he threw in the towel; but because, when he had to get on the tail of an adversary and pass him, he was evidently afflicted not so much by what might perhaps appear to be a sort of inferiority complex as by a state of nerves that prevented him from showing his class to the best advantage.' What Ferrari was saying, effectively, was that Ascari was a wonderfully fast driver who was not particularly good at overtaking, a part of the racing driver's craft that is often overlooked by those who have never tried it. What Ferrari had loved about Nuvolari and Moll – and, as it happened, Ascari's own father – was that they fought hard from whatever position they were in. It would probably not be wrong to suggest that his admiration of them was so fervent because they were doing something he himself had never truly mastered, while knowing enough to recognise it as the supreme test.

Not that Alberto Ascari was soft. Indeed it was Ferrari's own sentimental attitude to children that one day made him question Ascari about why he behaved so harshly towards his young son and daughter. 'Every time I come back from a race,' the driver replied, 'I always bring them something that will make them happy, and I usually try and give them everything they need – even if it's only to satisfy a whim. All the same, though, I think it's right to be severe with them. I don't want them to get too fond of me. One of these days I may not come back and they will suffer less if I've kept them a bit at arm's length.' As he may have remembered, Ferrari himself had been standing in the background when Antonio lifted the six-year-old Alberto into the cockpit of his winning Alfa at Monza in 1924, the year before his death.

Ascari's comfortable build led Italians to call him *Ciccio*, or Tubby. In fact he had a disciplined fitness regime, which was rare in those days, and there was no stopping him at the beginning of 1953. He dismissed the renewed challenge from

Fangio by starting with consecutive wins at Buenos Aires, Zandvoort and Spa, giving him a total of nine grand prix victories in a row – a record that had still not been beaten when Michael Schumacher became Ferrari's first world champion of the next millennium. But his run was broken by a comparative novice, a young Englishman. After Ugolini and Lampredi had watched Mike Hawthorn put his outclassed Cooper-Bristol on the front row at Zandvoort the previous season, alongside Ascari and Farina, they brought his name to Enzo Ferrari's attention. Born in Yorkshire but brought up in Surrey, Hawthorn was twenty-three years old when he joined Ferrari and took with him the sort of carefree image popularly associated with the Battle of Britain pilots. He wore Harris tweed jackets, he smoked a pipe, he liked a beer, he had an eye for the girls and he appeared to be going through life without taking anything too seriously. He also wore a bow-tie when he raced, which led the French to christen him *Le Papillon*. In Stirling Moss's words, he was still in 'the rather trying days of his extreme youth, when he was a little given to squirting soda siphons in pubs'. What was less obvious was that he was suffering from a long-term kidney disease, which had made him ineligible for national service – something that brought on a brief outburst of indignation in the tabloids, which argued that if he could travel all over Europe to drive racing cars, he could do his time in uniform. Yet his patriotism was hardly in question. Before he made his British debut for the Scuderia Ferrari, he bought a new green windcheater. 'If I can't drive a green car,' he told a friend, 'at least I can wear a green jacket.' Hawthorn, in short, had accepted the opportunity that Moss, intentionally or otherwise, had spurned, and in the fourth grand prix of 1953, over the ultra-fast five-mile triangle of *routes nationales* that formed the Rheims circuit, he was able to show his English rival what he had missed. While Moss struggled with a Cooper-Alta, Hawthorn went head-to-head with Fangio.

The weekend started badly for Ferrari when Umberto Maglioli appeared to have won the twelve-hour sports-car race, which started on Friday night and ended on Saturday morning, only to be disqualified for switching off his headlights before the appointed time, even though the morning sun had been shining brightly. When Ugolini rang Enzo Ferrari to break the news, the response was straightforward. Pull the cars out, Ferrari ordered. The threat of the team's withdrawal from the grand prix created panic among the organisers, and it was said that Ferrari's starting money had to be doubled before he agreed to allow his cars to participate in what *Autosport*'s report the following Thursday was to call 'the race of the century'.

Four Ferraris – Ascari, Villoresi, Farina and Hawthorn – faced the four Maseratis of Fangio, González, Felice Bonetto and a third Argentine, Onofre Marimon. The remaining nineteen starters might as well have been in another race. González made the first move, shooting from the third row of the grid into the lead. With his fuel tanks only half full, he was able to pull out a small lead. Behind him, however, the battle was already white-hot. In the days before chicanes and aerodynamic devices, a circuit such as Rheims was made for slipstreaming. At the end of the twenty-fourth lap, for instance, just before half-distance, Ascari, Villoresi, Hawthorn, Fangio, Farina and Marimon whistled past the pits in a tight phalanx, weaving in and out of each other's slipstreams as they looked for an advantage. After González had refuelled, the only one of the leaders to make a pit stop, the battle for the lead was fought between Fangio, Ascari and Hawthorn, until Ascari dropped back slightly. Lap after lap until the end of the race the Argentine champion and the English newcomer crossed the line abreast. Afterwards Hawthorn wrote of the experience of looking across at his opponent and exchanging grins as they tore along the straight side by side, both crouched down in the cockpit to minimise wind resistance. As they came out of Thillois Hairpin, the last corner, for the final time, Hawthorn got the drop on Fangio and made it to the line a second ahead, while the Argentine was almost pipped in the last hundred metres by his compatriot, the amazing González, who had caught and passed everyone else after his stop. The crowd's tumultuous reaction showed their gratitude for an afternoon's remarkable entertainment.

What it did not mean was that Hawthorn was ready to be world champion. Ascari reasserted himself at Silverstone and won again in Switzerland, where, needing only third place to become champion, he ignored Ugolini's instruction to hold station and roared past the surprised Hawthorn and the hugely displeased Farina to win, afterwards claiming that the low sun had prevented him from seeing the pit board. Farina's only win of the season came in Switzerland, while Ascari was leading the Italian Grand Prix, the last of the season, until Fangio swept past on the last corner of the final lap to take a small consolation for Maserati, giving the other Modenese manufacturer their only victory in the two years of Formula Two grands prix. Ferrari also won a prize of seven million lire offered by the organisers to any constructor who would enliven the entry by bringing along two of next season's grand prix cars. The new models looked lower but more bulbous, and when Ascari tried one of them in practice he was two seconds off his own pace.

This was also the year in which Roberto Rossellini had a stab at the Mille Miglia. The director drove a 3-litre Touring *barchetta*, one of no fewer than twenty-eight Ferraris in the field, with his collaborator Aldo Tonti wielding an 8 mm movie camera from the passenger seat. They got as far as Rome, reaching the control point at the piazza Tuscania in just under seven and a half hours, almost two hours more than the winner would take. There Ingrid Bergman was waiting to greet her husband as he swung into the control point under a temporary grandstand built along the road running by the northern side of the Villa Borghese. Rossellini switched off the engine, climbed out, and embraced his wife. 'Let's go home,' he said. Giannino Marzotto won the race for the second time, in a Vignale spyder, beating Fangio's Alfa Romeo.

At six-thirty on the morning of 11 August 1953, barely three years after his last race, Tazio Nuvolari died in his wife's arms at his home in Mantua, aged sixty-one. He had spent his last days in the room of his dead son Giorgio, among the boy's model cars and aeroplanes, from time to time asking to look through the albums containing photographs of his races. 'Bury me in my uniform,' he had asked on the night before he died, and he was laid in his casket in the yellow shirt with the monogram and the woven tortoise, and the blue helmet and trousers. Two days later, after a service in the fourteenth-century basilica of Sant'Andrea, at which Ascari was among the pallbearers, Nuvolari was buried in Mantua's municipal cemetery, in a fine marble mausoleum surrounded by grass and trees, with an inscription over the arch, said to have been the words of St Paul used by the priest administering the last rites: *Correrai ancor' piu veloce per le vie del cielo*. You will travel even faster along the roads of heaven.

'He had been a solitary man,' Ferrari wrote, 'embittered by the cruel way fate had treated him in the things he cared most about. At the same time, and I mean nothing disrespectful, he was always acutely aware of the effect he was making on his audience. More than most, he understood the crowd, knew what the crowd wanted, and expertly fuelled the Nuvolari legend.' Their relationship had not been easy, but the races at the Nürburgring in 1935 and around the Mille Miglia course in 1948 had defined most people's idea of what motor racing could and should be: heights of passion, conflict, skill.

Before the end of 1954, there were rumours that Enzo Ferrari intended to withdraw from grand prix racing. He was tired, it was said, and was worried about Dino's deteriorating health. At the traditional end-of-season banquet he lifted some of the clouds by announcing that Scuderia Ferrari would be competing during the forthcoming season, but only in the major events, as a protest against what he felt was a lack of appropriate support from the state and from Italian industry. In truth, after two years of almost unbroken triumph, he was worried about the threat posed by Mercedes-Benz, who had announced their intention to return to Formula One. Ferrari remembered the effect of their arrival in the 1930s, when government subsidies had helped them develop the technical and organisational capacity to smash and humiliate the poor little Italian teams such as his own. Now the Germans were coming back, and with Juan Manuel Fangio at their head.

By 29 December, when he went to Maranello for a meeting to discuss contracts, Alberto Ascari had already posed for photographers by the side of the Ferrari with which he would attempt to win his third world championship in a row. His existing contract was due to expire on 30 April 1954. Now Enzo Ferrari wanted to offer him an extended deal to cover the full season. In Ascari's version, Ferrari pushed a contract in front of him, saying that he had to sign it there and then. Ascari, who had in any case not been happy with his remuneration, answered that he had received several other offers, and was not prepared to agree to anything without thought. But Ferrari was firm, and the meeting was over. 'I returned to Milan with a heavy heart,' Ascari said. 'I had made too many sacrifices for the company and the collaboration had given me too much satisfaction to be able to close a chapter as passionate and attractive in my life without having some regrets.' Back at home, he called Villoresi and together they started looking through some of the other proposals. Villoresi had not been hard to persuade. He and Ferrari had never really enjoyed each other's company. He remembered winning the Modena Grand Prix for the team in 1952. 'Ferrari actually said "Thank you",' he recalled. 'That didn't happen very often.' The next morning the two drivers left for Turin, where they spoke to Gianni Lancia and told him that their services were available. Lancia had been planning a Formula One team since the middle of 1953, and his workers were apparently well advanced with Vittorio Jano's latest design. The car had a V8 engine and one significant design feature: petrol tanks mounted as pontoons on outriggers either side of the bonnet and between the front and rear wheels, intended to improve the sensitivity of the car's handling by placing most of the weight within the wheelbase. Ferrari issued a communiqué announcing the immediate end of the relationship with Ascari. Three weeks later the two drivers signed their deals with Lancia, and were followed on to the books by Eugenio Castellotti. On 12 March 1954 the cover of *Autosport*, the British weekly magazine, carried a photograph of Ascari having a first run in Jano's striking new machine, the D50, on a runway at Turin's Caselle airport. In May, the manslaughter charge from 1951 having been recently dismissed, he was winning the Mille Miglia in a Lancia D24, a lovely sports car powered by another Jano engine, a V6, despite having to use a rubber band in place of a broken throttle return spring for some of the distance. Gianni Lancia, the son of Vincenzo Lancia, the racing driver who founded the company back in the days of the pioneers, had taken a big and expensive gamble in launching his new team, and it seemed to be coming off.

At Maranello, in the wake of the drivers' departure, chaos reigned. Ferrari had allowed Lampredi – who, after all, had hardly made a wrong guess of any significance since he replaced Colombo – to spread his bets. Among the designer's new ideas was that if four cylinders had been better than twelve in a 2.5-litre engine, then perhaps two would be even better than four. He built a couple of prototypes, just to prove himself wrong. Then he drew up a new four-cylinder engine, plus a straight-six for the sports cars. Lancia, however, had a V8, while Mercedes were returning to the grand prix scene with a straight-eight. At Maserati, Gioachino Colombo and Alberto Massimino had teamed up to build a new straight-six. Bugatti and Gordini, too, were said to be on the way back with eight-cylinder power-plants. But the problem with Ferrari's 1954 Formula One cars was not really the engines: it was the chassis – the least important part of the design, at least in the view of Enzo Ferrari. For a team that had grown accustomed to domination, 1954 was to provide a chilling corrective.

No one was ready when the grand prix season started in

Buenos Aires in January. Mercedes allowed Fangio to drive for Maserati until they felt prepared to unveil their cars. Lancia had only just signed Ascari, and their D50 was untested. Ferrari's new chassis was not ready either, so Lampredi bolted new four-cylinder engines into four of the previous year's Formula Two chassis, called them 625s, gave them to González, Farina, Hawthorn and Maurice Trintignant, a wine-grower from Provence, and hoped for the best.

At Buenos Aires' spectacular new autodrome Fangio ran away from the Ferraris in the new Maserati 250F, a machine designed by Gioachino Colombo which proved the adage that if it looks right, it is right. A slender fuselage, a well-engineered frame, good suspension and a classic engine made it a pleasure to drive fast. Fangio put it on pole and won the race by more than a minute from Farina, followed by González and Trintignant. A protest by Ferrari, concerning the number of mechanics seen working on Fangio's car, was unsurprisingly rejected by the Argentine stewards.

When the new Ferrari turned up at Spa, it proved that what looks wrong usually is wrong. The 553's strange shape led it to be nicknamed the Squalo, or Shark, but it certainly lacked teeth. Farina hated it for the way its unpredictable handling compromised his elegant driving style. González, perhaps predictably, managed to wrestle more performance out of it. But engines and chassis were being constantly shuffled in an attempt to find a combination that worked. The other drivers generally seemed happier when they were given the old-fashioned 625s, which were not terribly fast but were at least reliable in their habits. When Fangio and two German team mates, Karl Kling and Hans Hermann, turned up at Rheims for the third race of the season with a trio of dramatically streamlined Mercedes and scooped the first two places without seeming to break sweat, the game appeared to be up. Nevertheless it was with a 625 that González registered his second British Grand Prix win at Silverstone, profiting when Fangio discovered that the Mercedes' all-enveloping bodywork prevented him from seeing the apexes of the corners and placing his car properly. González also used the older type of car to take second place at the Nürburgring and Bremgarten, and in September – since the Lancias were still not ready to race – Ascari was loaned back to Ferrari and actually managed to lead the Mercedes around the combined road and track circuit before a valve broke. Hawthorn finished the season on a more optimistic note by winning the Spanish Grand Prix in a Squalo, observing that at last, after a year of frantic development, it had become 'a very nice little car', and earning kisses on both cheeks from a relieved Ugolini. More significant that day, so it seemed, was the arrival of the Lancia D50. Ascari celebrated its long-delayed appearance by putting it straight on pole in Barcelona, ahead of the Mercedes of Fangio, who had already wrapped up his second title, and he was pulling away from the field at the rate of two seconds a lap when the car broke. Villoresi's sister car lasted just one lap, which said little for the team's work during a year of preparation. Consolation for the deposed Ascari came when, at the wheel of a D24, he ended Ferrari's run of six consecutive victories in the Mille Miglia, but González pulled off a wonderful win in the 1954 Le Mans race in a 4.9-litre car, co-driving with Trintignant. The conditions were dreadful, culminating in a Wagnerian thunderstorm which accompanied the final frantic chase of the big Ferrari by the D-type Jaguar of Duncan Hamilton, who finished barely a minute behind the winner.

For the grand prix team, the increased strength of the opposition meant that 1955 promised to be even worse than 1954. The Lancias would be ready for the start of the season, and Moss had joined Fangio at Mercedes. Lampredi seemed to have nothing new to offer beyond further permutations of largely discredited equipment. As for the drivers, González had gone back home to Argentina while Hawthorn had opted to sign with Tony Vandervell's new Vanwall team in order to spend more time helping out with his family's garage business in Surrey. That left only Farina and Taruffi, both aged forty-eight, and Trintignant, thirty-eight, all of them still solid but unlikely to be spectacular, plus a new recruit, Harry Schell, a popular Franco-American from a racing family, with a devil-may-care attitude and a moderate talent, but already in his mid-thirties and equally unlikely to reinvigorate the team. And yet, after Fangio had taken the Argentine Grand Prix, run in such raging heat that the second- and third-placed Ferraris each required the rotation of three drivers, the first European championship round of the season produced something of a miracle. Dapper little Maurice Trintignant, starting from the fourth row of the grid in an old 625, trundled round Monte Carlo to win Prince Rainier's cup. Moss and Fangio had broken down after running first and second and Alberto Ascari, who inherited the lead with less than twenty laps to go, then locked his Lancia's brakes at the chicane, shooting off the track and straight into the harbour. Just missing a moored yacht, he had to be rescued by frogmen. 'Our boss must have the luck of the devil,' Trintignant remarked to Ugolini. 'He must have put a spell on Mercedes and Lancia to stop them.'

The truer picture, however, was provided when Mino Amorotti, the Scuderia's technical director, invited the team's reserve driver, the Belgian journalist Paul Frère, to take over a car that Taruffi had abandoned at the pits in despair. Frère's judgement gives an interesting insight into the management culture at Maranello, into the atmosphere of barely suppressed paranoia and the fear of taking responsibility that tended to envelop the team in times of failure. 'The car was a real beast to handle around Monaco,' Frère reported. 'It just wanted to plough straight on at the two tight hairpins. I hinted that it might be a good idea to disconnect the front anti-roll bar, but Amorotti was responsible for technical matters at the races and I'm sure he was really upset by my suggestion. He didn't want to take the responsibility for modifying something which was part of the original design – for which he was not responsible. If he had taken my advice and something had gone wrong, he most certainly would have been held responsible for it back at the factory. He just wasn't prepared to do it.'

Trintignant's little blaze of glory was doused by the news, the following Thursday, that Alberto Ascari had been killed at Monza. After a two-night stay in hospital following his ducking in the harbour, Ascari had gone home to Milan, where the Italian Motor Nautical Federation presented him with a life jacket for future races and a society of frogmen made him an honorary member of their organisation. On the Wednesday he visited the local Lancia dealer and took a call from Castellotti, who said that he would be testing his Ferrari 750S sports car at Monza the next day and issued an invitation to Ascari to go and watch. On Thursday Ascari was at the track by noon. It was a warm spring day and after a light lunch with friends in the grandstand restaurant he accepted Castellotti's suggestion to try the car, probably on the basis that someone who has just fallen off a horse should get back in the saddle as soon as possible. Lacking his own helmet, goggles and gloves, he borrowed Castellotti's kit – a decision already surprising to those who knew of his profoundly superstitious attitude to such things – and set off. He had not driven a Ferrari for several months. He had never driven on Englebert tyres. The 750 Monza was known to be unforgiving of the slightest error. Ascari took the first couple of laps slowly, and then speeded up. When he reached the fast Vialone curve, where he had personally persuaded the track managers to add an extra yard of concrete to the exit so that it could be taken flat out, the car got away from him, flicked sideways and overturned, throwing him out as it bounced away down the grass verge and into the bushes. He died before the ambulance could get him to hospital.

No definitive explanation of the crash was ever found. Ferrari listened to the theory that a broken nasal septum, suffered in the Monaco crash, had affected Ascari. He also heard the patently absurd story that a track labourer, thinking that everyone was taking a lunchtime break, had tried to cross the circuit in the path of the approaching Ferrari, forcing the driver to brake violently. 'All we could find on the track were the signs of sudden, violent braking,' Ferrari said. 'It was also clear that the car hadn't strayed a millimetre off line. Indeed it looked as if the front wheels had dug in, just as they would if the driver had braked to avoid an object that had just appeared in front of him.' Ascari's funeral, at San Carlo al Corso in Milan, drew tens of thousands. He was buried next to his father in the family tomb. Enzo Ferrari wrote a letter of condolence, to which Mietta Ascari, Alberto's widow, replied: 'So far everything seems to be only an ugly dream, and I still have the impression that he will be back from one of his trips and that everything will again be as it was before.'

Castellotti raced alone at Spa, retiring at half-distance, and Gianni Lancia contacted Mike Hawthorn, who had been having a bad time at Vanwall, and signed him up as Ascari's replacement. But the shadow cast by Ascari's death had blighted the team, compounded by a financial crisis which was soon to lead to the entire Lancia company passing into the hands of a cement baron with little interest in racing and no interest in spending money on it.

Now it was that Ferrari's threat to quit grand prix racing, made during his long sulk at the beginning of 1954, bore unexpected fruit. Stuck with hopeless cars and over-the-hill drivers, he glimpsed his opportunity. Renewing his claims of poverty, he talked to his friends at Fiat — to Professor Vittorio Valletta, who had taken over as chairman from the late founder, Giovanni Agnelli, and to Valletta's designated successor, Agnelli's grandson Gianni, a playboy lawyer who was on his way to becoming the most powerful man in Italy. Gianni Agnelli was already a Ferrari customer. He had bought an early 166 *barchetta*, painted dark blue and dark green; in 1952, aged thirty-one and a vice-president of his grandfather's company, he had smashed into a meat truck in a Monte Carlo street at five o'clock in the morning while driving home from a party. His leg had been broken in six places, but he evidently bore no malice towards the car's manufacturer. Since Fiat's business and interests were becoming inextricably linked with those of the state, Valletta and Agnelli could see the national as well as the commercial sense in helping the smaller concern to preserve and perhaps extend its reputation. The company whose chief designer had once sent Enzo Ferrari jobless and tearful into the streets of Turin now came to his rescue. Fiat would pay Lancia an annual sum, believed to have been about £30,000 a year, which would enable Enzo Ferrari to take over all the stock of the Scuderia Lancia – its cars, its spares, its tools, its drivers and engineers – to do with as he wished. Six sparkling and barely used Lancia D50s arrived at Maranello, along with Mike Hawthorn, Eugenio Castellotti, Vittorio Jano and Luigi Bazzi, Ferrari's old collaborator. It was a remarkable stroke of good fortune, and it was enough to pull the Scuderia Ferrari round.

While Ferrari spent the rest of the Formula One season working out how to deploy his new resources, Fangio and Moss dominated the remaining races, giving the Argentine his third championship. But in any case the second half of the season was entirely overshadowed by a tragedy at Le Mans. On a Saturday evening in June, Pierre Bouillin, a forty-nine-year-old motor trader and brush manufacturer from Paris racing under the pseudonym of Pierre Levegh, swerved his Mercedes-Benz to avoid Hawthorn's Jaguar in front of the pits and hit the back of Lance Macklin's Austin-Healey. The impact launched the Mercedes over an earth banking and into the crowd, killing Levegh and eighty-two spectators. Instantly the whole of motor racing was on trial. The Vatican condemned the sport, and Switzerland banned it for good. Back in Stuttgart, the Daimler-Benz board held an emergency meeting, withdrew their cars from the race, and then decided to withdraw from all racing at the end of the season. Juan Manuel Fangio, three times world champion, would be looking for new employment.

Enzo Ferrari, test driver Martino Severi, team manager Federico Giberti and
Peter Collins (in cockpit) at the factory, 1957.

Seven

Françoise Sagan was eighteen when she wrote *Bonjour Tristesse*. With the proceeds of her mildly scandalous international bestseller, the story of a young girl's awakening, she bought a leopard-skin coat and a Jaguar XK120. She drove too fast, and a crash put her in hospital. The car was a write-off. When she had recovered she paid a visit to Maranello and to Enzo Ferrari, who told her that, with regret, he could not supply a new convertible for her to drive straight away. But he was obviously intrigued by the girl, and they talked about her crash. The Jaguar's steering, he suggested, had probably been too heavy for her delicate wrists to control once the accident had begun. Then, having told a small but courteous lie about the extent of his knowledge of her work, he asked how one so young could have come by so much knowledge of life.

'*Mais non, monsieur,*' Sagan replied. '*C'est seulement de la fantaisie!*'

A little while later she asked if she could try one of his cars. When she returned, she was full of exhilaration.

'Monsieur Ferrari,' she said, 'it's the greatest car in the world!'

'Mademoiselle,' he replied, 'you are being generous. I hope you haven't been using your *fantaisie* again.'

Sagan certainly loved speed. 'The plane trees at the side of the road seem to lie flat,' she wrote in her memoirs. 'At night the neon lights of petrol stations are lengthened and distorted; your tyres no longer screech, but are suddenly muffled and quietly attentive; even your sorrows are swept away: however madly and hopelessly in love you may be, at two hundred kilometres an hour you are less so. Your blood no longer congeals around your heart; it throbs to the extremities of your body; to your fingertips, your toes and your eyelids, now the fateful and tireless guardians of your own life. It's crazy how your body, your nerves and your senses hold you in the grip of life. For who has not thought that life was not pointless without that other person, and put his foot down on the accelerator, at once resistant and responsive? Who has not then felt his whole body tense, one hand moving to stroke the gears while the other grips the steering wheel, legs outstretched, deceptively relaxed, but ready for a violent jolt, ready to swerve and brake? And while taking these precautions to remain alive, who has not thrilled to the awesome and fascinating silence of imminent death, at once a rebuttal and a provocation? Whoever has not thrilled to speed has not thrilled to life – or perhaps has never loved anyone . . .'

By some mysterious process the cars built by Enzo Ferrari had come to embody this fevered commingling of sex and death, these emotions as violet as the ink in which he signed his name. The name Ferrari meant speed, but now much more than that. It meant the unspeakable glamour of the sudden death of the young and beautiful. Of all the racing-car manufacturers, Enzo Ferrari had become the most easily identifiable, even though he never attended races. His remoteness had increased his allure. He was the one who sent young men out to their deaths, helmeted and gauntleted, in cars painted the colour of blood, a knightly shield emblazoned on their flanks.

Now those shields were to be found on the sides of cars that had not been born in the Maranello stable. Ferrari faced 1956 with a squadron of cars built by Lancia and modified by his own engineers, nominally under Jano, although the old designer was annoyed when Ferrari insisted on moving the D50's fuel tanks from the pontoons to a more conventional location in the tail. Lampredi, humiliated by the tacit acknowledgement of his failure with the Squalo and its derivatives, left for Fiat, where he worked on road cars. And Ferrari began to rebuild his team of drivers – although without the advice of Nello Ugolini, who had performed the unforgivable act of accepting Omer Orsi's offer to run the Maserati team, for a salary twice that on offer at Ferrari. Ugolini crossed the via Emilia, never to return.

Ferrari gained Castellotti from Lancia, but lost Hawthorn, who had insisted on continuing to drive for Jaguar in sports-car races, to which Ferrari would not agree. To replace him he hired another young Englishman. Peter Collins, twenty-three, came from Kidderminster and had made an impression since his first outings in the tiny motorcycle-engined Formula Three cars. Two years younger than Moss and Hawthorn, he had been a team mate of the former in the HWM Formula Two team and was the best friend of the latter. The three of them were the glamour boys of British racing – Moss small and keen, Hawthorn large and informal, Collins youthful and debonair, on his way to marriage with a Hollywood actress.

Castellotti was not the only Italian in the team, which had also been joined by Luigi Musso, a thirty-year-old Roman, a diplomat's son who had worked his way up with Maserati sports cars. Castellotti and Musso: the protagonists of a classic Italian duel, of north versus south. And both with actress girlfriends: Castellotti with the blonde Delia Scala, already a star, Musso with the dark-haired Fiamma Breschi, *una bimba*, twenty-one years old. Castellotti was self-conscious about his lack of height; he was nervous and intense. 'Eugenio hated publicity,' Delia Scala said. 'There was an ingenuousness about him. He was an only child. Every time he left for a race, his mother would say, "Drive carefully".' Musso, taller and more self-confident, sometimes wore polo shirts edged with the maroon and orange of AS Roma, his favourite football club. 'He had the face of a child, and the heart, too,' Fiamma Breschi remembered. 'For him, life was always a game.'

But if these two looked like the product of some breeding programme intended to produce archetypal Ferrari drivers of the 1950s, another addition to the team was perhaps the most natural Ferrari driver of the lot. Don Alfonso de Cabeza Vaca, the seventh Marquès de Portago – Fon de Portago, for short – had been born in London twenty-seven years earlier and was an Olympic fencer, Grand National rider, Cresta Run competitor, multilinguist, smoker of cigarettes through a long holder, and a lover of beautiful women – in fact a Porfirio Rubirosa with the talent and the desire to make a deserved place for himself in the upper echelon of racing drivers. Ferrari was both fascinated and mildly repelled by the well-born de Portago's dishevelled appearance, remarking on 'his air of personal neglect with his stubbly chin, his hair in need of a cut, his shabby leather jacket and his loose-jointed gait . . .' But he added, with a shrug, 'It cannot be denied that he made quite an effect on the women, for he was tall and good-looking. In my mind's eye I always see him as a rare and perfect gentleman, despite the deliberate roughness of his outward appearance.'

The supporting cast to these front-line drivers included Trintignant and Olivier Gendebien, a Belgian gentleman driver, a civilised and cultured man and a specialist in sports cars. But the greatest star of all, and to Ferrari the most necessary but the least welcome, arrived in the shape of Juan Manuel Fangio. Ferrari sensed, as soon as he saw Fangio at work in his first summer in Europe back in 1949, that here was a star, but the two had never warmed to each other. Before their negotiations began, Ferrari knew the discussions were going to be unusually awkward. Fangio had driven for Alfa, Maserati and Mercedes; he was wise in the ways of motor racing, and he had a shrewd idea of what he was worth. He was also in certain financial difficulties back home, thanks to the fall of the Perónist government, to which he had been closely aligned, and he needed the best terms he could get. He sent his agent, Marcello Giambertone, to do the job, which irritated Ferrari, who liked to have the freedom to seduce or bully drivers without obstruction when trying to get their signatures on a contract. From Fangio's point of view, Ferrari was wasting time trying to beat him down. But they needed each other. Fangio was the world's best driver, and his presence provided the clearest guarantee of a championship that season. Ferrari had the Lancia cars, which, for all the delays surrounding their initial appearance and the fragility of their early performances, promised to be the class of the field, particularly if their advanced design could be backed up by Ferrari's solid engineering. In Enzo Ferrari's account it sounds as though he agreed to the deal – twelve million lire a year, plus a cut of the prize money, plus extras – just to avoid a further round of negotiations, so that he would not have to listen to the irritating sound of Fangio's high, tinny voice or have 'that inscrutable expression marked by the shadow of an indefinable squinting smile' hanging around his office.

Fangio, too, was accompanied by a woman, the gamine Doña Andreina, known as Beba, who was at his side throughout his career in Europe. Sometimes he described her as his wife; later he said they had never married. Fiamma Breschi described her as 'a primadonna, both in the pits and out shopping'. She had a reputation for collecting every titbit of gossip and reporting it back to her man, helping to create an atmosphere of distrust within the team. Ferrari, of course, had firm views about drivers' wives. The good ones either stayed in the background and gave unquestioning support, like Carolina Nuvolari ('a shining example of sweetness, of understanding, of tolerance for whatever her husband was undergoing'), or came to the races and made themselves useful with stopwatches, like the two wives of Rudi Caracciola, Charly and Baby. The bad ones were a distraction. And it was his experience that when a driver died, there were always two women left bleeding.

The story of Ferrari, Fangio and the 1956 season turned into one of constant accusations of treachery and double-dealing, which started with Ferrari's customary refusal to name a number-one driver, a policy that infuriated Fangio and was still causing problems within the team forty-five years later, long after Ferrari's death. 'It's impossible to pre-arrange a result,' Ferrari said in explanation of his philosophy, 'and for me the number one is always the one who wins.' Yet whatever conflicts the two men's temperaments may have provoked, the unwilling partnership produced the desired championship. In Argentina, Fangio took over Musso's car after his own engine gave trouble and outran the Maseratis; in those days two drivers were allowed to share a car, each taking half the championship points. Moss, now the Maserati team leader, won at Monaco, Fangio swapping cars with Collins to finish second after his own developed a suspension problem. Back in Europe, Collins won the Targa Florio and Castellotti the Mille Miglia before the grand prix season resumed. Then Collins won at Spa, after Fangio's transmission had broken when he looked a certain winner, and again in France, where Fangio drove brilliantly into third place after a split fuel line had sprayed petrol into his face. After Spa, Ferrari had been delighted for Collins, 'a fine-looking lad with a pleasant, open face' and, of course, someone who, unlike Fangio, was young and new enough to be grateful simply for the opportunity of driving for Mr Ferrari. But on the eve of the French Grand Prix, on 30 June, Dino Ferrari died at the family home in Modena, and his father's world changed utterly.

Dino was twenty-four. After the illness had curtailed his studies at Bologna University he had gone to work at the factory, in the design office, helping with the engines. He moved into a flat above the Ristorante Cavallino, opened in the old Cavani farm building across the road from the factory gates. His father gave him a 2-litre sports car, which he occasionally took for a spin around the Modena autodrome. Most mornings he visited Sergio Scaglietti's works on the viale Monte Kosica in Modena, checking on the progress of the bodywork for some car or other. He had a fiancée, Ines. The Marzotto brothers had taken him on a trip to Le Mans. When he became bedridden, Peter Collins would visit him to describe the story of the movie he had seen the previous night, a gesture the boy's father never forgot. 'I had always deluded myself – a father always deludes himself – that we should be able to restore him to health,' Enzo Ferrari wrote. 'I was convinced that he was like one of my cars, one of my engines.' He and Laura were constantly protective, attentive to the minutest detail. They ensured that he never sat in draughts, and they would make him put on extra clothes when he went out. Strangers sometimes thought their precautions exaggerated, but they had not lived through the boy's decline. Enzo drew up graphs to keep a daily record of Dino's food intake and its effect. 'Until one evening, in the notebook in which I put down all these particulars, I simply wrote, "The game is lost."'

In a procession befitting one who, in his father's eyes, had been destined to become an outstanding engineer, Dino's coffin was carried from the funeral service on the shoulders of overalled mechanics from the factory. He was buried in a new tomb in the cemetery of San Cataldo, where his grandfather was also reinterred and spaces were allocated for the surviving family members. And the following year, when he launched a new Formula Two car with a V6 engine of 1.5 litres, Ferrari announced that it would be called the Dino, claiming that his son had been responsible for its concept and had worked with the engineers on the early plans. This highly successful engine was to be the first of several memorials, which included a new technical school in his name in the centre of Maranello, the naming of via Ing. Alfredo 'Dino' Ferrari, and, eventually, the renaming of the grand prix circuit at Imola in memory of the father and the son. 'The conviction has never left me', Enzo Ferrari once said, 'that when a man says to a woman, "I love you," what he means is, "I desire you," and that the only real love possible in this world is that of a father for his son.'

Ferrari's mourning was loud and long, and had barely begun when Fangio won the next two grands prix, at Silverstone, after Moss had dropped out of a comfortable lead, and at the Nürburgring. When the teams arrived at Monza for the season's finale, any one of three drivers – Fangio, Collins and Moss – could win the title. No fewer than five Ferraris were on the starting grid, piloted by Fangio, Castellotti, Musso, Collins and de Portago, preparing for what turned out to be a dramatic contest. Fangio knew that he needed only a third place to clinch the title, that the two Italians were desperate to win their home race, and that their Englebert tyres would not stand up to much abuse on the combined road track and banked oval. He went to Castellotti and Musso shortly before the start and suggested that if they took it easy for most of the race, he would let them through to battle it out over the last ten laps. Inevitably they ignored him, and within five laps they were both back in the pits, having chewed up their tyres while fighting furiously against each other. But Fangio's steering arm broke on the twentieth lap, putting his title in danger, particularly with Moss in the lead. Castellotti had spun off and damaged his car too badly to continue, and when Musso, charging back through the field, came in for a pit stop, he was invited to hand his car over to Fangio. Having given up his drive in Buenos Aires at the beginning of the season, this time he remained in his seat, staring straight ahead and affecting not to hear. Before long he would be back in the lead. Beba dashed up to Fiamma Breschi. 'You don't treat a champion of the world like that,' Fangio's companion told Musso's girlfriend. But when Collins came in, his Ferrari in third place and chasing Moss's Maserati, he responded to the request very differently, stepping out without a word and letting the maestro climb in. He was young enough, he said later, to know that his chance would come again. Musso had his first grand prix victory dashed from his grasp when a steering arm and a tyre burst as he came off the banking four laps from the end, leaving Moss to take the flag ahead of Fangio. Twenty-five years later the historian Michael Lynch made a strenuous attempt to prove that Fangio did not need the extra points in order to win the title, and that Collins' gesture was therefore statistically meaningless; but the fact remains that had Collins stayed in the car, and had Moss – who was suffering from a split petrol tank – retired, he would have been world champion, at the age of twenty-four. Instead Fangio, forty-five, claimed his fourth title.

But the arguments had only just begun, and were to last for years. On his client's behalf, Marcello Giambertone produced a litany of allegations of internal sabotage, beginning with complaints that during the Mille Miglia the mechanics had cut holes in Fangio's car designed to let the rainwater in rather than out, and reaching a climax with the claim that Eraldo Sculati, Ugolini's successor, had refused to ask Collins to give up the car at Monza but had quit the pits and gone to the press stand in order to avoid the issue, leaving Giambertone to make the request. Ferrari responded with measured fury. 'Fangio was a really great driver,' he wrote, 'but afflicted by a persecution mania. I was not the only one against whom he entertained all kinds of suspicions.' Even his appreciation of the champion's skill was infused with poison: 'I think it unlikely that we shall ever see a champion capable of such a series of sustained successes. Fangio did not remain loyal to any marque; he was conscious of his ability, he invariably used every endeavour to ensure that he should if possible always drive the best car available at the moment; and he was successful in this, placing his self-interest – which was quite legitimate and natural – before the affection which has, instead, kept other great drivers faithful to certain makes through good and ill fortune.'

In other words this driver thought himself more important than the car, a blatant breach of Ferrari's cardinal principle. The mutual dislike and distrust, however entertaining to others, could not be sustained at close quarters for another season. Fangio left the Scuderia, crossing the via Emilia to take up the leadership of Maserati. A typically logical career move, it was also the most provocative of farewell gestures. But many years later Fangio backtracked, in several directions. His memoirs, he claimed, had been written by Giambertone, his manager; he had never so much as read them before they were published. And when he and Ferrari encountered each other, Fangio told his old boss: 'I'm no longer married. I see things in a different light now.' To Fiamma Breschi, when they met in Monte Carlo three decades after his year with Ferrari, he mentioned Beba and said: 'She was the biggest burden of my life.'

★

[193]

That Sunday afternoon they had walked up from the village of Guidizzolo, a distance of just over a mile. In the morning they had stood outside the cafés and watched the smaller cars going through, tyres squealing as they braked and slalomed around the dark red church building on their way to Brescia, less than thirty miles distant. Now, outside the village, the big cars would be at their maximum speed. Fields stretched away into the distance on either side of the ditches bordering the ruler-straight two-lane road running through this flat countryside. It was a May day in 1957, and the trees were barely in leaf. The villagers stood on the bank, looking over the ditch that lay between them and the road, and waited.

The red Ferrari with the number 531 on its bonnet would have been doing around 175 mph, close to its maximum, when it approached them from the direction of Mantua, a distant droning dot quickly growing bigger and louder. Did they see, before its left front tyre burst, the white helmet of the driver and the darker one of his passenger? The car, travelling at more than 250 feet per second, swerved and slewed and tumbled end over end as it mounted the bank and flew into the air, the aluminium panels shaped by Scaglietti's artisans disintegrating as it smashed against the trees before coming to rest in the water-filled ditch, most of its bodywork gone. Today the names of the nine spectators who were killed by the Ferrari, five of them children, are inscribed on a white marble memorial standing in a small copse at the point where it left the road. Also there, on an adjacent slab, are the names of Alfonso de Portago, the driver, and Edmund Nelson, his navigator and a former lift operator at the Plaza Hotel in New York; both were also killed instantly in the accident. Seven people had died in the previous year's race; this new tragedy was enough to spell the end of the Mille Miglia.

Piero Taruffi won the race in a Ferrari. He was fifty years old and had first taken part in the Mille Miglia in 1932, at the wheel of one of the Scuderia's Alfas. He had never won it before, and his failure had become an obsession. In 1955 he had left Ferrari after an episode in which he felt brusquely treated. Now, two years later, Ferrari had made him an offer. Drive one more Mille Miglia for me, he said, but you must promise your wife that if you win, you will retire from racing. Taruffi booked into a Modena hotel and made himself ready. Ferrari prepared a car in which he could drive one complete reconnaissance lap, spread over two days, with his wife Isabella as passenger on the second day. Taruffi was not really expected to win. His team mates, Collins and de Portago, a late substitute for Musso, who had caught hepatitis in Syracuse, and Wolfgang von Trips, a count with an ancient title and a *schloss* near Cologne, were younger and faster. But win Taruffi did, after Ferrari had instructed von Trips not to attack him in the final stretch. Waiting at the Bologna refuelling stop, he had told all his drivers to hold station. De Portago, he believed later, had listened to a journalist who told him that he had fallen behind and needed to speed up. De Portago's current girlfriend, the American actress Linda Christian, had kissed him during the brief halt at the Rome control and had then been driven to Ciampino airport to take a flight to Brescia, so that she could greet him at the finish. Twenty-four minutes behind Taruffi at Bologna, de Portago reached Mantua in ten hours and three minutes, three minutes ahead of the Italian and six minutes faster than von Trips. There were those who said that a mechanic had noticed a tyre rubbing against the damaged coachwork of Ferrari number 531 at the last checkpoint and wanted to change the wheel but had been waved away by the impatient driver. Another version suggested that the tyre had been cut by an imperfectly laid cat's-eye somewhere between Mantua and Guidizzolo. It was Taruffi's fourteenth Mille Miglia, the most joyful and the saddest, the fulfilment of a dream and the end of a legend.

Missing from the team that day was Eugenio Castellotti, killed in March testing a new Tipo 801 grand prix car at the Modena autodrome. He and Delia Scala had announced their engagement, and he had been with her in Florence, where she was appearing in a play. A few days earlier, in Modena, Ferrari had noticed some tension between this glamorous and popular couple. When he asked Scala about it, she said that Castellotti wanted to get married, but also wanted her to give up her career. Why, she said, shouldn't she ask him to give up *his* career? Ferrari, perhaps an unlikely marriage-guidance counsellor, told Castellotti that they should not try to impose change on each other: 'Try to understand one another better and try, too, each of you, to understand also yourself better.' But once in Florence, Castellotti was not overjoyed to be rung up and told that his presence was required in Modena the next day, since Jean Behra was setting new records at the *aeroautodromo* with the latest Maserati, and that he would need to arise from his bed at dawn to drive to the track and defend the team's honour. Within a few laps he had made the mistake that killed him.

'He was going through a confused and conflicting time emotionally,' Ferrari said, 'and probably his reflexes failed him for a moment.' Fiamma Breschi remarked that when Ferrari needed to find a scapegoat for the failures of his machines, the feelings of men and women were not taken into consideration. 'Especially of women,' she added. Castellotti and Delia Scala had met a year earlier, outside a nightclub, when the actress noticed that the blue of the driver's trousers matched the shade of his Cadillac convertible. 'I was his girlfriend for a year,' she said. 'The circumstances were very complicated. He was racing, I was performing – both very demanding. The tragedy happened twenty-five days before our wedding.'

Ferrari liked his drivers to womanise, so that they could tell him all about it afterwards, but was sometimes not so keen when they established grown-up relationships. Take Collins, for example. After Dino's death, Ferrari had given the Englishman the boy's apartment, which allowed him to move out of the Hotel Real. But when, in February 1957, Collins suddenly married Louise Cordier, a blonde American actress known professionally as Louise King, Ferrari claimed to detect a change in the driver's mood. They had married in Coconut Grove, Miami, where the bride was appearing in *The Seven Year Itch*. A few weeks later they celebrated at El Morocco in New York with de Portago, von Trips and other team mates. Collins' parents disapproved, and so did his employer. Ferrari thought Louise's love of partying had drawn Collins into a world of excessive drinking, which damaged his reflexes. 'They had met a year earlier in Monte Carlo but she had made no impact on him,' he wrote. 'She was the type of girl you find in the pits. But a trip to Florida changed all that. She intrigued and seduced him. So Peter phoned his father and they got married. Collins still preserved his old enthusiasm and skill, and was still outstanding, but a change nevertheless became evident in his happy character. He became irritable and friends whispered that America had robbed him of his sleep.' Ferrari lent the couple his villa outside Maranello, but was displeased when they announced their intention to live on a boat in Monte Carlo. His general view was that marriage and children slowed a driver by dividing his concentration. A mass of firm evidence already existed both to support and to demolish his case.

Collins was certainly pleased by the return to the team of his chum Hawthorn, with whom he could still get into bachelor-boy scrapes. But the grand prix season began with an effortless victory for Fangio in Argentina, leading a Maserati sweep of the first four places; the six Lancia-Ferraris fell out or fell away. Once again, only eighteen months after receiving the gift of a complete race team, the Scuderia had surrendered the initiative. Sculati, evidently too terrified to make the telephone call back to Italy with the bad news, was taken out to lunch and fired on his return. He was replaced by Romolo Tavoni, a former journalist who had been acting as Ferrari's press secretary. Not that this switch of personnel could halt the decline, which grew more apparent when the Vanwall team, absent in Buenos Aires, made their appearance at Monaco. Moss, their number one, jumped into the lead but made a mistake at the chicane on the third lap, starting an accident which also eliminated Collins and Hawthorn. Fangio, who had been hanging back in his Maserati, picked his way through the debris with the delicacy of a cat on a crowded mantelpiece. He won again at Rouen, but had to give way at Aintree to Moss and Tony Brooks, who shared a Vanwall to become the first British drivers to win a proper grand prix in a British car since Sir Henry Segrave in 1923.

At the Nürburgring the huge crowd watched Fangio produce the drive of his life, at Ferrari's expense. Having practised over the fourteen-mile circuit in a time a quarter of a minute under the lap record, he started the race with his 250F's tank only half full and built up a lead of thirty seconds over Hawthorn and Collins before coming in for fuel and new rear tyres. The poorly executed stop took almost a minute, causing Ugolini to tear his hair out, but within eight laps Fangio had clawed back the deficit and was on the tails of the two Ferraris. On the twentieth lap he clocked a time twenty-four seconds below the lap record and the next time round he overtook first Collins and then Hawthorn, shoving them aside as though they were children in soapbox carts. Hawthorn tried to take the fight back to him, but this was Fangio – held in universal admiration and affection by his fellow competitors, if not by Enzo Ferrari – at his most ruthless, the bareknuckle racer who had been raised on those thousand-mile marathons across the Altiplano. 'Even though Peter and I had been beaten,' Hawthorn generously reflected, 'we had enjoyed every minute of it.'

Intense criticism following the Mille Miglia accident had been directed chiefly at Ferrari, portrayed as the lethally cynical old man who sat at home sending young men out to mow down women and children. He was charged with manslaughter, the indictment focusing on his decision to fit the car with Englebert tyres allegedly unsuited to its capabilities. As with the charge against Ascari in 1951, the process a consequence of a legal system which insisted that all deaths must be investigated and possible causes put to the fullest test. If the demands of the system appeared to offend against a rather nebulous set of sporting values, then they certainly enshrined the emotional requirements of the families of the dead, acknowledging their right to the most thorough investigation of circumstances and blame. Like Ascari, Ferrari was exonerated after four years of rumour and uncertainty. But his immediate reaction to the charge was to respond to the perceived affront with one of his melodramatic gestures.

The grand prix teams were moving on to Pescara, where, since the Suez fuel crisis had forced the cancellation of several earlier races, the old circuit, taking in seaside promenade and mountain roads, was being used for the first and only time as a world-championship course. Ferrari announced his intention to stay away as a sign of his displeasure with the Mille Miglia witch-hunt. Only the pleas of Musso, desperate for the points he needed in order to take second place in the championship, persuaded him to send a single car down to the resort on the Adriatic. Musso got away to a wonderful start as the cars streamed up into the hills, and managed to come past the pits in the lead at the end of the first lap, but Moss soon took charge, holding the Italian at bay until the Ferrari ran out of oil. 'Musso's performance that day', the historian Alan Henry wrote, 'epitomised the role of the dauntless, patriotic, hard-trying Italian Ferrari driver, pulling every trick in the book to try and make up for a combination of car deficiency and a shortage of natural flair.' Moss came home a comfortable winner, more than three minutes ahead of Fangio in what could be seen as the last grand prix of the era of motor races held over public roads, taking in urban and rural settings and accepting the surroundings as they existed, lampposts and ditches and brick walls and all. In that sense, it was the end of the heroic age.

Nothing could be done at Monza either, where the season ended with a sign of things to come: three green British Vanwalls on the front row alongside Fangio, the fastest Ferrari, driven by Collins, no higher than seventh on the grid. An untouchable Moss won the race, the cars from Maranello betrayed by lack of speed and hopeless unreliability. The best result went to von Trips, two laps behind the winner in third place. And Fangio had his fifth title, at the wheel of a car drawn up by Colombo, in a team managed by Ugolini, for a company on its last legs after a series of business disasters for the Orsi family. The Scuderia Maserati may have won the title, but it was on the brink of making its last appearance in grand prix racing.

In Buenos Aires four months later, at the start of the 1958 season, there was an even more vivid signal of the changing of the old order when, in the absence of his Vanwall, Moss turned up to challenge the Italian teams with a privately entered rear-engined Cooper with a 2-litre engine based on the powerplant of a fire pump. The thoroughbreds – Collins, Hawthorn and Musso in Ferraris, and Fangio, Behra and Schell in Maseratis – were humbled by a mongrel. Moss and his mechanic, Alf Francis, won the race with a splendid gambit, lulling the pursuing Musso and Hawthorn in the final stages by putting fresh tyres out against the pit counter as though they were planning to make a stop, but then running straight through to the end, with the tyre treads worn almost to the canvas beneath. It was a piece of pure pickpocketing, the sort of inspired improvisation to which the Ferrari team, riven with paranoia and jealousy, was never able to aspire. Nor did Enzo Ferrari see the writing on the wall when he looked at photographs of the Cooper in the next morning's *Gazzetta dello Sport* and listened to Tavoni's explanations on the telephone. Nature must be respected. Even when Trintignant took the same Cooper and won the next race, at Monaco, Ferrari did not budge. The ox must still pull the cart.

The team did, however, have new cars at last, and they bore Dino's name, being powered by an enlarged version of the V6 engines that were said to have sprung from his initial inspiration. A prototype Dino 246 had already killed one of its designers, Andrea Fraschetti, who had lost control during a test at the Modena autodrome. Now they were in the care of Carlo Chiti, an imposingly plump engineer who arrived from Alfa Romeo to replace Fraschetti and took up residence in an apartment next to Ferrari's, on the first floor of 11 viale Trento e Trieste. The Dino 246, lighter and more responsive than the Lancia-Ferrari, turned out to be the equal of the latest 250F and of the Vanwall, which would lead to a season's close racing, albeit one over which, in the end, it was hard to enthuse. Moss won in Holland and Brooks in Belgium, establishing the credibility of the Vanwall's challenge, but when Hawthorn won at Rheims it was against a background of new tragedy.

On 11 May, Luigi Musso had triumphed in the Targa Florio for Ferrari. It was to be his last victory, although not his last moment of greatness. At Monza in June the second Race of Two Worlds was held, in which Indianapolis cars came to challenge the European grand prix teams on the banked oval at Monza. It was an interesting idea, but flawed: whereas the American cars were ideally suited to the *pista alta velocità*, the Europeans were not. Effectively, they had shot themselves in the foot as bizarrely as had the Americans when they created a twisty circuit on which to hold the Vanderbilt Cup race in 1936. Nevertheless local pride forced Maserati to build an Indianapolis-style special for Stirling Moss, subsidised by an ice-cream maker and named the Eldorado Special, while Ferrari took the 4.1-litre V12 engine from de Portago's Mille Miglia wreck, bolted it to an old 375 Formula One chassis, and handed it to Musso.

When she met Luigi Musso, three years earlier, Fiamma Breschi had been reading the poetry of D'Annunzio. She dreamed of meeting a man who was 'tall, self-confident, elegant, fascinating, with a penetrating gaze and a fine head of hair, living a life of adventure and passion'. Musso was all those things, she thought. He, in turn, felt strongly enough to leave his wife and two children for this eighteen-year-old beauty. And in addition to all the qualities she had noted, he was, as the spectators at Monza that weekend discovered, incredibly brave. After setting the fastest practice lap at an average speed of 175 mph, in the race he fought for the honour of Italy, his car bucking and jolting over the bumps on the banking's uneven concrete, straining every sinew to stay on terms with the Americans. The fact that he was overcome by fumes in the attempt merely added to the honour he gained that day, even in the eyes of those who did not consider him to be a driver of the very first rank. Of his courage there could be no more doubt.

Two weeks later he was at Rheims for the French Grand Prix, the season's best-rewarded race, in financial terms as well as in the cases of champagne awarded for the fastest laps in practice and the race. The previous year he had won enough money to buy Fiamma a little grey Fiat *Seicento*. But now the atmosphere in the Ferrari camp had deteriorated. Musso accused Hawthorn and Collins of operating a sort of cartel to divide up the prize money between them. Collins had been ordered to stand down from the grand prix and drive in the Formula Two race instead. This, so it was said, constituted a punishment for purposely frying his clutch soon after the start the previous week at Le Mans, where he and Hawthorn had been overheard joking that they would be 'home for Sunday lunch'. Mino Amorotti, a man with no love for the English, had passed the story back to Ferrari – who, it was alleged, had responded: 'Collins will pay for that.' Musso was also said to be under extra pressure from creditors to repay debts incurred in setting up an agency to import Pontiac cars into Italy. The starting money and prizes at Rheims could make a big dent in that debt. The winner, for example, would take home £10,000.

Collins had argued his case with Tavoni effectively enough to be reinstated by the time the race started, but all eyes were on Hawthorn and Musso, first and second in the opening laps. Musso was on the Englishman's tail as they passed the pits for the sixth time, pushing hard. Beyond the brow of the hill lay a right-hand kink, usually taken with only the slightest lift of the accelerator pedal but which the best and bravest – Fangio, for example – could negotiate at full throttle. A slower Maserati was ahead, about to be lapped by the leading duo. As they went through the kink at about 150 mph, Musso lost the car. In his mirror, Hawthorn saw the Ferrari suddenly going broadside, then disappearing in a cloud of dust. By the time Fiamma Breschi reached the hospital, her boyfriend was dead. Had he and Hawthorn touched as they approached the kink? There were no reliable witnesses. No doubt they were racing each other, in the way that Ferrari always preferred. That was why he was always reluctant to designate a number one. He believed that the drivers had to fight it out for themselves, and the best would emerge. Or survive. To Ferrari, Musso was 'the last in a line of Italian stylists that began with Nazzaro and Varzi'.

Fiamma went home to her family in Florence. After a while, letters began to arrive from Maranello. At first sporadic, then almost daily. A few months later Enzo Ferrari invited her to meet him in Modena, at the Hotel Real. She was met by Tavoni, who took her to a restaurant, La Baia del Re. There Ferrari was waiting, with Peppino Verdelli at a nearby table. They talked about her future and his obsession with cars. He cried when she told him about the recent suicide of her widowed grandmother. She said something about how he himself had endured 'terrible joys' pursuing his destiny; three years later, she noted, the phrase turned up as the title of his memoirs. When lunch was over he took her to Maranello and introduced her to Dan Gurney, Musso's crew-cut successor. And afterwards he drove her to Bologna station, in a Ferrari, with Peppino squashed in behind the front seats. Before long he had set her up with a shop in Bologna and taken to paying her regular visits; later, after she had returned to Florence, he would mention the possibility of marriage, or so she claimed. 'She used to come to the factory, and to the races,' Brenda Vernor, Ferrari's secretary in later years, said. 'One of the many.'

Hawthorn celebrated the victory at Rheims, at first unaware that Musso was dead. That night there was a party, the usual sort, with horseplay involving a hosepipe. But there was an outcry from those who thought motor racing amounted to ritualised murder. *L'Osservatore Romana*, the official Vatican newspaper, published an editorial aimed directly at establishing the guilt of the man in whose cars Ascari, Castellotti, De Portago and others had died. The writer drew a parallel between Enzo Ferrari and a Greek myth. 'A modern Saturn,' he wrote, 'that is to say a Saturn who has become a captain of

[203]

industry, continues to devour his own sons. As in the myth, so it is, unhappily, in reality. The latest of his victims is Luigi Musso . . .'

At Silverstone, the British crowd saw Collins win, with Hawthorn second. Moss broke down and Brooks in the second Vanwall was slowed by a mechanical problem, but with Musso and Castellotti gone, and with Fangio having departed quietly into retirement after finishing fourth at Rheims, the championship was now certain to be won for the first time by an Englishman. The likelihood of it being an Englishman in a Ferrari was halved at the Nürburgring, where Brooks had overtaken Collins to take the lead on the eleventh lap when tragedy struck the Ferrari team yet again. Chasing the Vanwall out of a dip and into a climbing right-hander, trying to stop Brooks from making a break, and with Hawthorn sitting back to watch the battle, Collins made a slight error. Accelerating hard in second gear, the car drifted wide of the usual line, the left rear wheel mounted the grass verge, and suddenly the car was flipped into the air, throwing its driver out. Hawthorn braked, almost stopped, looked round, then accelerated away. After a few more kilometres, his clutch failed. He asked a marshal to telephone the pits and was told that Collins had merely suffered a few bruises. At the end of the race he was driven back to the paddock, stopping at the scene of the crash to collect Collins' helmet and gloves but unable to get any sense of what might have been his team mate's fate. Not until he and Louise arrived at the specialist neurology clinic at Bonn University that night were they told that Collins had hit a tree when he was thrown from the car and had died in the hospital from head injuries.

In Portugal three weeks later they raced on the streets of Oporto, criss-crossed with tramlines. In barely a year Hawthorn had lost four of his team mates, one of them his best friend. Only two Ferraris lined up for a race which Moss won easily, with Hawthorn falling further and further behind in second place, his rapidly fading brakes causing him to spin and stall the car on the very last lap. He and Collins had been complaining about their old-fashioned drum brakes all season, comparing them unfavourably with the disc brakes fitted to the British cars. Now he got out and tried to push-start the Ferrari against a slight gradient, without success. Moss, passing by on his lap of honour, saw what was happening and shouted at him to push it downhill, against the direction of the circuit. Hawthorn turned the car round, did as Moss suggested, and secured his second place. However a track marshal had watched the manoeuvre and, believing it to be against the regulations, reported Hawthorn to the stewards, who held an immediate inquiry. Hawthorn told his story, followed in front of the tribunal by Moss, who said that his rival had only pushed the car on the pavement, which was not against the rules. After a long deliberation *in camera*, the stewards announced that Hawthorn would be allowed to keep his six points for second place. Moss's testimony on his behalf had convinced them.

There were two more races to go, and the championship hung in the balance. Before the Italian Grand Prix, Hawthorn persuaded Enzo Ferrari to allow his car to be fitted with disc brakes by Dunlop technicians with whom he had worked at Jaguar. Collins had paved the way by fitting his road-going Ferrari with discs, and then leaving it at the factory for the engineers to inspect and evaulate. Ferrari himself was reluctant, even when the technicians had arrived at Maranello, but after a day of argument the job was done. The widely circulated story that the brakes had been taken from Collins' GT car and fitted to Hawthorn's race car turned out not to be true. But again Ferrari had been forced into accepting progress.

He had received Louise Collins in Maranello after her husband's death, wept with her, and invited her to go with him to the Italian Grand Prix, promising that he was going to make his last race-day appearance there and suggesting that it might be good for her to be back among her old friends. She went. He, however, failed to turn up, although he had attended the practice days, as was his habit. Only 20,000 spectators paid to watch the race, a fraction of the usual number. The deaths of Castellotti and Musso had drained their enthusiasm, and they were not prepared to allow it to be rekindled by the sight of two Englishmen fighting for the title, even if one of them was in a Ferrari. Although Ferrari was the leading Italian team, it had certainly not acquired the pre-eminent position in the fans' emotions that it was to be granted in decades to come. The race, as it happened, was a fine one. Hawthorn was second to a Vanwall again, this time in the hands of Brooks. The Californian driver Phil Hill, previously noted for his success in sports cars, made his debut in a grand prix Ferrari, and caused a minor sensation by leading the first lap, setting the pace in an attempt to lure Moss to mechanical destruction. The Vanwall's gearbox broke, Moss took no points from the race, and the title would be decided at the Moroccan Grand Prix, on the outskirts of Casablanca.

During the five-week gap between the races, Enzo Ferrari called Hawthorn into his office. He wanted him to stay for 1959, he said. And he would let him write his own contract. It is not hard to imagine that Ferrari had been shocked by the loss of so many drivers, and particularly by that of Collins, who had been kind to his dying son. Ferrari had wanted Collins to stay close to him, in Maranello. Now the nearest thing to Collins that was left was Hawthorn. He must have seemed worth hanging on to, whether or not he became champion. Hawthorn replied that he would not commit himself until after the final race.

The terms of the showdown were simple. Moss had to win and to score the extra point for the fastest lap in the race; and his team mates, Brooks and Stuart Lewis-Evans, had to keep Hawthorn out of second place. Any other outcome would mean the title was Hawthorn's. Moss did his part, but Phil Hill performed more effectively than the Vanwall leader's lieutenants, holding second place until the time came to accept a signal to pull over and let Hawthorn through. That allowed Hawthorn to win the title by a single point – in effect, a point awarded when Stirling Moss, who was never to become champion, came to his aid in Oporto. Would Hawthorn, the carefree party animal, have done the same for Moss, the dedicated professional? And if he had, what would Enzo Ferrari have said? He might have saluted a remarkable example of sportsmanship, or he might not.

But even in its denouement, this season had bad cards to deal. As the race in Casablanca drew to a close, a pillar of black smoke rose above the desert. Lewis-Evans' car had crashed and caught fire, burning him so badly that he died a week later. And three months after Hawthorn's day of triumph, three months after he accepted Romolo Tavoni's post-race congratulations in the pit lane at Casablanca with the announcement that he was, at that very moment, already a retired racing driver with plans only to work in his family's garage business, the new world champion lost control of his Jaguar saloon in the rain while racing a friend on the Guildford bypass, clipped the tail of an oncoming truck, left the road and hit a tree, and died within moments.

Laura and Enzo Ferrari with (from left) the British constructors John Cooper and Colin Chapman and Porsche's competitions manager, Huschke von Hanstein, during practice for the Italian Grand Prix at Monza on 11 September 1961.

Eight

Phil Hill was the first of the Americans. Born in 1927, he was brought up in Santa Monica, California, where his father was the city postmaster. Of his childhood, he said: 'I was far more interested in my mother's shiny Marmon Speedster than in learning to play the piano.' He grew up hot-rodding Fords and Chevys, but his sister's boyfriend had a father who liked exotic foreign cars and he soon became familiar with Bugattis and Zagato-bodied Alfas. As soon as he was old enough he competed in everything he could get his hands on, from dirt-track midgets to MGs and XKs and a pre-war Alfa 2900 from the factory Mille Miglia team. In 1952, one month past his twenty-fifth birthday, he called Luigi Chinetti in New York and used $6,000 from an inheritance to buy a Ferrari 212 Export, the very car in which a French driver called Larivière had died at Le Mans in 1951, decapitated by a strand of barbed wire when he slid off the road at Tertre Rouge. It had been rebuilt in time to win that year's Tour de France rally. There were so few Ferraris in those days that each one seemed to come with a history attached. In his first race in the car, Hill finished second at Golden Gate Park in San Francisco.

Hill was hooked on Ferraris. He loved everything about them. In the next few years he drove many different models for many different owners, at Pebble Beach and Elkhart Lake and Watkins Glen and Torrey Pines and the various US Air Force bases and civilian airports – Sebring, McDill, Beverly, Moffett, Oakes Field – at which the Sports Car Club of America, the California Sports Car Club and the United States Auto Club organised their meetings. This was a time when rich men like

Briggs Cunningham, Temple Buell and Allen Guiberson loved getting hold of Ferraris and hiring brave young men to drive them. Tony Parravano, an immigrant from Naples who had made a fortune in construction and housing development in Detroit and Los Angeles, sent the Texan driver Carroll Shelby on frequent missions to Modena to buy Ferraris direct from the factory. Until his unexplained disappearance in the late Fifties, Parravano provided a series of top-line Ferrari sports cars in which young hotshots could make their reputations. Parravano himself even made trips to Maranello, where he was welcomed by Enzo Ferrari. But usually Chinetti was at the centre of all such transactions, creating the network and fostering the mystique. 'You have to admit that Luigi Chinetti is responsible for Ferrari's success in the United States,' said René Dreyfus, who drove for the pre-war Scuderia before becoming a successful New York restaurateur. When Bill Harrah of Reno bought the West Coast Ferrari dealership from Johnny von Neumann, he paid Chinetti a royalty on every car sold. Bob Grossman, a driver and a dealer in exotic imported cars in Nyack, an upstate New York community, was typical of the men who made deals with Chinetti to rent drives in the North American Racing Team's Ferraris at Sebring and Le Mans and the other major long-distance races. 'It was chaos,' he remembered, talking before Chinetti's death. 'Complete confusion. You never knew where you stood until half an hour before the race started. You didn't know who you were going to drive with, or if you'd drive at all. But he's one of the shrewdest guys I've ever met in the automobile business. He's a fox.'

In 1953 Hill competed in the Carrera Panamericana with his friend Richie Ginther, a Korean War veteran, and the following year they won it. Their open 4.5-litre Ferrari, distinguished by its white paint and a dramatic tail fin, beat Umberto Maglioli's factory-entered 4.9-litre coupé. Hill met Enzo Ferrari in Europe the following year, Chinetti's support earning him a works drive at Le Mans in 1955 and another in the Buenos Aires 1,000-kilometre race at the start of the following year, a chaotic race in which he and Olivier Gendebien finished second. Afterwards he was offered a contract for the season. Disappointingly, he spent the next two years kicking around the sports-car team, hoping in vain for a chance to break into Formula One. It was a time of frustration, in which his eyes grew less starry at the mention of Enzo Ferrari's name. But over the end of 1957 and the start of 1958 he and Peter Collins won the sports-car Grand Prix of Venezuela, the Buenos Aires 1,000 km and the Sebring 12-hour race, and he was reunited with Gendebien to win at Le Mans. And at Monza and Casablanca, he finally got his shot at grand prix racing.

For 1959 Enzo Ferrari needed virtually a complete new team. His experienced drivers were dead, and one of his new stars, Wolfgang von Trips, had briefly fallen from favour. Hill was still there, now hoping to make the most of the promotion fate had offered him, and so was Olivier Gendebien, the sports-car specialist. Maserati's financial troubles had put an end to the works team, while a grieving Tony Vandervell had folded the entire Vanwall operation in the aftermath of Lewis-Evans' death, so Ferrari was able to profit from the availability of Jean Behra, the aggressive Frenchman, and Tony Brooks. A trained dentist, a quiet man not at all in the obvious Spitfire-pilot mould, Brooks had suffered in career terms from falling under the shadow of Stirling Moss, the golden boy of the British press and public. Nevertheless he had, at the wheel of a car built at the Connaught garage in Surrey, won the non-championship race at Syracuse in 1955, becoming the first British driver to win a Continental grand prix in a British car since the war; and in 1958 he had won three grands prix at three classic circuits, Spa, the Nürburgring and Monza.

The least familiar of the new boys was another Californian, Dan Gurney, a former GI and the latest Chinetti protégé, who arrived in Modena in his VW Beetle with his wife and two sons and performed so brilliantly in his test at the autodrome in front of Ferrari and Tavoni that he was offered a contract on the spot. Not, it was true, a notably generous one. The cost of living in

Emilia was still low, but Gurney's stipend of $163 a week, plus 50 per cent of the prize money, could hardly be termed magnificent. But to drive a Ferrari was what men came out from California to do, and for a while, anyway, the money was beside the point.

Ferrari remained impervious to the suggestions of Chiti and the drivers that mid-engined cars like the Cooper represented the future of racing. 'I remember', Chiti said, 'that he always listened attentively to his most important customers, who used to tell him what their ideas were about how an ideal car for taking part in the Formula One world championship should be made; of course it had to have a front engine. Even the chemist Nello, one of Ferrari's long-time friends, predicted a difficult future for him if he should ever decide to race with a car similar to those dreadful horrors they were producing in England.' Ferrari ordered Chiti and his engineers to develop the previous year's Dino 246 cars. In some cases this meant literally taking the old cars apart and cannibalising them to build the new ones. None of the 1958 cars was sold to a private customer, and none remained in existence. Like the Lancia-Ferraris and their derivatives, their remains were left to gather dust in a corner of the factory until the scrap dealer came to gather them and take them on a last ride to the knacker's yard. The only car that interested Ferrari, as he often said, was the next one that proved itself a winner. The 1959 Dinos came cloaked in beautiful bodies by Medardo Fantuzzi, Modena's own Michelangelo of aluminium panel-beating, whose work had distinguished the last of the grand prix-winning Maserati 250Fs, the gorgeous lightweight model of 1957.

Lightweight was not the word to describe the new Dino. The English constructors, led by Colin Chapman and John Cooper, were producing cars that were pared to the bone, and then (at least in Chapman's case) going even further to improve the ratio between power and weight. To Ferrari, development generally meant adding things. In isolation, the Dino looked like a classic grand prix car. Placed next to the Coopers or

Chapman's Lotuses, it looked like a piece of Edwardiana. High-speed circuits, where the four-cam V6 could overcome the deficiencies of the chassis, suited it best, and Brooks won at Rheims, with Hill second. That was also where Behra left the team, in colourful circumstances. Nursing a grievance over Ferrari's customary refusal to nominate a number-one driver, a status to which he felt entitled, he had made an official complaint in which he claimed that he was being given cars with frames welded together from crash-damaged chassis. The team members were infuriated by the slur, and even more so when he seemed to go out of his way to blow up his engine at Rheims, as a gesture of disaffection. At the party to celebrate Brooks' win, he accused Tavoni of making him drive with wrecks and aimed a couple of punches at the *direttore sportivo*. When Ferrari heard about it, Behra was summarily sacked. Four weeks later, driving his own Porsche in a sports-car race at Avus, he lost control on the steep banking, flew over the edge, was hurled against a flagpole, and died. 'We had completely abandoned that man to himself,' Chiti reflected thirty years later. 'We had obliged him to take refuge in his own desperation.' Also years afterwards, perhaps in atonement, Ferrari rather surprisingly claimed that Behra was 'matched only by Wimille as the greatest of French drivers'.

At the Nürburgring, Brooks repeated his victory of the previous year, ahead of Gurney and Hill, who completed a sweep of the first three places, a tribute to the car's ruggedness over the long and difficult track. But at Monza, where Brooks really expected to win, the Ferrari's clutch burnt out on the starting line. Instead the Coopers were the story of the season, Brabham winning three races in the works car and Moss two in Rob Walker's private entry. Brooks forfeited his chance of the championship in the last round, at Watkins Glen, when von Trips ran into the tail of his car and he came into the pits to have the damage checked, eventually finishing third. The Italian press did not stint itself in criticism of his decision to stop, which had effectively given Brabham the title. 'I think that taking an uncalculated risk could lead to what amounts to suicide,' Brooks said, 'and I have a religious conviction that such risks are not acceptable.' To the Italians, the acceptance of such risks was a part of being a Ferrari driver. Ferrari's own attitude was made clear when, three years later, he wrote: 'Brooks, who has left racing to be a car salesman or a dentist – I am not sure which – appeared in the limelight as a great stylist and a man who used his brains. Subsequently, although possessing ability and skill, he became far too cautious, both for himself and others.' Brooks, who was married to an Italian woman and spoke the language well but recalled meeting Ferrari only two or three times during his time at Maranello, left the team at the end of the year. Two more seasons in Formula One produced no more victories, but he lived to tell the tale and always thought of the 1959 Dino as the best car he ever drove, the pinnacle of the evolution of the classic 1950s front-engined grand prix car.

Unfortunately for the drivers, it was still around in 1960. The registered name of the company had changed, the title SEFAC (Società Esercizio Fabbriche Automobili e Corse) Ferrari at last replacing the old Auto-Avio Costruzioni, reflecting the change to limited-liability status that Ferrari had made, fearing lawsuits, after the Mille Miglia crash of 1957. But the cars would hardly differ from the previous year's lumps, and for Dan Gurney it was too much. He was off to BRM. But if that particular Californian could see no future in Ferrari's adherence to the old technology, yet another one was ready to take his place. Richie Ginther, Hill's co-driver in the Mexican races, was a small, crew-cut enthusiast with diligent attitude and an enquiring mind. He joined the team as a junior driver but established a good rapport with Chiti and his assistant, Franco Rocchi, who recognised his sensitivity to the machinery and were happy to give him the bulk of testing duties at the autodrome. Soon, too, there was the attraction of the first rear-engined prototype, an acceptance of the inevitable which, on its debut in Ginther's hands at Monte Carlo in 1960, managed to look like not much more than an old Dino turned back to front. But as Brabham hurled his Cooper to a second title, the Scuderia managed only a single victory, and that a somewhat hollow one. When the British manufacturers refused to risk their featherweight machines, developed on the smooth asphalt of their flat aerodrome circuits, on the Monza banking and announced a boycott of the Italian Grand Prix, Hill profited from their caution, leading home Ginther and Willy Mairesse, a newly recruited Belgian, in a clean sweep. Fifth came von Trips, in a rear-engined Formula Two Ferrari, a sign of things to come.

Since Ferrari chose to send no cars to the US Grand Prix, the final round of the championship, the one-two-three at Monza represented the last hurrah of the front-engined grand prix cars, and of the 2.5-litre Formula One, although not of the name Dino. When the new cars appeared for the first race of the 1961 season, in which the new regulations stipulated a maximum engine capacity of 1,500 cc, the lightened, lowered and generally improved rear-engined Ferrari, a development of von Trips' 1960 Monza machine, continued to carry a V6 engine which gave the car its name: the Dino 156. Its nickname, however, was derived from the twin nostrils with which Chiti and Fantuzzi had endowed its long nose: it became known, universally and for all time, as the Sharknose Ferrari. Like many ideas associated with Ferrari, this styling tweak was not an original thought. It had previously been seen on a couple of Maserati 250Fs owned by the American entrant Temple Buell, on which Fantuzzi, in a vain attempt to draw a last ounce of speed from an ancient design, had bestowed a notion more cosmetic than scientific in its effect.

The Sharknose may have had its engine behind the driver, but it needed no aesthetic gestures in order to impress and prevail. The English constructors had confused themselves by objecting to the change in regulations and by agreeing – with, or so they believed, Enzo Ferrari, among others – to maintain the old regulations in a parallel series, to be known as Formula Intercontinental. While they prepared cars to meet both types of competition, Ferrari quietly changed his mind and concentrated on the official Formula One. The wisdom of his decision was on display all season, and his cars, in the hands of Hill, von Trips, Ginther and Mairesse, dominated the championship. The extent of their superiority could be gauged very precisely at Rheims, when Ferrari lent a spare car to a new organisation called the Federazione Italiana Scuderie Automobilistiche, formed by a group of lesser team owners who had banded together in an effort to promote new Italian driving talent to replace the lost generation of Ascari, Castellotti and Musso. Their first candidate, Giancarlo Baghetti, the twenty-five-year-old son of a Milanese industrialist, actually gave the Dino 156 its debut, in a non-championship race at Syracuse, and won, beating Gurney's Porsche. And at Rheims, in his first world-championship race, he profited from the mechanical failure of all the works cars, winning the race after a tense and spectacular wheel-to-wheel battle with the Porsches of Gurney and Jo Bonnier in the closing laps. 'It seemed quite impossible that such a newcomer to big-time racing could go on battling against more experienced drivers without making the mistake of a missed gearchange, an error in braking or a misjudgement of speed into a corner, or getting elbowed out of line by his superiors,' Denis Jenkinson of *Motor Sport* wrote admiringly. Ferrari described Baghetti as 'probably a Varzi who had yet to acquire the latter's grimness of purpose'. He never did acquire it, if that was what it took. Rheims was to be his only grand prix success, and he went down in history as the only man to win the race in which he made his world-championship debut.

If Baghetti reminded Enzo Ferrari of Varzi, then twice that season his memories of the great Nuvolari were also evoked. On both those occasions, however, it was when his cars were getting beaten. He had already formed a high opinion of Stirling Moss's talents, and regretted the chance he had missed in 1951. Now he was forced to watch the black and white pictures on the television at his home in Modena as Moss, in a privately entered four-cylinder Lotus-Climax of an already obsolescent design, working without team mates, used all his virtuosity to defeat the assembled Ferrari squad at Monte Carlo and the Nürburgring – the two circuits at which, as the legendary hand-to-hand battles of the 1930s had proved, driving skill and racing wisdom counted above all.

At thirty-one years of age, four times a runner-up in the championship but several times the moral victor, Moss was ready to produce his masterpieces. For the Monaco Grand Prix he planned to counter the superior power and numbers of the Ferraris by stripping the side panels off his car to reduce its weight. For two and three-quarter hours he drove it at what racing drivers of that era called 'ten tenths', in other words at the absolute maximum, without a single instant of relaxation. That year there would be no kisses blown to the blonde in the pale pink lipstick who sat at a table outside Oscar's Bar, on the descent from Casino Square to Mirabeau. Not during the race, anyway. The Ferraris hounded him all the way, but after the most torrid of chases Richie Ginther was still three and a half seconds behind at the flag, with Hill and von Trips lost in the distance. There are pictures of Ginther that afternoon, being lifted from the Ferrari's cockpit at the end of the race, demon-strating perhaps better than any ever taken the agony and exhaustion that defeat in a race can inflict. Another photograph, taken of Moss from above his cockpit as he turns the car into one of Monaco's tight bends, shows him guiding the car with his fingertips, as though it were a violin from Cremona rather than a racing car from Cheshunt. And in Germany, Moss did it again. This time a more streamlined body camouflaged the ageing mechanicals of his old Lotus, and he had the advantage of rain showers to exaggerate the distinction between his skills and those of the men chasing him in the Ferraris. Only two of them, von Trips and Hill, could follow him to the finish, trailing by more than twenty seconds.

Elsewhere, on circuits where horsepower counted for more than sheer skill, and whenever Moss paid the price for his perverse insistence on switching from one kind of car to another and tinkering with already inferior machinery, von Trips and Hill were dominant. By the time they reached Monza, the penultimate race of the year, the aristocrat had won in Holland and Britain, the postmaster's son in Belgium. Either man could take the championship in a race which the Ferraris were expected to win as they pleased. Once again the banked oval was being used, as well as the road circuit; and this year the English teams were in attendance. As usual there were no team orders in the Scuderia Ferrari, or any sense of precedence, but there was a surprise when a nineteen-year-old turned up for his debut with the team and put his car on the front row alongside von Trips in the first two-by-two grid seen in grand prix racing. This was Ricardo Rodriguez, who, with his brother Pedro, two years his senior, had been wholeheartedly encouraged by their father, a rich man from Mexico City who admitted to spending $80,000 a year subsidising their racing – much of it with Chinetti, who brought them to international notice when he put them in his cars at Sebring, Le Mans and the Nürburgring. Both were gifted, both were fearless, and Ricardo, at least, seemed likely to join the all-time greats when he erupted on to the scene at Monza. Like the rest of the Ferraris, however, his car had been fitted with a high back-axle ratio, in the belief that they would be so much faster than the opposition that it would be sensible to give them a gearing which would enable them to maintain high speeds with the least possible strain. This meant that their starts were less than rocket-like, and accounted for the presence among them of Jim Clark in his four-cylinder Lotus-Climax on the first lap, as part of a leading group which, in the old Monza slipstreaming tradition, could be covered by a tarpaulin. Clark's brilliance, in his second grand prix season, had already been widely noted, but it was clear that his equipment would not allow him to keep up with the Ferraris for long. Coming into the Parabolica, the 180-degree turn leading on to the pit straight, for the second time, Hill, Ginther and Rodriguez were in the lead as they prepared to complete the lap. Just behind them, von Trips went past Clark on the inside and then appeared to move wide in order to adopt his usual line through the corner. The two cars touched, which sent the Lotus into a spin. But the Ferrari flew off to the left, towards the spectator enclosure, somersaulting across the grass. As it bounced against the chain-link fencing, fourteen spectators suffered fatal injuries. Von Trips, who had been thrown out, was also dead.

'It looked bad, but no worse than others,' Hill thought as he raced past the scene. 'I didn't really worry because people had been crashing all season and there had been no fatal accidents. I turned my thoughts to the job at hand: winning the Italian Grand Prix.' He won the race, and the championship with it, the first American to do so, but the pleasure was muted by the tragedy, and the celebrations were stifled by the renewed uproar of protest against motor racing in general and Ferrari in particular. It made little difference to the critics' perceptions that in the next two days there were two air crashes involving commercial airliners, sixty-eight people dying in a DC8 and seventy-seven in a Caravelle. Hill and Ginther acted as pall-bearers at von Trips' funeral, the cortège proceeding in the rain from the dead man's medieval castle, Burg Hemmersbach, to the church, the casket carried in von Trips' Ferrari convertible as a band played Chopin's *Marche funèbre*. In the wake of another tragedy, and another legal involvement, and with the title already won, Ferrari decided not to send a team to the last race of the season, the United States Grand Prix at Watkins Glen. So the first American world champion was denied the chance to take his crown home.

Enzo Ferrari had never really cared for Phil Hill. The Californian was too nervy, too twitchy, for his taste. In his memoirs, he described the man who brought him the 1961 title as 'not outstanding' – but then Ferrari probably thought, with some justification, that he had brought Hill the title. Yet he could hardly ignore the new world champion, a driver who had also won at Le Mans three times in his cars, and Hill was offered a new contract for 1962. He signed it, only to discover afterwards that most of those with whom he had been working were on their way out of the door.

Inside Maranello, there had been a revolt. In the closing weeks of 1961, eight members of the senior staff had resigned en masse: the engineers Carlo Chiti, Giotto Bizzarrini, Federico Giberti and Fausto Galazzi; Romolo Tavoni, the team manager; Gerolamo Gardini, the commercial manager; Ermanno Della Casa, the financial administrator; and Enzo Selmi, the personnel manager. In a communiqué hastily contrived to minimise any sense of scandal that might attach itself to an undeniably spectacular multiple defection, Ferrari told the world: 'These resignations were motivated by an act of solidarity towards the accountant Gardini, who had been asked not to attend the firm any more because of accusations which were considered disrespectful to Ferrari and were uttered in a public place in the presence of Mr Luigi Chinetti, general director of Ferrari for the USA. Therefore there is no question of a union-based conflict, or of economic reasons . . . It is clearly a matter of the over-inflation of marginal issues which have nothing to do with the normal life of the company.'

In fact the revolt had been precipitated by a slap in the face. After staying in the background while her son was alive, Laura Ferrari had suddenly come to the fore in the day-to-day life of the company. She had been spending more time at the Maranello works, intervening in policy issues, particularly those concerned with financial matters, and making her presence felt in ways that were thought by several senior executives to be conducive neither to interpersonal harmony nor constructive work. They had become fed up with her interference. For reasons that none of them could fathom, her husband made no attempt to restrain her until it was too late. 'She often descended unannounced on the factory,' Oscar Orefici, Chiti's authorised biographer, wrote. 'She also claimed to be in charge of the financial management of the firm. She was present at all the official business deals, when she never failed to astonish people with her very original notions.'

'She was a strange woman,' Brenda Vernor remembered. 'She'd come up to Maranello in the van to save money and bring her salami roll and sit in the *cantina*, and eat with the mechanics. Crazy thing, all to save money. And she used to drive Tavoni nuts.' Chiti himself observed: 'She was a woman completely devoid of any diplomatic sense. She had none of the characteristics needed to live alongside a man of the stature of her husband. But Ferrari was a great sentimentalist, and he allowed her to get away with a great deal – far too much, in fact – just because she was the mother of his son.'

One day in the Modena office she ended a noisy row with Gardini and Della Casa by slapping the former in the face. That brought other grievances to a head. Ferrari had rewarded his surviving drivers for their triumphant season by attempting to cut the pay of Hill and Ginther, and when the latter responded by announcing that he was leaving for BRM, Ferrari ordered the security guards to search him on his way out. Ferrari had also forbidden Tavoni and Chiti to attend von Trips' funeral, although Chiti later came to understand that it may have been to protect them – and the company – from giving unguarded answers to journalists' questions about the Monza disaster. At the end of 1961, these matters were all combining to raise the internal temperature of the organisation. But money, inevitably, was at the heart of the matter, along with a sense of self-worth and collective value. Some of the senior managers had asked for a rise, thinking that the season's successes might persuade Ferrari to set aside his habitual stinginess. They were wrong. Ferrari could be persuaded to pay the going rate, but only when he had convinced himself that there was no alternative. Otherwise his employees would be well advised to understand that there were plenty of others keen to take their places. Now, faced with a letter which they had all signed, complaining about his refusal to improve their terms and about the way things were going in general, he turned his face, shut his door, and let them all go to hell.

Giberti and Della Casa were back within thirty days, pledging their loyalty for the rest of their working lives, and were apparently allowed to resume their work as if nothing had happened. But they were the old guard. The rest of the deserters were on their own in the wilderness. It would be a year before Chiti and Gardini were ready to reveal plans for a new company formed to build and run grand prix and sports cars, with backing from three rich men: an aristocrat, Count Giovanni Volpi di Misurata, who had run Ferraris with his own team, Scuderia Serenissima; a Tuscan industrialist, Giorgio Billi; and Jaime Ortiz Patino, the Bolivian tin-mine king. There were some who claimed that the announcement provided the proof that Gardini and Chiti had been fired because Ferrari discovered their plot to mount a coup and seize control, an allegation strenuously denied by those involved.

Meanwhile Ferrari licked his wounds and tried to rebuild the company's superstructure. Six hundred road cars would be manufactured in 1962, he announced, double the output of only two years earlier. There, at least, he could be sure of applause as the lovely 250GTs and 410 Super Americas rolled out of the factory, with dramatic bodywork by Scaglietti of Modena, Touring of Milan or Pininfarina of Turin. After all, the supplicants were still coming to Maranello: Marcello Mastroianni and Monica Vitti, the pianist Arturo Benedetti Michelangeli and the conductors Arturo Toscanini and Herbert von Karajan, royalty and aristocrats such as the Shah of Persia, ex-King Leopold of Belgium, Princess Maria Gabriella of Savoy and, most loyal of all, Prince Bernhard of the Netherlands, who sent a telegram after every grand prix victory and was said by his wife to refer to Maranello as the capital of Italy.

That winter, one visitor to Maranello in particular might have provoked a swift change in Ferrari's fortunes. While entertaining Stirling Moss to lunch at the Ristorante Cavallino, Ferrari offered the Englishman something he had never offered any driver before, not even Nuvolari: tell me what sort of a car you want, he said, and I will build it. Since the altercation in

Bari ten years earlier, Moss had seldom driven Ferraris. Two victories in the Tourist Trophy at Goodwood at the wheel of Rob Walker's 250GT, the second of them so easy that he claimed to have had the car's radio on throughout the race, were the most significant of the few meetings between England's most talented driver and the products of the world's most famous racing-car manufacturer. Unlike Fangio, Moss had seldom made wise decisions over which team to join. He had finished second in the world championship four years in a row and then third three years in a row. Like Moss's fans, Ferrari could see that this incandescent talent might never receive its reward. But Stirling Moss's nature was every bit as independent as Enzo Ferrari's. I'll drive your car, he replied, if you will allow it to be entered and run by Rob Walker's team, and painted in Walker's dark blue livery, while you simply supply and maintain it. Remarkably, Ferrari said yes. The agreement was made in principle, and they also talked about plans for him to drive the company's sports and GT cars. One way or another, Stirling Moss would be a Ferrari driver at last. As a sort of preface to the deal, on 25 March 1962 he shared Chinetti's 250 Testa Rossa sports car with Innes Ireland at Sebring, where they went well but were disqualified from the twelve-hour race for changing the brake pads earlier than the regulations permitted. But on Easter Monday, 24 April, exactly one month before he was due to arrive on the Monaco grid in a Ferrari for the start of the grand prix season, he unaccountably ran off the track at Goodwood while driving a Lotus in a minor meeting, suffering head injuries. Moss was generally as quick to return after injury as Nuvolari, but this accident involved something more serious than a few broken bones. After more than a year of recovery and convalescence, and much speculation about his future, one morning he took a Lotus sports car back to Goodwood and gave himself a few laps to see how he felt. What he learned prompted him to announce an end to his career, at the age of thirty-two. So now no one would ever know if Moss and the prancing horse were really meant for each other.

To replace Chiti, Enzo Ferrari promoted Mauro Forghieri, a studious and inventive young engineer whose father, Reclus Forghieri, had been with Ferrari before the war, starting with work on the Tipo 158. In the 1950s Reclus had supervised the installation of the first foundry in the factory, a highly significant step in the company's evolution as a manufacturer, since it enabled cylinder blocks and gearbox casings to be produced without the aid of outside suppliers, increasing the sense of self-sufficiency. Enzo Ferrari, it was said, had paid for young Mauro's education at the University of Bologna, where he graduated in mechanical engineering. With a nudge from his father, Ferrari called the boy in, persuaded him to abandon his ambition to become an aeronautical engineer with Lockheed in California, and offered him a job in the engine department. Now Mauro was twenty-six years old, he had worked with Chiti on the V6 grand prix engine, and perhaps Ferrari looked at him and remembered his hopes for his own first son. But if the startling promotion for Forghieri was to infuse the team with a more youthful spirit, and to provide many long-term benefits, the arrival of Eugenio Dragoni as team manager was to have a very different effect.

Dragoni, a wealthy man from the proceeds of a cosmetics and pharmaceuticals business in Milan, had run a small racing team, the Scuderia Sant'Ambroeus. His mission on earth was to discover and promote the heir to the thwarted destiny of Castellotti and Musso. Baghetti, the first of his candidates, had already won the French Grand Prix on his debut. The second, Lorenzo Bandini, an ambitious but likeable Milan garage owner, twenty-five years old, joined Scuderia Ferrari for 1962 alongside Hill, Mairesse, Baghetti, Gendebien and Ricardo Rodriguez. Only a few months after one of its drivers had won the world championship, however, this was an organisation in a state of disintegration. Once the English manufacturers had acquired engines with as much power as Ferrari's, the game was up. Forghieri did his best to revise the 156, but the modifications that arrived race by race were little more than ineffective fiddling. By comparison with the new Lotuses,

[224]

BRMs and Coopers, Chiti's old chassis was a dog. None of the drivers was capable of providing the sort of feedback that the engineers had enjoyed from Ginther, whose inventive spirit had been responsible for the creation of the tail spoiler seen on the 1961 sports cars, an innovation widely copied on road cars. Not even Hill, who scored a second place and two thirds in the opening three races but then watched the Scuderia collapse into such disarray that Ferrari seemed relieved when a metalworkers' strike prevented the team from entering the French Grand Prix. With two races to go, he wrote to his drivers informing them that the industrial unrest meant the Scuderia would not be sending cars to the United States or South Africa, or to Mexico City for a non-championship race. Once again a team that had been virtually omnipotent a year earlier had degenerated into a rancorous shambles. Only the sports cars maintained the company's reputation, with wins in the Sebring 12 Hours, the Targa Florio, the Nürburgring 1,000 km, and – for the fourth year in a row – the 24 Hours of Le Mans: a clean sweep of the classics. But in Mexico City the twenty-year-old Ricardo Rodriguez, one of the team's great hopes for the future, was killed at the wheel of a privately entered Lotus, crashing at the banked Peraltada turn while trying desperately to win pole position in front of his home crowd.

Hill had known his time with Ferrari was over at Spa, only three races into the season. He had limped home in third place, more than two minutes behind Clark's Lotus. That evening he overheard Dragoni making his usual call to Ferrari.

'*Commendatore?*' the team manager was saying. '*Si. Si . . . si. Si. Ma il tuo grande campione non ha fatto niente. Niente.*' Your great champion didn't do a thing.

'You son of a bitch,' Hill thought.

At the end of the season, in despair, he accepted Chiti's offer to sign up with the new company, ATS. It turned out to be the worst decision Hill ever made, but he had no regrets about saying farewell to Maranello. 'Enzo Ferrari never understood me,' he concluded. 'I wasn't his type, not gung-ho enough. I wasn't willing to die for Enzo Ferrari. I wasn't willing to become one of his sacrifices.' The first of the Americans, and the most devoted, was gone.

The two Englishmen arrived only weeks apart, but from opposite directions. The elder of them, Mike Parkes, was the Haileybury-educated son of the chairman of Alvis, from whose eyes, while serving an engineering apprenticeship with the Humber car company, he had hidden the evidence of his early amateur racing career. The younger, John Surtees, grew up watching his father prepare and race motorbikes and had left school to begin a career that would see him win seven world championships on two wheels. Parkes joined Ferrari as a development engineer but wanted to be a grand prix driver. Surtees joined Ferrari as the team's leading driver but believed that his experience and technical knowledge would benefit the team as it prepared for reconstruction. When they met in Maranello, at the end of 1962, the collision was unavoidable.

Parkes' father hadn't wanted him to race. His MG, and the cups that had been won with it, were secreted in a barn. Later, when it was all out in the open, he won races in a 250GT entered by Colonel Ronnie Hoare of Maranello Concessionaires, Ferrari's British distributor. 'I think Colonel Hoare introduced him to Ferrari,' Brenda Vernor, Parkes' girlfriend during his early years in Modena, remembered. 'The Old Man liked Mike a lot because he was very down to earth. No beating about the bush. What he had to say, he had to say. A typical English gentleman. And Mike was a very good engineer. Everybody loved him because he spoke the Modenese dialect and he treated everybody the same, whether the head of the department or not. No airs and graces.'

Surtees had been approached two years earlier, a year after he had switched from bikes to cars. He was already a great hero in Italy, where he was known as *Il Grande John*, thanks to his association with Count Domenico Agusta's MV team, and to

Ferrari the idea of hiring a motorcycle champion to drive his cars was a reminder of the days of Nuvolari, Varzi and Ascari. 'I first went out to Modena at the end of 1960,' Surtees said. 'I met him at the *assistenza clienti*, the original building. I remember a longish office, quite dark, and a picture of Dino with a light over it. Mr Ferrari was wearing dark glasses, even though you could hardly see a thing. He said, "We'd like you to join us – you'd do testing and you'd do sports cars and you'd drive the Formula One, all the cars. Road cars, too. We have these drivers" – he listed them all – and I thought, why do they want me? He said, "Come out to Maranello and see." So I was taken there, I was shown through the racing department, all familiar to me, really. A typical Italian scene, and one I liked rather a lot. But I thought, where's the specific programme? Where does this fit in? Chiti was still there, and I wasn't sure about what he was doing. And I said, "No, some other time." It was too early for me. I wanted to learn my trade a little more first. They said, "Mr Ferrari doesn't ask a second time." I said, "No, when I'm ready." It wasn't too well received.'

He had been expecting to spend the next season driving a Lotus for Colin Chapman, but he was let down. Instead he drove a privately entered Cooper in 1961, forced to watch from the middle of the grid as Phil Hill's Ferrari walked away with the championship. The following year he formed a team with Eric Broadley of Lola, using sponsorship he had arranged himself. It gave him the satisfaction of an involvement with the engineering and the management sides, in addition to his driving duties, but at the end of 1962, just as the prospects were looking bleak, another call came. 'This time it was quite different. They said, "We want you to be team leader, do all our testing, all the old people have gone, we're building a new team." I thought, yes, the time is right.' There was a bit of haggling over money. 'They said, "We don't pay a lot. We put all our money into the team." I knew that Phil Hill had been on virtually board and lodging. They said, "Well, the advantage is that you get good discounts." I lived at the Hotel Real Fini for

1,800 lire a day, full board – just under a pound a day. Of course the Real Fini restaurant was the *haute cuisine* of Modena. And if you went into other restaurants in Modena it was all, "*Ah, pilota Ferrari! Formula Uno! Disconto! Cinquanta per cento!*" They all warmed to you. That's what I love about the Italians.'

He met Mauro Forghieri, the technical co-ordinator; Franco Rocchi and Angelo Bellei, the successors to Colombo and Lampredi; Walter Salvarani, the gearbox man, who had not joined the revolt; Michael May, a young Swiss engineer who was working on the fuel-injection project; and the senior mechanics Ener Vecchi and Giulio Borsari. His main team mate was going to be Willy Mairesse, the dark-browed little Belgian, fast but inconsistent; he had a reputation for crashing too often and for sometimes involving other people in his accidents. And, unavoidably, Surtees met Eugenio Dragoni. 'Ah, the perfume manufacturer. He had some connections. I never quite got to the bottom of it.'

Those connections, he came to suspect, reached as far as Turin, where Fiat's directors had been alerted by the news that Ferrari was looking at the possibility of selling part of his company and had received an offer of $18 million from the Ford Motor Company in exchange for 90 per cent of the entire operation. The reasons that led Ferrari to contemplate a sale, after more than twenty years of independence, were threefold. First, there was the poor condition of the Italian economy, not helped by an extended period of industrial unrest which frequently affected his suppliers, if not his own shopfloor. Second, the cathartic effect of the mass defection at the end of 1961 exhausted a man aged sixty-three more than it exhilarated him. Third, the removal of his wife from an involvement in the business affairs of the factory disturbed the difficult balance between his working life and his domestic existence for a while. There were several months of increasingly public speculation, during which a group of managers flew in from Ford's headquarters in Dearborn, Michigan, to undertake a top-to-bottom audit of the company. On 20 May 1963, after twenty-two days of talks, the sticking-point was reached over Ford's stipulation that Ferrari would have to submit, 'for quick approval', an application to obtain any increase to the racing-team budget over 450 million lire, which equalled $250,000 at the time, the amount of Ferrari's race budget for the 1963 season. According to Franco Gozzi, who was present, Enzo Ferrari exploded when he came across the provision during a negotiating session, underlining the words 'submit' and 'to obtain' twice with his violet ink. This clause, Ferrari said, 'seriously compromised the total freedom I had been promised as racing-team director'. He then filled the room with a string of insults – using words which Gozzi said 'you would not find in any dictionary'. It was ten o'clock in the evening. Eventually Ferrari turned to Gozzi and said quietly, 'Let's get something to eat.' They walked out, leaving the fourteen-member Ford delegation sitting speechless. On being told of the rebuff, Henry Ford's response was straightforward: 'Okay then, we'll kick his ass.'

At their offices in the Lingotto plant, Fiat's top executives had noted the widespread opposition to the sale of a jewel of Italy's patrimony to the Americans, and decided that both Ferrari and public opinion might now be receptive to an approach from a benevolent Italian corporation. They began to make friendly overtures at a variety of levels, official and informal. For example, Dragoni's squad of drivers for 1963 included Ludovico Scarfiotti, who was a nephew of Gianni Agnelli, the man only a rung away from the top of the Fiat tree. And it soon became clear that the success of Scarfiotti's career was of unusual importance to the team manager.

But the first shock for Surtees, when he arrived to take up his job, was the realisation that the sports cars had automatic priority over Formula One. 'I'd only driven a sports car once, when I had a test with Aston Martin, but my first task was to go to Modena and sort out the sports prototype. In hindsight, I think it was all a question of money. There were a lot of wealthy clients and dealerships all willing to pay good money for the sports-car programme. It was something that kept all the Chinettis happy.' So he would test and sort out the works cars at the autodrome, only to discover when he got to a race meeting that they had been passed on to Maranello Concessionaires for Graham Hill to drive or to Chinetti to enter for Pedro Rodriguez. And Surtees would be given the newest car, the one there hadn't been time to test, to race as the factory's lead car. 'That was always a point of frustration. And it was obvious that there just wasn't the money to do it all properly.'

The biggest casualty was the grand prix programme. Forghieri had looked at what Lotus and Cooper were doing and had modified the single-seater chassis accordingly. In Surtees' first season he won the German Grand Prix, which was an improvement on the previous season's form, but the programme to develop a new engine was running hopelessly late while engineers devoted their time to preparing cars for Sebring and Le Mans. 'I said at one point that if we wanted to do Formula One properly, we had to stop sports cars completely,' Surtees said. 'But that wasn't possible. The success of the sports-car programme, and its close association with the road-car business, was very important in Mr Ferrari's mind. Those important private owners all put a lot of money in.' And, whereas the grand prix cars were floundering, the sports cars were winning big races – the Sebring 12 Hours, the Nürburg-ring 1,000 km and Le Mans again, all in Surtees' first year. He would have won Le Mans himself, partnered by Mairesse, but for a stroke of bad luck. They were leading comfortably with less than four hours of the twenty-four left when Surtees came into the pits to hand over to his team mate. 'They filled the car up and he went out of the pits and round the corner and up to the Dunlop Bridge, and when he put the brakes on the car caught fire. It had been overfilled, and the fuel ran out and the stoplight switch ignited it. It was so unlucky. Apart from the fact that we could have won the race, there was Willy all burnt. And it was nothing to do with him.'

Mairesse recovered in time to rejoin the team for the German Grand Prix, but while Surtees was winning his first world championship race for Ferrari, the Belgian made an error of judgement as he came over one of the Nürburgring's famous humps and ran off the road, killing a medical attendant and smashing his own arm in several places. 'He was a driver of indomitable will and immeasurable courage,' Enzo Ferrari said. 'Everything he did was enveloped in some sacred flame.' But he never granted the Belgian another opportunity to drive a Formula One Ferrari. Although Mairesse recovered, his career dwindled away. One September day in 1969, a year after another bad Le Mans crash, this time in a Ford, had put him in a coma for a fortnight, he committed suicide with a handful of pills in an Ostend hotel room. 'Willy was a nice character,' Surtees remembered. 'A good driver. Not the most talented. You were a bit worried that he might have a little lapse, a little moment. Unfortunately, and you've seen it in so many instances, Willy had let his motor-sport career be the sole thing he lived for. Being in a motor race and sitting in a racing car was the only world he knew. And when he found that it was beyond him, I don't think he could stand it.'

Despite all the problems, Surtees managed to take the world championship in 1964, his second season with the team, although it took only two wins, at the Nürburgring and Monza, to bring him the title, beating off the challenge of Jim Clark and Graham Hill. Curiously, he won the points that clinched the title in the final round at Watkins Glen while driving a Ferrari painted not in the traditional red but in the blue and white of the USA. As a part of a squabble with the FIA and the Italian automobile association, who had refused to recognise Ferrari's new 250LM coupé as eligible for competition in the grand touring-car class despite visiting the factory to verify the numbers being produced, Enzo Ferrari renounced his entrant's licence and sent the car to the United States Grand Prix in the name and the livery of Chinetti's North American Racing Team. Surtees needed the help of his team mate Lorenzo

Bandini to get the points he needed: after Bandini had nudged Graham Hill's BRM into a spin, he was told to let his team leader go by, thus giving him the vital points.

Surtees' earnings in his championship season amounted to £25,000, but there was continued frustration over the lack of commitment to developing the Formula One cars. In 1965 the team continued to use the previous year's V8 engine instead of pushing ahead with the development of Forghieri's new flat-twelve, which Surtees believed would have enabled them to win more races and take the title more convincingly. Nor did he mind making his feelings known on such matters. 'The engineers would take it as personal criticism, but basically the Old Man was always quite receptive. At the same time he could be dogmatic. "That worked for Alfa Romeo", he'd say, "and it will work for us today." Then Jano would come in and they'd talk it over and they'd come up with solutions, but largely old-fashioned solutions.'

Yet Enzo Ferrari was more famous than ever. When the American director John Frankenheimer arrived at Monza to shoot sequences for a feature film called *Grand Prix*, starring Yves Montand and Françoise Hardy, one of the central characters was an Italian racing-car constructor with a morbid, ruthless, Machiavellian cast of mind. He was played by Adolfo Celli, a fine actor best known outside Italy for his portrayal of a Bond villain, Largo, opposite Sean Connery in *Thunderball*. Celli had a strong face, a hooked nose, white hair and piercing eyes. Invited on to the set, Ferrari was introduced to the actor. He couldn't see the resemblance, he said. But he had noticed that the photographers who clustered around him on his increasingly rare public appearances always wanted a scowl from him rather than a smile. In the building of the Ferrari myth, they wanted to play their part. And he obliged them, not least by permanently adopting a pair of dark glasses, even indoors, which enhanced his air of withdrawal and mystery.

In 1965 Porfirio Rubirosa made his final contribution to the legend. His early racing adventures had encouraged him to maintain an involvement with Ferrari, usually through Luigi Chinetti. After his divorce from the heiress Doris Duke, he had enjoyed an affair with Zsa Zsa Gabor, who posed for photographers in the cockpit of the big 375 MM coupé that Rubi drove for Chinetti's team at Le Mans in 1954. Then came Barbara Hutton, his fourth wife; he was her fifth husband, the next in line after Prince Igor. With the Woolworth fortune she wrote him a cheque for three million dollars and gave him a converted Boeing B25 bomber as a personal plane and a string of polo ponies. And more cars. He became a regular participant in the Sebring 12 Hours and in the Nassau Speed Weeks, the Bahamas' only contribution to motor-racing history, one part sporting competition to two parts social event and greatly enjoyed by the likes of de Portago and Moss as an out-of-season break among the beautiful people of the late 1950s. But in the Sixties, and particularly after the assassination of the Dominican dictator Trujillo, his friend and patron, in 1961, Rubirosa lived a quieter life, commuting between Texas, California, Paris and the Riviera, mostly staying out of the gossip columns. He provided his final story while driving through the Bois de Boulogne on his way home from an all-night party in the early hours of the morning of 6 July 1965. On the Avenue de la Reine Marguerite he lost control of his car, a pale grey Ferrari 250GT cabriolet with red leather upholstery, and smashed straight into the trunk of a medium-sized tree. The impact threw him into the steering wheel and the windscreen. The pictures of the crash were in the following day's newspapers, with the appropriate headlines. He was fifty-six years old, and he had played his part.

Now, after forty years, Enzo and Laura Ferrari had moved out of the apartment above the old Scuderia headquarters and bought a property around the corner. The big, dark, four-storey town house was on the corner of a block in the Largo Garibaldi, a spacious square perhaps 800 metres long and 200 metres wide, just outside the city walls on the via Emilia Est. He and Laura set up home there, with his mother in her own set of rooms on an upper floor. Adalgisa choked to death on a hard-boiled egg one October day in 1965, aged ninety-three, and went to join her husband and her first grandson in the family tomb. To her, Ferrari said, he had been 'both her pride and joy and her daily torment'; she had given him 'a lifetime of tender devotion'.

Most mornings were now spent in the office at the *assistenza*, going on to the factory in the afternoon. He had recently attended the opening of his new school in Maranello, the *Istituto professionale de stato per l'industria e l'artigianato Alfredo Ferrari*, created in collaboration with the Corni technical institute, where both Dino and Piero had studied. Now Piero, too, was working at the factory, following his graduation, and that itself had been a source of argument. Adalgisa, before she died, had been all for it. Laura was firmly against. Only once had she even caught sight of the boy, when she walked into Gozzi's office in the *assistenza* – one of her unexpected arrivals – and found this thin, shy boy there, and saw the eyes and the nose and knew instantly at whom she was looking. Enzo had found Lina and Piero an apartment in the via Vittorio Veneto, not far from his new house, on the edge of a park; and he was spending more and more time there, often eating his evening meal with his second family. Nevertheless Lina's life was hardly perfect. 'I've spent thirty years with one man', she told Margherita Bandini, Lorenzo's wife, 'and we've never been out to the cinema or the theatre together. At Christmas he gives me the usual diamond. I've got a shoebox full of jewels. But what I'd like most of all would be if, just once, he'd take me on his arm, without hiding, into a restaurant.' Nevertheless there were weekends together in Pavullo, an old village of which they were both fond, in the mountains above Maranello, and visits to her three sisters, among whom they were accepted as man and wife.

Once a year he went to Monza to attend the first day's practice for the Italian Grand Prix, and occasionally he would get Peppino to drive him to the Modena autodrome to watch the first trials of a new car. Not for years, however, had he been in direct contact with the evolution of racing-car design as practised by the new pioneers like Chapman and Cooper. He depended on others to bring him news. 'The Old Man had isolated himself,' Surtees said. 'He didn't get the right stories. People were either covering themselves or telling him what they thought would fit in with his philosophy. He was out of touch and relying on second- and third-hand information.'

In an attempt to drag the team into the same world as that inhabited by the British constructors who were setting the pace, Surtees successfully introduced Ferrari to a British company specialising in fibreglass mouldings, which in time meant an end to the beautiful single-seater bodies hand-beaten in aluminium by Medardo Fantuzzi and his band of Modenese artists. No doubt that sort of thing created local resentments. When the team needed help to combat the loads imposed on their tyres by the Monza banking, Surtees made an approach to the Firestone company, whose Indianapolis experience solved the problem, beginning a fruitful relationship that lasted through the remainder of the decade. And Surtees even asked Ferrari for permission to let him run his own team of Lola sports cars in America, on the grounds that they would not be competing against Ferraris and would provide him with regular access to more modern design philosophies than those still prevailing in Maranello. Against the advice of some of his lieutenants, Ferrari gave his assent.

But the covert resentments began to fester. Dragoni was constantly undermining Surtees, criticising him to Ferrari and to Italian journalists, trying to implant the notion that Bandini was the faster driver and was being held back only by the obligation to give the Englishman the better equipment. When Surtees was asked to try out a new road car called the 275GTB, on which Parkes had done the development work, he delivered a damning opinion and offered a list of suggested improvements. Nor did he like sharing a sports car with Parkes in endurance races; the other Englishman was six feet five inches tall, and the need to change seats along with drivers cost valuable time at pit stops. He preferred to be partnered by Ludovico Scarfiotti, or

Lorenzo Bandini, who were of similar dimensions. But towards the end of the 1965 season, before the last two world-championship rounds, Surtees crashed his Lola-Chevrolet heavily at Mosport Park in Canada, almost killing himself. Back at the factory, Giulio Borsari, his chief mechanic, read the headline in the early edition of *Il Corriere Lombardo*: 'Surtees paralysed or dead'. The later edition was more categorical: 'Surtees is dead'. He wasn't, to Borsari's great relief, but there were those in Maranello whose dominant reaction was the thought that to have an accident in a car other than a Ferrari represented a form of treason.

The company took care of Surtees' personal insurance without question, even though he had not been at the wheel of their car, an interesting contrast with the falling-out between Ferrari and Luigi Villoresi over the question of compensation for the death of Mimi Villoresi in an Alfa Corse car almost thirty years earlier. And Ferrari, on discovering that Surtees' injured foot was the left one, half-jokingly promised to build him an automatic. Surtees' relationship with the Old Man was still good. Occasionally at the weekend Peppino would drive them down the via Emilia to Ferrari's villa by the beach at Viserba, on the Adriatic coast, just above Rimini. During the time he owned a Mini-Cooper, the Old Man liked to do the driving himself. 'He loved that car,' Surtees remembered. 'For a while it was the hottest thing since sliced bread. It's a wonder the next Ferrari didn't come out with rubber suspension. I think eventually the engineers persuaded him not to.' In Modena Surtees would dine sometimes with Ferrari and Laura, sometimes with Ferrari and Lina. 'He normally had a fair twinkle in his eye when we were together. We didn't necessarily agree with each other all the time but we respected each other. That's why the Dragoni people had to stage a conspiracy to get me out.'

The plot gathered momentum, he believed, when he returned from his convalescence at the beginning of 1966 and was told to shake down a sports car that he was due to share with Parkes at the Monza 1000 kms. 'I tried it, came back, and said,

"It ain't right." Forghieri didn't like that, and Parkes liked it even less. I told the Old Man and insisted we did a quick rehash of some of the aerodynamics. We made some improvements and it went quicker and it was better to drive. But it had created some problems. During the race it poured with rain and the windscreen wiper broke. I couldn't do anything about it, but I found that by going faster than you really wanted to go, it created enough of a wind effect to keep the screen clear. Michael carried on in the same vein. After the race, Dragoni put in his report to the Old Man. "Surtees would have stopped and not used the car," it said, "if it hadn't been for me and Michael Parkes."'

Then Surtees got a sight of the new V12 Formula One car, known as the 312, built to the three-litre regulations which were coming in at the start of 1966 in an effort by the governing body to make grand prix cars more powerful and spectacular. 'Instead of being the totally new car I'd been told was being built, they'd compromised on the engine. All they'd done was make a short-stroke version of the sports-car engine. So it was overweight, and instead of the 320 horsepower they'd claimed, it had 290. When I told them that I wanted to drive the V6 car with the previous year's chassis, which was two and a half seconds a lap faster round Modena, Dragoni kicked up.'

The lines had been drawn for the final battle. 'I'd just moved into a flat belonging to the Old Man, opposite the Real Fini. I'd decided to move to Italy instead of going backwards and forwards from England. I went to Syracuse and just scraped a win. I said, "This car doesn't go." I said, "At Monaco, I'm driving the old car." They said, "No, you're not." "But I want to win the race. I can win the race with it." "No, you've got to drive the new car." I said, "If I drive it in a manner to try and make it go quick, it will break." Sure enough, I led the race for fifteen laps and it broke. Then Rocchi came up with a revised cylinder head for Spa, which took it to 320 hp, again a wet race, a tactical race which you wanted to win at the slowest pace. I did win. I led at the start, then sat behind Jochen Rindt's

[237]

Cooper for a while because he had a tyre with a bit of a deeper groove, and I considered it was better to let him make the pace. Then after two-thirds of the race I went by him and disappeared.' It was among Surtees' greatest victories, in the light of the fact that halfway round the long circuit on the opening lap the cars ran into a cloudburst which eliminated seven of the runners straight away. 'The mechanics were very happy, but Dragoni never even came up and said, "Good show." So the next day I went off to Le Mans.'

For the previous two years, but with increasing difficulty, Ferrari had managed to hold at bay the Ford threat to their primacy at Le Mans. Henry Ford's men had yet to make good the threat to 'kick his ass', and Surtees was left in no doubt of the urgency of the mission. 'At the Le Mans test day our people came to me and said, "John, you've got to do a better time than the Fords. Only you can do it." The Fords were there in strength and there was hostility over the fact that Ford had been going to buy Ferrari and then the Old Man turned them down. I put in a Formula One-type effort and set the fastest time. Then I said, "We've got to prepare the car to do the race like a grand prix. These Americans are here to race us. We've got to push them early on to get them to break." OK, that's agreed. But when I get there, Dragoni comes up to me and says, "You're not starting." I say, "What?" He says, "No, Mr Agnelli is coming, and he'd like to see Ludovico start." I said, "What are you talking about? What are we doing? I can't drive the fastest car at Monaco, I can't do this . . ."'After a furious exchange, Surtees walked out and Dragoni was able to pair up Parkes and Scarfiotti in the big 4-litre 330 P3. Five hours into the race, the Italian tangled with two smaller cars and the crash eliminated the Ferrari. Fords finished first, second and third, the next four positions filled by Porsches. The Americans had taken the first instalment of their revenge for Ferrari's temerity in refusing their offer.

'I was there in '66 at Le Mans', Brenda Vernor remembered, 'when there was all that fuss with Surtees and they gave Mike the drive. John is a nice guy, but he's a funny guy. I remember at the airport when we were coming back we saw John. Mike said, "Hello, John," but John wouldn't speak to him.'

'Of course the Fords won.' On a chilly afternoon more than thirty years later, the words came in a suddenly impassioned burst from a white-haired man sitting at his office desk on a small industrial estate in Surrey, the county in which both John Surtees and Mike Parkes were born, albeit at opposite ends. 'I went back to see the Old Man', Surtees continued, 'and we talked things over. It was in the middle of a delicate time with the Fiat situation, and there were other forces at work somewhere. I said, "That's it." Sad. Sad to this day, in some ways.'

Lorenzo Bandini tests the 1965 grand prix car at Modena, attended by Giulio
Borsari, the Scuderia's chief mechanic, with Enzo Ferrari and Don Sergio
Mantovani in the background.

Nine

'I know what I'm losing,' Enzo Ferrari said when John Surtees' departure was announced. 'What I don't know is how much I'd be losing if I kept him on.' He liked Mike Parkes and Ludovico Scarfiotti, although he knew their limitations. Both were excellent sports-car drivers, as the likes of Franco Cortese, Clemente Biondetti and Olivier Gendebien had been in previous generations. They also got on well with each other. Either might, given appropriate luck, win one or two grands prix. Neither, however, was likely to make the big step to become a true champion. Not even 'Lulu' Scarfiotti, despite his Agnelli connection and the promotional efforts of Dragoni and an ambitious Signora Scarfiotti. The big hope was Lorenzo Bandini.

He had first arrived at Ferrari in the difficult year of 1962, a keen young driver from Milan who had graduated through Formula Junior, sports cars, and the Formula One Cooper-Maseratis run by the Scuderia Centro Sud, where he befriended a young mechanic, Giulio Borsari, who moved to Ferrari a month or two before Bandini arrived. By the end of 1963 Bandini had become an established member of the grand prix squad, moving in after Mairesse's Nürburgring accident had removed him from contention, and in 1964 he graduated to the status of number two to Surtees – in fact if not in writing – in a team of only two cars. Although Dragoni constantly promoted his case above that of the Englishman, Bandini and Surtees remained good friends and colleagues. But after Surtees was fired, the spotlight turned squarely on the Italian. 'Lorenzo just about cried when he knew I was leaving,' Surtees said. 'He didn't want to be put in that position. Being an Italian, it wasn't the right time or the right place for him to be.'

He was a handsome, pleasant man, without guile, born in Libya during the Italian occupation, and from humble origins. In 1964 he had married Margherita Freddi, the daughter of the Milan garage owner who had given him his first opportunities to work with cars and to race. Like Surtees, he knew enough about the mechanical side to make himself useful. In his first race as team leader, the French Grand Prix at Rheims, he was leading with ease when his throttle cable broke and the car stopped, but in a nearby field he found a piece of baling wire and rigged the throttle so that he could open and close it by pulling the wire over his shoulder, while steering with one hand. This piece of improvisation got him back to the pits, where the mechanics could set to work on a proper repair – although too late to enable him to finish the race in a decent position. But if a result could not be achieved, it was the effort and the will-power that counted. Parkes, at last promoted to the Formula One team, finished second, and followed up by putting his car on pole position for the Italian Grand Prix, with Scarfiotti alongside him and Bandini on the second row. A broken fuel line cost Bandini a long stay in the pits, but his team mates were able to exploit the extra power provided by a new cylinder head. They raced each other for victory in front of a delirious home crowd which went home even happier after the Italian took the decision, caring little that only the special conditions of the ultra-fast Monza track had enabled the team to score its one–two win. To them, Scarfiotti was simply the first Italian to win their grand prix in an Italian car since Ascari in 1952. The true situation was reflected in Ferrari's refusal, once again, to send a car to the final race of the year, the Mexican Grand Prix.

At the end of 1966, Ferrari finally dismissed the manipulative Dragoni, whose reign had been so rancorous. To fill his place he hired Franco Lini, an experienced and admired journalist, and previously one of Ferrari's most trenchant critics. 'Maybe that was the reason I was asked,' he told the journalist Graham Gauld. 'One day Enzo called and said that because we were so much in opposition to each other, joining forces might produce a positive reaction. To be honest, at that time Ferrari needed someone to rebuild the team's image. It was not popular with the other teams, nor with race organisers and the press in particular, so he asked me especially to do something about it.'

The restoration of a decent *esprit de corps* would be the minimum requirement. For 1967 the team of Bandini, Scarfiotti and Parkes was augmented by Chris Amon, a New Zealander who had arrived in Europe as a twenty-year-old prodigy four years earlier. Meanwhile he had driven privately entered Lolas and Lotuses in Formula One with little success, but had shown better form in sports cars, driving for Ford at Le Mans and for Bruce McLaren's team in the Can-Am series. Amon, too, wanted to be a grand prix driver, but he had a difficult baptism with the team when, after his first few laps in a Formula One car during a test session at Monza in November 1966, he crashed heavily. The car he was driving turned out to be the one that Scarfiotti had used to win the grand prix two months earlier. The engineers believed that Scarfiotti had hit a guard rail during the race, damaging the suspension, which had not subsequently been inspected. Nevertheless Amon got the 1967 season off to a fine start when, in company with Bandini, he won the Daytona 24 Hours and the Monza 1,000 km in the handsome 330 P4. At Daytona, in fact, the Ferraris finished in the first three positions, doing to Ford on their own home ground what the Americans had done to Ferrari in Europe. 'This was everything I expected from Ferrari, perhaps more,' Amon said. He found Bandini 'a true sportsman' and was also pleased by his developing relationship with Enzo Ferrari – 'just like father and son'. He was young enough not to mind that he had signed a contract entitling him to not a single lira in regular salary or guarantees, but awarding him 50 per cent of the prize money. 'That was fine by me,' Amon reflected.

Wisely, Franco Lini discarded Scarfiotti and Parkes for the first championship grand prix of the season, at Monaco. Mauro Forghieri and Franco Rocchi had produced a new version of the

312, a well-muscled device distinguished by its tangle of white-painted exhaust pipes running along the top of the exposed engine. Two examples were trucked over the border to the principality for the use of Bandini and Amon. Determined to justify his new standing in the team, Bandini put the car on the front row of the grid, with a time beaten only by Jack Brabham in one of his own cars. Everybody liked Bandini. 'He had a fine engineering background, just the right amount of nonchalance in his driving, and quite exceptional pride,' Ferrari wrote. 'His strength of will, his confidence and his great loyalty to the team won my affection.' When Louis Chiron, the Scuderia's old driver, dropped the flag to start the race, Bandini used the Ferrari's horsepower to grab the lead as the field funnelled around Sainte-Devote and up the hill to Casino Square. Halfway round the lap, however, Brabham's engine blew up, coating the area around the Station hairpin with oil, and over the next few laps Bandini was overtaken by Denny Hulme, in the second Brabham, and Jackie Stewart in a 2-litre BRM. Chasing furiously after these nimbler opponents, Bandini saw Stewart retire with a transmission problem, and pressed on in pursuit of Hulme. But on the eighty-second lap, after two hours of intense racing in tiring heat, two hours of manhandling a big, powerful car around a circuit better suited to more agile machines, two hours of trying his best to justify his position as an Italian carrying the standard for an Italian team, Lorenzo Bandini made a mistake.

Entering the chicane, the point where the circuit comes on to the harbour front, where Ascari had shot into the water in 1955, Bandini allowed his right front wheel to clip the barrier on the outside of the turn. The car was thrown across the road, hit the barrier on the opposite side of the track, lost two wheels, somersaulted, and came crashing down on the edge of the harbour, landing on straw bales. Almost immediately it caught fire, the straw adding kindling to the conflagration. Nevertheless marshals were making efforts to extinguish the flames and release the driver, and they might have been successful had a helicopter carrying a television camera crew not swooped down to capture pictures of the accident. As it hovered at low level, the downdraught from the helicopter's rotor blades fanned what remained of the fire, which reignited with a new ferocity. In that moment, Bandini was done for. Once the helicopter had been shooed away, the marshals were able to turn the car over and get him into an ambulance. 'I was in my office in Maranello watching the final stages of the race on television,' Ferrari wrote. 'When I saw that cloud of black smoke floating grimly above the bay, I could just feel, even before the TV reporter began to explain the catastrophe depicted on the screen, that the car in flames was one of mine. And although I can't now say why, I guessed that Bandini was in that fire, and that I'd never see him again.' Three days later, in the Princess Grace Hospital, the driver succumbed to his burns. In the next ward, his wife had suffered a miscarriage. No more would straw bales be seen at a grand prix circuit. The development of fire-retardant fuel systems and flameproof clothing for drivers and marshals was accelerated. Never again would a TV crew be allowed to fly a helicopter low over a burning car.

At Zandvoort a month later the future of grand prix racing presented itself in the shape of a new V8 engine produced by Ford, Ferrari's nemesis. For an investment of a mere £100,000 with the Cosworth engine-building company of Northampton, the American giant received an engine that would win more than 150 grands prix in cars built by Lotus, McLaren, Brabham, Tyrrell, Williams, Ligier and others. Like the Coventry Climax engine of the late Fifties, the 3-litre Cosworth DFV made life much easier for the English firms who built their own chassis but then bought a Ford engine and a Hewland gearbox to complete the package. At Ferrari, there was real and justifiable pride in creating virtually the entire organism. The foundry at Maranello, where craftsmen cast the alloy cylinder blocks, was still the heart of the operation; although it was also, in a sense, the company's greatest handicap, since the English designers were able to concentrate on their special expertise in chassis construction without having to worry, as Forghieri did, like his predecessors and successors, about whether the engine and transmission would also work.

Installed in Colin Chapman's Lotus 49, and driven by Jim Clark, the Ford-Cosworth DFV engine won its first grand prix. That was on 4 June. There was worse to come only a week later, when the Ferrari sports-car team arrived at Le Mans to face a squadron of Fords which had been sent with the specific mission to take the defeat they had inflicted on the Italians a year earlier and turn it into a genocide. Twelve Fords confronted seven Ferraris, and although the result was not a massacre, it certainly left a bitter taste in Enzo Ferrari's mouth. Dan Gurney, his old pilot, and A. J. Foyt, the Indianapolis maestro, had combined to outrun the Ferraris in one of the new Ford Mk IVs. The best of the Italian cars, the P4 driven by Parkes and Scarfiotti, finished second after featuring in a desperate chase through the final hours. That disappointment was still being digested a week later when Parkes, restored to the Formula One team for the Belgian Grand Prix at Spa, smashed into the guard rail at Blanchimont, a 150 mph left-hander, his tyres having picked up oil blown out of Jackie Stewart's BRM. If you happened to be standing at the top of Eau Rouge, on the other side of the pits, you could see his car rear into the air and explode into scarlet fragments. Parkes was half-ejected and dragged along behind the disintegrating chassis. Amon, driving past, was sure he must be dead. In fact his head injuries put him into a coma that lasted a week. His broken bones would take six months to heal, but when he came back all he could think of was getting into a racing car. Ferrari refused permission, instead offering him a succession of more senior engineering jobs. But in 1971 Parkes left Maranello to race for a private team, Scuderia Filipinetti. Later he worked for Fiat on the rally-car programme and for Lancia, developing the Ferrari-engined Stratos. He was thinking of moving on again when, while driving to Turin one day in 1977, he was hit by a truck and killed.

The trouncings at the hands of Ford increased Ferrari's need for help and Fiat's belief that they could provide it. Links had been strengthened the previous year, when Ferrari announced that Fiat would be building a sports car using the Dino engine, which would be manufactured in sufficient numbers to allow him to use it in a Formula Two car. In May 1965, Pier Ugo Gobbato arrived at Maranello. He was the son of Ugo Gobbato, the pre-war general manager of Alfa Romeo, who had helped Ferrari run the Scuderia, then paid him money to set it aside and run Alfa Corse instead before sacking him at the end of 1938. Talks began between Maranello and Turin that would create a formula to ensure the Scuderia's survival, both in the immediate emergency and, more distantly, after its founder's death. On a practical level, the Dino-engined Fiat coupé had been a success, although it had not done as much for Ferrari's prestige as the subsequent launch of his own Dino, a little two-seater coupé with its V6 engine located transversely behind the driver (if a Ferrari did not have rubber suspension, then at least it had one important feature copied from the Mini-Cooper). The Dino 246 was the ultimate café racer of 1967, and served the commercially useful purpose of broadening the ownership of Ferraris without diluting the essence. Over the company's first twenty years, the road cars had become bigger and bigger: for all their sophistication, the 365GTB/4 Daytonas and the 410 Super Americas were what the Americans called muscle cars. The Dino 246 represented a return to the scale of the early 166 models. It carried the name of a championship-winning Formula One car, and its low Pininfarina body made it look like something that would be at home racing in the Targa Florio or around the Nürburgring, even though its destiny was to cruise the King's Road. And it was the first of a series of cars which, more effectively than any of the other memorials, would carry the dead son's name into the consciousness of future generations.

With Bandini gone and Amon still finding his feet, Ferrari needed a top-line driver. 'I remember after Bandini died at Monaco', Franco Lini said, 'we were looking for another driver and Jackie Stewart's name came up.' The idea came from the competitions manager of Shell, who had Stewart under contract at BRM. The Scot was invited to share a Ferrari with Chris Amon in the BOAC 500 sports-car race at Brands Hatch, where their second place gave the team the sports-car championship for 1967. The next day Lini took Stewart to Maranello to meet Enzo Ferrari. Before their arrival he warned the driver, who was already noted for his interest in the business side of driving racing cars, that Ferrari was an old man set in his ways, and that he didn't need to be told anything he already knew. 'But when the discussions began, Jackie forgot all that. He told Ferrari that he had spoken to his lawyer before coming to Maranello. At this Enzo turned to me and muttered, "He had to go and see his lawyer before he comes to see me?" Then Jackie went through a list of things that he would like to have, and once again Ferrari turned to me and said, "What does he want? The factory?" It was clear to me that we were not going to get anywhere, and we didn't. The last straw for Mr Ferrari came when he muttered to me something about the "*Inglese*" and this was picked up by Jackie, who responded, "I'm Scottish!" And that was it.' Instead Stewart went to start a new team with Ken Tyrrell, a Surrey timber merchant, with whom he was to win three world championships over the next half-dozen years. Ferrari's instinctive dislike had quite possibly cost his team those titles; perhaps Stewart could have pushed the Scuderia to the sort of success for which two other drivers also noted for their financial acumen and lack of romantic notions, Niki Lauda and Michael Schumacher, would be responsible in decades to come.

Lini's tenure as *direttore sportivo* lasted only a single season. Before the start of the 1968 season he was replaced by Franco Gozzi, whose experience as Ferrari's press secretary made him equally sensitive to the requirements and prejudices of the media. Gozzi had met Ferrari ten years earlier, when he was twenty-two years old. He had qualified in law, he was looking for a job, and he had asked his future father-in-law, Ferrari's barber, for a letter of introduction to the manager of the local office of the Banco San Geminiano e San Prospero. Ferrari, who had launched the Scuderia with a loan from that very branch, offered to help. The bank had nothing to offer the young man at that moment, but Gozzi was struck by the copious apologies the manager made for his inability to assist Enzo Ferrari's young acquaintance. 'I told him that it didn't matter and I would wait,' Gozzi said. 'He repeated that it wasn't easy. You don't know Ferrari, he said. I promised that I would tell Ferrari that he had made every possible effort, but he was very worried and went on repeating: "It won't be enough, but you tell him, I beg you. I promise you that in six months I'll find you a job. I'll start now – but please tell him." So it was that I saw the first sign of the strength of Ferrari's personality: a bank manager was terrified because he could not satisfy his request.'

The following year, Gozzi helped Ferrari's press agent, Giorgio Crestani, with press releases announcing the changeover from a private company, Auto-Avio Costruzioni, to the Società Esercizio Fabriche Automobili e Corse Ferrari, the joint-stock company. When Crestani resigned at the end of the year, complaining of overwork, Ferrari sent his barber to tell his prospective son-in-law that there was a full-time job for him at Maranello, if he wanted it. Gozzi had just begun work as a clerk in a notary's chambers, but he took leave of absence and never went back. And what he learned was that Ferrari required loyalty and commitment far beyond the norm. 'It's not true to say that Ferrari was a slave-driver, as someone once said,' Gozzi observed, 'but the fact is that at Ferrari it wasn't enough to give 100 per cent, or 110. The minimum was 130 per cent. Whoever thought that he only had to give 100 per cent was out by a third. It was not due or required, but if you wanted to be a part of it, that was the share. Among Ferrari's virtues were his concern for life on the factory floor and a collective spirit. In the workshop, from the foreman to the most junior mechanic, they accepted everything, even working on seven or eight cars at a time. It was like having it in the blood, having it in your DNA – everything was secondary to work and the needs of the company. It wasn't always recognised and rewarded as it should have been, and sometimes it hung by a thread. But Ferrari had a great sense of timing. Just before you started to complain, you got a pat on the back. At Christmas, for example, he never forgot to give presents to the wives, as a way of saying sorry for their husbands' absences during the year.'

Families were important. A wife who felt that her husband's livelihood depended on Enzo Ferrari might tend to be more understanding when he worked late or over the weekend, rushing to finish cars urgently needed by the *gestione sportiva*. And if the men from Formigine and Sassuolo and Castelvetro could be made to feel valued, then Ferrari would retain the most precious quality of his labour force, the feeling that they were somehow infused with the spirit of the region's artisan tradition, and that this spirit found its highest expression in the construction of the world's most admired and coveted sports and racing cars. Families were important, indeed. And on 10 February 1968, Piero got married to Floriana Nalin, a pretty girl from Cesena, near Forli. It was a formal affair, with the bride in white and the groom's mother in an elaborate hat. Piero was now twenty-five, and had been working in the factory since his graduation from the Corni institute. He loved engines, as his half-brother Dino had, and it was inevitable that he would take some sort of a role in the company, but he was still known to the outside world as Piero Lardi, the name on his birth certificate, and his patrimony was not acknowledged. Within a year he and Floriana had given Ferrari and Lina a granddaughter, Antonella. By the age of two, she was at the wheel of a plastic pedal car with a prancing-horse shield on the bonnet.

Enzo Ferrari kept his distance from unlucky people, and unlucky drivers in particular. Chris Amon stayed with Ferrari for two more seasons. In all, the New Zealander competed in twenty-seven grands prix with the team, and won none of them. By the end of his career he had started ninety-five grands prix in eleven makes of car, and had still not won one. He came second three times and finished third on eight occasions, and in his heyday he led races quite often before the intervention of any number of species of misfortune, which could be as trivial as the breaking of the strap securing his goggles. There were those who believed him to be inherently as fast as any of the stars of his day – Clark, Stewart, Gurney or Rindt. But in the end Ferrari's opinion of the man who had fondly believed them to enjoy a father-and-son relationship was clouded by his personal interpretation of Amon's luck. His verdict was not without admiration, yet somehow disdainful: 'Chris Amon was the Nazzaro of the Sixties,' he observed, 'but without the sincere human warmth of that unforgettable artist of the steering wheel. In the three years he drove for Ferrari he never achieved the success he deserved. He was a good, indeed an excellent test driver, unfussy and intuitive, but on the race track he didn't have what it takes and his strength often seemed to run out when it was needed.' And there was a harsh postscript. 'After his time at Ferrari he drifted from team to team in a vain attempt to overcome the adversities that he was constantly encountering,' Ferrari concluded. 'In the end he went back to his native New Zealand and devoted himself to his family. I wonder if his children – he had twin sons in 1980 – believed him when he told them how very near he had been to becoming a motor-racing legend.'

Jacky Ickx was another matter. The son of a distinguished Belgian motoring journalist, twenty-three years old, he had demonstrated at the Nürburgring in 1967 his considerable talent by pushing his little 1,600 cc Matra up among the Formula One giants in the German Grand Prix. The Matra had been entered into the race by Ken Tyrrell, a renowned talent scout and the first significant figure to identify Ickx's ability. Ferrari offered the Belgian a retainer for 1968, which upset Amon, who was still receiving only a proportion of the prize money. In Ickx's fifth race with Forghieri's latest 312, which featured the innovation of a little adjustable wing mounted behind the driver's head, he brought the team its first win since Scarfiotti's victory at Monza almost two years earlier. It was the French Grand Prix, at the demanding Rouen-les-Essarts circuit, and Ickx won because,

[251]

when it started raining just as the drivers set off on their parade lap, he was the only one whose car had been fitted with wet-weather tyres. He also happened to have a particular genius for driving in the rain, a quality not shared by all grand prix drivers, including the New Zealander in the other Ferrari. The chore of testing never excited Ickx's imagination; he left Amon to do the donkey work and to earn Forghieri's admiration as perhaps the best test driver the Scuderia had employed – which was not what Amon wanted to hear. That season Ickx also scored three thirds and two fourth places, enabling him to finish fourth in the championship, well ahead of Amon. But at the end of the season he left to join Brabham, mainly because he wanted to drive in sports-car races for John Wyer's Gulf team. Ferrari, mindful of conflicting oil and tyre sponsorships, and perhaps remembering what had happened when he gave John Surtees permission to drive for another sports-car outfit, would not allow it.

Ferrari made another mistake at the end of 1968 when he transferred Mauro Forghieri away from the racing team and replaced him with Stefano Iacoponi, who had been developing sports cars for the hillclimb events which remained a part of the European calendar. Forghieri had led Ferrari's technical team into an unaccustomed position among the leaders in the fast-changing world of Formula One design. His V12 engine had plenty of power, the chassis handled well, and he had led the way in the use of aerofoils, an idea he had borrowed from the Swiss engineer Michael May, who had tried bolting a wing on to the back of his Porsche Spyder in the early Sixties. May had been working at Ferrari on fuel-injection systems during the Surtees years, and his earlier innovation inspired Forghieri to try an idea which became and remained universal. But they had won only one race, and Forghieri refused to accept the ensuing criticism. In an age of increasing specialisation, he was one of the last men alive capable of designing virtually every component of a racing car, but Ferrari sent him back to the old workshops in Modena, where he sat in a drawing office designing the Boxer, a rear-engined grand touring car, and a new gearbox for the 312.

By comparison with what Forghieri achieved in his time as technical director, Iacoponi had little to offer. Only a single car was entered in the early races of the 1969 season, and Amon found plenty to complain about as he lost ground against its rivals. At Silverstone in July he was at last given a team mate, Pedro Rodriguez, and the two-car entry made the team look a little more serious in its endeavours; but in the practice sessions Amon's car kept jumping out of gear and he gave up in disgust, leaving the team before the race. Ferrari accepted his decision. 'Our collaboration had started far more gloriously than it finished,' Amon concluded. Rodriguez ran in the remaining rounds of the championship, seldom emerging from mid-field anonymity, and the team ended the season on its lowest note since entering grand prix racing twenty years earlier.

Unquestionably, Ferrari's mind was elsewhere. Despite its growing fame, the company's finances were strained. To keep it going for almost a quarter of a century had required ingenuity and a certain flair for drama. The historian Luigi Orsini described Ferrari as 'a stable which managed to base its fortune on races rather than being crushed by them, as was often the case'. With his old rivals and sometime coevals at Maserati, for instance, just one catastrophic race at Caracas in 1957, when four of their big, expensive sports cars were destroyed in crashes, had been enough to push their finances over the edge and the company into virtual oblivion, at least as a racing team. At the very moment when Fangio was giving Maserati its first world championship, the firm was going into survival mode. It was fated never to recover its position in the world of racing, and would spend decades trying to establish itself as a manufacturer of road cars. Few of the many other local car builders, such as Vittorio Stanguellini in Modena and Giovanni Minardi in Faenza, had progressed much beyond the stage of cobbling together specials made out of Fiat saloons. Ferrari succeeded on a far grander scale because he never made the mistake of confusing business with sentiment, or that of making an ambitious commitment without ensuring an escape route. 'With Ferrari', the pre-war French ace René Dreyfus remembered, 'I learned the business of racing, for there was no doubt that he was a businessman. Enzo Ferrari was a pleasant person and friendly, but not openly affectionate. There was, for example, none of the sense of belonging to the family that I had with the Maserati brothers. At Maserati, confidences were shared; there was banter back and forth; I never hesitated to suggest or cavil. At Bugatti, I did likewise. One never got the impression that Ettore Bugatti resented such conversations. In truth, I'm not sure that Enzo Ferrari would have resented them, either. It just never occurred to me to have them. One tended to believe that Enzo Ferrari was much happier going about his business without intrusion from his racing drivers. And so one didn't intrude.'

Of course it had been difficult for Ferrari, and there had been times when he felt like giving up the struggle – even if not as many times as he had said so to the reporters in order to start a scare: 'Ferrari to quit!' As early as the 1930s he had needed all his powers of persuasion to make Alfa Romeo give the Scuderia the cars that would make them competitive. In 1955, when early success had dwindled away, his team had been effectively relaunched by the Lancia handover, thanks to Fiat's intervention. And now it was time to accept the overtures that Fiat had been making ever since the successful agreement to manufacture the sports car carrying the Dino engine four years earlier.

There were long negotiations between Turin and Maranello, and eventually a deal emerged. In Ferrari's words, it was 'the culmination of a story that had developed under the pressure of any number of external and internal pressures'. The terms were straightforward but imaginative, given the special requirements of the smaller of the two concerns. Fiat would buy 40 per cent of the company. Ferrari would keep 50 per cent, which would be ceded to Fiat on his death. Piero would be given 10 per cent, which would become the Ferrari family's holding after the founder's demise. Fiat would take control of the road-car division, at that time producing fewer than 1,000 cars a year and occupying more than half of the company's 700 workers, while Ferrari would maintain absolute command of the firm's racing activities. Thus he achieved exactly what Ford's negotiators had denied him, while retaining the company in Italian ownership – a factor possibly less important to him than to those in the world outside.

The deal was signed in Turin on 18 June 1969. Ferrari, who suffered from claustrophobia in elevators, made everyone walk up to the eighth floor of the Fiat office on the Corso Marconi. Piero and Gozzi went with him. 'We were ushered into the office of Gianni Agnelli,' Ferrari remembered, 'a man I'd first met twenty years earlier but only four times, years apart, since then.' On one of those occasions, Agnelli had arrived at Maranello to take delivery of a car with a special body built by Pininfarina, incorporating a central seat for the driver. And it had been in a Ferrari that, during his playboy days, he had broken his legs on the way home from a Riviera party, leaving him with a lifetime's legacy of wearing an orthopaedic shoe on one foot and, in later years, of walking with a cane – both of which somehow added to the distinctively rakish appeal of a man who came to dominate Italian business and political life.

'Ferrari,' Agnelli said, 'I'm here to listen.'

His visitor started talking, and he talked for a long time, just as, thirty-five years earlier, he had made his impassioned pitch to the manager of Banco di San Geminiano e San Prospero in Modena, when he asked for a million-lire loan to build a headquarters for his new Scuderia. Now, to Agnelli, he spoke of his company's origins, and of its achievements, and of the dangers and opportunities that presented themselves. 'I told him of my past and my present, of the things I wanted for my factory, and I was able as never before to express what I really thought about things.' Then it was Agnelli's turn. 'Twenty years younger than me,' Ferrari recalled, 'he exuded all the power of a thoroughly modern man, of the businessman, politician and diplomat, an alertly intelligent observer of the world he lived in. His questions

[255]

were short and to the point, in the manner of a man who needed to know and to understand. Eventually he brought in his people and summed it all up.'

'Well, Ferrari,' Agnelli said, 'I suppose we could have come to this agreement before now. Perhaps we've wasted time. So we'd better start making up for it.'

The press release was a model of enigmatic economy. 'Following a meeting of the president of Fiat, *Dottore* Giovanni Agnelli, with *Ingegnere* Enzo Ferrari, the prominent intent of it being to ensure the continuity and development of Ferrari automobiles, it has been decided that the past technical collaboration and support will be transformed within the year to a joint participation.' The price, it was rumoured, was in the region of 7 billion lire. About $11 million, in other words, or £8 million. The new managing director, replacing Ferrari himself in the role, would be Francesco Bellicardi, the general manager of the Weber carburettor company, bought by Fiat after the 'disappearance', in the post-war turmoil of vengeance and retribution, of Ferrari's friend and collaborator Edoardo Weber. Bellicardi would remain at his post in Bologna, visiting Maranello when required. The appointment of someone already a member of the extended family, as it were, reassured those both inside and outside the factory that Fiat would not be threatening the continuity or the integrity of the Ferrari tradition. In an extension of the deal, the new Ferrari Spa (*Società per azione*) would take over the Carrozzeria Scaglietti, the body-building concern created by Ferrari's friend Sergio Scaglietti, whose workmen had created the outer skins for some of the finest of his cars. And that night Enzo Ferrari returned to Modena, the business he had built with such passion and such agony suddenly rendered impregnable.

He brought Forghieri back in from the cold in time for 1970, and Jacky Ickx also returned, after spending a season doing well with Brabham. The Belgian was not universally loved; some found him aloof and pretentious. 'Ickx was a mixture of fiery emotion and ice-cold intellect,' Ferrari said. 'I retain the impression of a boy who had grown up fast, and the memory of his skilful daring in the rain. For four years we pursued the dream of a title amid gossip of disagreements that were often purest fantasy.' And sometimes, presumably, not fantasy at all.

With Forghieri's 312B1, now powered by the first flat-twelve engine in Ferrari's history, Ickx won in Austria, Canada and Mexico, but was pipped to the title by Jochen Rindt, who had won enough points to be declared champion despite being killed at Monza in practice for the Italian Grand Prix. Ickx's team mates were Ignazio Giunti, a member of a wealthy Roman family, who finished fourth in his first grand prix, at Spa, and Gianclaudio 'Clay' Regazzoni, a Swiss-Italian from Ticino whose aggressive driving, a motorised version of bareback riding, won the hearts of spectators and made a great contrast with the precise, unruffled style of Ickx. Regazzoni, too, won a race in 1970, the Italian Grand Prix at Monza, and also took three second places, allowing him to finish third in the championship behind Rindt and Ickx. The night of his Monza victory, Regazzoni treated the mechanics to dinner at the team's usual base near Monza, the old Albergo Sant'Eustorgio in Arcore. The telephone rang. It was *Domenica Sportiva*, the Sunday-night national television sports magazine, asking him to travel a few miles to Milan to appear live on the programme. Regazzoni was having fun, and said no. A day or two later Enzo Ferrari invited him to lunch at his country house, with Lina and Piero. Regazzoni's priorities, like his driving, came from another, more spontaneous age.

The story was less satisfactory in 1971 when Peter Schetty, the son of a Basle textile manufacturer and a graduate in economics and political science, took over as *direttore sportivo*. Schetty had done well as a driver in the European hillclimb championship, working hard with Ferrari's engineers to develop a special sports car, the 212 E, which became unbeatable in a series that still enjoyed a measure of prestige. Perhaps, when he put Schetty in charge of the Formula One team, Ferrari saw in him a memory of the part played by Didi Trossi in the early days of the Scuderia – the role filled by the gifted amateur whose decisions and loyalties would not be distorted by considerations of financial gain or personal glory. To Schetty, too, Ferrari was like 'a second father'; they would drive off into the hills around Maranello, stopping for a lunch of local ham and a glass or two of Lambrusco.

The year got off to a dreadful start when Giunti was killed in a freak accident in the sports-car race at Buenos Aires in January, his Ferrari ramming into the back of a Matra which Jean-Pierre Beltoise was pushing back to the pits. 'He had talent and passion and we all loved him,' Ferrari wrote. To Forghieri, the Roman had given evidence of the ability to become a world champion. And so another potential Italian champion had been erased from the lists. The season held only two wins: one for Ickx, in Zandvoort, and another for Mario Andretti, an Italian-American from Nazareth, Pennsylvania, who had become one of the biggest stars of the US track-racing scene. Andretti was born in 1940, near Trieste; after the war, when his region of Italy became part of Tito's Yugoslavia, his family had been sent to a displaced persons' camp near Lucca in Tuscany. His first sight of a motor race had been the Mille Miglia, which passed by not far from their home; his boyhood hero was Alberto Ascari. In 1955 the Andrettis had taken a ship to America and before long young Mario and his brother Aldo were serving their racing apprenticeship on the dirt ovals of Pennsylvania. Like Nuvolari, Fangio, Moss, Clark and a very few others, Andretti could win races in any kind of car. He was already a major figure in US single-seater racing when he marked his Ferrari debut by winning the South African Grand Prix at Kyalami. He was mature enough, nevertheless, to see that however strong was the emotional appeal of Ferrari to his ethnic and romantic instincts, he would stand a better chance of winning a championship surrounded by the cooler heads of an English team. The fact that he was both Italian and American enabled him to perceive the reality behind the legend with a clarity seldom given to those who looked at the question from only one of those perspectives. And, having been steeped in the unpretentious attitudes of the American track-racing scene, he spotted very quickly the sort of games that were being played at Maranello. Unlike other drivers, for instance, he never telephoned Enzo Ferrari after a race to give him his own version of what had gone right or wrong. Partly that was because he lived on the other side of the Atlantic and did not have an intimate relationship with Ferrari. But there was a more profound reason, which reached down into the causes that lay behind the team's seasons of consistent failure. 'My own observations', Andretti said, 'would have contradicted what his engineers told him.' He raced a dozen times for Ferrari in 1971 and 1972, in both Formula One and sports cars, but never got back on the podium in a grand prix. For a while he returned to concentrating on American teams and American racing, but in 1976 he joined Lotus, and two years later, in Colin Chapman's innovative Lotus 79, he became the second American, after Phil Hill, to win the drivers' world championship.

Endless mechanical problems associated with Forghieri's latest car, the 312B2, blighted most of 1971. There was little improvement in 1972, although now the team was able to test its cars at home in Maranello, where a little figure-of-eight track had been built across the road from the factory, on land that Ferrari had acquired over the years in the hamlet of Fiorano, from which the circuit took its name. None of its rivals enjoyed such an advantage. Now Ferrari could test every day of the year, with all the team's development and manufacturing facilities on site. The inhabitants of the houses and apartment blocks surrounding the Aeroautodromo di Modena would no longer have the sound of twelve-cylinder Ferraris assailing their ears; before long the old track would be torn up, the site eventually turned into a public park bearing Enzo Ferrari's name. But the free entertainment of testing was still available to those who were prepared to drive to Maranello, park their cars on a bridge overlooking the track, and get out their binoculars to watch the engineers, mechanics and drivers at work in the little garage next to the farmhouse in which Enzo Ferrari had established his new base.

Ickx broke the 1972 drought at the Nürburgring, leading from start to finish. Regazzoni came second, having repulsed Jackie Stewart's efforts to pass him on the last lap by easing the Scot's Tyrrell into the barrier. But once again the sports cars were more successfully upholding the company's honour, a multinational cast of star drivers – Ickx, Andretti, Regazzoni, Ronnie Peterson, Brian Redman, Carlos Pace, Carlos Reutemann and Tim Schenken – winning many races and dominating their series in the fast and nimble 312P, basically the grand prix car thinly disguised with a full-width sports-car body. Their superiority over their rivals was so pronounced that at Watkins Glen, in the six-hour race which finished off the season, Schetty told the two cars, one driven by Ickx and Andretti and the other by Peterson and Schenken, that they could throw caution to the wind and race each other to the finish. The mechanics made bets on the winner, with bottles of Lambrusco as the prizes, and there was great celebration in half the Ferrari pit as the Belgian–American pairing triumphed. Schetty left at the end of the season, returning to Basle to help run his family business.

As he approached his seventy-fifth birthday, Ferrari's health was beginning to deteriorate. He was suffering from diabetes, and refused to have a straightforward operation to treat an inguinal hernia because of his morbid fear of going under the surgeon's knife. His doctors managed to persuade him to stop smoking his mentholated Kool cigarettes and to cut down on heavy foods, while the demands of managing his diabetes also brought about a change of diet.

His supervision of the day-to-day operations of the company was becoming less stringent, and the effect was felt most keenly in the grand prix team. A new designer, Sandro Colombo, formerly of the Fiat-owned Innocenti mini-car company, had come in to work with Forghieri, who resented the intruder. Towards the end of 1972 Forghieri produced the prototype of a radical new car, the 312B3, nicknamed the *spazzaneve*, or snowplough, because of the flat, shovel-like contours of its nose. The car pursued a design notion originally explored in Jano's

Lancia D50 and it was supposed to form the basis of the 1973 effort. But the signs of discord were evident when Regazzoni's contract was not renewed and he was told that the team would be entering only one car in future. Ickx disliked Forghieri's new car, and he was not the only one. So did Arturo Merzario, a diminutive and enthusiastic Italian driver brought in as a tester and a back-up to the Belgian. So once again Ferrari removed Forghieri from the Formula One project, instructing Colombo to produce his own variation, also investing him with the responsibility of *direttore sportivo* – the first time the two roles had been handled by a single man, and an indication of the lowered status of the racing department. In another significant departure from previously unquestioned traditions, Colombo ordered the monocoques of the first three cars to be constructed in England, by a company based near Northampton. Whether motivated by the inconvenience of constant industrial action in Italy or by a genuine desire to bring the expertise of the small British specialist racing-car construction companies to his own team, Ferrari approved the commission.

In terms of results, however, Colombo's 312B3 may have been the least successful Formula One car in the entire history of Ferrari, swiftly plunging to a nadir at Silverstone in 1973, when a forlorn Ickx qualified for the British Grand Prix in a humiliating nineteenth place and finished an utterly undistinguished eighth. Ferrari announced that he was withdrawing from grand prix racing, pending improvements to the car. Ickx proclaimed that he didn't care what Ferrari intended to do: he would be driving at the Nürburgring in a McLaren. The team missed the Dutch and German races, returning in Austria with Merzario in the cockpit – but only after Ferrari had removed Colombo and recalled Forghieri, at the behest of Fiat, whose executives were seriously concerned about the poor performance and deteriorating image of a company in whose reputation they had made a large investment only four years earlier. Once again Enzo Ferrari was casting around for the inspiration that might jump-start a stalled team.

Enzo Ferrari confers with Mauro Forghieri, his chief designer and the son of one of his factory workers, during a test at Fiorano in 1975.

Ten

Luca Cordero di Montezemolo was born in 1947, the year the first Ferrari car appeared. His family lived in a villa in the hills south of Bologna, on the road up to the Futa pass, and as an infant he was taken to watch the Mille Miglia go by. He remembered it as resembling a scene from a Fellini film, whole hillsides crowded with people buzzing with excitement as they waited for the parade to arrive. His own first car was a Fiat Nuova 500, tuned up by a friendly mechanic. As a law student at the University of Rome he developed his interest in cars, entering rallies with a Fiat 124 and eventually moving on to international events like the San Remo Rally, in which he finished seventh. In that world he met men such as Jean Todt, a young Frenchman who was the navigator for one of the world's best drivers, Hannu Mikkola of Finland, and Cesare Fiorio, one of Italian motor sport's leading *hommes d'affaires*, who invited him to join the official Lancia team.

By the time he graduated, Montezemolo was already a figure noted for a self-presentation which blended a certain flamboyance with impeccable manners. His direct gaze and apparent candour contributed to his ability to charm and persuade strangers. His first contact with Enzo Ferrari came as a result of his appearance on a popular radio programme, *Chiamate Roma 3131* (Call Rome 3131), when he became engaged in a discussion on the current fortunes of the Ferrari grand prix team and found himself mounting a resolute defence. Ferrari, who sometimes kept the radio on when he was writing letters, heard the broadcast. Three days later Montezemolo received a package in the post. Inside was a copy of Ferrari's memoir, *Le*

[263]

mie gioie terribili, inscribed by the author: 'To Luca di Montezemolo, who has the courage of his words and his actions.' Montezemolo went off to New York to study international relations at Columbia University, with the ambition of becoming a diplomat, but on a visit home to Bologna over Christmas 1972 he telephoned Ferrari to request a meeting. 'I need someone like you,' Ferrari responded. 'It's a pity you're going back to America.' When Montezemolo indicated that he might be prepared to give up his studies, Ferrari told him to finish his course. In June 1973, aged twenty-six, Montezemolo returned to Italy and arrived for his first day's work at Maranello, installed as *direttore sportivo*.

Inevitably, scepticism greeted the appointment of such a young and untested figure to so prominent a position in Formula One's senior team. Some observers took an instant dislike to his easily caricatured suaveness, and to the fluency and conviviality that made him a natural public-relations man on Ferrari's behalf. A few of them thought that such gifts had no place in the Formula One paddock. The gossips claimed that he was a Fiat appointment, and possibly even a member of the Agnelli clan. This was strenuously denied by Montezemolo himself, although as time went by it became clear that he enjoyed some form of quasi-filial relationship with *l'Avvocato*, as Gianni Agnelli had become known throughout Italy.

Just ten days after Montezemolo's arrival, the Silverstone debacle gave him his first experience of attending a race meeting with the team. 'I arrived in the middle of a farce,' he said. 'The car was practically undrivable.' After qualifying he made a call to Maranello, where Ferrari told him to forget about the race – just get the mechanics to put the car on a truck and bring it home. Montezemolo persuaded him to allow the car to take part, but it was obvious that big changes were needed and that anyone insisting on taking a summer holiday would be in receipt of disapproving looks from the *capo*.

The first step was to bring back Mauro Forghieri, with instructions to rework the car from stem to stern. The next was to find the right man to drive it. The initial candidate was James Hunt, the young Englishman who had been showing outstanding form in a car privately entered by Lord Hesketh, an English aristocrat whose flamboyant patronage seemed a throwback to a long-forgotten era when gentlemen amateurs could take on the professionals. Hesketh arrived at Maranello in a private plane, surrounded by a gaggle of longhaired English friends and collaborators, and Ferrari was entertained by their company at lunch. But there was no business to be done. Hesketh wanted to hold on to Hunt.

There was more luck with the second candidate. Niki Lauda, a thin-faced twenty-six-year-old Austrian, had impressed Montezemolo with his performance in a BRM at Silverstone, where he shot from ninth place on the grid to second by the time the field had reached the first corner. After an indifferent debut season with March, Lauda was paying for his drive at BRM, a second-rate team, simply in order to maintain his tenuous foothold in Formula One; he was in debt to the tune of around £120,000 when Montezemolo called him on the telephone, encouraged by a warm recommendation from Clay Regazzoni, who was also driving for BRM that season and was on the brink of agreeing terms for a return to Maranello the following year. Enzo Ferrari had also noticed the way Lauda's abilities had shone through an unpromising environment, and approved the idea of an approach from Montezemolo. The driver and the new *direttore sportivo* met in secret at a bar near Heathrow airport, in order to keep away from the eyes of the Italian press. Having established the terms of an agreement, Lauda then drove his Ford Capri to Modena, where he met Ferrari at the old Scuderia headquarters in the viale Trento e Trieste. It was agreed that Lauda would try the Formula One car for a few laps at Fiorano, and then give his impressions.

Piero acted as the translator for the meeting, using the English that Brenda Vernor had taught him. But old ways of thinking persisted at Maranello. When Lauda, young and direct, told the Old Man that the car was a disaster, Piero butted in.

[265]

'You can't say that!' he exclaimed. Lauda wanted to tell Ferrari that his car wouldn't go round corners efficiently. But so unused was Ferrari to direct criticism, and so accustomed to hearing his team managers blaming poor performances on the drivers, that Piero had to persuade Lauda to temper his language, and to say that the problems could be fixed. Forghieri told Ferrari that the necessary work would take a week. In that case, Ferrari said to Lauda, if you are not at least one second a lap quicker this time next week, you can say goodbye to Maranello.

Lauda and Forghieri spent the next few days together, working on the modifications. At the end of the week the Austrian took the car around Fiorano again, and was soon setting times comfortably inside the target Ferrari had set for him. He was in. And, as it turned out, his timing could not have been better. From a shambles of a team, Scuderia Ferrari was about to build a strong and lively new organisation from which the evasions and excuses of former regimes were more or less banished. Montezemolo, Forghieri, Lauda, Regazzoni, and the mechanics Ermanno Cuoghi and Giulio Borsari formed a compact and highly motivated unit whose interest in the myths and legends of the past was entirely subordinated to a concern with writing a new page in the company's history. The unsentimental, realistic Lauda set the tone. There would be no more hand-wringing over failures, just a determination to put things right. But there was no shortage of sceptics, at least until results were available to prove their case.

Lauda did not have to spend much time at Maranello before he recognised how profoundly Enzo Ferrari's remoteness from the racing scene had damaged the team's level of performance. 'When you see all the facilities at the team's disposal,' he said, 'it's a little difficult, at first glance, to understand why they don't win every race without any difficulty.' But the Old Man was too ignorant of the real state of play, and too easily influenced by those operating according to their own agendas and playing expertly on his love of intrigue and melodrama. The young driver's impressions of Ferrari as a man in old age were also enlightening. 'He could exude great dignity making a public entrance, but in a more intimate circle he was less impressive.' Lauda remarked unfavourably on his habit of scratching himself and of hawking and spitting into a large handkerchief. 'He still had all his wits about him, however, and his remarks were perceptive and amusing. In the midst of all the dog-like devotion he seemed to engender, he retained a fine sense of gentle irony.'

From his farmhouse in the middle of the test track, Ferrari kept a close eye on Forghieri and Lauda as they laboured through the winter of 1973–74 to produce a car capable of redeeming recent disasters. If the Old Man was absent, Lauda would cross the road to the factory, knock on his office door, and walk in. In this way he short-circuited those who had been used to exerting influence without taking direct responsibility. And Montezemolo's Agnelli connections gave him a particular authority and independence within the set-up, as well as guaranteeing the sympathy of the parent company. 'He was young,' Lauda said of Montezemolo, 'but he was good.'

When the new 312B3 appeared in Buenos Aires for the first race of the 1974 season, all the months of hard work that had gone into it were immediately apparent. Regazzoni, the elder of the drivers by ten years and the senior partner by virtue of his previous experience with the team, put the car on the front row, next to Ronnie Peterson's Lotus. Peterson and Jacky Ickx in Colin Chapman's cars, Emerson Fittipaldi and Denny Hulme in the McLarens, Hunt in his March and Carlos Reutemann in a Brabham were going to be the class of the year's field, all using Ford's Cosworth engine. Apart from the BRMs, which were to be found at the back of the grid, only the shriller sound of the Ferrari flat-twelve broke the aural monotony of the blaring V8s. Reutemann took the lead in Buenos Aires and would have won a magnificent victory in his home race had his petrol tank not run dry on the last lap, leaving hundreds of thousands of local fans desolate and presenting the victory to Hulme – with Lauda in second place and Regazzoni third. In a single bound, it seemed, the team was fully competitive again. Lauda achieved their first victory of the year from pole position at Jarama in Spain, after Peterson's engine had given up while he was in a commanding lead. When Montezemolo rang Maranello, Ferrari was more inclined to remark that, while watching on television, he had admired his *direttore sportivo*'s new blue jacket. But he did add, apropos of Lauda, 'That boy is quick. That boy is *very* quick.' The Austrian won again at Zandvoort, and this time it was a Ferrari one-two. Regazzoni won at the Nürburgring, but picked up so many second and third places that he was able to take the runner-up position behind Fittipaldi in the final championship table. Lauda, who finished fourth, might have won the title in a closely contested season had he possessed the maturity to prevent himself from crashing out of the lead in Germany and Canada, and had a puncture not cost him the British Grand Prix at Brands Hatch. After his scratchy introduction to Formula One with March, and his promising display with BRM, suddenly he was not far away from presenting a fully fledged talent.

There was no doubt about it in 1975. For the third race of the season, in South Africa, Forghieri produced a new car, the 312T, with a gearbox mounted transversely behind the engine, which was delivering almost 500 horsepower. In Lauda's opinion this car constituted Mauro Forghieri's masterpiece, and the satisfaction was all the greater for his own intimate involvement in its development. Two races later, at Monaco, Lauda began a sequence of victories which saw him win five out of the season's remaining ten races, enough to give him the title – the first for a Ferrari driver since John Surtees in 1964 – with a big lead over Fittipaldi, the defending champion. Regazzoni won at Monza again, on the day Lauda clinched the championship by finishing third. The Swiss had done his bit to help Ferrari win the constructors' championship and he was able to drink anew from the adulation of the Italian fans, although he could do no better than fifth in the table at the end of the season. He had more or less accepted the fact of Lauda's primacy;

occasionally he grumbled to Montezemolo about it, but on balance he and the Austrian were as close to an ideal pair of team mates as Ferrari had employed since Ascari and Villoresi twenty-five years earlier.

In the circumstances, it seemed natural enough that Montezemolo should bow out after two and a half years spent rebuilding the team's structure and its morale. Now, surely, the foundations were in place for a sustained run of success. While retaining an informal link with Ferrari, he could go off on further missions in other corners of the Agnelli empire, which some said were designed with the long-term aim of grooming him as *l'Avvocato*'s successor, although it would always be hard for many of those within Formula One to comprehend the existence of a world beyond the perimeter wall of the grand prix paddock.

Also gone, at a more intimate level, was Peppino Verdelli, who had died in 1974 after half a century of watchful service to Enzo Ferrari, ready at his beck and call every day of the year except Easter Sunday morning. His eventual replacement, Dino Tagliazucchi, a former policeman, was to prove just as devoted and reliable, but what he knew of Ferrari's life was nothing compared to the decades of history that Peppino had absorbed and never released.

Perhaps Montezemolo had been the real second son, after all. Piero was never in with a genuine chance of replacing Dino. He worked at the factory, he was taken to the meetings and his presence was accepted in the inner councils, but his father never took him seriously or let him show what he could do. At the meetings he would say something and the Old Man would interject, 'Oh, you be quiet,' and he would ask Forghieri for his opinion instead. He trusted Forghieri's judgement more than his own son's. Combined with that sort of reaction, Piero's naturally introverted character made him frightened to say anything. He would not defend himself. In the view of those close to the centre, never a day went by that Piero was not made aware that, for the Old Man, Dino had been everything, and still was. And his mother was not the sort to propel him to the foreground. After all, she had never pushed herself forward. She would never argue or speak unkindly about anyone. She would cover it up and say something nice, perhaps to disguise the suffering her position created. And Piero was the same.

For the next season, Forghieri produced an even neater and faster version of his *trasversale* car, the 312T2, and Lauda began with a bang, winning the opening races in Brazil and South Africa and finishing second to Regazzoni in Long Beach. The cars had appeared for the first time in South America with Fiat logos on the sides of the engine covers, apparently at the request of the local Fiat agents, which set some observers wondering about a possible intention to prepare the way for a wholesale identity change. But things began to go wrong before the fourth race of the season. Lauda, driving a miniature tractor in the garden of the house he had bought on the Fuschlsee, near Salzburg, turned the machine over while moving a mound of earth, and broke two ribs. His injuries might easily have been more serious, but there was little sympathy issuing from the direction of Italy, either from the factory or the press. When it was announced that he would probably be missing from the next race, some believed the incident had been invented to cover up a row with Ferrari. Others took a view reminiscent of the furore over Surtees' near-fatal crash: what did he think he was doing, having an accident in anything other than a Ferrari, even a garden tractor?

This time there was no Montezemolo to mediate between the driver, the Old Man and the newspapers. The two men who had replaced him, Guido Rosani and Daniele Audetto, were not up to the task. Audetto, another Agnelli protégé and a former manager of the Lancia rally team, had come in via a route similar to that taken by Montezemolo, but he was unable to strike up a similar rapport with Lauda or the staff, who called him 'Timex' because he tended to call on Ferrari at inopportune moments. Too anxious to curry favour, and perhaps keen to establish himself as independent from the Montezemolo legacy, he fell into the kind of intrigue that had been rooted out and silenced three years earlier. There was talk that Lauda would be replaced for the next race by Maurizio Flammini, a promising Italian Formula Two driver. Audetto, it seemed, was repeating the old and destructive pattern established by Eugenio Dragoni's patronage of Lorenzo Bandini. When he heard the rumour, Lauda made remarks to a reporter from the *Gazzetta dello Sport* that were highly critical of the regime at Ferrari. And, after intensive treatment, he returned to action in time for the next race, making his point by putting the car on the front row at Jarama next to James Hunt's McLaren and finishing second, half a minute behind the Englishman. The discontent rumbled on, but wins from pole position in Belgium and Monaco made a second title look like a certainty, particularly when Hunt, his chief rival, was disqualified from victory in his home race, the British Grand Prix, leaving victory to Lauda.

By the time he arrived at the Nürburgring for the tenth of the season's sixteen races, Lauda had amassed sixty-one championship points to the twenty-six of his nearest competitors, Hunt and Patrick Depailler. A recent contract renegotiation had involved a stormy and sometimes hilarious lunch with Ferrari in the private room at the Cavallino, at which Piero refused to translate when Lauda wanted to tell Ferrari that the company would never have won the championship again without him, and both parties threatened to call the relationship off that very instant. Clearly the two men took great enjoyment from their spats, which gave Lauda the chance to exercise his natural directness and Ferrari the opportunity to scream at somebody who dared to answer him back. Eventually, in the usual way of such negotiations, they reached a compromise that satisfied both Ferrari's love of drama and Lauda's pleasure in making a good deal. Lauda's typically unorthodox analysis of the final agreement: ' "Okay, *ebreo*," says Ferrari. Okay, Jew-boy. He's entitled to say that – he's paying.'

But the full price of a grand prix driver's life was almost paid at the Nürburgring. The incomparable fourteen-mile *Nordschlief* circuit, with its 175 corners and endless changes of camber and gradient, had become a magnificent anachronism. First used in 1927, it had been the scene of many heroic deeds. Tazio Nuvolari and Juan Manuel Fangio had used it as the canvas on which to create their greatest works of art. The souls of Rosemeyer, Caracciola, Varzi, Ascari and Moss sang through the trees of the dark Eifel mountain forests through which the grey ribbon of track unwound. Lauda was fascinated by the challenge it posed but horrified by the inability of the circuit's administrators to provide adequate safety facilities – not out of any lack of will but because fourteen miles of track could not be properly protected by anything short of an army of marshals and a fleet of ambulances and helicopters. At the instigation of the safety-conscious Jackie Stewart, before his retirement in 1973, a three-year plan to rebuild the trackside barriers and increase the number of marshals had been undertaken, but nothing could really make the Nürburgring as safe as the modern ethic of sporting risk demanded. Earlier in 1976, at a meeting of the Grand Prix Drivers' Association, Lauda had proposed a boycott of the track, which had not endeared him to purists who believed that a Ferrari driver should be prepared to accept the same risks that had confronted his predecessors. He was outvoted, in any case, and the German Grand Prix took place in its spiritual home on 1 August.

Despite his reservations, he put the Ferrari on the front row, next to Hunt. There was a threat of rain, and he started on wet-weather tyres. One of the problems at the Nürburgring was that the length of the circuit made a parade lap impractical, so the drivers had no means of making a full reconnaissance in which to assess the conditions immediately before the race. Another danger was that, like Spa, it could be raining heavily on one part of the track and bone-dry on another. This time he discovered, after the race had started, that the track was dry all the way around and the possibility of rain was receding. Again, the sheer length of each lap meant that no risks could be taken, so he stopped at the end of the first lap and switched to slick tyres before charging out again to try and regain lost ground. He had almost reached the Bergwerk corner when his car suddenly pitched itself to the right and penetrated a barrier of wire netting before hitting an earth bank and slewing back on to the track, its fuel tanks ruptured and a blaze about to engulf it. The impact with the barrier had exerted one curious effect: Lauda's helmet came off, thanks, it was said, to a sudden shrinkage of the cranium which was a reflex response to the trauma of the impact. The result was that as the car burned the trapped driver could not help but inhale toxic smoke and petrol vapour, scorching his lungs while his face and head were seared by the flames. Four cars which he had overtaken since leaving the pits – the Surtees of Brett Lunger, a DuPont heir, the Williams of Arturo Merzario, the former Ferrari number two, and the two Heskeths of Guy Edwards and another Austrian, the sometime journalist Harald Ertl – stopped at the scene of the crash. The drivers leapt out and tried to help the marshals extricate the unconscious Lauda. Eventually he was freed and taken by ambulance to a hospital in Mannheim, where a priest administered the last rites as doctors fought to save his life.

There was consternation at Maranello. Ferrari, watching on the television, got on the telephone to Luca di Montezemolo. 'When Niki Lauda was badly burnt at the Nürburgring,' Montezemolo recalled more than a decade later, 'one second later Ferrari said to me, "Luca, who are we going to get to replace him?" He was demonstrating on one hand a sense of professional priorities, on the other a certain cynicism. But a minute later he was preoccupied with Lauda's condition.' When the storm broke over the accident, and commentators began alleging that it had been caused by a breakage of some component or other on the car, Ferrari remembered the troubles he had endured after the Mille Miglia disaster of 1957, the deaths of Musso and Collins in 1958, the von Trips accident of 1961 and the Bandini accident of 1967, and announced his intention to quit.

For a month, he kept his word. No statement was ever forthcoming from the factory on the probable cause of the accident, and there were indeed no Ferraris at Zeltweg for the Austrian Grand Prix, while Lauda was still fighting for his life. Lauda was furious when he heard that Audetto had tried to get the race cancelled. But at Zandvoort the team sent Regazzoni out to finish second in a lone entry, and in the meantime, at Montezemolo's request, Ferrari had been negotiating to sign Carlos Reutemann. The Argentine was so anxious to leave Brabham and join Ferrari that he bought himself out of his contract with Brabham's owner, Bernie Ecclestone, and joined his new team in time for the Italian Grand Prix on 12 September, six weeks after Lauda's accident. But, to Ferrari's amazement, Lauda announced his intention to compete at Monza, forcing Ferrari to field three cars, one each for Lauda, Reutemann and Regazzoni, the last of the trio just beginning to realise – although no one was willing to tell him so – that his time at Ferrari might be drawing to a close. Lauda, arriving at the track for the first practice session an incredible thirty-three days after his accident, his badly burnt head swathed in bandages to protect still-weeping wounds, drove in great pain but nevertheless finished fourth, twice setting the fastest lap in the closing stages. Reutemann came ninth, finding the cockpit of the 312T2 too small for his lanky frame; he solved Ferrari's overmanning problem by spending the rest of the season testing while Lauda and Regazzoni got on with competing in the last three races, at Mosport, Watkins Glen and Mount Fuji.

Lauda's eyelids had been burnt away, and there was severe damage to his ears and the skin on both sides of his head. But he was desperately keen, for whatever combination of possible motives, to prove that he could come back to Ferrari and defend his title, for which Hunt was now the favourite. A suspension problem slowed him in Canada, where he finished eighth, and at Watkins Glen he came third behind Hunt's McLaren and Jody Scheckter's Tyrrell, unable to match their pace but collecting points that kept the championship in the balance. His readiness to drive through pain ensured that when the team arrived at Fuji in the shadow of the snow-capped peak he still had a three-point lead over Hunt, and was facing his last chance to hold on to his title against a background of whispers from people in and around the Ferrari camp who blamed him and his accident for the deterioration in the team's performance.

He qualified the car third on the grid, behind Hunt's McLaren and Mario Andretti's Lotus. If he finished ahead of Hunt, or if neither of them completed the race, he would be champion. The race started in a downpour just about as bad as anyone could remember. For a while the drivers refused to go out, with the exception of Regazzoni and an equally crazy Italian, Vittorio Brambilla, in a March. A black rain fell on the slopes of Mount Fuji, sluicing the hills and streaming across the track. As they toured round on their parade lap, cutting bow-waves as they went, it looked more like a speedboat race. And yet, traditionally, racing drivers do their job whatever the conditions. Some of them, in fact, have tended to revel in such conditions of natural adversity. These were the *garibaldini* whom Ferrari so admired, the men who would take a race and shake it by the throat until it did their bidding. Lauda was not one of those. He was too clever, too calculating. And, having just struggled back from the brink of death, perhaps he had a better appreciation of the value of life. At the first corner he went into a lurid aquaplaning slide that almost took him clean off the circuit. The field tiptoed round, their deep-grooved wet-weather tyres useless in the surreal conditions, and at the end of the second lap Lauda pulled in, popped the catch on his seat belts, climbed out, and retired from the race. 'In the wet, you have to call on additional reserves of motivation and endurance,' he reflected. 'I had no such reserves. I was finished. The rain had totally destroyed me.' A quarter of the way through the race, the rain stopped and the track started to dry out. Hunt had his problems, but finished third, which was good enough to give him the title by one point. If Lauda had stayed out there, taken it easy, and then pushed when the rain stopped, he would have needed to finish only fifth in order to retain his championship. The telephone conversation with Enzo Ferrari at Tokyo airport was short and brusque. '"Do you want to go on driving? What's wrong? What can I do? What's our next move?" These were some of the questions', Lauda wrote, 'that Enzo Ferrari never once asked.' When Lauda was back at home, and preparing for his surgery, Ferrari offered him the job of team manager for the following season. Lauda could see that he no longer had the boss's trust; and he could also see that his presence alongside Reutemann would create an embarrassing conflict. He didn't care about that. Embarrassment was never an emotion that gave Niki Lauda much trouble. Eventually he waved his recently signed contract under Ferrari's nose, only to be told, yes, you can stay on, but Reutemann will have priority. The number one, Lauda replied, will be the one who goes fastest and wins the most races.

Audetto left at the end of 1976, replaced by Roberto Nosetto, a long-serving Ferrari man noted for his habit of wearing green suits. By this time, however, Lauda was beyond notions of warm and constructive relationships with Ferrari managers. He just wanted to beat Carlos Reutemann and get his title back. Reutemann made the better start to the season, winning the Brazilian Grand Prix at Interlagos. But Lauda, having been left on the sidelines during the winter testing, insisted on getting involved in a major development programme which resulted in several significant modifications to the cars – and in wins for him in South Africa, Germany and Holland. These, together with the points for second places in Monaco, Belgium, Britain and Italy, were enough to give him his second title. But he had grown to dislike the atmosphere at Ferrari so much that, with several of the season's races still to go, he secretly signed an agreement to drive one of Bernie Ecclestone's Brabhams in 1978, for £500,000 a year, the kind of guaranteed money that was certainly not available at Maranello.

Lauda was quite happy when the news leaked out. He had wanted it to be a slap in Enzo Ferrari's face. He had already won the championship, and the team had won the constructors' title. But it was all over. 'It wasn't really a fair fight,' he said. 'I was young, I was strong. He was seventy-eight, surrounded by self-serving "advisers", and he got his information at second or even third hand. I really enjoyed turning down surely the most generous offer he has ever made.' Lauda was even more contemptuous when he discovered that Ferrari, hearing that Ermanno Cuoghi would be going to Brabham with Lauda, had summarily sacked the head mechanic. On the eve of the Canadian Grand Prix, with two races left in the season, Lauda walked out. '*Ciao*, Enzo,' he said as he left, the only man ever to address the boss with such disdainful informality.

Ferrari's subsequent verdict on a man who brought him two championships when all seemed lost, and with whom he shared a certain sardonic cast of mind, was wholly typical: 'When Lauda raced, he looked confident and determined right from the start, meticulous in his preparation of both himself and the car. He showed himself to be a great and intelligent driver, there can be no doubt about that. He did a lot with Ferrari and he could have done a lot more. As for his character, I'm disinclined to judge people . . .'

Before the end of the year, Enzo Ferrari had found a new favourite. While Carlos Reutemann was contracted to be his team leader for 1978, Ferrari was already harbouring doubts about the Argentine's temperament, although none about his intrinsic talent or his gift of turning women's heads, another quality he admired. 'The first time Reutemann walked into the office', Brenda Vernor remembered, 'I nearly died. So handsome. Those blue eyes, that tan. I nearly fell off my chair. Such a charming guy. But he lived in a world of his own. Never knew what day it was.' Year after year, in its descriptions of the drivers, the programme for the Monaco Grand Prix summed up Reutemann in a single eloquent phrase: '*Physique d'un séducteur du cinéma*'. In Ferrari's view, he was 'a driver with an athlete's

[277]

physique and real talent' who 'suffered from a difficult temperament that made others suffer, too. He could fight his way out of the toughest situations and even compensate for mechanical difficulties, but he was apt to let his emotions lose him races that he had been slated to win.'

As his number two, to replace Regazzoni, who had belatedly been informed that there would be no room for him, Ferrari had hired Gilles Villeneuve, a French-Canadian star of Formula Atlantic who had driven just once in a grand prix, at Silverstone that summer, where he had qualified a McLaren on the fifth row of the grid, less than half a second slower than James Hunt's pole-position time, and had shown himself capable of running with the pacesetters in the race itself. He had been recommended to Ferrari by Walter Wolf, a Canadian construction and oil tycoon who was running his own Formula One team and had become so friendly with Ferrari that his cars and his leading driver, the South African Jody Scheckter, were allowed the occasional use of Fiorano's testing facilities. Chris Amon, who had watched Villeneuve drive Wolf's Can-Am sports cars, endorsed the recommendation. Villeneuve had also attracted interest from John Hogan of the Philip Morris tobacco company, manufacturers of Marlboro cigarettes. Hogan had been extending his company's sponsorship of Formula One teams and drivers, and was keen to find a way of getting involved with Ferrari. He had heard about Villeneuve from James Hunt, another Marlboro-affiliated driver.

At twenty-seven, Villeneuve could easily be taken for ten years younger. He had a soft and almost angelic face, but he turned out to be the very definition of a *garibaldino*, not just a spectacular driver but a real racer, someone who would give it everything no matter how unfavourable the circumstances. 'Well, young man,' Ferrari asked at their first meeting, to which an astonished Villeneuve had been summoned by telephone from his home in Berthierville, near Québec, 'how much do you need to be content?' They got on well, although no deal was concluded. Ferrari had another meeting that day, with Niki

Lauda, after which the Austrian told the world of his intention to leave. Among those widely tipped to replace him were Mario Andretti and Jody Scheckter. It was Villeneuve, however, who got the job, and with it John Hogan got his chance to put the distinctive red and white chevron of the Marlboro packet on a Ferrari grand prix car – even if, at this stage, it was only the driver's helmet. The deal, by which Villeneuve was to receive $75,000 a year, plus a quarter of sponsorship income, plus $15,000 travelling expenses for his wife and two small children, was done in time for him to make his Ferrari debut in the final races of the 1977 season. He failed to finish the first race, in front of his home crowd at Mosport Park. The handling of the Ferrari did not suit his style, and after spinning the car he broke the driveshaft when flooring the throttle as he tried to restart. At Fuji he miscalculated his braking and ran into the back of Ronnie Peterson's Tyrrell, sending his car flying into the air and then down into a crowd of onlookers, killing a marshal and a photographer and injuring several others. Villeneuve and Peterson were questioned by investigators but allowed to go, pending an investigation which eventually determined that they had driven in accordance with the rules of their sport and that no crime had been committed. 'He has been unlucky,' Ferrari said of Villeneuve at his end-of-season press conference, 'but I still think he has the ability to grow.'

Laura Domenica Garello Ferrari died on 27 February 1978, aged seventy-seven. She had been bedridden for several years, suffering from the final emergence of the muscular dystrophy that had killed her son more than twenty years earlier. The widower mused on their long life together, on their triumphs and their disagreements over a span of almost sixty years, on her curious and difficult personality, and on the sad fate of their son. He remembered their first encounter under the arches in Turin, he remembered the wedding attended by her disapproving family, and he remembered all the nights he had gone home to eat one of her less than enthusiastically prepared meals, to be assailed by scornful accusations that no doubt he would soon be up and out of the door and off to eat a second and more acceptable meal with his second family.

'Her innate frugality, her desire to carry out tasks quickly, often involving changes and agreements normally requiring time and reflection, and her daily criticisms of my smallest decisions caused irritating arguments, but also revealed the reality of such situations,' he said. There had been times when her active presence among the staff, however abrasive and irksome to others, had left him free to concentrate on the day-to-day business of the factory. And she had certainly been conscious, even to a fault, of the need to observe a strict economic regime, although her unconstrained behaviour in that direction had provoked the mass defection at the end of 1961. 'In a strange way our daily arguments strengthened the bond between us,' Ferrari wrote, 'though sometimes harsh things were said that made us consider separation. But in the end we stayed together, despite adversity. Not even the tragedy of our son's death could separate us.' Ferrari mourned his wife, and buried her in the family tomb, and then began the preparations that, within two years, would see Lina, Piero and Floriana, and their daughter Antonella move into the house in the Largo Garibaldi. His lawyers also began the procedures that would give Piero's family the Ferrari name, following a legal adoption, something he had pledged to reserve until after Laura's death.

There were other losses in 1978. A young engineer, Giancarlo Bussi, who had worked with Forghieri and Franco Rocchi in the engine department, disappeared while on holiday in Sardinia. Since he came from a branch of a wealthy family, there was a belief that this represented a kidnap and ransom attempt. But no demands were forthcoming, or at least none was publicised, and Bussi was never heard of again.

This was also Carlos Reutemann's final season with Ferrari. In terms of exerting an appeal to the public and to his co-workers, Gilles Villeneuve had become everything Reutemann could not be. The Argentine had the talent and the looks, but his brooding temperament failed to bring a response from either the spectators or his team, and in particular the new *direttore sportivo*. Marco Piccinini was a member of an old Roman banking and commercial family and a far more adroit politician than many of his predecessors. This was another whom Ferrari trusted, according to one of his staff, like a son. He was also to last ten years in the job, a record. 'For me, Enzo Ferrari was like a prime minister surrounded by advisers,' said Reutemann, who would eventually return to Argentina to launch a political career that took him to the governorship of his native Santa Fé province. 'I always had the feeling that several people had spoken to him before our meetings, and that several more would speak to him afterwards. Unfortunately I never got the impression that he believed what I was telling him.'

Reutemann won four races for Ferrari in 1978, at Rio de Janeiro, Long Beach, Brands Hatch and Watkins Glen, finishing third in the table behind Mario Andretti and Ronnie Peterson, both of them driving Colin Chapman's revolutionary ground-effects Lotuses. But there was no real enthusiasm on either side: 'Like Fangio,' Ferrari said, 'Reutemann left us when he was offered a car which he believed would give him a better chance of winning the title. He didn't manage it.' Reutemann had a nickname – *Lole* – but the fans never used it. He was Reutemann, that was all. His team mate was different. 'Villeneuve's personality was such that he captured the crowd right away and became known simply as Gilles,' Ferrari noted. Reutemann remarked, perceptively and without rancour, that the relationship between Ferrari and Villeneuve, with fifty years between them, was like that of a grandfather and a grandson. Ferrari loved Villeneuve's lightness of spirit. And at the very end of the 1978 season, returning to Mosport Park and performing for his compatriots, Villeneuve won the Canadian Grand Prix, his first for Ferrari.

Behind him, in second place, was a Wolf driven by the man who would be his team mate the following season, Jody

Scheckter. An unpretentious individual, with the brusqueness that had marked his arrival as a prodigy in Formula One five years earlier now smoothed away, the South African had made it clear that he expected to be recognised within the team as the number one driver, and Ferrari had agreed. Villeneuve was still too new to expect anything different, and was happy to accept the position. By the third race of the season Forghieri's men had delivered a new car, the 312T4, still using the flat-twelve engine but distinguished by its strange, flying saucer-ish arrangement of bodywork and front wing. It looked horrible but it certainly did its job, carrying Scheckter and Villeneuve to three wins apiece – Belgium, Monaco and Italy for the former, Kyalami and the two United States races, East and West, for the latter. Scheckter won the title at Monza, where Villeneuve played the faithful number two, shadowing his colleague to the finish line even though he might well have been able to outrace him, and evoking memories of Collins' selfless gesture to Fangio twenty-odd years earlier. Like Collins, Villeneuve was thinking: my time will come.

Not, however, in 1980. Where the 312T4 had been an efficient machine, the T5 was hopeless. Unreliable, unable to exploit its Michelin tyres, the T5 was so bad that Scheckter, the reigning champion, had completely lost interest by the middle of the season, and was busy planning his retirement. Nor was the internal politicking at an end. Brenda Vernor was now one of Ferrari's personal secretaries in the racing department, charged with special responsibility for English-language work. 'I remember in the era of Scheckter and Villeneuve,' she said, 'he got those two after every grand prix to send him a telex. He wanted their report on the race and what they thought was or wasn't right. I think from this moment he realised that someone wasn't telling him the real truth. So he got the drivers every Monday to sent a telex describing what they thought about the race and the car.' Villeneuve soldiered on, still in love with the idea of driving a Ferrari, but able to do no better than two fifth places. Meanwhile the Ford-powered Williams and Brabham cars shared the victories between them; and the new turbocharged Renaults, which had made their first appearances in 1977, were looking so promising that Ferrari and Forghieri decided to follow suit and build a turbocharged engine.

Ferrari himself was not exactly overwhelmed by Scheckter's fulfilment of a lifetime's ambition. He knew the truth, or so he believed: the car had won the championship. Scheckter received no telegram, no congratulatory phone call, no special gift to mark the occasion. He thought himself lucky, the next time he passed through the factory and encountered the Old Man, to receive a brisk greeting: *Ciao, campione*.

Enzo Ferrari with Gilles Villeneuve, the last of his favourites, during a practice
session at the Imola circuit for the 1979 San Marino Grand Prix.

Eleven

The final years passed quietly, for the most part. In his farm-house he could act the grandfather, emerging from time to time to see how the boys were getting on with their cars. Every now and then he would amuse himself by giving someone's strings a tug, just to get them dancing.

At the beginning of the 1980s, the factory was turning out forty cars a week. Fiat took care of all that. He no longer bothered to meet the television stars and footballers who bought the Testarossas that carried his name. But of the company's 700 workers, 200 were employed in the *gestione sportiva* and remained under his direct control. To the secretaries and the others who worked in his office, he could be a charming old man who loved a joke. 'He was very observant,' Brenda Vernor said. 'When he saw me, he'd always say something like, "Oh, aren't you elegant tonight, you've got this or that on." He could tell you what you'd been wearing at the office the day before. He noticed everything. I remember once I did a letter for him and he sent it back and said to me, "The address is wrong – they haven't lived there for three years." And he gave me the proper address. Right up to the last few months, he still had a terrific memory.'

He had a way, she said, of earning loyalty without overdoing the praise or the perks. 'The pay wasn't particularly good. Everybody thought that because you worked for Ferrari you must be on a fabulous wage, but it wasn't like that. It was a privilege to work for Ferrari. And if you did something good, he wouldn't come and say, "Oh, thank you very much, that was wonderful, you did a good job." Never. I remember once he gave me a long telex to send, miles of it. He said to me, "Put it down, and when you've done it bring it and show it to me." Then he said, "This paragraph should go there and put that there and put this there." I did exactly as he told me. He was at Cavallino having lunch. I went across and showed it to him. I sat down. He said, "Would you like something to eat?" I said, "I've eaten." He said, "Have a *macedonia*." Very kind, very thoughtful. He got hold of the telex, took it, and suddenly he started shouting at me. I said, "*Ingegnere, scusi,* may I say something, you told me to do this, and this, and I put this there . . ." "Hmm. Send it off." He wouldn't say sorry. He wouldn't say, "You're right." Yes, it was irritating, but you accepted it from Mr Ferrari. Anything you did for Ferrari was a pleasure, and also a privilege. Once he came in, and a guy had come in with these Ferrari scarves, I was in the office with Gozzi, when we were still in the old factory, and he said, "You're the only woman around here – let's have your opinion. What colour scarves should we choose?" I said, "That one and that one and that one." He said, "Okay, we'll take that one and that one and that one." Completely the opposite of what I said. Typical. Just being bloody awkward. You'd feel like saying, "What the bloody hell did you bother asking me for?" But you wouldn't dare. And he could be generous. Another time I did something for him and he sent Dino Tagliazucchi here with a watch for me, to say thank you.'

His generosity could be considerable, on many different scales. He funded medical research at the Mario Negri Institute in Milan, he founded a Dino Ferrari diagnosis and treatment centre at Milan University, and he paid for a magnetic resonance imaging scanner to be installed at Modena's Polyclinic, a machine which speeds up the identification of certain conditions, including muscular dystrophy. He also subsidised the further education of the sons of some of his employees. 'If you asked the Old Man for something, he would never say no. But I never had the courage to ask him. I remember one of the heads of department said that there was a mechanic who needed a specialist for his son who was very ill. The Old Man said why didn't he come and ask him himself? But nobody would dare. Deep down he was very human. For me, because he came from nothing, had nothing and knew what it was not to have anything, he understood people who were in the same position. Although he became very famous and very rich, he still understood what it was to have nothing and to be in need. Deep down he was, I think, a sensitive person. If someone in the family, a mechanic or somebody, had a problem financially or they needed a specialist and there was a six months' waiting list, they'd go and ask him and he'd phone up and make an appointment and sometimes even say, "No, I don't want any money." He'd pay for it. But no one had to know. He would answer every letter he received, even if it was just with a postcard to say thank you, always signed with that violet ink. To a child, or a handicapped person, he would send a little present. When people wrote to him from prison asking for money, he would send something – 20,000 lire, 50,000 – without anybody knowing, until one of his aides said, "You'd better stop – they're passing the word around."'

At its best, Brenda Vernor remembered, the Scuderia Ferrari was an extended family. 'When the guys were preparing the cars for a race, I used to go down there late at night, to take them Lambrusco and a cake or *pannini* and sit with them. You couldn't do that now. Now there's a guardhouse. It's like trying to get into Alcatraz. It's Fiat, not Ferrari. Somebody like me, who can't keep their mouth shut, I wouldn't last two weeks. So different. When Mr Ferrari was there, he was the boss, and you were part of Ferrari. As long as he was there, he was the one who made the decisions. Agnelli used to come every now and then. He was nice, too. He'd come into the racing department and say hello to everyone.'

But being a member of the family entailed obligations. 'For example in August, when everybody goes on holiday in Italy, Mr Ferrari never went away and he couldn't understand why other people did. He used to get angry in August because nobody was there. He wanted people around him. There had to be somebody. So every August, and especially 15 August, which is a big holiday here, it's *Ferragosto*, all that week Mike and I were always going out to dinner with him. Every evening he'd invite us because he wanted company. The factory closed but the racing department didn't because there were always three races in August. And when there was a race on Saturday and Sunday, he wanted people to be there.'

To him, the drivers were simply men employed to do a job. 'He used them. He needed them. He paid them so they had to do a job for him and they had to do it well. He didn't dislike anybody, I think. I know Phil Hill had an argument with him, but . . . It all depends. If they'd had a bad day and he thought they'd made a mistake, he'd tell them. "You bloody idiot!" But you never knew with the Old Man.'

And there were always exceptions to his objectivity. Campari, Moll and, for a while, Collins had been among them. Now there was Villeneuve. 'With Gilles he went . . . I wouldn't say berserk, exactly, but he really loved Gilles. For him, Gilles was like a son. He liked Bandini, because Bandini was a bugger for the women, too. And he liked Scarfiotti. But not to this point. Probably it was because Gilles was spectacular. I mean, everybody loved Gilles. In terms of cars, you could give anything to Gilles. He just put his foot down and if it went, it went. He couldn't care less. He was a racer. He could do anything with a car. Look at the time he came into the pits with no wheel on the back. The old man used to laugh his head off. He really enjoyed it. He admired Gilles.'

Villeneuve had made him laugh in 1979 when he completed a lap of the Zandvoort circuit in Holland with a shredded tyre disintegrating on the rim of his left rear wheel. He made him laugh that same year when he raced René Arnoux's Renault to the line at Dijon, the two of them banging wheels as they fought for every corner. They were contesting only second place, but it would have made no difference to them if it had been twenty-second. Villeneuve went round corners with the tail of the car hanging out wide, in the old style – or at least he did as soon as he could get Forghieri to amend the handling of the cars to suit his approach. He drove with emotion, and he made that emotion visible to the fans, just as Nuvolari had.

He required all his skill and brio in 1981, when Forghieri's turbo car, the 126C, demonstrated that it had plenty of power but a chassis with the sort of agricultural characteristics that had been plaguing Ferrari thirty years earlier. The 126C was a crude piece of machinery, and Villeneuve needed to use every ounce of cunning available to him to bring off two wins that season, at Monaco and Jarama, where he stayed in front of faster cars by driving without making the kind of minor imprecision that would have given them openings to get by. He made Ferrari laugh again towards the end of the season when he completed the Canadian Grand Prix in fourth place, minus his car's front wing, which had broken off and flown over his head. His performances that season made an interesting contrast with those of his new team mate, Didier Pironi, a twenty-eight-year-old Parisian from a wealthy background, with family origins in Friuli. Pironi had won a grand prix for Ligier and had always looked quick. Ferrari reckoned he was a born fighter, but after managing nothing more than a couple of fifth places in 1981, the Frenchman was finding life at Ferrari frustrating.

In an effort to import British chassis technology in support of the powerful V6 turbo, Ferrari hired Harvey Postlethwaite, an English engineer who had designed the cars Alexander Hesketh provided for James Hunt and the Wolf cars driven by Jody Scheckter. A deceptively chilly, schoolmasterish type, Postlethwaite was something of a throwback to Mike Parkes in that he felt at home in the Italian environment, quickly learnt to speak the Modenese dialect, and got on well with the mechanics. He redesigned the 126C and had its carbon-fibre monocoque manufactured in Belgium, since Ferrari lacked the necessary technology, just as the company had in 1973. 'The team was a long way behind,' he said.

The season began with a good row in which Enzo Ferrari,

even at his advanced age, could play a leading role. When Renault, on deciding to enter Formula One, calculated that a turbocharged 1.5-litre engine could be persuaded to give a great deal more power than a normally aspirated 3-litre engine, the British constructors could see that the days of their reliance on the Ford–Cosworth V8 were numbered. The first of Formula One's Concorde agreements had been signed in Modena in January 1981, settling the regulations and the rewards for the teams, but there were still disputes over the control of the sport, and one of them blew up over ruses invented by the British teams in order to prolong the competitive life of the DFV engine. One trick was trying to get under the formula's weight limit by carrying a water tank, ostensibly used for cooling the brakes. In fact the water was merely ballast and would be allowed to flow away as soon as the race started. While ingenious, this scheme clearly contravened the spirit of the regulations, but when the governing body's appeals court threw it out, disqualifying Nelson Piquet's Brabham and Keke Rosberg's Williams from the first two places in the Brazilian Grand Prix, the British constructors organised a boycott of the next race, under the aegis of Bernie Ecclestone's Formula One Constructors' Association. These were the teams that Ferrari had once called 'garage owners', insinuating that they built their mongrel cars out of bits taken from here and there – which was indeed how the earliest of them had started out. On the other side, and known as the 'grandees', were Renault and Ferrari, the two biggest teams in Formula One, in the sense that both represented significant slices of the European passenger-car market. And on the grandees' side was Jean-Marie Balestre, the choleric and controversial president of the FIA. With Max Mosley, later to succeed Balestre to the presidency, giving legal advice to the British teams, the boycott held firm and none of the garage owners turned up at the 1982 San Marino Grand Prix at Imola, which became effectively a contest between the Ferraris of Villeneuve and Pironi and the Renaults of Arnoux and Alain Prost. And when the Renaults fell away, the Ferraris were left to cruise home to a one-two finish, apparently under orders that, in those circumstances, they were not to jeopardise the team's chances by racing each other. Unfortunately no one seemed to have told Pironi, or if they had he took no notice, since he spent the last few laps launching vigorous attacks on Villeneuve and frequently taking the lead, much to the chagrin of the French-Canadian, who believed that the agreement gave him the right to the victory. Every lap he worked at finding a way back past Pironi, hoping to make him see sense and desist from this internecine struggle. But the calming influence of Forghieri was not available in the pits that weekend, thanks to a family problem, and on the last lap Pironi took advantage and nipped ahead once more, refusing to be overtaken before they saw the chequered flag. Villeneuve was furious with the man who was supposed to be his team mate. For all Pironi's protestations of innocence, Villeneuve's mind went back a few weeks to Pironi's wedding, at which the *direttore sportino* Piccinini had been best man and to which Villeneuve himself had not been invited. It looked very much like a revival of the Maranello's traditional political infighting, the sort of thing that had blighted the careers of so many drivers. Ferrari himself offered no view, at least in public.

Two weeks later Villeneuve presented himself at Zolder for the Belgian Grand Prix in the very worst state of mind to participate in a Formula One race. He was angry, but what he imagined to be an icy rage had run hot and out of control. His only thought was to get back at Pironi by humiliating him on the track. The two men had stopped speaking after Villeneuve had been practically shoved bodily on to the podium at Imola to share the celebrations of his team mate's victory. Now the gloves were off. Never, however, was Villeneuve to be given the opportunity to repay Pironi in kind. With fifteen minutes of the final hour of the last qualifying session to go, Forghieri showed him the 'In' signal. Villeneuve had used all his special qualifying tyres, and had set a time he was unlikely to beat. On that last lap, the lap in which he was supposed to come into the pits,

Villeneuve charged over the brow of a hill at around 140 mph and came upon Jochen Mass's March, travelling much more slowly. Mass moved to the right to let the flying Ferrari go past, but as it did so the two cars appeared to touch. The impact launched the Ferrari as if from a ramp, and it was airborne for over a hundred metres before smashing down on its nose, sending debris flying. As the car disintegrated, the driver, his seat and his steering wheel became detached, were hurled into the air, and penetrated two layers of catch fencing. Villeneuve's helmet had been torn off. When the medics got to him, he was unconscious. They took him to the intensive-care ward of a hospital in Louvain, only a few miles away, and just after nine o'clock that night he was declared dead. Pironi and the rest of the team withdrew from the race, packed up their equipment and started for home. Nobody thought that for Villeneuve to take such a risk on a slowing-down lap was anything but typical. That was the way he drove, on the road as well as on the track. 'He was great,' Postlethwaite said. 'Given the choice between being in the lead and destroying his tyres, and going carefully and finishing third, Gilles would always choose the former. Jody would always choose the latter and he became world champion. Gilles didn't. It wasn't that he couldn't do it. There was something in him that wouldn't allow him to do it.'

Ferrari understood his value better than anyone. 'He made Ferrari a household name,' he said, 'and I was very fond of him.' It had become the practice for teams to stick with the same racing numbers throughout the season, and Villeneuve had raced for the previous two years with the number 27 on his car. For the next fifteen years, no grand prix – particularly in Italy – was complete without Ferrari flags and banners incorporating the number 27 in their design, a homage of extraordinary intensity and duration to a star who won only six grands prix during his four and a bit seasons with Ferrari, but whose driving made such a vivid impression that it blazed in the memory and ignited imaginations long after he was gone.

★

Patrick Tambay replaced Villeneuve, and was moved to tears on the grid at Zandvoort when he found a Canadian maple leaf painted on the track at the point from which he would start the race. Pironi won the Dutch Grand Prix, but in Germany three races later, in the pouring rain, he ran into the back of Prost's Renault at high speed during untimed practice and suffered multiple breakages to both his legs. '*Arrivederci mondiale*,' Ferrari was said to have muttered. Bye–bye, championship. Pironi would never race a grand prix car again; five years later he crashed in a speedboat race off the Isle of Wight and was killed. At Hockenheim, Tambay pulled the team round and won the race, and Mario Andretti came back to fill the vacant seat at a couple of late-season grands prix.

Tambay stayed with Ferrari for 1983, joined by René Arnoux to form another all-French team, and won at Imola on the anniversary of the fight between Villeneuve and Pironi, which seemed a form of homage to his friend, if not exactly vengeance. Arnoux won a couple of races, enough to give Ferrari the constructors' championship, but the drivers could do no better than third and fourth in the final table. Against the wishes of some team members, who found him sympathetic and highly professional as well as fast, and admired the work he had done to bring the team together in the wake of the accidents to Villeneuve and Pironi, Tambay was replaced for 1984 by Michele Alboreto, a twenty-eight-year-old from Milan who had won the European Formula Three championship and two grands prix at the wheel of a Tyrrell-Ford. This was Piccinini's doing, but the *direttore sportivo* was spending more and more of his time acting as Enzo Ferrari's emissary in the continuing war between Balestre's FIA and Bernie Ecclestone's FOCA. At one point Ferrari commissioned Gustav Brunner, a talented Swiss engineer who had recently joined the team, to build a car to race at Indianapolis; this was by way of making a veiled threat to the Formula One authorities that if Enzo Ferrari did not get his way, he would leave European racing and take his famous red cars to the United States. The bluff was never called, and the car never raced; it was to spend its life first as a curiosity, then as a museum piece. Meanwhile Piero Lardi Ferrari had been given the role of general manager of the racing department, as part of an attempt to find him a meaningful senior role in the company. His close friendship with Postlethwaite, however, created a rift with Forghieri, who resented the Englishman's presence. Eventually their roles were switched, Postlethwaite taking overall control of the racing department while Piero ran a special advanced research team, but the result was little more successful in terms of creating a lasting harmony within the superstructure of the *gestione sportiva*.

Alboreto was the team's first Italian driver since Merzario, more than ten years earlier. His talent had persuaded Ferrari to ignore his belief that to have an Italian in one of his cars was to invite constant criticism from the national newspapers and to run the risk of further trouble from the direction of the Vatican and the popular press in the event of a bad accident. But Alboreto, who was as level-headed as he was gifted, ensured that those fuses were never lit. As Arnoux's performances declined, so those of the Italian increased in authority. He won his first race for the team in 1984, and two more victories and four second places the following year made him runner-up in the championship to Alain Prost, although he could reasonably feel that only a late-season run of mechanical unreliability cost him the title. Arnoux's increasingly erratic performances and behaviour had led to an uncomfortable interview with Ferrari, and to his replacement in the middle of the season by Stefan Johansson, a young Swede who showed great promise but never quite lived up to expectations. He stayed for 1986, but at the end of that season was replaced by Gerhard Berger, an Austrian from a small town near Innsbruck, where his father ran a trucking company. Alboreto had stopped winning races by this time, the sharp edge having gone from his talent, and it was Berger's turn to make the best of a car which was now being developed by not one but two British engineers. Postlethwaite had been joined by John Barnard, designer of the formidable

McLaren-TAG cars which had given Niki Lauda his last championship and Alain Prost his first. 'Joined', however, was perhaps not the operative term, since it was agreed that Barnard stay in England. Ferrari funded the building of something called the Guildford Technical Office, in which Barnard and his team would work on their computers, sending their data down the wire to Maranello, where their designs would be turned into aluminium and carbon fibre. It was an ambitious and risky notion, and no one was ever really happy with it, least of all Postlethwaite, who was thoroughly enjoying the experience of living and working among Italians and failed to see why another Englishman should not do the same. Forghieri was so alienated by the whole process that he finally left the company his father had joined half a century earlier, and with which he himself had enjoyed so many seasons of glory but even more of embarrassment. 'The problem at Ferrari was always that Ferrari is a theatre,' he grumbled. And now, whenever there were problems, Barnard's operation was the obvious scapegoat. 'It's like trying to do brain surgery down the telephone,' an exasperated Alboreto told the correspondent of *L'Equipe*. And Barnard hated giving in to the necessity of showing his face at the occasional race, his presence required by those who believed he ought to be there to shoulder or deflect the blame. But as efficient as it may have seemed on paper, in practice the liaison between Maranello and Guildford was a terrible idea. Ferrari, of all teams, was supposed to represent the organic unity of a car designed, built and tested almost entirely on the premises. That was its virtue, even in those times when it was being torn apart by internal strife. A Ferrari designed by computer from an anonymous building in Surrey sounded like a plan that had no right to succeed; all that really came out of it was Barnard's seven-speed semi-automatic gearbox, operated by fingertip paddles located behind the steering wheel, another innovation which quickly became universal.

And yet for Gerhard Berger, 1987 was to be the most enjoyable year of his long career as a driver. He achieved the team's only wins of the season in the last two races, at Suzuka and Adelaide, but he also remembered the part played by Enzo Ferrari. Berger would go back to Maranello after a race to do some testing, and the Old Man would give him lunch in his farmhouse or at the Cavallino and ask him about the car. Then they would talk, in rather greater technical detail, about girls, on which subject the Austrian was the paddock's resident expert. 'In 1987 I went to the circuit in the morning', he said a few years later, 'not knowing which set-up I had on the car, and I'd put it on pole or lead the race. I didn't know what I was doing but I was always in front. And I was so young and free in my mind that I didn't even know I was happy.'

That year also saw the fortieth anniversary of the first appearance of a Ferrari car, and of Franco Cortese's first race victory in the 125S at the Terme di Caracalla that Roman spring. One celebration took the form of a launch of the F40, a startling mid-engined café racer which Ferrari himself, tiring of the increasing blandness of the firm's road cars, had ordered to be designed and built *con emozione* – with feeling. It was as close to the racing machines as the 125s and 166s had been in the dawn of the company.

Late in the year his surviving drivers assembled at Maranello for a celebration, and Ferrari exchanged greetings with all of them, those who had played significant parts in the story, such as González and Villoresi, and those with whom he had not always enjoyed such cordial relations, including Fangio. Most of the pre-war stars were long dead, but Taruffi, who had raced for him first in 1931 and last in 1957, when he won the final Mille Miglia and kept the promise to his wife, was there, and so was Trintignant, who had given him an important victory in Monaco at an unexpected time, and Serafini, one of the last of the motorcycle racers turned four-wheel aces. A place of honour was found for Mietta Ascari, the widow of his first world champion. And as Phil Hill, another champion, shook hands with the Old Man, did he remember the words with which he had summed up their relationship? 'Since his cars were so directly an extension of Ferrari's own being, to admit fault in them was to admit fault in himself,' he wrote. 'That was something he could not do. As I look back, all my years at Ferrari seem to be a macabre dance, by everyone concerned, to avoid blame. The mechanics, the engineers – yes, even the drivers. No one wanted to be stuck with *mea culpa*.'

Enzo Ferrari at the Monza autodrome, 1976.

The Last Enemy

On 14 January 1988, with Piero at his side, he signed an agreement with the Mayor of Modena to bulldoze the old Scuderia building and redevelop the site on the viale Trento e Trieste as a multistorey car park, incorporating shops and a suite of offices. A fortnight later, attended by Gozzi, he received the scroll of an honorary degree in physics from Modena University. On 18 February, his ninetieth birthday, he sat down to lunch with 1,800 employees and members of the extended family in a marquee erected at Maranello. Three days later Antonella, Piero's daughter, gave birth to a son, whom she named Enzo. On 7 May the original Enzo Ferrari sat at a table outside Sergio Scaglietti's *carrozzeria* to watch the annual Mille Miglia parade of historic cars go by. And on 4 June, the Pope came to visit Maranello.

The experience of journeying to meet Enzo Ferrari in Modena or Maranello had often been compared to that of an audience with the Holy Father in the Vatican. The waiting, the whispering, the ranks of cardinals and *consiglieri*, the bowing and the scraping, the prayers, the confessions, the absolutions and the excommunications all had their equivalents in the long and rich life of the factory. Now John Paul II made the pilgrimage as part of a tour of the region, but although he was given a ride in a Ferrari Mondial cabriolet around the *pista* Fiorano, with Piero at the wheel, he was not granted an audience with the Old Man. Ferrari was too ill to leave his home in Modena, and the two spoke on the telephone. Ferrari's account of their conversation sounds as though it could have been written by Giovanni Guareschi as an exchange between Don Camillo, the worldly priest, and Peppone, the communist leader.

'Here I am, Ferrari,' the Pope said. 'I've given a kiss to little Enzo and I hope you'll be better soon.'

'Thank you, your Holiness,' Ferrari responded. 'I'm not a good Catholic and I've never prayed, but every night before I go to sleep I think about the people dear to me, the ones I've lost and those I still have around me. And since I saw the television pictures of you in St Peter's Square after the assassination attempt, I've always included you in my thoughts. I'm sorry not to have met you.'

Perhaps he was, too. His health had entered its final decline, thanks to a combination of diabetes and pleurisy and other effects of the advancement of old age. Sometimes, nonetheless, he had enjoyed such state visits. When Sandro Pertini, the President of the Republic, paid a call, they had argued about the respective merits of Brilli-Perri and Nazzaro, the heroes of their childhood. But perhaps the idea of two pontiffs in Maranello was too much. Or maybe he remembered how, twenty years earlier, the Vatican newspaper had compared him to a Saturn devouring his own children, and the hypocrisy was unbearable, even for him. He was pleased that the event meant so much to his devout employees and family members, but for him the occasion had no more significance than the award of yet another honorary degree.

He died at six o'clock on the morning of Sunday 14 August in his small bedroom on the first floor of the house in the Largo Garibaldi. That weekend, Modena was in the grip of a heatwave; by midday the temperature would reach 35 degrees. The following day was *Ferragosto*, the Feast of the Assumption, a day on which he used to gather up all the people in the racing department who had not committed the minor treason of going on a summer holiday, and take them out to lunch. So that day, a public holiday, there were no newspapers to report his passing.

The early-morning funeral was immediate and quiet, attended only by Piero, Floriana, Gozzi, Scaglietti, Benzi and Tagliazucchi. He was committed to rest by Don Sergio Mantovani, and by seven o'clock in the morning he was in his grave. There was no public ceremony or procession through the streets of the town, as there had been for so many of the drivers who died in his cars, and even for his own first son. No overalled mechanics or uniformed knights of the track carried Ferrari's coffin to its resting place. The streets were so quiet that no one even noticed as the hearse left the Largo Garibaldi, bearing the body of Modena's most famous citizen.

He was interred without drama in the cemetery of San Cataldo, where the white marble arch above the doorway of the family tomb bears a single name, FERRARI, and an epigram: *Ad maiora ultra vitam* – Towards greater things beyond this life. Inside, a hexagonal chamber contains an altar on which stand a heavy steel crucifix and four tall white candles. On each of the side walls, the names of the deceased are inscribed on tablets of striated brown marble cut in an asymmetrical design. Alfredo Ferrari and Adalgisa Bisbini Ferrari, his parents, are there, and so is his wife, Laura Domenica Garello Ferrari. Enzo Ferrari shares a tablet with Dino, the first of his sons.

A month later the *trigesimo*, the mass said thirty days after the death, was held in Modena's cathedral, that jewel of the early Renaissance. On a warm and sunny afternoon in early autumn they arrived to pay their respects, filling the Duomo and spilling out into the Piazza Grande. Gianni Agnelli, walking with the stick that was the legacy of a youthful indiscretion at the wheel of a Ferrari, was received by the mayor in a private meeting before the service, along with Sergio Pininfarina and his two sons, and Piero Ferrari and his family. The cathedral was full of the people among whom Enzo Ferrari had lived and worked, from his barber and his cook and his secretaries and his three doctors to the men who had built and driven his racing cars, among them Forghieri, Alboreto, Merzario, Vaccarella and Arnoux. Lina Lardi, however, stayed at home. The bishop of

Modena performed the rite, assisted by Don Sergio. Traditional in form, devoid of personal valedictions or eulogies, it lasted no more than half an hour.

All season, Gerhard Berger and Michele Alboreto had been unable to stay on terms with the McLaren-Hondas of Alain Prost and Ayrton Senna. As they were outpaced or broke down in race after race – even in Canada, where the two cars competed immediately after receiving the Pope's blessing during his visit to Maranello – it seemed a win would never come.

He had been dead four weeks when the cars were taken in their massive red Fiat trucks along the via Emilia to Monza for the Italian Grand Prix. Here, many years earlier, Enzo Ferrari had last watched a motor race in person. This time there was no old man watching on television in the farmhouse in the middle of the *pista* Fiorano as Prost led the race in his McLaren, before dropping out. Then Senna, his team mate, took over. Berger and Alboreto held second and third places, but that was small consolation for the *tifosi*. There seemed no chance of the Ferraris catching the McLaren. With only a few laps to go, however, Senna tried to lap an inattentive back-marker at the tight first chicane, collided with the other car, and spun off the track. Unable to restart, he climbed out and walked back to the pits. Berger and Alboreto roared past, into first and second places. As they crossed the line for the final time, they made a fitting salute to the Old Man's memory: the sight of two red cars, in close formation, greeted by the chequered flag on the great old autodrome where Nuvolari and Ascari and Phil Hill and Surtees and Scarfiotti and Regazzoni and Scheckter had won for him, and where Campari and Ascari and von Trips had perished in his machines. The fans went wild, spilling out of the grandstands and on to the track, waving their red flags with the yellow shield and the black horse. That night Don Erio Belloi rang the bells of his parish church in Maranello, celebrating the victory as he always did. Perhaps now, after a long drought, there would be more to come.

Non mi piacciono i monumenti, Enzo Ferrari said. I don't care for monuments, myself. This was only in part an affectation. He hardly discouraged mythmaking, but he was careful not to lend his own overt participation. Sentiment must never divert attention from the business at hand, the business of winning the next race; and that, too, became part of the myth. Visitors to his factory in the 1960s and '70s were astonished to see, jumbled together in a dusty corner, parts of cars that had once written the chapters of the legend but were now simply waiting for the arrival of the knacker's cart. His favourite car was always the one that would bring home the next victory. But if you wished to see his monument, you had only to switch on the television on a Sunday afternoon and watch the sea of red banners rippling in response to the successes of the team he created, a phenomenon that his own death did nothing to diminish.

Notes on Sources

An Agitator of Men

Who am I in this world? Fiamma Breschi, *Il Mio Ferrari* (Mursia, 1998).

See also Lycia Mezzacappa, *Il Mio Drake – Dalle confidenze del barbiere personali di Enzo Ferrari, Massimo D'Elia* (Il Fiorino, 1998); Enzo Biagi, *Enzo Ferrari – The Drake* (Rizzoli, 1980 / RCS 2001); Gianni Cancellieri, interview with Sergio Scaglietti, *Ferrarissima* (January 2001).

One

Perfect north Italy . . . Jonathan Keates, *An Italian Journey* (Picador, 1992). **We were awakened . . .** Enzo Ferrari, *My Terrible Joys* (Licino Cappelli, 1963). **I found these events . . .** EF, *My Terrible Joys.* **I will be a racing car driver . . .** reported in Giulio Schmidt, *The Roaring Races* (Libreria dell'Automobile, 1988). **I can still remember the weight . . .** Enzo Ferrari, *Una Vita per l'Automobile* (Conti Editore, 1998). **That left me desperately alone . . .** EF, *Una Vita per l'Automobile.* **Reputedly intended for incurables . . .** EF, *Una Vita per l'Automobile.* **I was back where I started . . .** EF, *Una Vita per l'Automobile.* **A stalwart man . . .** EF, *My Terrible Joys.* **A young man who has been around a lot . . .** reported in Schmidt, *The Roaring Races.* **We found ourselves in a blizzard . . .** EF, *My Terrible Joys.* **We became close friends . . .** EF, *My Terrible Joys.* **The unspoken understanding . . .** EF, *My Terrible Joys.* **Swarthy of complexion . . .** EF, *My Terrible Joys.* **Antonio was a man . . .** EF, *Una Vita per l'Automobile.* **From this meeting . . .** EF, *My*

Terrible Joys. **Audacious and ready** . . . From *Il Paese Sportivo*, 1919, reported in Schmidt, *The Roaring Races*. **He should be considered** . . . From *La Gazzetta dello Sport*, 1920, reported in Schmidt, *The Roaring Races*. **I can't honestly swear** . . . EF, *Una Vita per l'Automobile*. **Ferrari had too great a respect** . . . Gino Rancati, *Enzo Ferrari – The Man* (Haynes, 1988). **I was one of the first** . . . EF, *Una Vita per l'Automobile*. **I climbed up to an apartment** . . . EF, *My Terrible Joys*. **Bazzi had described him** . . . EF, *Una Vita per l'Automobile*. **Ascari's first lap** . . . Giovanni Canestrini in *La Gazzetta dello Sport*, reported in Schmidt, *The Roaring Races*. **I really made my name** . . . EF, *Una Vita per l'Automobile*. **Lap after lap** . . . EF, *My Terrible Joys*. **After the practice laps** . . . EF, *Una Vita per l'Automobile*. **My indisposition** . . . EF, *My Terrible Joys*. **The truth is that I was sick** . . . EF, *My Terrible Joys*. **If he came upon a technical problem** . . . EF, reported in Karl Ludvigsen, *Alberto Ascari – Ferrari's Double Champion* (Haynes, 2000). **Some day you will** . . . Griffith Borgeson, reported in Ludvigsen, *Alberto Ascari*. **The Mille Miglia was** . . . EF, reported in Schmidt, *The Roaring Races*.

See also Valerio Moretti, 'Enzo Ferrari The Driver', and Giovanni Lurani: 'The Prancing Horse Iconography', both in *Ferrari: Opera Omnia* (Automobilia, 2000); Luigi Fusi, Enzo Ferrari, Griffith Borgeson, *Le Alfa Romeo di Vittorio Jano* (Edizioni di Autocritica, 1982); Valerio Moretti, *Enzo Ferrari Pilota* (Edizioni di Autocritica, 1987).

Two

I pushed my way . . . EF, *My Terrible Joys*. **I think a radiator hose** . . . EF, *My Terrible Joys*. **Alfa Romeo never saw** . . . EF, *Una Vita per l'Automobile*. **It was in front of the basilica** . . . EF, *My Terrible Joys*. **You should be a** . . . Giovanni Lurani, *Nuvolari* (Cassell, 1959). **They told me you were** . . . EF, *My Terrible Joys*. **At the first corner** . . . EF, *My Terrible Joys*. **Those who saw Nuvolari** . . . From *Il Littoriale*, 1931, reported in Schmidt: *The Roaring Races*. **Pull in the belt, Decimo** . . . Lurani, *Nuvolari*. **Unlike just about all drivers** . . . EF, *My Terrible Joys*. **A beautiful contrast** . . . Piero Taruffi, *Works Driver* (Temple Press,

1964). **Although the Scuderia** . . . Taruffi, *Works Driver*. **He was a unique character** . . . EF, *Una Vita per l'Automobile*. **Certainly money talked** . . . Taruffi, *Works Driver*. **He had created** . . . Lurani, *Nuvolari*. **They were still just as different** . . . Taruffi, *Works Driver*. **Typically, in his half brusque** . . . Taruffi, *Works Driver*.

See also Luigi Orsini and Franco Zagari, *La Scuderia Ferrari* (Olimpia, 1979); Giorgio Terruzzi, *Achille Varzi – Una Curva Cieca* (Nada, 1991); Valerio Moretti, *When Nuvolari Raced* (Veloce, 1994); Valerio Moretti, *Grand Prix Tripoli 1925–1940* (Automobilia, 1994); Gioachino Colombo, *Origins of the Ferrari Legend* (Haynes, 1987).

Three

Varzi the driver . . . EF, *My Terrible Joys*. **The newspaper** . . . EF, *My Terrible Joys*. **That day** . . . EF, *My Terrible Joys*. **I was amazed** . . . EF, *My Terrible Joys*. **In fact he resembled Nuvolari** . . . EF, *My Terrible Joys*. **Jano was good at that sort of thing** . . . René Dreyfus, *My Two Lives* (Aztex, 1983). **Jano wasn't directly involved** . . . Fusi / Ferrari / Borgeson, *Le Alfa Romeo di Vittorio Jano*. **As far as I'm concerned** . . . Gino Rancati, *Ferrari – A Memory* (Motorbooks International, 1989). **You could only be sure** . . . Dreyfus: *My Two Lives*. **Of course I wouldn't** . . . Dreyfus: *My Two Lives*. **The magic show is over** . . . Valerio Moretti: *Grand Prix Tripoli 1925–1940* (Automobilia, 1994). **When I arrived in Modena** . . . Colombo, *Origins of the Ferrari Legend*. **We spent many Sundays working** . . . Federico Giberti interviewed by Daniela Zacconi in *Ferrari World* (No. 9, 1990). **Giorgio will be able** . . . Lurani, *Nuvolari*. **He appeared almost surreptitiously** . . . EF, *My Terrible Joys*. **He was not a great believer** . . . EF, *My Terrible Joys*. **Neubauer says thanks** . . . George Monkhouse, *Mercedes-Benz Grand Prix Racing 1934–1955* (White Mouse Editions, 1984). **Why to Hockenheim** . . . Hermann Lang, *Grand Prix Driver* (Foulis, 1953). **My reception at the pits** . . . Lang: *Grand Prix Driver*. **Some people** . . . George Monkhouse, *Motor Racing with Mercedes-Benz* (Foulis, 1948). **I was sacked** . . . EF, *Una Vita per l'Automobile*. **Ferrari claimed the incident** . . . Luigi Villoresi: interviewed in *Ferrari:*

Che Gente, No 1 (Ruoteclassiche, 1995). **My return to Modena . . .** EF, *My Terrible Joys*.

See also Orsini and Zagari, *La Scuderia Ferrari*; Terruzzi: *Achille Varzi – Una Curva Cieca*; Rancati, *Ferrari – A Memory*; Aldo Santini, *Nuvolari – Il Mantovano Volante* (Rizzoli, 1983); Chris Nixon, *Racing with the Silver Arrows* (Osprey, 1986).

Four

Scuderia Ferrari was a joint-stock company . . . EF reported in Franco Varisco, *815 – The Genesis of Ferrari* (Ferrari World, undated). **Though I have to say . . .** EF, *Una Vita per l'Automobile*. **He made me such a ridiculous offer . . .** Varisco, *815 – The Genesis of Ferrari*. **I therefore set to work . . .** EF, *My Terrible Joys*. **For what were perhaps . . .** EF, *My Terrible Joys*.

See also Brock Yates, *Enzo Ferrari – The Man and the Machines* (Doubleday, 1991); Angelo Titi Anselmi, *Tipo 166 – The Original Ferrari* (Libreria dell'Automobile, 1984 / Haynes, 1985); Gianni Rogliatti, *Maranello – Ferrari e la sua Gente* (Comune di Maranello, 1995); Francesco Genitoni (ed.), *Maranello – Un Paese, la sua storia, la sua anima* (Editrice Telesio, 1996); Luigi Orsini/Corrado Millanta, *Carambola!* (Le Edizione dell'Opificio, 1996).

Five

Monogamy does not come naturally . . . Charlotte Chandler, *I, Fellini* (Bloomsbury, 1994). *Lei e matto . . .* Rogliatti, *Maranello – Ferrari e la sua Gente*. **Colombo, Ferrari said . . .** Colombo, *Origins of the Ferrari Legend*. **In my view . . .** Colombo, *Origins of the Ferrari Legend*. *Caro Colombo . . .* Colombo, *Origins of the Ferrari Legend*. **I have always paid more attention . . .** EF, *Una Vita per l'Automobile*. **Broken dreams . . .** Yates, *Enzo Ferrari – The Man and the Machines*. **Once again Nuvolari . . .** *Motor*, 13 July 1947. **At the end of that lap . . .** *Auto Italiana*, 15 July 1947. **Now**

I went and sat . . . EF, *My Terrible Joys*. **Some of the customers** . . . EF, *My Terrible Joys*. **Don't be downhearted, Tazio** . . . EF, *Una Vita per l'Automobile*. **He was a man on whom drama** . . . EF, *My Terrible Joys*. **It was the sort of technical immorality** . . . Colombo, *Origins of the Ferrari Legend*. **Gigi Villoresi was** . . . EF, *Una Vita per l'Automobile*. **He who has good health** . . . Biagi, *Enzo Ferrari – The Drake*. **Ferrari is a man who instils** . . . Angelo Titi Anselmi, *Tipo 166 – The Original Ferrari*. **By this well-balanced decision** . . . Colombo, *Origins of the Ferrari Legend*. **You're starting two minutes behind Fangio** . . . Franco Andreatini, *Dorino Serafini – Storia e Leggende di Un Asso Pesarese* (Fondazione della Casa di Risparmio di Pesaro, 1997). **The details required** . . . Cesare De Agostini, interview with Giannino Marzotto in *Ferrari 1947–1997: The Official Book* (Nada / Haynes, 1997).

See also Luigi Orsini and Franco Zagari, *Maserati – A Complete History from 1926 to the Present* (LDA, 1980); Jonathan Thompson, interview with Luigi Chinetti (*Road & Track*, 1982); Graham Gauld, *Modena Racing Memories* (MBI, 1999); Moretti, *When Nuvolari Raced*; Giovanni Lurani, *Mille Miglia 1927–1957* (Edita, 1981); Chris Jones, *Road Race* (George Allen & Unwin, 1977); David Owen, *Targa Florio* (Haynes, 1979); Lurani, *Nuvolari*; Santini, *Nuvolari – Il Mantovani Volante*; *Ferrari, Opera Omnia 1947–2000* (Automobilia, 2000); Jonathan Thompson, *The Ferrari Formula One Cars 1948–1976* (Aztex, 1976); Hans Tanner with Doug Nye, *Ferrari* (Haynes, 1989); Alan Henry, *Ferrari – The Grand Prix Cars* (Hazleton, 1989); Walter Guadagnini / Michele Smargiassi, *La Ferrari e Modena* (Edizioni Armo / Galleria Civica di Modena, 1997); Juan Manuel Fangio, *My Twenty Years of Racing* (Temple Press, 1961), Juan Manuel Fangio with Roberto Carozzo, *My Racing Life* (Patrick Stephens, 1990); Denis Jenkinson, *Vanwall* (PSL, 1975); Colombo, *Origins of the Ferrari Legend*; David Hodges, *The Le Mans 24 Hour Race* (Temple Press, 1963); Christian Moity, *The Le Mans 24 Hour Race 1949–1973* (Edita, 1974); Marcel Massini, 'Porfirio Rubirosa' (article in *Cavallino* 102, 1997/1998); Dean Batchelor, *Ferrari – The Early Berlinettas and Competition Coupés* (Batchelor, 1974); Terruzzi, *Una Curva Cieca*.

Six

Whereas Fangio . . . EF, *My Terrible Joys*. **I cried for joy** . . . EF reported in Yates, *Ferrari – The Man, The Machines*. **We seemed to get on** . . . Stirling Moss with Doug Nye, *My Cars, My Career* (PSL, 1987). **Tremendously human** . . . EF, *My Terrible Joys*. **When leading** . . . EF, *My Terrible Joys*. **Every time I come back** . . . EF, *My Terrible Joys*. **If I can't drive a green car** . . . Chris Nixon, *Mon Ami Mate – The Bright Brief Lives of Mike Hawthorn and Peter Collins* (Transport Bookman, 1991). **He had been a solitary man** . . . EF, *Una Vita per l'Automobile*. **The rather trying days** . . . Mark Kahn, *Le Mans 1955* (Barrie & Jenkins, 1976). **I returned to Milan** . . . Ludvigsen, *Alberto Ascari – Ferrari's Double Champion*. **Ferrari actually said 'Thank you'** . . . Biagi, *Enzo Ferrari – The Drake*. **Our boss must have the luck** . . . Trintignant quoted in *Ferrari 1947–1997: The Official Book*. **The car was a real beast** . . . Paul Frère reported in Henry, *Ferrari – The Grand Prix Cars*. **All we could find** . . . EF, *Una Vita per l'Automobile*. **So far everything** . . . Ludvigsen, *Alberto Ascari – Ferrari's Double Champion*.

See also Steve Small, *Grand Prix Who's Who* (Travel Publishing, third edition, 2000); Fangio with Carozzo, *My Racing Life*; Jones, *Road Race*; Thompson, *The Ferrari Formula One Cars 1948–1976*; Hans Tanner with Doug Nye, *Ferrari*; Alan Henry, *Ferrari – The Grand Prix Cars*; Anthony Pritchard, *Maserati – A History* (David & Charles, 1976); Alan Friedman, *Agnelli and the Network of Italian Power* (Harrap, 1988).

Seven

Mais non, monsieur . . . EF, *My Terrible Joys*. **The plane trees** . . . Françoise Sagan, *With Fondest Regards* (W. H. Allen, 1986). **Eugenio hated publicity** . . . Delia Scala in Biagi, *Enzo Ferrari – The Drake*. **He had the face of a child** . . . Fiamma Breschi in Biagi, *Enzo Ferrari – The Drake*. **His air of personal neglect** . . . EF, *My Terrible Joys*. **That inscrutable expression** . . . EF, *My Terrible Joys*. **A primadonna** . . . Breschi, *Il Mio Ferrari*. **A shining example of sweetness** . . . EF in Biagi, *Enzo Ferrari –*

The Drake. **It's impossible to pre-arrange a result** . . . EF in Biagi, *Enzo Ferrari – The Drake*. **I had deluded myself** . . . EF, *My Terrible Joys*. **The conviction has never left me** . . . EF, *My Terrible Joys*. **You don't treat a champion** . . . Breschi, *Il Mio Ferrari*. **Fangio was a really great driver** . . . EF, *My Terrible Joys*. **She was the biggest burden** . . . Breschi, *Il Mio Ferrari*. **Try to understand** . . . EF, *My Terrible Joys*. **He was going through** . . . EF, *My Terrible Joys*. **I was his girlfriend** . . . Biagi, *Enzo Ferrari – The Drake*. **Even though Peter and I** . . . Mike Hawthorn, *Challenge Me the Race* (William Kimber, 1958). **Musso's performance** . . . Henry, *Ferrari – The Grand Prix Cars*. **Tall, self-confident** . . . Breschi, *La Mia Ferrari*. **A modern Saturn** . . . From *L'Osservatore Romana*, quoted in EF, *My Terrible Joys*.

See also Michael T. Lynch, 'Peter Collins and the Myth of Monza', *Cavallino* 64 (Aug/Sept 1991); Taruffi, *Works Driver*.

Eight

I was far more interested . . . Phil Hill quoted in William F. Nolan, *Phil Hill – A Yankee Champion* (Brown Fox, 1962/1990). **You have to admit** . . . René Dreyfus quoted in Albert R. Bochroch, 'Ferraris in America' from *Ferrari: The Man, The Machines* (Automobile Quarterly/Dutton, 1975). **It was chaos** . . . Bob Grossman quoted in Bochroch, 'Ferraris in America' from *Ferrari: The Man, The Machines*. **I remember that he always listened** . . . Carlo Chiti quoted in Oscar Orefici, *Carlo Chiti – Sinfonia Ruggente* (Autocritica, 1991). **We had completely abandoned** . . . Carlo Chiti quoted in Orefici, *Carlo Chiti – Sinfonia Ruggente*. **I think that taking an uncalculated risk** . . . Tony Brooks quoted in Henry, *Ferrari – The Grand Prix Cars*. **Brooks, who has left racing** . . . EF, *My Terrible Joys*. **It seemed quite impossible** . . . Denis Jenkinson, French Grand Prix report (*Motor Sport*, August 1961). **Probably a Varzi** . . . EF, *My Terrible Joys*. **It looked bad** . . . Phil Hill quoted in Nolan, *Phil Hill – A Yankee Champion*. **She often descended** . . . Orefici, *Carlo Chiti – Sinfonia Ruggente*. **She was a woman completely devoid** . . . Carlo Chiti quoted in Orefici, *Carlo Chiti –*

Sinfonia Ruggente. **Commendatore? Si . . .** Phil Hill in *Ferrari, The Man, The Machines*. **Enzo Ferrari never understood me . . .** Phil Hill quoted in Nolan, *Phil Hill – A Yankee Champion*. **I've spent thirty years with one man . . .** Margherita Bandini in Biagi, *Enzo Ferrari – The Drake*.

See also Robert Daley, *The Cruel Sport* (Studio Vista, 1963); Denis Jenkinson, 'An Unhappy Ferrari Win' (*Motor Sport*, October 1961); Guy Mangiamele, Interview with Mauro Forghieri, *Cavallino* 49 (1989); Mark Hughes, 'Mike Parkes', *Motor Sport* (May 1999); Franco Gozzi (*Automotive News Europe*, August 1998); Marcel Massini, 'Porfirio Rubirosa', *Cavallino* 102 (1997/98)

Nine

Maybe that was the reason . . . Graham Gauld, www.theautochannel.com. **This was everything I expected . . .** Chris Amon in *Ferrari 1947–1997, The Official Book*. **That was fine by me . . .** Henry, *Ferrari – The Grand Prix Cars*. **He had a fine engineering background . . .** EF, *Una Vita per l'Automobile*. **I was in my office . . .** EF, *Una Vita per l'Automobile*. **I remember after Bandini . . .** Gauld www.theautochannel.com. **I told him that it didn't matter . . .** Genitoni, *Maranello – Un Paese, la sua storia, la sua anima*. **It's not time to say . . .** Genitoni, *Maranello – Un Paese, la sua storia, la sua anima*. **Chris Amon was the Nazarro of the Sixties . . .** EF, *Una Vita per l'Automobile*. **Our collaboration . . .** Chris Amon in *Ferrari 1947–1997, The Official Book*. **A stable which managed to base . . .** Orsini, *Carambola!* **With Ferrari, I learned . . .** René Dreyfus, *My Two Lives* (Aztex, 1983). **We were ushered into the office of Gianni Agnelli . . .** EF, *Una Vita per l'Automobile*. **Ickx was a mixture . . .** EF, *Una Vita per l'Automobile*. **He had talent and passion . . .** EF, *Una Vita per l'Automobile*. **My own observations . . .** Mario Andretti in *Ferrari, Opera Omnia 1947–2000*.

See also Alan Henry, 'Lorenzo Bandini' (*F1 Racing*, August 1999); Mark Hughes, 'Mike Parkes' (*Motor Sport*, May 1999); Giacomo Sironi, *Lorenzo Bandini* (Omnia, 1997); Giulio Borsari with Cesare De Agostini, *La Ferrari in Tutta* (Autosprint, 1980).

Ten

I need someone . . . Luca di Montezemolo with Marco Franzelli, *Le Grande Vittorie Ferrari* (Bompiani Overlook, 2001). **You can't say that** . . . Niki Lauda with Herbert Völker, *To Hell and Back* (Stanley Paul, 1986). **When Niki Lauda was badly burnt** . . . Enzo Biagi, interview with Luca di Montezemolo in *Enzo Ferrari, Una Storia* (RAI TV, 1997). **When Lauda raced** . . . EF, *Una Vita per l'Automobile*. **A driver with an athlete's physique** . . . EF, *Una Vita per l'Automobile*. **Well, young man** . . . Gerald Donaldson, *Gilles Villeneuve* (MRP, 1989). **For me, Enzo Ferrari was like a prime minister** . . . Carlos Reutemann in *Ferrari 1947–1997, The Official Book*.

See also Niki Lauda, *For the Record* (William Kimber, 1977).

Eleven

The team was a long way behind . . . Henry, *Ferrari – The Grand Prix Cars*. **He was great** . . . Henry, *Ferrari – The Grand Prix Cars*. **He made Ferrari a household name** . . . EF, *Una Vita per l'Automobile*. **The problem at Ferrari was always that Ferrari is a theatre** . . . Mauro Forghieri, *Cavallino* 49 (1989). **In 1987 I went to the circuit** . . . Richard Williams, *Racers* (Viking, 1997). **Since his cars were so directly** . . . Phil Hill in *Ferrari: The Men, The Machines*.

The Last Enemy

Here I am, Ferrari . . . EF, *Una Vita per l'Automobile*. **Non mi piacciono** . . . EF, *Una Vita per l'Automobile*.

See also Lycia Mezzacappa, *Il Mio Drake*; Gianni Cancellieri, interview with Sergio Scaglietti, *Ferrarissima*.

Acknowledgements

Thanks go first of all to the historians, principal among them Doug Nye, Hans Tanner, Alan Henry, Luigi Orsini, Chris Nixon, Jonathan Thompson, Luigi Fusi and Valerio Moretti, whose diligence and enthusiasm ensured the preservation not just of facts but of hundreds of wonderful stories.

Then to the photographers, notably Ferruccio Testi, Odoardo Gandolfi, Luigi Orlandini, Louis Klementaski, Peter Coltrin, Corrado Millanta, Jesse Alexander, Franco Zagari, Robert Daley and Geoff Goddard, whose images form an inspiration and a wonderful record.

To Denis Jenkinson of *Motor Sport*, Henry N. Manney III of *Road & Track*, and Nigel Roebuck of *Autosport*, whose enthusiasm fed my own.

To Piero Ferrari and Franco Gozzi for allowing me to enter the family tomb in San Cataldo cemetery in 1989.

To Brenda Vernor.

To Chris Rea.

To John Surtees.

To Stephen Wood, of *Condé Nast Traveller*, whose commissioning enabled me to drive the entire 1957 Mille Miglia route in an Alfa Romeo (in three and a half days), to walk the length of the Monaco Grand Prix track (in about six hours, including lunch), and to drive a Ferrari from the Bois de Boulogne to the steps of the basilica of Sacré-Coeur at dawn (in seventeen minutes).

To the sports editors who allowed me to write, from time to time, about Ferraris, in particular Ben Clissitt at the *Guardian*, and his predecessor, Mike Averis; Paul Newman at the *Independent*; and Simon Kelner and Simon O'Hagan at the *Independent on Sunday*.

To Emma Matthews, Christopher Petit, Paul and Pauline Smith, John Hooper, Elizabeth Jobey, Matt Sinclair and Karen Frankel, for logistical, linguistic and technical support at critical moments.

To Pino Allievi and Giancarlo Galavotti, distinguished correspondents of *La Gazzetta dello Sport*.

[313]

To Rachel Cugnoni, this book's publisher and editor, and to David Godwin, my agent.

We all have our Rosebuds. Mine include a Dinky Toy model of the Maserati 4CLT/48 'San Remo' given to me by my grandmother, the late Sarah Jane Williams, and the memory of being read the stories of Don Camillo and Peppone by my grandfather, the late Harold Steer. They, as much as anyone, are responsible for the existence of this book.

Index

Figures in italics indicate captions.

12 Heures de Paris, Montlhéry
    152

Abruzzi, Duke of 33
Abyssinia 89, 91, 115
AC Milan 15
Acerbo, Professor Count
    Giacomo 33, 62–3
Acerbo, Tito 62–3
Adami, Peppino 43
Adelaide 296
Adenau 89
Agnelli, Gianni 182, 229, 238,
    241, 255–6, 264, 287, 301
Agnelli, Giovanni 16, 182
Agnelli family 264, 267, 269, 270
Agusta, Count Domenico 226
Aintree 198
Alboreto, Michele 293, 294, 295,
    301, 302
Aldrighetti, Giordano 64
Alexander the Great 5
Alfa Corse 99, 100, 102, 103, 104,
    106, 107, 113, 145, 169, 247
Alfa Romeo 51, 54–5, 117, 138,
    188, 200, 232, 254
    F orders a G1 model 23
    F joins the team 23
    works occupied 24
    Ascari's business relationship
        with 25

four-leafed clover badge 26,
    102
Sivocci joins 26–7
Bazzi joins 27
F sells their cars in the Modena
    area 28, 34
Jano joins 30–1
wins the Italian Grand Prix 31,
    34, 36
retires from grand prix racing
    36, 41
special relationship with the
    Coppa Acerbo 42
relationship with Scuderia
    Ferrari 44–5, 54, 69–70, 95
finances 65
state protection 66
reduced investment in racing
    82
viper and cross badge 84
Jano sacked 99, 125
takes over Scuderia Ferrari
    99–100
F sacked 107, 164
Colombo falls out with 128,
    134
and Busso 128, 137
non-participation in grand prix
    (1949) 144–5, 146, 150
refuses *Temporada* offer 145
Colombo returns to (1951) 157

[315]

and Ferrari's first grand prix
victory (1951) 163–4
withdrawal from grand prix
racing (1952) 168, 169
Alfa Romeo cars 18, 20, 22, 24,
25, 32, 34, 48, 52–3, 64, 68,
69, 79, 81, 84, 111, 115,
126, 130, 133, 144, 157,
163, 171, 174, 194
6C–1500SS 36
6C–2300 79
8Cs 62, 63, 65, 66, 94, 98
8C–35 89–91
8C–2300 Monza 55–8, 65–7,
75
8C–2900 sports cars 91, 92
12C–36 models 92, 93, 94, 97,
98
1500 series 45, 63
1600 series 36
1750 series 36, 45, 48, 56, 57,
58, 60, 63, 66, 79, 95
2300 series 55, 60
2500 model 113
2900 model 209
Bimotore 83–4, 85, 112
Giulietta car 100
Mussolini's 35
P1 29, 30, 31
P2 31, 32, 33, 35, 36, 41, 47,
48, 49, 51, 52, 53, 95
P3 (Tipo B) 64, 65, 66, 69, 70,
72, 75, 76, 79, 82, 83, 84, 90
RL SS model 38
SS model 45
Tipo 158 Alfetta 99, 101, 102,
105, 106, 109, 112, 114,
126, 136, 143, 156, 165, 224
Tipo 159 161, 162
Tipo A 55

Tipo RL/Targa Florio sports
car 31
Zagato-bodied 209
Allemano 139, 140
Amilcars 42
Amon, Chris 243, 244, 247, 248,
250–3, 278
Amorotti, Mino 118, 180, 202
Anderloni, Felice Bianchi 112,
150–1
Andreina, Doña (Beba) 189, 192
Andretti, Aldo 258
Andretti, Mario 258–9, 260, 275,
279, 281, 293
Angiolini, Mario 133
Anonima Lombarda Fabbrica
Automobili 23
Aquila car 19
Arcangeli, Luigi ('Lion of
Romagna') 40, 42, 45, 46,
52, 53, 55, 135
Argentina 145–7, 156, 164, 190,
197
Argentine Automobile Club 150,
162
Argentine Grand Prix 180
Arnoux, René 288, 290, 293,
294, 301
Ascari, Alberto 34, 35–6, 110–14,
137, 140, 142, 143, 146–50,
157, 158, *160*, 161–5, 167,
169–82, 198, 199, 203, 216,
227, 242, 244, 258, 269,
272, 302
Ascari, Antonio 19, 22, 24–5, 28,
29, 31, 33–6, 41, 49, 63,
110–11, 159, 171
Ascari, Mietta 182, 296
Astaire, Fred xi
Aston Martin 229

ATS 225
Audetto, Daniele 270–1, 274, 276
Auriol, Vincent 152
Austin-Healey 183
Austria 257, 261
Austrian Grand Prix 274
Auto-Avio Costruzioni
    F prohibited from using Ferrari
      name for four years 109
    founded (1939) 109
    Bellentani joins 109–10
    first customers 110–11
    war work 116–18
    decision to return to building
      sports cars 124–5
    change to SEFAC 214, 249
    see also Maranello factory
Auto Union cars 77–81, 83–7,
    90–3, 96, 97, 99, 103, 126
Autodromo Enzo e Dino Ferrari,
    Imola 115
Automobile Club of Argentina
    150, 162
Autosport 173, 177
Avanzo, Baroness Maria
    Antonietta 63, 126
Avus 77, 85, 97, 117, 213

Badoglio, Marshal 120
Baghetti, Giancarlo 216, 224
Bai (mechanic) 94
Balbo, Air Marshal Italo 32–3, 92,
    104–5
Balestre, Jean-Marie 290, 293
Ballot car 20
Banco di San Geminiano e San
    Prospero, Modena 54, 119,
    248–9, 255
Banco Sella 62, 119
Bandini, Lorenzo 224, 231–2,

234, 236, *240*, 241–5, 271,
    273, 288
Bandini, Margherita (née Freddi)
    234, 242, 245
Bar Nord, Turin 17
Baracca, Count Enrico 25
Baracca, Francesco 15, 25–6, 65
Baracca, Countess Paolina 25
Barbieri, Nando 70
Barcelona 179
Bari 165, 223
Barnard, John 294–5
Barracano centre, Bologna 16
Baumer, Walter 114
Bazzi, Luigi 1, 27, 29, 30, 33, 34,
    41, 53, 70, 75–6, 83, 84, 94,
    97, 100, 125, 128, 132, 133,
    136, 139, 183
Behra, Jean 170, 196, 200, 211,
    213
Belgian Grand Prix 246, 271, 276,
    282, 291–2
Bellantani, Vittorio 109–12
Bellei, Angelo 228
Bellicardi, Francesco 256
Belloi, Don Erio 302–3
Beltoise, Jean-Pierre 258
Beltracchini, Enrico 114, 133
Benzi, Carlo 4, 120, 301
Bergamo 89
Berger, Gerhard 294, 295–6,
    302
Bergman, Ingrid 148, 174, 175
Bernhard, Prince, of the
    Netherlands 3, 222
Berretta, Nino *8*, 19, 20, 21
Besana, Gabriele 138
Besana, Soave 138
Bianchi 18, 50, 59
    Freccia Celeste motorcycles 50

Biella 89
Billi, Giorgio 222
Biondetti, Clemente 60, 102,
    139–42, 151, 241
Birabongse, Prince ('B. Bira')
    142–4
Bizzarrini, Giotto 220
BMW cars 113, 114, 133
BOAC 500 sports-car race,
    Brands Hatch 248
Boccoleri, Archbishop 155
Boillot, André 20, 21, 22
Bologna
    F sets up an office in 34
    Casa del Fascio 43
Bologna University 190
Bonacini, Romolo 17
Bonetto, Felice 142, 150, 151,
    173
Bonmartini, Count 32
Bonnier, Jo 216
Bordino, Pietro 27, 42, 47
Borgeson, Griffith 30
Borrani 65
Borsari, Giulio 228, 236, *240*, 241,
    266
Borzacchini, Mario (Baconin) *40*,
    43, 51, 52, 53, 56, 57, 63,
    65, 69, 71
Bosch 45, 54
Bouillin, Pierre ('Pierre Levegh')
    183
Brabham 244, 245, 252, 256, 267,
    274, 276, 277, 282–3, 290
Brabham, Sir Jack 213, 214–15,
    244
Bracco, Giovanni 137, 167
Brambilla, Vittorio 275
Brands Hatch 248, 268, 281
Brauchitsch, Manfred von 78, 87,

88
Brazil 147, 270
Brazilian Grand Prix 276, 290
Breda aircraft and armaments
    company 77–8, 117–18
Breda, Ernesto 117
Bremgarten 143, 156, 169, 179
Breschi, Fiamma 187, 189, 192,
    193, 196, 201, 202, 203
Brescia 16, 112, 113
Brickyard track 169
Brilli-Perri, Gastone 36, 38, 46,
    300
British Grand Prix 163–4, 178,
    261, 268, 271, 276
Brivio, Antonio 65, 84, 91, 94
BRM (British Racing Motors)
    147, 150, 165, 166, 168,
    214, 221, 248, 268
BRM cars 170, 225, 232, 244,
    246, 265, 267
Broadley, Eric 227
Brooklands 26, 27, 85, 144
Brooks, Tony 198, 201, 204, 206,
    211, 213–14
Brunner, Gustav 293
Buell, Temple 210, 215
Buenos Aires 146, 164, 172, 178,
    192, 197, 200, 210–11, 258,
    267–8
Bugatti 29, 136, 254
Bugatti cars 18, 32, 42, 43, 53, 55,
    60, 71, 75, 94, 96, 97, 177,
    209
    horseshoe-shaped radiator
        grilles 26
    Type 35 51
    Type 51 67, 68
Bugatti, Ettore 254
Bühler, Dr Joseph 92

Bussi, Giancarlo 280
Busso, Giuseppe 128, 131, 132, 136, 137, 143

California Sports Car Club 209
Calzoni foundry, Bologna 111, 116
Campari, Giuseppe 20, 22, 24, 28, 29, 31, 32, 33, 35–6, 41–2, 45, 46, 48, 52, 55, 70, 71, 74, 288, 302
Can-Am series 243, 278
Canada 257, 274, 302
Canadian Grand Prix 277, 281, 289
Canestrini, Giovanni 31, 37, 38
Caniato, Alfredo 43, 46, 55, 62
Caniato, Augusto 40, 43, 44
Capelli, Ovodio 105
Caracas 253
Caracciola, Baby 189
Caracciola, Charly 189
Caracciola, Rudolf 45, 52, 55, 79, 84, 87, 104, 105, 168, 189, 272
Carpi 9
Carraroli, Guglielmo 22, 30, 46
Carrera Panamericana 167, 210
La Carrozza d'oro (film) 167
Carrozzeria Emilia 28, 54
Carrozzeria Italo-Argentina 18
Carrozzeria Scaglietti 256
Carrozzeria Touring of Milan 111
Casablanca 211
Caserta 48
Casoli, Giuseppe 54
Castagneto, Renzo 37, 38, 109
Castelbarco, Count Carlo 70
Castellotti, Eugenio 158–9, 177, 181, 182, 183, 187, 190,

191, 192, 195–6, 203, 204, 206, 216, 224
Castelvetro 250
Castoldi, Achille 127
Cavalleri, Lina 41
Ceirano 54
Celli, Adolfo 232
Chapman, Colin 170, 208, 212, 213, 227, 235, 246, 267, 281
Chevrolet cars 145, 209
special 145
Chiamate Roma 3131 (Call Rome 3131) (radio programme) 263
Chiarli, Anselmo (F's godfather) 13
Chinetti, Luigi 93, 129–31, 151–5, 167, 169, 209, 210, 211, 218, 223, 225, 230, 231, 233
Chiribiri 31, 48
Chiron, Louis 70, 76–9, 84, 85, 91–2, 244
Chiti, Carlo 200, 212–15, 220, 221, 222, 224, 225, 227
Christian, Linda 195
Chrysler 42
Ciano, Count Galeazzo 115
Circuito del Garda 51
Circuito del Pozzo 43, 51
Circuito delle Tre Provincie 43, 56–8, 61
Circuito di Alessandria 36, 42, 43, 47
Circuito di Bologna 13–14
Circuito di Cremona 31
Circuito di Modena 36–7, 42, 81, 89
Circuito di Mugello 42, 43
Circuito di Parma 136

Circuito di Pescara 31–3
Circuito di Piacenza 114, 132,
    133
Circuito di Polesine 31
Circuito di Savio 25, 29, 31, 36,
    48
Cisitalia 132, 135, 136, 140
Cisitalia-Porsche 150, 168
Clark, Jim 170, 218, 225, 231,
    246, 251, 258
CMN (Costruzioni Meccaniche
    Nazionali) 8, 18–22, 26
CMN cars 8, 20, 21
    CMN Tipo 15/20 tourer 18,
    19
Collins, Louise (née King) 204,
    205
Collins, Peter 184, 187, 190–3,
    195–200, 202, 204, 205,
    206, 211, 273, 282, 288
Colombini, Augusta 119
Colombini, Dante 119
Colombo, Gioachino 95, 96–7,
    102, 122, 125–8, 131, 134,
    136, 137, 143, 146, 148,
    149, 153–4, 157, 161, 164,
    168, 177, 178, 199, 201, 228
    Volpe (Fox) 134
Colombo, Sandro 260, 261
Comminges Grand Prix 70
Compagnia Nazionale
    Aeronautica 116
Compagnoni, Decimo 51, 57–8,
    64, 69, 86, 89, 98, 140
Conelli, Count Carlo Alberto 19
Connaught garage, Surrey 211
Connolly, Joanne 155
Conti, Michele 24
Convoglio farm, Maranello 119
Cooper 165, 200, 212, 214–15,

    225, 227, 230, 237
Cooper, John 170, 208, 212, 235
Cooper-Alta 172
Cooper-Bristol 172
Cooper-Maserati 241
Coppa Acerbo (Pescara) 31, 41,
    53, 63, 65, 70, 79, 89
Coppa Alberto e Giorgio
    Nuvolari 142
Coppa Ciano 40, 51, 52–3, 56,
    59, 69, 84, 93, 102, 115
Coppa della Mille Miglia 37–9,
    41, 45–7, 50–1, 55, 63, 64,
    67, 69, 76–7, 91, 97, 109,
    110, 111, 113–14, 140–2,
    149, 151, 157, 158, 161,
    167, 174–5, 177, 179, 190,
    193, 194–5, 198, 199, 214,
    258, 263, 273, 296, 299
Coppa Frigo 60
Coppa Galenga 62
Cordier, Louise ('Louise King';
    later Collins) 196–7
Corni Institute of Technology,
    Modena 149, 234, 250
Cortese, Franco 117, 118, 124,
    132–5, 137, 140–1, 150,
    241, 296
Costatini, Meo 104, 106
Cosworth engine-building
    company 245
    DFV engine 245
Coupe du Président de la
    République 152
Coventry Climax engine 245
Crestani, Giorgio 249
Cuneo–Colle della Maddalena
    hillclimb 52
Cunningham, Briggs 152, 210
Cuoghi, Ermanno 266, 277

Czaikowski, Count 70–1

Da Zara, Leonino 14
Daily Express Trophy, Silverstone
    149, 161–2
Daimler-Benz 183
D'Annunzio, Gabriele 82, 86, 201
Dante Alighieri 5
Darracq factory, Portello 23
Darrieux, Danielle 154
Daytona 24 Hours 243
De Dion Bouton car 13, 21
De Palma, Ralph 14
de Portago, Don Alfonso de
    Cabeza Vaca, seventh
    Marquès 187–8, 191, 194,
    195, 197, 201, 203, 233
Dearborn, Michigan 228
Delages 96, 113, 137, 152
Delahaye cars 97, 130, 152
D'Elia, Antonio 1–2, 159
D'Elia, Massimo 2
Della Casa, Ermanno 220, 221
Depailler, Patrick 271
Diatto Torpedo car 15
Dijon 288
Dino Ferrari diagnosis and
    treatment centre, Milan
    University 286
D'Ippolito, Guido 65
Domenica Sportiva (television
    sports magazine) 257
Donington Park 103, 144
Dragoni, Eugenio 224, 225, 228,
    229, 235–8, 241, 242, 271
Dreyfus, Pierre-Louis 'Ferret' 152
Dreyfus, René 82, 84, 90, 91,
    210, 254
Duesenberg 66
Duke, Doris 154, 233

Dundrod 170
Dunlop 85, 205
Dusio, Piero 135
Dutch Grand Prix 293

Ecclestone, Bernie 274, 276, 290,
    293
Edwards, Guy 273
Eifelrennen 93
Englebert tyres 83, 93, 181, 192,
    198
ERAs 94, 96, 126, 144
Ertl, Harald 273
Etancelin, Philippe 129
European Formula Three
    championship 293
European Grand Prix, Monza 51

Fagioli, Luigi ('Abruzzi Bandit')
    70, 74, 79, 80, 84, 87, 99,
    157, 161
Fairfield, Pat 94
Fangio, Juan Manuel 145–6, 150,
    156–7, 158, 161–6, 169,
    170, 172, 173, 174, 176,
    178, 179, 180, 183, 188–93,
    197–200, 202, 204, 223,
    253, 258, 272, 281, 282, 296
Fantuzzi, Medardo 212, 215, 235
Farina, *Dottore* Giuseppe ('Nino')
    91, 92, 94, 98, 105, 132,
    133, 136, 142–7, 149, 156,
    157, 161, 162, 169, 172,
    173, 174, 178, 179
Farina, Giovanbattista 'Pinin' 167
Farina, Sergio 167
Fascist Party 115–16, 120, 125
Fédération Internationale de
    l'Automobile (FIA) 168,
    290, 293

Federazione Italiana Scuderie
    Automobilistiche 216
Fellini, Federico 123–4, 263
Ferrari *see* Società Anonima
    Scuderia Ferrari; Ferrari cars
Ferrari, Adalgisa (née Bisbini; F's
    mother) 15
  F's fear of 9
  marries Alfredo 9
  pleads for F to return home
    (1918) 16
  and F's return to Modena 27–8
  stormy relationship with Laura
    28
  death 233–4
  family tomb 301
Ferrari, Alfredo ('Dino'; F's son)
    1, 6, *108*, 123, 227
  birth (1932) 61
  illness 73, 98, 149, 151, 159,
    175
  taught by Scapinelli 149
  interest in the technical side of
    the business 149, 250
  appearance 149
  education 190, 234
  works at the factory 190
  memorials 191
  death (1956) 7, 190–1, 279
  Collins given his apartment
    196
  family tomb 301
Ferrari, Alfredo (F's father)
  birth (1859) 9
  background 9
  marries Adalgisa 9
  metal fabricating business 9,
    12, 15
  personality 12
  his cars 12–13

takes his sons to their first
    motor race 13
  beats F over a school report 14
  dies of pneumonia (1916) 15
  legacy to F 17
  family tomb 301
Ferrari, Alfredo, Jr ('Dino'; F's
    brother)
  birth (1896) 10
  childhood with F 1, 14
  education 12
  sees first motor race (1908) 13
  war service 15, 25
  death (1916) 15
Ferrari, Enzo Anselmo
  birth (20 February 1898) 10
  his routine 1–5
  personality 4, 5–7, 9, 96, 254,
    285–8
  Swiss bank accounts 4
  appearance 6, 123, 131
  honours 7, 299
  in his first race *8*, 18–19
  education 10, 14
  ambition to be a racing driver
    12–15, 18
  sees his first race (1908) 13–14
  beaten by his father 14
  a published writer 14, 78
  death of his father and brother
    15
  war service 15–16
  turned down by Fiat 17, 138
  tests and delivers cars for
    CMN 18
  wins first race (1923) 25
  Lombardini a 'second father' to
    him 27
  meets and marries Laura 27–8,
    279–80

sells Alfa Romeo cars 28, 34
his calibre as a racing driver
    28–9
retreat from Lyons 33–4, 37
and Mussolini 35
friendship with Nuvolari 48
last appearance as a racing
    driver 56
his marriage 61–2, 73–4, 280
begins a relationship with Lina
    62
becomes chairman of the
    board 91
becomes an employee of Alfa
    Romeo 100
loathes Ricart 100–101
dispute with the Villoresi
    family 106–7, 147, 236
sacked from Alfa Romeo 107,
    164
Fascist Party membership
    115–16
and *Temporada* 145
memoirs (*Le mie gioie terribili*)
    152–3, 203, 263–4
Colombo on 153–4
effect of son Dino's illness on
    159, 175
Moss incident 165–6
rebuilds his team of drivers
    186–7
and Dino's death 190–1, 279
charged with manslaughter
    198–9
offer to Stirling Moss 222–3
dark glasses 232
buys a town house in Modena
    233
death of his mother 233–4
isolates himself 234–5

meets Stewart 248
transfers Forghieri 252, 261
ill health 260, 299, 300
unused to direct criticism 266
Lauda on 266–7, 277
treatment of Piero 269
on Lauda 277
and Laura's death 279–80
birth of his great-grandson 299
speaks to the Pope on the
    telephone 299–300
death (14 August 1988) and
    funeral 300–301
family tomb 301
Ferrari, Floriana (née Nalin) 250,
    280, 301
Ferrari, Laura Domenica (née
    Garello; F's wife) *40*, 56,
    119, *208*
meets and marries F 27–8,
    279–80
stormy relationship with her
    mother-in-law 28
appearance 37
her marriage 61–2, 280
personality 62, 279
and Dino's illness 73, 74,
    190–1
involvement in F's life 73–4
involvement in the factory
    220–1, 228, 280
purchase of a Modena town
    house 233
opposes Piero working at the
    factory 234
and Surtees 236
death (1978) 4, 279–80
family tomb 301
Ferrari, Piero Lardi (F's son) 3,
    257, 299

birth (1945) 123
brought up by his mother,
    Lina 4, 5
personality 4, 269, 270
education 234
works in the factory 234, 250,
    269
appearance 234
marries Floriana 250
Fiat–Ferrari deal 255
translation for Lauda 265–6,
    271
change of name and adoption
    280
general manager of the racing
    department 294
close friendship with
    Postlethwaite 294
drives for the Pope 299
and his father's death 301
Ferrari, Saracco 45
Ferrari cars 177, 202, 205,
    209–10, 218, 246, 272,
    290–1, 292
3-litre Touring *barchetta* 174
125 131, 156, 296
125GPC 143, 144, 149–50
125GPS 146–7
125S 126–36
126 296
126C 289
159 137
166 157, 247
166 *barchetta* 182
166 F2 150
166 Formula Libre 162, 169
166 Inter 151, 158
166 MM Spider 151, 155
166 Spider Corsa 138, 139,
    140, 142, 152

212 E 257
212 Export 209
212 Inter 167
250 MM Berlinetta 168
250 Testa Rossa sports car
    223
250GT 222, 226, 233
250LM coupé 231
275GTB 235
312 237, 244, 251, 252
312B1 257
312B2 259
312B3 (*spazzaneve*
    (snowplough)) 260–1, 267
312P 260
312T 268
312T2 270, 274
312T4 282
312T5 282
330 P3 238
330 P4 243, 246
330GT 3
365GTB/4 Daytona 247
375 161, 162, 169, 201
375 MM coupé 233
410 Super America 222, 247
500 169
553 (Squalo) 178, 179, 186
625 178, 179
750S sports car 181
815 111–15, 116, 133
Berlinetta coupé 140, 141, 142
Boxer 252
Dino 191, 212–13, 214, 246–7,
    254
Dino 156 (Sharknose) 215,
    216, 224–5
Dino 246 200–201, 212, 247
F40 296
'Ferrari Special' 169–70

Grant Piston Ring Special 170
Mondial cabriolet 299
Rob Walker Ferrari 250GT
    Berlinetta 223
supercharged *122*, 136
'Thinwall Special' 147
'Thinwall Special' (2) 162
Ferrari Spa 256
FIA (Federation Internationale de
    l'Automobile) 231
Fiat (Fabbrica Italiana Automobili
    Torino) 26, 29, 30, 111,
    182, 183, 228, 239, 246,
    254, 260, 261, 264, 285
    Nazzaro and Lancia work for
    13, 17
    commitment to a racing
    programme 16–17
    turns down F 17, 138
    deal with F 33, 254–6
    Lampredi joins 186
    links with Ferrari 229, 246–7,
    254
    logos 270
Fiat Grand Prix (1914) 19
Fiat-Stanguellini 134, 135
Fiat cars 63, 111, 113, 132, 134,
    253
    124 263
    508C 111
    1100 special 114
    501 model 16
    Cinquecento 111
    Dino-engined coupé 246–7
    Nuova 500 263
    Seicento 202
    Topolino 111, 113
Fiorano 5, 259
Fiorano test track 119, 259, *262*,
    266, 278

Fiorio, Cesare 263
Firestone tyre company 235
Fittipaldi, Emerson 267, 268
Flammini, Maurizio 271
Florio, Count Vincenzo 19, 22
FOCA (Formula One
    Constructors' Association)
    290, 293
Fochi, Luciano 128
Fondo Cavani, Maranello 119,
    120
Fontanile farm, Maranello 119
Ford, Henry 229, 238
Ford-Cosworth engines 246, 267,
    290
Ford cars 209, 231, 238, 239,
    246
    Capri 265
    Mk IV 246
Ford Motor Company 228, 238,
    243, 245
Forghieri, Mauro 224, 228, 230,
    232, 237, 243–4, 245, 251,
    252, 253, 256–61, *262*, 264,
    266, 267, 268, 270, 280,
    282, 283, 289, 291, 294,
    295, 301
Forghieri, Reclus 224, 295
Forli 9, 135
Formigine, near Modena 118,
    250
Formula Atlantic 278
Formula Libre category 83
Formula One 156, 168, 176,
    177–8, 183, 211, 212, 214,
    216, 229, 230, 242, 243,
    246, 251, 252, 257, 259,
    261, 264, 265, 268, 269,
    278, 282, 290–3
    Concorde agreements 290

Formula One Constructors'
    Association (FOCA) 290,
    293
Formula Three 165
Formula Two 150, 156, 165, 168,
    174, 202
Fornaca, Guido 27
Foyt, A.J. 246
Francis, Alf 200
Franco Bahamonde, General
    Francisco 94
Frankenheimer, John 232
Fraschetti, Andrea 200
Frazer-Nash 152
French Grand Prix 13, 27, 33, 35,
    163, 190, 202, 224, 225,
    242, 251–2
Frère, Paul 180

Gabor, Zsa Zsa 233
Galazzi, Fausto 220
Galetto, Attileo 128
Gardini, Gerolamo 120, 220, 221,
    222
Gardner, Ava xi
Garelli, Marco 18
Garibaldi, Giuseppe 13, 159
Gatti, Corrado 116–17
Gauld, Graham 242
Gavéa 92–3, 147
La Gazzetta dello Sport 14, 78,
    200, 271
Gendebien, Olivier 188, 211,
    224, 241
German Grand Prix 55, 85, 93,
    230, 231, 251, 272
Germany 78, 276
Ghersi, Mario 64
Ghersi, Pietro 79
Giacosa, Dante 111

Giambertone, Marcello 188,
    192–3
Giberti, Federico 97, 128, 133,
    163, 169, 220, 222
Gilco company 128
Ginther, Richie 210, 214–19,
    221, 225
Giovannoni (F's employer in
    Turin) 17–18
Giunti, Ignazio 257, 258
Gobbato, Pier Ugo 247
Gobbato, Ugo 66, 69, 89, 90, 99,
    100, 101, 107, 116, 121, 247
Golden Gate Park, San Francisco
    209
González, Amalia 163
González, José Froilàn ('Canuto';
    'Montemaro') 162–3, 164,
    173–4, 178, 179, 296
Goodwood 223
Gordini cars 143, 170
Gozzi, Franco 2, 4, 5, 6, 229, 234,
    248, 249–50, 255, 299, 301
Gran Premio del Norte 145
Gran Premio delle Nazioni,
    Monza 50
Gran Premio Eva Duarte Perón
    146
Gran Premio Reale, Rome 51
Grand Prix (film) 232
Grand Prix de Marseille, Miramas
    75
Grand Prix des Nations, Geneva
    157
Grand Prix Drivers' Association
    272
Grand Prix of Europe 31
Grand Prix of Venezuela 211
Grossman, Bob 210
Guareschi, Giovanni 5, 299–300

Guiberson, Allen 210
Guidotti, Gianbattista 46, 47
Guildford Technical Office 295
Gulf team 252
Gurney, Dan 203, 211–14, 216,
    246, 251

Hamilton, Duncan 179
Hanstein, Huschke von 114, *208*
Hardy, Françoise 232
Harrah, Bill 210
Hawthorn, Mike 172–4, 178,
    179, 182, 183, 187, 197,
    198, 200–207
Henne, Ernst 80
Henry, Alan 199
Herrmann, Hans 178
Hesketh 273
Hesketh, Lord Alexander 265,
    289
Hewland gearbox 245
Hill, Graham 230, 231, 232
Hill, Phil 206, 209–11, 213–21,
    224–7, 259, 288, 296–7, 302
Hispano-Suizas 130
Hitler, Adolf 78, 92, 109, 112,
    115
Hoare, Colonel Ronnie 226
Hockenheim 104, 293
Hogan, John 278, 279
Holland 276
Howe, Earl 94
Hubach, Ilse *see* Pietsch, Ilse
Huhnlein, *Korpsführer* Adolf 86,
    88–9, 98
Hulme, Denny 244, 267
Humber 226
Hunt, James 265, 267, 271, 272,
274, 275, 278, 289
Hutton, Barbara 138–9, 233
HWM 165, 187

Iacoponi, Stefano 252, 253
Ickx, Jacky 251–2, 256–7, 258,
    260, 261, 267
Imola 191, 290, 291
Indianapolis 14, 66, 106, 169,
    170–1, 235, 293
Innocenti mini-car company 260
Interlagos 147, 276
Internal Liberation Committee
    125
Internazionale Football Club 2,
    14–15
Ireland, Innes 223
Isotta Fraschini 18, 22, 36, 132
Istituto di Ricostruzione
    Industriale (IRI) 66
Itala 18, 42, 59
Italian Air Force 15
Italian automobile association 231
Italian Grand Prix 29, 31, 34, 36,
    53, 55, 64, 70, 81, 149, 165,
    174, 205–6, 215, 219, 234,
    242, 257, 274, 276, 282,
    302–3
Italian Motor Nautical Federation
    181
Italy
    enters World War I 15
    Fascism 23, 34, 92
    invades Abyssinia 89, 91
    neutrality in 1939 109
    open-road racing banned
        (1938) 110
    declares war (1940) 115
    surrenders (1943) 120
    economy 228

Jaguar 183, 187, 205, 207
    D-type 179
    XK120 185
Jano, Rosina 30
Jano, Vittorio 30–1, 33, 34, 36,
    48, 49, 51, 54, 64, 82, 83,
    90, 91, 92, 95, 99, 102, 125,
    126, 176–7, 183, 186, 232,
    260
Jarama, Spain 268, 271, 289
Jenkinson, Denis 216
Johansson, Stefan 294
John Paul II, Pope 299–300, 302
Jung company 117

Karajan, Herbert von 222
Kavan, Anna: *World of Heroes* xi
Keates, Jonathan 11
Kissel, Dr 103
Klemantaski, Louis 162
Kling, Karl 168, 178
Kramer, Stanley xi
Kyalami 258, 282

Lake Garda 144, 165
Lampredi, Aurelio 128, 132, 146,
    148, 149, 153, 156, 157,
    158, 161, 168–9, 172, 177,
    178, 179–80, 186, 228
Lancia 45, 99, 125, 178, 180, 182,
    183, 187, 246, 254, 270,
    113, 179, 189
    Aprilia 110, 114, 133
    D24 177, 179
    D50 176–7, 178, 179, 183, 186,
    261
    Stratos 246
    transporter 54
Lancia, Gianni 176–7, 177, 182
Lancia, Vincenzo 13, 17, 177

Lancia-Ferraris 197, 200, 212
Landi, Chico 150
Lang, Hermann 97, 104, 105
Lardi, Lina (F's mistress)
    brings up Piero 3–4, 5
    F begins relationship with 62
    gives birth to Piero (1945) 123
    F buys her an apartment 234
    and Surtees 236
    and Regazzoni 257
    and F's treatment of Piero 270
    moves into F's house 280
    and mass for F 301
Larivière 209
Lauda, Niki 248, 265–77, 278–9,
    295
Lausanne 165
Le Mans 24-hour race 38, 93,
    113, 129, 151, 152, 153,
    155, 161, 168, 179, 183,
    190, 202, 209, 210, 211,
    218, 219, 225, 230, 231,
    238–9, 243, 246
Lee, Tommy 152
Lehoux, Marcel 75
Leiningen, Prince von 80
Leopold, ex-King of Belgium 222
Levi, Enzo 43, 53–4
Lewis-Evans, Stuart 206, 207, 211
Leygonie, Pierre 155
Ligier 245, 289
Linas–Montlhéry 35
Lingotto plant 229
Lini, Franco 242–3, 247, 248
Livorno 89
Lola 227, 235, 243
Lola-Chevrolet 236
Lolli, Marco 78
Lombardini, Mario 27, 69
Long Beach 270, 281

Lotus cars 213, 223, 224, 225, 227, 230, 243, 245, 267, 275, 281
  Lotus 49 246
  Lotus 79 259
  Lotus–Climax 216, 217, 218, 219
Lucas, Jean 152
Lunger, Brett 273
Lurani, Count Giovanni 68, 98, 110
Lynch, Michael 192
Lyons 33, 37, 61

McGriff, Hershel 167
Machiavelli, Marchese Lotario Alfonso Rangoni 110, 111, 113–14
Machiavelli, Niccolò: *The Prince* 5
Machiavelli, Marchese Rolando 114
Macklin, Lance 183
McLaren 245, 261, 267, 271, 274, 278, 302
McLaren, Bruce 243
McLaren-Hondas 302
McLaren-TAG cars 294–5
Maggi, Count Aymo 36, 37, 38
Maglioli, Umberto 172–3, 210
Magnani, Anna 148, 167
Mairesse, Willy 215, 216, 224, 228, 230–1, 241
Mambelli, Paride 52, 94
Mantovani, Don Sergio 155, *240*, 301, 302
Maranello Concessionares 226, 230
Maranello factory 2, 7, 119, 120–1, 140, 176, 303
  described 3, 139

  workforce 138, 285
  visitors 148, 185, 203, 210, 222
  Dino's interest in 149
  increasingly voluptuous bodywork 167
  management culture 180
  in revolt (1961) 220–2
  Istituto professionale de stato per l'industria e l'artigianato Alfredo Ferrari 234
  foundry 245
  Gozzi on the labour force 249–50
  Montezemolo becomes *direttore sportivo* 264
  output 285
  F's ninetieth birthday celebrations 299
Maranello, near Modena 118–19
  parish church 302
March 267, 268, 292
Marchetti, Adelmo 132
Maria Gabriella, Princess, of Savoy 222
Maria Luisa, Duchess of Parma 19
Marimon, Onofre 173
Marinoni, Attilio 70, 83, 92, 94
Mario Negri Institute, Milan 286
Marlboro 278, 279
Marne Grand Prix 69
Marseilles 169
Marzotto, Count Gaetano 158
Marzotto, Giannino 158, 174
Marzotto, Vittorio 157
Marzotto brothers 190
Masarykring, Czechoslovakia 61, 65
Maserati, Alfieri 102
Maserati, Bindo 125
Maserati, Ernesto 125

Maserati, Ettore 125
Maserati brothers (Scuderia
    Maserati) 26, 45, 53, 66, 69,
    91, 102, 125, 135, 137, 145,
    155, 169, 174, 177, 178,
    187, 188, 193, 199–200,
    211, 253, 254
Maserati cars 43, 51, 53, 64, 69,
    70, 80, 81, 96, 103, 105,
    125, 126, 129, 132, 133,
    137, 142, 144, 145, 149,
    168, 170, 173, 190, 192,
    197, 200, 202
  trident of Bologna badge 26
  8CLT/48 143
  8CM 69
  8CTF 106
  250F 178, 212, 215
  3500GT (Vignale) Spyder 175
  Eldorado Special 201
  Tipo 26M 45, 46
Masetti, Count 32
Mass, Jochen 292
Massimino, Alberto 51, 97, 109,
    111, 112, 125, 143, 177
Massina, Giulietta 124
Mastroianni, Marcello 222
Materassi, Emilio 42, 46, 51
Matra 251, 258
May, Michael 228, 252
Mazzotti, Count Franco 37, 38
Meazza, Stefano 94, 132, 133,
    146, 169
Medio Circuito della Madonie
    20–1
Mellaha 84–5, 92, 103
Mercedes-Benz 45, 74, 91, 106,
    176, 178, 179, 180, 188
Mercedes-Benz cars 32, 52, 55,
    78, 79, 83–7, 91, 92, 98,

103, 126, 178, 179, 183
  three-pointed star badge 26
  300 coupé 168
  SSK 45
  W25 78, 90
  W125 97
  W163 162
  W165 104, 106
Meregalli, Guido 24
Merosi, Giuseppe 24, 27, 29, 30,
    31, 36, 38
Merzario, Arturo 261, 273, 294,
    301
Mexican Grand Prix 242
Mexico 167, 225, 257
MG 66, 209, 226
Michelangeli, Arturo Benedetti
    222
Michelin tyres 282
Mikkola, Hannu 263
Milan
  F works for CMN 18
  Cimiterio Monumental 35
Minardi 253
Mini-Cooper 236, 247
Minoia, Nando 38
Minozzi, Giovanni 113
Misurata, Count Giovanni Volpi
    di 222
Modena 129–30, 300
  Ferrari's town house 1, 233
  Alfredo Ferrari's workshops 1,
    9–10
  F's workshops 2, 99–100, 116,
    129, 155, 265, 299
  history 10–11
  Cathedral of San Geminiano
    11
  Palazzo Ducale 11
  Teatro Ducale 11

described 11–12
San Carlo Hotel 53
Ristorante Boninsegna 60, 74
aeroautodromo 155–6, 190, 195,
    196, 200, 211, 230, 234,
    259
Scaglietti works 190
San Cataldo cemetery 191, 301
Polyclinic 286
Duomo 301
Modena, Bishop of 301–2
Modena, Mayor of 299, 301
Modena Automobile Association
    14
Modena Grand Prix 176
Moll, Guy 75–80, 117, 166, 171,
    288
Momberger, Christian 80
Monaco Grand Prix 67–9, 84,
    91–2, 142, 165, 182, 190,
    197–8, 217, 223, 237,
    243–5, 247, 268, 271, 276,
    277–8, 282, 289, 296
Monkhouse, George 103
Montand, Yves 232
Monte Carlo 67, 156, 180, 214,
    217
Montenero 76, 93, 136
Montezemolo, Luca Cordero di
    263–71, 273, 274
Montlhéry 26, 79, 110, 129, 151
Monza 26, 29, 31, 34, 36, 49, 50,
    51, 70, 80–1, 90, 92, 102,
    103, 106, 144, 149, 150,
    156, 157, 164, 170, 171,
    181, 191–2, 193, 199–200,
    201, *208*, 211, 213, 215, 218,
    221, 231, 232, 234, 236,
    242, 243, 251, 257, 268–9,
    274, 282, *298*, 302

Monza Motorcycle Grand Prix
    59
Moroccan Grand Prix 77, 206,
    207
Morris Minor 165
Mosley, Max 290
Mosport Park, Canada 236, 274,
    279, 281
Moss, Stirling 32, 165–6, 172,
    179, 180, 183, 187, 190,
    191, 192, 198–201, 204–7,
    211, 213, 216–18, 222–3,
    233, 258, 272
Motor magazine 135
Motor Sport 216
Motori Aero Cicli e Sports 61
Mount Fuji 274, 275, 279
Musso, Luigi 32, 187, 190, 191,
    192, 195, 199, 200–204,
    206, 216, 224, 273
Mussolini, Benito 33, 34, 35, 65,
    89, 94, 95, 109, 112–13,
    115, 116, 120, 121
MV 226

Napoleon Bonaparte 5
Nardi, Enrico 102, 112, 113, 116,
    126
Nasi, Angelo 97, 127
Nassau Speed Weeks 233
Navicello 14
Nazzaro, Felice 13, 17, 24, 203,
    251, 300
Nello (F's chemist friend) 212
Nelson, Admiral Lord Horatio 5
Nelson, Edmund 194
Neubauer, Alfred 85, 88, 103,
    104, 106
Neumann, Johnny von 210
New York 94–5, 97–8

North American Racing Team 210, 231
Norton motorcycles 59, 64, 69
Nosetto, Roberto 276
Nuovo farm, Maranello 119
Nürburgring (*Nordschlief*) 55, 78, 79, 85, 87, 88, 89, 93, 97, 164, 170, 175, 179, 191, 198, 204, 211, 213, 217, 218, 225, 230, 231, 241, 247, 251, 260, 261, 268, 271, 272–3
Nuvolari, Alberto 140, 142
Nuvolari, Arturo 49
Nuvolari, Carolina (née Perrina) 50, 175, 189
Nuvolari, Emma 49
Nuvolari, Giorgio 50, 98, 142, 175
Nuvolari, Giuseppe 49, 50
Nuvolari, Tazio 31, 36, 42–3, 46–7, 54, 55, 59, 65–71, 75, 76–7, 80–1, 84, 90–5, 113, 115, 125, 140–2, 149, 166, 171, 216, 222, 223, 227, 258, 272, 289, 302
    friendship with F 48
    early life 49–50
    early races 50–1
    debut with the Scuderia 52
    driving on bends 56–7
    personality 58
    signs with Maserati 69
    Varzi replaces 74, 81
    returns to Ferrari 81–2
    drives the *Bimotore* 83
    one of the greatest drives in grand prix racing 85–9
    bombarded with offers 97
    death of his son Giorgio 98

    in the Auto Union team 99, 103
    and the Porsche family 132
    returns to Ferrari 135–6
    ill health 135, 140
    his last Mille Miglia 140–2
    last ride for Ferrari 142
    death 174–5

Offenhauser engines 168–9
Oldsmobiles 167
OM 45
On the Beach (film) xi
Opel 18
Oporto 204–5
Orefici, Oscar 220–1
Orlandi, Renzo 62, 97
Orlando, Vittorio Emanuele 21, 22
Orsi, Count Omer 145, 187
Orsi family 102, 200
Orsini, Luigi 253
L'Osservatore Romana 203–4

Pacchiani 16
Pace, Carlos 260
Packard 63, 126
Pallavicino, *Ingegnere* Cesare 78, 117
Parkes, Mike 226, 235–9, 241, 242, 243, 246, 288, 289
Parma–Poggio di Berceto hill-climb 8, 18–19, 22
Parnell, Reg 162
Parravano, Tony 210
Patino, Jaime Ortiz 222
Pau Grand Prix 89, 91, 104, 161, 169
Pedralbes 144, 157, 164
Penya Rhin 92

Penya Rhin Grand Prix 144, 157
Perón, Eva 164
Perón, Juan 145, 150, 164, 188
Perón Cup 162
Persia, Shah of (Mohammad
    Reza Pahlavi) 222
Pertini, Sandro 300
Pescara 98, 199
Petacchi, Clara 121
Peterson, Ronnie 260, 267, 268,
    279, 281
Peugeot 20, 21, 26
Philip Morris tobacco company
    278
Piacenza 82
Piccinini, Marco 281, 291, 293
Piemonte, Principessa di 64
Pierce-Arrow 23
Pietsch, Ilse (née Hubach) 81,
    136
Pietsch, Paul 81
Pina (F's cook) 5
Pininfarina 222, 247, 255
Pininfarina, Sergio 301
Pintacuda, Carlo 84, 92, 93, 97
Piquet, Nelson 290
Pirelli 27, 44, 45, 54, 55, 69
Pironi, Didier 289–93
Pius XII, Pope 156
Poellto, Rossene 50
Pola, Julio 144
Pontedecimo hillclimb 53
Pontiac cars 202
Porsche 135, 213, 216, 238
    Spyder 252
Porsche, Dr Ferdinand 77, 86,
    125
Porsche family 81, 132
Postlethwaite, Harvey 289, 292,
    294, 295

Primavera Romana dei Motori
    134–5
Pro Parma club 19
Prost, Alain 290, 293, 294, 295,
    302

Racconigi, near Turin 27
Race of Two Worlds, Monza 201
Ramponi, Giulio 25, 42, 53,
    136
Rancati, Gino 29
Ravenna 25, 151
Red Cross 15
Redman, Brian 260
Regazzoni, Gianclaudio 'Clay'
    257, 260, 261, 265–8, 270,
    274, 275, 278, 302
Renault 2–3, 26, 170, 283, 288,
    290, 293
Renoir, Jean 167
Reutemann, Carlos 260, 267,
    274, 276, 277–8, 280, 281
Reville, Rémy 20
Reynolds, R.J. 155
Rheims 143, 156, 162, 170,
    172–4, 178, 201–4, 213,
    216, 242
Ricart, Wilfredo 100–101, 107,
    126
Righetti, Ferdinando 132, 135,
    137
Rimini, Giorgio 23, 26, 28, 29,
    30, 34, 36
Rindt, Jochen 251, 257
Rio de Janeiro 281
Ripamonti (mechanic) 20
Ristorante Cavallino, Modena 3
Rizzi metalworks 9
Rocchi, Franco 214, 228, 237,
    243–4, 280

Rodriguez, Pedro 218, 230, 253
Rodriguez, Ricardo 218, 224,
    225
Rol, Franco 141
Rolls-Royce 130
Romeo, Nicola 23, 30, 34
Rosani, Guido 270
Rosberg, Keke 290
Rose, Mauri 94
Roselli, Arnaldo 83, 114
Rosemeyer, Bernd 87, 91, 93, 97,
    98, 99, 272
Rosier, Louis 148
Rossellini, Roberto 148, 174
Rouen 170, 198
Rouen-les-Essarts 251
Rovelli, Nino 133
Royal Grand Prix, Rome 59
Royal Italian Automobile Club
    64
Rubirosa, Porfirio 154–5, 232–3
Rudge motorcycles 64

Sagan, Françoise 185–6
    Bonjour Tristesse 185
Sailor, Max 106
Salvarani, Walter 228
San Cataldo cemetery, Modena 2,
    191, 301
San Marino Grand Prix, Imola
    114–15, 290–1
San Martino farm, Maranello 119
San Remo Rally 161, 263
Sanesi, Consalvo 141, 143
Santoni, Antonio 24
Sassuolo 250
Satta, Ingegnere Orazio 100
Scaglietti, Sergio 4, 256, 299, 301
Scaglietti works, Modena 190,
    194, 222

Scala, Delia 187, 195–6
Scapinelli, Sergio 140, 149
Scarfiotti, Ludovico 229, 235–6,
    238, 241, 242, 243, 246,
    251, 288, 302
Scarfiotti, Luigi 45, 46, 63
Scarfiotti, Signora 241
Scheckter, Jody 274, 278, 279,
    281–2, 283, 292, 302
Schell, Harry 180, 200
Schenken, Tim 260
Schetty, Peter 257–8, 260
Schumacher, Michael 172, 248
Scuderia Centro Sud 241
Scuderia Ferrari see Società
    Anonima Scuderia Ferrari
Scuderia Filipinetti 246
Scuderia Nuvolari 48, 51
Scuderia Sant'Ambroeus 224
Scuderia Serenissima 222
Sculati, Eraldo 193, 197
Seaman, Dick 98, 103, 165
Sebring 210, 211, 218, 223, 225,
    230, 233
SEFAC see Società Esercizio
    Fabbriche Automobili e
    Corse
Segrave, Sir Henry 198
Selmi, Enzo 220
Selsdon, Lord 152
Sempione Park 93
Senigallia hillclimb 53
Senna, Ayrton 302
Serafini, Dorino 157–8, 296
Seria, Diego 17
Severi, Francesco 102
Severi, Martino 155–6
Shaw, Wilbur 106, 169
Shelby, Carroll 210
Shell 45, 54, 64, 247–8

Siena, Eugenio 31, 32, 46, 52,
    63–4, 65, 74, 76, 93
Silver Arrows 85
Silverstone 149, 156, 161–2, 164,
    170, 174, 178, 191, 204,
    253, 261, 264, 265, 278
Simca-Gordini cars 146
Sivocci, Ugo 18, 20, 22, 26,
    29–30
Società Anonima Scuderia Ferrari
    119, 130, 148
  garage at Modena 5, 45,
      99–100
  prancing horse device 25–6,
      65, 69, 84, 102, 109, 117,
      133, 169, 223, 250, 302
  founded 43–4
  finances 43–4, 53–4, 62, 69–70,
      222, 228, 229
  relationship with Alfa Romeo
      44–5, 54, 69–70, 95
  F's achievement 44–5
  first podium position 47
  successful first year 53
  new headquarters 53–4
  growth in scale 55–6
  Taruffi joins 59–60
  brochures 61, 74
  the Acerbo visit 62–3
  diversifies into motorcycles 64
  first fatality 70
  Lehoux and Moll join 75
  direttore sportivo appointment 78
  takeover by Alfa Romeo
      99–100, 109, 169
  annual magazine 116
  a privately owned business 125
  first ever Ferrari one–two (at
      Parma) 136
  F recruits personnel 125

  lessons of first grand prix
      season 144
  deals with Ascari and Villoresi
      147
  growth of 155
  first grand prix victory (1951)
      163–4
  first world champion 172
  Fangio leaves 193
  Behra sacked 213
  Laura Ferrari's involvement
      220–1, 228, 280
  mass defection (1961) 221–2,
      228, 280
  industrial unrest 225, 228
  Hill leaves 225–6
  Ford's offer 228–9
  links with Fiat 229, 246–7
  loss of Surtees 238–9
  deal with Fiat (1969) 254–6
  monococques made in
      England 261
  strong and lively new
      organisation 266
  anniversary year 296
Società Esercizio Fabbriche
    Automobili e Corse
    (SEFAC) 214, 249
Soffietti (amateur driver) 64
Sommer, Raymond 75, 93, 94,
    98, 99, 129, 137, 144
Soria, Diego 138
Sortenna di Sondrio 15
South African Grand Prix 258,
    268, 270
Sozzi, Carlo 46
Spa 65, 69, 93, 137, 148, 156,
    162, 170, 172, 178, 182,
    190, 211, 225, 237, 246,
    257, 272

Spanish Civil War 94
Spanish Grand Prix 179
Sport Nazionale 110
Sports Car Club of America 151,
  209
Stanguellini, Vittorio 134, 155,
  253
Stefani (mechanic) 94
Steinbeck, John 5
Stella, Cavaliere Ugo 23
Stendhal 5
Sterzi, Bruno 139
Stevenson, Adlai 152
Stewart, Jackie 244, 246, 247–8,
  251, 260, 272
Stockholm Grand Prix 142
Stuck, Hans 78, 79, 81, 85
Sunbeam 26, 29
Surtees 273
Surtees, John 3, 226–32, 235–9,
  241–2, 252, 268, 270, 302
Suzuka 296
Swiss Grand Prix 89, 98–9, 143,
  149, 162, 165, 169
Syracuse 161, 169, 211, 216, 237

Tadini, Mario 43, 46, 48, 62, 91,
  92
Tagliazucchi, Dino 2, 4, 269, 286,
  301
Talbot 42, 46, 51, 91, 97, 148,
  168
Tambay, Patrick 293
Targa Abruzzo 24-hour race,
  Pescara 79–80
Targa Florio 18, 19–22, 24, 28,
  29, 47, 51, 55, 77, 84, 107,
  139–40, 161, 190, 201, 225,
  247
Taruffi, Isabella 195

Taruffi, Piero 58–60, 63–9, 71,
  113, 140, 151, 157, 162,
  166, 167, 169, 170, 179,
  180, 194–5, 296
Tavoni, Romolo 197, 200, 202,
  203, 207, 211, 213, 220, 221
Temporada 145–6, 150, 156, 165,
  169
Terme di Caracalla 135, 165
Testi, Dottore Ferrucio 44, 61, 74,
  74, 168
Thomas, René 20
Todt, Jean 263
Tonti, Aldo 174
Toscanini, Arturo 222
Touring 36, 112, 113, 114, 151,
  174, 222
Tourist Trophy, Goodwood 223
Tre Fontane 48, 59
Trieste–Opicina hillclimb 52, 79
Trintignant, Maurice 178–81,
  188, 200, 296
Tripoli Grand Prix 51, 77, 92,
  103, 104–6
Trips, Wolfgang von 195, 197,
  199, 211, 213, 215–19, 221,
  273, 302
Trossi, Count Carlo Felice
  ('Didi') 62–3, 69, 91, 119,
  136, 143, 258
Troubetzkoy, Prince Igor
  138–40, 142, 233
Trujillo, Flor de Oro 154
Trujillo, Rafael 233
Tunis Grand Prix 66, 84
Turin auto show 151
Turin Grand Prix 89, 137
Tyrrell 245, 260, 274, 279
Tyrrell, Ken 248, 251
Tyrrell-Ford 293

Ugolini, Nello 78–9, 87, 94, 100, 169, 172, 173, 174, 179, 180, 187, 193, 198, 199
United States Auto Club 209
University of Bologna 7, 224
US Grand Prix 215, 219, 231

Vaccarella, Nino 301
Vailati, Silvio 112
Val Seriana 15–16
Valentini, Valdemaro 4
Valentino Park 137, 143–4
Valletta, Professor Vittorio 182
Vanderbilt Cup 93–4, 115, 201
Vandervell, Tony 136, 147, 162, 179, 211
Vanwall 32, 147, 179, 182, 197, 198–201, 204, 206, 211
Varese 135
Varzi, Achille 43, 46, 47–8, 51, 52, 53, 55, 59, 67, 68–9, 72, 74–81, 84, 92, 93, 115, 136, 143, 145, 158, 203, 216, 227, 272
Varzi, Norma 143
Vatican 2, 79, 183, 203, 299, 300
Vecchi, Ener 228
Vercelli 135
Verdelli, Peppino 1, 2, 4, 14, 45, 203, 234, 236
  first works with F 37
  F's successes with him as mechanic 42
  and Taruffi 60
  death 269
Vernor, Brenda 203, 221, 226, 238–9, 265, 277, 282, 285–8
Vigevano 135
Villeneuve, Gilles 278–9, 280–2, 284, 288–91

Villoresi, Emilio 'Mimi' 102, 105, 106, 147, 236
Villoresi, Luigi 'Gigi' 102–7, 137, 142–8, 157, 158, 159, 161, 163, 165, 166, 167, 169, 173, 176, 179, 236, 269, 296
Villoresi family 106
Viserba (F's villa) 236
Vitti, Monica 222
Vittorio Veneto–Cansiglio hillclimb 52
voiturette racing 96, 101, 102, 103
VW Beetle 211

Wagner, Louis 33, 34
Walker, Rob 213, 223
Watkins Glen 213, 219, 231, 260, 274, 281
Weber, Edoardo 64, 121, 256, 274
Weber carburettor company 256
Whitehead, Peter 147
Williams cars 245, 273, 282–3, 290
Wimille, Jean-Pierre 94, 136, 143–6, 213
Wolf, Walter 278
Wolf cars 281, 289
World War I 15–16, 63
World War II 101, 106, 109, 112, 115, 116, 120–1, 123
Wyer, John 252

Yates, Brock 129

Zagato 36, 65
Zandvoort 170, 172, 245, 258, 268, 274, 288, 293
Zeltweg 274
Ziegler, Enrico 64
Zolder 291